Reminiscences of an Elephant

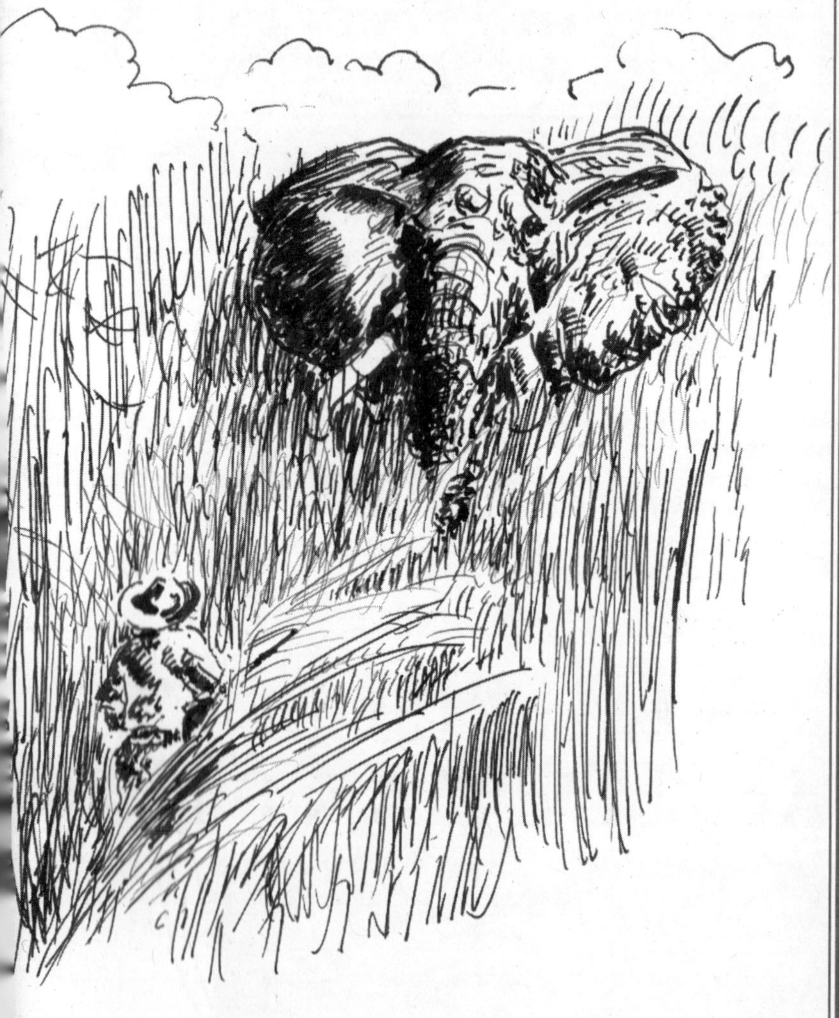

REMINISCENCES OF AN ELEPHANT HUNTER

THE AUTOBIOGRAPHY OF
W. D. M. "KARAMOJO" BELL

SAFARI PRESS

REMINISCENCES OF AN ELEPHANT HUNTER, The Autobiography of W. D. M. "Karamojo" Bell © 2018 Walter Dalrymple Maitland Bell from his unpublished diaries and Safari Press. Artwork © 2018 Clive Kay and W. D. M. Bell. All rights reserved. No part of this publication may be used or reproduced in any form or by any means without permission from the publisher.

The trademark Safari Press® is registered with the U.S. Patent and Trademark Office and with government trademark and patent offices in other countries.

Bell, Walter Dalrymple Maitland

Second edition

Safari Press

2018, Long Beach, California

ISBN 978-1-57157-502-9

Library of Congress Catalog Card Number: 2017945953

10 9 8 7 6 5 4 3 2 1

Printed in Canada

Readers wishing to see Safari Press's many fine books on big-game hunting, wingshooting, and sporting firearms should visit our website at www.safaripress.com.

This Book Is Dedicated to

My Wife

Without Whose Help It Would Have Made

Much Livelier Reading

Table of Contents

Foreword by Ludo J. Wurfbain VII
Introduction by Townsend Whelen XIV
Timeline of the Life of W. D. M. Bell 1880–1954 XVIII

Part I	The Life and Times of W. D. M. Bell	1
Chapter 1	Early Misadventures	3
Chapter 2	I Take a Sailing Ship to the Other Side of the World	12
Chapter 3	New Zealand in the 1890s	28
Chapter 4	Swagging and Other Adventures	44
Chapter 5	My Escape from Germany	52
Chapter 6	One Foot in Africa, 1897	62
Chapter 7	Another Foot in the Yukon	84
Chapter 8	Back to Africa and the Boer War	110
Chapter 9	Into the Unknown	120
Chapter 10	Karamojo	134
Chapter 11	Abyssinia under Menelik	144
Chapter 12	The Lado Enclave	152
Chapter 13	Rubber and Whales, an Interlude	158
Chapter 14	Liberia, Where the Black Man Rules	166
Chapter 15	French Equatorial Africa	176
Chapter 16	I Join the Royal Flying Corps (R.F.C.)	196
Chapter 17	The War Years	204
Chapter 18	Another Go at Africa	226
Chapter 19	Home in the Highlands	238
Chapter 20	Postscript	254
Chapter 21	The Obituary of Capt. W. D. M. "Karamojo" Bell by Major Kinloch	258
Part II	Original Stories by W. D. M. Bell	265
Chapter 22	Walter Bell's Handbook on African Big Game	266
Chapter 23	The Repulsive Saurian	272
Chapter 24	The Nandi Epic	282
Chapter 25	The Somali Virgin	298
Chapter 26	A Sojourn among Practicing Christians	302
Chapter 27	Among Friends	310
Chapter 28	A Whaling Project	316
Chapter 29	Hunting with the Waboni	332
Chapter 30	Slaving and Raiding in Karamojo	336
Chapter 31	The Film Party	350
Chapter 32	Miscellaneous Misadventures and Reminiscences	356

Foreword

In 2015 we came across Walter Bell's diaries through a very fortuitous encounter. As soon as I could, I sat down and read every page of these "lost" materials, and I then re-read all three of Bell's earlier books. I felt like a child in a candy store.

At the same time, though, I was struck by the discrepancies and inconsistencies I was finding between Bell's diaries and his published works. Some of these discrepancies can be explained away by the mere fact that Bell wrote many versions of the same event over several decades, and, memory being what it is, variances naturally will creep into the different narratives.

I realized that there were two key unresolved mysteries in Bell's unpublished diaries. These involve what Townsend Whelen knew when he edited Bell's autobiography, *Bell of Africa*, and why Bell was so successful in Karamojo.

It was obvious from reading some 1,800 hand- and typewritten pages from Bell's lost works that Townsend Whelen used only a fraction of Bell's autobiographical materials. The first question, therefore, involves why Townsend Whelen chose to use so little of Bell's autobiographical materials when creating *Bell of Africa*.

Townsend Whelen said in his introduction to *Bell of Africa*, "About *1950* he [Bell] wrote me of his desires to publish his *complete* memoirs." (Emphasis mine.) Whelen explains Bell could find no British publisher interested. Whelen, in his reply to Bell, suggested that he could possibly get Bell's book published in the United States and asked Bell to send him the manuscript.[1]

Whelen then goes on to explain that he received a cablegram that Bell had died, and two days later he says that he received Bell's manuscript. Whelen stated that the manuscript was not "consecutively arranged" and that it was a rather *"intimate story"* of his life. Furthermore Whelen says, "Bell left no exact record of the number of elephants he shot" and that "Bell was a personal friend of mine. We had corresponded for years. . . ."

---

[1] It is interesting to note that Whelen ultimately published *Bell of Africa* with Neville Spearman of London, obviously a British firm.

Upon examination of all Bell's materials, however, it became apparent to me that a number of things Whelen said seemed out of place and incorrect. Whelen stated that Bell wrote him "around 1950," and he gives the impression that Bell sent him the manuscript about that time. Whelen could not have received the cablegram advising him of Bell's death "shortly after" because Bell did not die till 30 June 1954. Whelen in his "Editor's Note" at the back of *Bell of Africa* states that Bell died in "1951." If Whelen and Bell were such good friends, how could Whelen have mixed up these dates so badly?

So, when did Whelen receive Bell's materials? Was it in 1951 or was it in 1954? Let's assume for a minute Whelen did not receive the manuscript till 1954. We know that *Bell of Africa* was published in 1960 by Neville Spearman of London and in 1961 by Charles Branford of Boston. Why did it take Whelen six years to get it published? And if he received the manuscript in 1951, why did it take him nine years? This seems an extraordinarily long time.

Also why did Whelen say Bell left no record of the exact number of elephants he shot when, in fact, Bell clearly did so in a number of letters and typed lists that could be found not only in Bell's unpublished materials, which Whelen surely had access to, but also from published materials that were pretty widely circulated at the time of Bell's death.

Readers will see that we have a new introduction by Townsend Whelen for this book, and in it he contradicts many of the statements given above. It was sent to us by a collector of big-game hunting books who found it in an archive and kindly alerted us to its existence. See extract on page VIII.

In it Whelen says that "in 1951" Bell wrote him to say he was working on his complete memoirs, and he also says that Bell died a week after a letter dated 24 June 1954. These contradict the two statements Whelen made elsewhere: the date he attributes to Bell's death as stated in *Bell of Africa* (1951) and when he received Bell's manuscript. This introduction also shows that Whelen knew the number of elephants Bell shot on his safaris in Karamojo and elsewhere.

What then can explain the contradictory nature of these discrepancies? We can only assume that the two introductions were written years apart and that Whelen either forgot about the one, did not like it, or simply decided to write a new one.

In the introduction to *Bell of Africa,* Whelen states that he took "no liberties with the text" except for "certain inconsequential matters." As you read this new autobiography of Bell, you will find that, in fact, a very large number of consequential facts were omitted in *Bell of Africa*. So what happened?

Whelen was born in 1877, and by 1954 he was seventy-seven years old. In the 1950s Whelen would have been considered an old man. While age in itself is not a good indicator of human productivity or functioning, nevertheless we cannot discount that age may have played a factor in his decisions on what to use of Bell materials. Whelen worked on Bell's manuscript for at least six years. Making major mistakes and omissions on a project that lasted six years is not hard to do.

Another possibility is that Whelen deliberately cut out large sections of Bell's autobiography. If this is the case, why would he have done so? It is noteworthy that Whelen stated he felt the manuscript was "rather intimate," yet *Bell of Africa* actually revealed very few intimacies about Bell, especially when compared with the memoirs that are now in your hands.

Bell himself perhaps offers a clue to why Whelen decided to leave out all the salacious bits from Bell's autobiography. As mentioned elsewhere, Bell wrote two complete autobiographies, expanding on different things in each one. In one version of his autobiography, Bell dedicated his life's story to his wife, Katie. The dedication, which is given in this frontal, states: "Dedicated to my wife, without whose help it would have made much livelier reading." It's possible that Whelen purposely left out a lot Bell's remarks about the fairer sex in deference to Katie Bell who was alive for part of the time Whelen worked on Bell's memoirs.

That still leaves the mystery as to why Whelen would have left out so much of Bell's other materials on New Zealand, South Africa, Ethiopia, the Yukon, and West and Central Africa. Let's look at the composition of *Bell of Africa* for a minute. *Bell of Africa* consists of 16 chapters and 231 pages without frontal matter and appendix. Whelen said that Bell had indicated that chapters V to XXII from *Wanderings of an Elephant Hunter* were to be included in this new book; these chapters represent 153 pages, or 66 percent of the total book by page count. In other words only 34 percent of *Bell of Africa* contains new material.

It is possible that Walter Bell, in the last months of his life, failed to send both autobiographical diaries to Whelen. Katie Bell would not have been much help to Whelen, either, for we know for a fact that Katie Bell was ill with uterine cancer after her husband died. Katie, who was fifteen years younger than Walter, died in 1957, barely three years after her husband. It's possible that Whelen simply didn't have access to all the materials and was left with creating an autobiography from only those that he had received.

Let's now turn to the second Bell mystery. Why was Bell apparently the only white elephant hunter in the Karamojo district in Uganda before 1907? About twenty-five years ago I read *Karamojo Safari* for the first time, and as soon as I was halfway through the book, I started wondering how it was that Bell had the entire Karamojo region in Uganda to himself—a virtual private hunting ground—for a period of approximately five years, from 1902 till 1907 or so. It was only while I was reading the materials that resulted in *Incidents from an Elephant Hunter's Diary* that answers began to shine through.

It is now clear that Bell had help from two, or possibly three, British officials. According to Bell, the Karamojo province fell under the "Outlying District Ordinance," and "no white man was allowed north of Elgon without a special permit." Uganda had become a British Protectorate in 1894; however, control over the northern parts was nominal when Bell arrived in 1902. Added to the general lawlessness of the area, the old slavers had set up their last stronghold in this "Closed District." British forces were spread thin, and the territory was in a slow simmer at the time of Bell's arrival in East Africa. Only a small match would ignite the lot. Here's what Bell had to say:

> Added to this sense of lawless chaos, everyone had a firearm except the owners of the land; they had only spears. When I drew into Mumias at the foot of the 14,000-foot Mount Elgon, this was the state of affairs in the area. Therefore, I was delighted to find my old friend P. in charge of the *boma*. A man of great independence of outlook, P. seized the chance of acquiring, without any cost to the Government, an unofficial agent who could be relied upon to confine his activities to the killing of four-footed game and whose presence in the disturbed area would restrain the activities of those who were more addicted to the pursuit of the two-footed sort. All these considerations played right into my hand.

It was Bell's friends, referred to in his earlier books as P., M., and O., who made it possible for Bell to be the sole white elephant hunter in the Karamojo region of Uganda for five long years. Without their help, Bell's story would have been very different. Bell was a friend, quite possibly a very good friend, of Hugh Basil Partington's and Sidney William Ormsby's, and he was acquainted with Walter Mayes.

A few snippets on these men shine through in this book and in *Incidents*. Through these friends, especially Partington, Bell gained what appears to have been exclusive access to Karamojo and its elephants. In exchange for this exclusive access, Bell was active in helping to stop cattle and slave raids, all of which served British interests in the area. Partington's world view, as you will see from the stories in this tome, was one of enlightened British self-interest.

If we study the history of Africa in the 1880–1920 era and read books from early ivory hunters from this same period, we can see that others would have entered Karamojo if there had been an opportunity to do so. Alfred Neumann hunted in East Africa as early as 1894 and John Boyes, no timid character when it came to unruly natives and "acquiring" ivory, was in Mombasa by 1898. Obviously there were others, and you can bet they cast long and wide to get themselves to the best possible hunting grounds for ivory. Bell's successes in Karamojo was thus predicated on the help he received from his friends who held positions of power over the area.

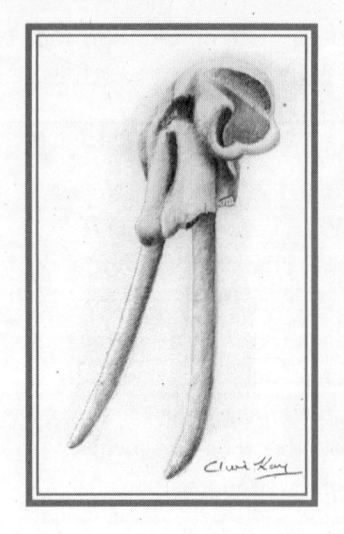

If you own a copy of *Incidents*, and you should, you will see that Bell listed having shot 42 elephants from Mount Elgon, 91 from Manimani, 63 from Dobesi, and 149 from Dabessa. At a total of 345 elephants, this means that Bell shot more than a third of all the elephants he took in his lifetime from the Karamojo region . . . and all of them in a period of five years.

Bell started hunting in Africa in 1897 and his last elephant hunt after World War I probably occurred in 1924 when he traveled with the Forbes brothers from Kano to Khartoum. Nowhere else was he as successful as he had been in Karamojo, and nowhere else did he return again and again to hunt elephants. Karamojo was a comparatively small area and shooting 345 elephants there was a fantastic result. Had access been granted freely to anyone wishing to hunt there, it is hard for me to imagine that Karamojo would not have been a "free-for-all" like other ivory hunting grounds where unlimited access occurred. Just look at what happened in the Lado Enclave where the large herds of elephants were reduced and "educated" rather quickly by the ivory hunters who entered it.

Bell, in fact, says as much in this book. Discussing his Bahr Aouk expedition, he states, ". . . we would make a base camp and bury all the ivory. None of it would we take out, for I had found from bitter experience in the past that if you did so, others immediately came in and spoiled your hunting. The Lado Enclave was a good example. A deluge of hunters and would-be hunters descended upon me there, spoiling not only the game but also the natives."

Exclusive access to Karamojo helped, but it must also be said that Bell was a phenomenal hunter, a man of great energy, and a great shot. As he said, he walked about "seventy miles" for every elephant he shot. These are not the accomplishments of a marginal hunter.

In ending this foreword, it is my hope that this analysis will give you, the reader, a foundation for understanding Bell's books. Bell was a highly enigmatic character who, even when compared to the other giants of his era, stands out as an exceptional individual of extraordinary skills. His life's story is testament to his bold, courageous, and persistent nature. Bell was the embodiment of rugged individualism. After reading the account of his life, I am sure you will agree with this assessment.

In closing I want to specifically thank Mr. Bill Kircher for generously supplying us with a copy of Townsend Whelen's second introduction to Bell's autobiography. I would also like to thank Mr. Peter Ayre of Somerset, England, for kindly letting us access his database of people of British descent who lived in Kenya up to 1939. It was through him that we learned the true identity of Bell's friends, the men who helped him so much during his hunts in Karamojo. Finally, I would like to thank Mr. Terry Castle of Omokoroa, New Zealand, for his unstinting help in providing us with the results of his years-long research into W. D. M. Bell.

Ludo J. Wurfbain
Publisher, Sports Afield
Huntington Beach, California
March 2017

Note from the editor:

In reading the nearly 1,800 pages of handwritten and typed diaries that Bell left, we found a treasure trove of stories and autobiographical notes that had not been previously published. We also discovered more than a few discrepancies—not only discrepancies within these pages but also between Bell's autobiographical writings and his previously published books. Whenever we discovered a discrepancy, we made a footnote to explain what we found.

Another revelation to us was the sheer number of redundancies in Bell's diaries and his previously published works. While we did our best to eliminate redundancies wherever we could, we decided that it was necessary to keep some of them in order to preserve continuity and to respect the importance of maintaining chronological order in the telling of his life's story.

Finally, we made certain decisions concerning the editing of this manuscript that may be of interest to the reader. First of all we decided to try to keep the orthography—as much as possible—the way Bell wrote it. We made this decision so that his autobiography would reflect the time in which he wrote. You will, therefore, see "Sudan" spelled "Soudan"; "river bank" spelled as two words rather than the current fused spelling "riverbank"; and "caribou" spelled "cariboo." We felt that maintaining the orthography (norms of spelling, hyphenation, capitalization, word breaks, etc.) of the period would make the manuscript "feel" more authentic for the reader. Second, as a convenience for the reader, we added dark lines to the maps at the beginning of the chapters to denote Bell's journey for that particular segment of his life.

INTRODUCTION

Walter D. M. Bell was the last of the African professional elephant hunters. During the first portion of this century [twentieth], he hunted all over Central Africa from coast to coast, and he shot over 1,000 elephants with his own rifle. On one of his expeditions lasting about a year, he shot 183 elephants, with an average weight of tusk of 53 pounds. From the sale of this, he realized £9,000. For that year the expenses of his outfit and safari were £3,000, realizing a profit of £6,000 ($29,000). And at the end, he said he still had a "full-power safari."

In the 1830s the Dutch settlers in the Cape started to trek northward where they came on great herds of wild animals. Besides providing them with food and clothing, the Dutch soon found that there was a profitable market for hides and ivory. The wonderful fauna of this region soon attracted a number of British sportsmen, among them Roualeyn Gordon-Cumming and W. C. Baldwin who wrote wonderfully of their experiences. Enthused by these books, a nineteen-year-old English boy, Frederick C. Selous, appeared on the scene in 1871, destined to eventually become the most celebrated and glamorous big-game hunter of all time.

In the mid-nineteenth century, the French and Belgians began the colonization of North and West Africa. The troops that pacified the continent and the settlers who followed them found a plethora of big game. These people started to live on the wildlife and to hunt for profit. Many men took up professional elephant hunting, which has continued in these regions almost to the present day.

The start of the twentieth century left only East Equatorial Africa as a virgin hunting country. The British started to penetrate this country about 1892, and they shortly thereafter undertook the construction of the railroad from Mombasa to Lake Victoria. But just before that, another celebrated British professional elephant hunter arrived in this region. Arthur H. Neumann started his first expedition from Mombasa in 1893 for the purpose of professional elephant hunting and continued his successful hunting for several years in the regions north of Mount Kenya and on the eastern side of Lake Rudolph. While he was followed by many other hunters in Kenya and Tanganyika, one was destined for fame. That man was Walter D. M. Bell.

Bell started his hunting life in Kenya. He first journeyed into the country to the west of Lake Rudolph about the time that the Uganda Railway was under construction, and from there he went into regions farther north and west, all the way to the Atlantic coast, all the while continuing to hunt elephants. This he persisted to do until very recent years.

Bell and his predecessors should not be confused with the present-day professional African hunters. Highly experienced and glamorous as these men are, they are mainly conductors and guides for the present-day safaris of wealthy sportsmen. They operate in country well known, and they have the advantage of motor transportation and a native population that is friendly and cooperative.

In the old days Bell and his predecessors set out for long periods—continuous years of hunting—on their own as the only white men in the areas they hunted. They utilized native porters and sometimes donkeys or oxcarts for carrying all their needs into the bush and for bringing out their ivory. Sometimes they found the natives deadly hostile. They had to rely on their rifles for their sustenance, maintenance, and sometimes for their very lives. They lived off the country, mainly on meat and native flour that they obtained in exchange for the animals they shot. They also traded beads and cloth with natives for ivory and plumes. If they were injured or fell sick, there was no one they could rely on but themselves and their native boys. Neumann was once seriously injured by a charging elephant and was brought back to health by the men of his safari. It was obvious that he had been in a helpless condition and was rescued by his men. Many died as the result of encounters with beasts, accidents, or disease; the lowly hyena acted as undertaker.

Bell was in many ways unique among the early professional hunters. Indeed, today you will often hear the old Afrikaner say: "There was only one Bell." Living and hunting for years as the only white man among a native population, much of it in entirely uncharted territory by any civilization, he came to know the natives—their character, habits, and their thoughts—as few men ever have, and in his writings he has given us a very true picture of the more fractious tribes. He also survived traveling alone, and because he was greatly respected by the locals, he was able to elucidate more intelligently than some others his understanding of the native Africa of his day, thus contributing to our present knowledge of the life of these people in the bush.

But he was perhaps best noted for his preference for the small-bore rifle and solid (full-jacketed) bullets to hunt all game, including elephants. He shot almost all his elephants with such calibers and bullets. There was a reason for such preference on his part: He was exceptionally skillful with the rifle; in fact, he was almost certainly the best and the most practiced rifle shot who ever hunted in Africa. He also had an accurate knowledge of the anatomy of all African beasts. Not only was he an exceptional bolt-action shot in placing his bullets with all the accuracy of which his weapons were capable, but he had an almost uncanny ability to time his shot placement, and that combination enabled him to place his bullet instantly and exactly where he wished.

When he first started to hunt in Africa, the small-bore, high-velocity, smokeless rifle had already been developed to a high degree of efficiency, and he mostly used the best rifles of British make. His preferences to all other rifles were the following: the .275 Rigby Mauser, shooting a 175-grain bullet at a muzzle velocity of 2,300 feet per second; a .303 British Lee-Enfield with a 215-grain bullet at a muzzle velocity of 2,000 feet per second; and a .256 Mannlicher-Schönauer rifle shooting a 160-grain bullet at a muzzle velocity of 2,400 feet per second.

The long, round-nose solid bullets of high sectional density these rifles used gave deep penetration and usually drove through flesh and bone accurately to the vital organs—the brain and heart—of elephants and other game when directed with the skill with which Bell was capable. The light weight, balance, handiness, and lack of recoil of such rifles, as compared with heavier rifles of larger bore, contributed greatly to Bell's accuracy, especially given the speed with which he could use them. Of course, even though the bullet be small and light, if it reaches the brain or heart, it will kill as quickly and surely as a larger bullet.

Apart from his inborn skill at hunting, which was such that he would consistently hit birds on the wing with a rifle, Bell made himself into the deadly and quick shot he was by continually practicing. Particularly he did a lot of "dry shooting" every day, and he used his rifle for exercising to develop familiarity with its feel and fit.

We feel it wise to state that we do not believe Bell's preference for the small bore is good advice for the average sportsman hunting in Africa, or indeed for any hunter in a dangerous-game hunt. This is a consensus by the vast majority of professional hunters of today who guide safaris in Africa. Not one hunter in a thousand has the ability to place his bullets quickly and accurately, nor does he have the knowledge of animal anatomy that Bell had. Again, "There was only one Bell." If the small-bore bullet does not quickly strike a vital organ "first crack," it has little or no stopping or turning ability. Thus, it is not a safe bullet in the hands of the average shot for large and dangerous game, nor a humane and sportsmanlike bullet for other game.

A rifle and ammunition should be selected that has penetration and stopping power adequate for the game on which it is used. The modern elephant rifle shooting a .450 to .470 bullet of 450 to 500 grains at a muzzle velocity of 2,200 feet per second will almost always stop or turn the charge of any elephant, buffalo, or rhino when striking near vital organs, even though it does not penetrate them. And for slightly smaller game—lion and the larger antelopes—rifles in the class of the .375 magnum are similarly adequate.

Walter and I corresponded regularly for many years. We had much in common. He had already published two books on some of his adventures in elephant hunting: *The Wanderings of an Elephant Hunter* and *Karamojo Safari*. In 1951, he wrote me to say that he was working on his complete memoirs that would include those adventures already published and many others from his long and active life in wild Africa. I encouraged him in this, and finally last year he sent me his manuscript.

He realized it was not in proper shape for publication, and he asked me if I would edit it for him. I told him that I hardly felt qualified as I personally have never hunted in Africa. But such was my interest in it that I finally, gladly agreed to do so. If the old African hunter finds certain discrepancies, I think he will make allowances. My last letter from Walter was dated 24 June 1954. A week later he passed over the Great Divide. Death came suddenly and painlessly in his sleep.

Townsend Whelen
Someday Farm
Woodstock, Vermont
Circa 1955

Timeline of the Life of
Walter Dalrymple Maitland Bell
1880–1954

1880 (8 September)
Born at Clifton Hall in Uphall, Linlithgowshire (West Lothian, near Edinburgh), Scotland, the second youngest of ten children. Bell's father, Robert Bell, was a pioneer in the coal and shale oil industries; he discovered sulfate of ammonia, a by-product of shale, and made a fortune in this industry.

1883 (23 April)
Bell's mother, Agnes Bell, dies of peritonitis and complications from childbirth. She was thirty-nine.

1887
Inspired by the heroics of "Dead Shot Dick," a dime novel superman, Bell walks away from home with barrels from a dueling pistol, a pocket watch, and some pennies to travel to America to hunt bison. Trip screeches to a halt at train station. He is seven years old. Bell expands his reading, now devouring the classic works on elephant hunting by Sir William Gordon-Cumming and others. Bell states: "Had my guardians realized what Gordon-Cumming's writings would do to me, they would have bought and destroyed every available copy of his works in a hundred-mile radius." Bell begins his lifelong love of hunting the African elephant.

1888
Sent to boarding school. Leaves school in 1889. Family in despair.

1892
Bell's family resort to the time-honored expedient of sending Bell to sea. Bell, now twelve years old, boards the sailing ship *Jupiter* bound for Tasmania, a 128-day journey. Bell learns basics of sailing from ruffian crew. Arrives in Hobart, Tasmania, where he "breaks his articles," thus forfeiting the premium his family had paid, and leaves the ship.

Works his passage to New Zealand, becomes enamored of an Irish widow, and finds work at a starch factory. Travels to Port Chalmers to find passage to Africa; instead, he lands a job on a fishing boat with a "blue-nose bastard" of a skipper. Bell's love of the sea and sailing is born.

Now thirteen years old, Bell hears he can get a ship to Africa from Invercargill. Bell has absolutely no money, and a fellow hobo teaches him how to snatch eggs from hen houses and how to jump trains. Jumps a train to Invercargill and gets caught; meets "Bill" who takes him in and clothes and feeds him. On failing to find a boat to East Africa, Bell takes the *Destiny*, a refrigerator steamer, bound for London.

1894
Robert Bell dies on 30 May of pleurisy and Bell's eldest siblings become his guardians, with his eldest brother in command. (Date of death erroneously indicated as 1887 or 1888 in Bell's diaries.) Robert Bell was born in 1827 in Wishaw, Lanarkshire, Scotland.

Fourteen-year-old Bell returns to Scotland from his trip to Tasmania and New Zealand. No records to indicate if this is before or after his father dies. Once more Bell entreats his family with the cry: "To Africa! To Africa!" Instead, they send him to Oxford Military College, which he escapes from as quickly as he can. Bell then sends a letter to his father's factor asking to borrow against the proceeds he expects to inherit from his father's will. Factor shows letter to guardians, and Bell's plan fails.

1896
Completely fed up with him, his guardians send Bell to boarding school in Germany. The Herr, Bell's school master, buys Bell a 12-bore hammer gun; Bell spends his time shooting small game; and he also shoots a roe deer for meat for the school.

Bell builds a kayak to escape from Germany. Bell embarks on his kayak on a tributary of the Weser River, which would take him to Bremerhaven, Germany, a port city on the North Sea. (The Weser is 431 kilometers (268 miles) from its source to Bremerhaven.) The kayak sinks in rapids before he reaches the Weser River; Bell manages to get to shore with his gun. A German family takes him in; Bell exchanges his gun for enough money to buy food and a rail ticket to Bremerhaven; once there, he finds a passage back to Scotland.

1897
Bell's guardians finally give in and outfit him for a trip to East Africa. Now nearly seventeen-years-old, Bell's eldest brother buys him a single-shot .303 and passage on the *Somali*, a German steamer bound for Mombasa. He is hired as a "hunter" by the Uganda Railway, also known as the Lunatic Express, and sent to Voi via the train. There he shoots lions and other game along the rail tracks. Exchanges his .303 for a .405 Winchester blackpowder, single-shot rifle. Later he finds the .405 to be inadequate as a lion killer because of the hollow-point bullets; gets acquainted with the 8-bore. Meets a German who hires Bell as an elephant hunter for his camp; German fails to show at rendezvous, and Bell is left stranded in Central Africa. Bell returns to coast, sells rifle, and goes home to Scotland.

1898–1899 (Bell's map of the Yukon says 1897–1898)
On arriving home, Bell's guardians refuse to advance funds for another African safari. Bell reads of the gold strike in the Yukon. Gets a .360 from his friend Daniel Fraser in Edinburgh. Leaves England on a steamer possibly to Seattle (accounts differ) and from there travels north; meets "Micky" en route. The pair travel on a scow from Whitehorse to Dawson. On arrival they meet Micky's brother who has a claim. Bell detests the backbreaking work of working claims and decides to use his rifle to shoot meat for miners, but finds game shot out everywhere near mining sites.

Meets "Bill" who tells him that all game shot out for at least 100 miles. He and Bill become partners in a meat-hunting business. They build a cabin 200 miles from Dawson in the Ogilvie Mountains. Bell shoots the meat and Bill transports it back to Dawson via dogsled to sell it. In the spring Bill takes the penultimate load to Dawson via dog sled and never returns; Bell abandons the meat he's shot as well as the cabin and hikes back to Dawson with a rifle and a few dogs.

1899
Bell hears that Canada is recruiting for the Boer War (Oct. 1899–May 1902), so he sells his .360 Fraser and dogs and goes to Calgary to enlist. He travels down the Yukon River via Nome and the Aleutians to reach Calgary. He is accepted into the 2nd Battalion Canadian Mounted Rifles (CMR) because he's the owner of a horse and has a Stetson! The troops travel by train to Quebec and then from the East Coast of Canada to Cape Town; he arrives there on 27 February 1900.

1900–1902
Bell partakes in Boer War using a .303 Lee Enfield. His pony is shot from underneath him; he's taken prisoner and then escapes. At the end of the war, he takes his discharge from what is now the 1st Battalion CMR, probably in May 1902, and goes back to England. Army money funds his first elephant hunting expedition in BEA. Buys two sporting-model .303s with 10-shot magazines.

In second half of 1902, Bell arrives in East Africa, travels via rail to Kisumu on Lake Victoria, takes a boat to the Ssese Islands, gathers a crew, and shoots buffaloes. Arrives in (B)Unyoro, western Uganda, in the midst of the Sudanese Mutiny. Meets Sydney Ormsby.ABell meets in Mumias. Gets faulty advice on using head shots to kill crop-raiding elephants; manages to kill an elephant with a heart shot but finds this upsets the herd. Obtains a saw from Ormsby's camp and cuts elephant skull in half, thus learning how to properly position shots to the brain of an elephant. All ivory is turned into the government. Ormsby refers Bell to Partington, whom Bell meets in Mumias.

1902–1907
Does a total of 4 expeditions into Karamojo during this time period. The last expedition is the subject of *Karamojo Safari* (Harcourt Brace, NYC, 1949). Shoots a total of 345 elephants from the Karamojo region in these years: 42 from Mount Elgon, 91 from Mani-Mani, 63 from Dobesi, and 149 from Dabessa.

1903
Partington allows Bell access to Karamojo, whose jurisdiction falls under the "Outlying District Ordinance" and, thus, is restricted to outsiders. While Partington stays in a hut near Nandi Boma (a government post), Bell embarks on his first expedition into Karamojo; he has twenty .577 Snider rifles for his crew to demonstrate a show of force against the raiders. Uses unruly steers as pack animals because donkeys are too expensive. Meets Pyjalé at Bokora village for first time; Pyjalé will become Bell's most faithful tracker as well as a man Bell much admires.

After first journey, Bell retreats, sells ivory, and sets up a much larger scale safari. Bell finds that giving cattle as a reward is the key to getting information on elephants from natives. Bell establishes a cattle farm near Partington in Nandi country.

1904
Bells leaves on second, much larger safari, again meets Pyjalé, and together they travel as far north as Sudan. Bell returns to Mumias with 14,000 pounds of ivory.

1905–6
Third safari into Karamojo, no details known.

1906–1907
Fourth, and last safari, into Karamojo is described in *Karamojo Safari*. Starts in Mumias, east of Mount Elgon, crosses the Turkwell River (which was the border between effective and ineffective British control), and hunts beyond Moru Akipi. Bell shoots a record one-day take of ivory: 1,463 pounds (also recorded as 1,493); 15 were single tusks; one bull had two broken stumps totaling 148 pounds.

At the end of this safari Bell describes shooting the largest tusker on this safari between Nabwa and Dodosi, a bull with tusks of 148 x 145 pounds. The entire safari yielded 354 tusks—an average of 53 pounds each—or a total of 18,762 pounds of ivory. He sells the ivory to traders for 7 rupees a pound. After paying expenses, he netted £6,000 sterling, which is £572,400 or $670,000 USD in today's money. The entire trip lasted 12 to 14 months (accounts differ) of which 6 were spent actually hunting and the rest consumed by travel. Bell returns to Mumias.

1908
Goes back to London. For his next African safari, Bell asks Thomas Cook's Tours to make arrangements to deliver four natives from his previous Karamojo expeditions to Djibouti. Bell arrives in Djibouti with Harry Rayne, and they travel via rail and horse to Addis Abba. After a horse-racing interlude in the Abyssinian capital, the party travels to Gore and then into western Abyssinia. Bell and Rayne pay an extortionate rate of tribute to the local ruler, Ras Tsama, in order to continue: ivory and gold dust as well as firearms, mules, camels, and liquor. They go to the Gambela Swamps where they shoot elephants, and then they take boats and descend the Pibor River till it joins the Sobat River. Their safari ends when they finally reach the White Nile at Tawfikia.

1908–09
From Tawfikia Bell travels to the Lado Enclave where he hunts for 9 months and shoots 210 elephants; he has a close brush with a rhino. Rayne travels to the coast of Kenya to start a rubber plantation in partnership with Bell.

1909–10
Bell returns on foot from the Lado Enclave to Lake Victoria, then travels to Kisumu and the coast. Visits Rayne and plantation; the partners decide to sell the rubber plantation. Bell explores possibilities of whaling between the Kenya coast and the Seychelles Islands. Bell goes back to London and orders a cachalot whaler and, after much trouble, kills a whale in the English Channel. Norwegian company gets whaling rights off the Seychelles Islands; Bell gives up whaling scheme.

1911
Takes steamer to Liberia and hunts in the interior.

1912–1914
Takes steamer to Brazzaville (D.R.C) and then goes upriver to Bangui (C.A.R). Orders a small boat with steam engine from his agent in Scotland, which takes a year to arrive. In the meantime he hunts in Congo Brazzaville and Ubangi-Shari and with Pygmies between the Ubangi and Sangha Rivers. He is brought to court in Bangui for shooting elephants without the permission of the French concession holders, but a sympathetic judge dismisses the case.

Continues to hunt and encounters man-eating leopards, slave raiders, and cannibals. Bell's thirty-five-foot steamer arrives in Bangui, and he arranges for two, large native canoes to be placed along its side with a platform on top so that it can accommodate a team of trackers. Holds elephant drives on the large islands of the Ubangi River. Continues east on the Ubangi River and then north on an unnamed side river; he stops at a French post on the way. Leaves the steamer and goes into the interior; hunts local crop raiders with the help from villagers. Deals with marauding hyenas and takes part in a "fire hunt" with natives.

Receives a note sent by native runners from the commandant of the French fort sheltering his steamboat that World War I had broken out between England/France and Germany five months earlier (July 1914–November 1918). Returns to Bangui, sells his ivory, and gets on a steamer bound for Bordeaux; from there Bell travels to England. Takes flying lessons so he can enlist as a pilot in Royal Air Corps.

1915–1917
Earns his wings and is sent to BEA; scouts and flies in the East Africa campaign. There is no German air opposition, so Bell asks to be transferred. He is sent to the Balkans via Egypt and is stationed in Macedonia. Shoots down an enemy plane and receives the Military Cross for this action. Goes on R&R leave to Egypt; his boat is torpedoed; and he is rescued and taken to a Greek island. On his return to war, he shoots down a French plane by accident.

Bell becomes ill, and in December 1917 he is invalided back to England to recuperate.

1918
Arrives back in England in late January and is hospitalized. After his release, Bell settles in London.

1919
Walter Bell marries Miss Kate Rose Mary Soares in London on 15 January 1919. Moves to Ross-shire, Scotland, and settles in Corriemoillie, his Highland estate.

In *Bell of Africa*, Bell leaves for Ivory Coast and hunts elephants in thick cover before meeting Wynne-Eyton in Nigeria. In the diaries Safari Press edited, he and Wynne-Eyton depart together for West Africa. Wynne-Eyton (last name mistakenly given simply as Eyton in *Bell of Africa*) has a .450 Rigby, a .318 Mauser, and a 12-gauge shotgun. Bell carries a .318 Mauser and a .22 LR.

The two hunters travel up the Niger River in their Peterborough canoes and then over to the Benue River. They enter the kingdom of Buba Gida (Rei) from whom they get permission to hunt in the land of the Lakkas. From there they arrange for a 100-mile portage of canoes to the Longue River. They descend the Longue toward Lake Chad, go upstream on the Chari River, and from there to the Bahr Aouk. Once there they trade hippo meat with natives for flour and fish. Shoots rhinos for their horns.

The pair intended to reach Lake Mamoun, but they never get there. They find ivory not as heavy as in other expeditions. Bell's best day is 10 elephants. Despite plans for an extended multi-year hunt, Bell and Wynne-Eyton return after one season.

1920
Bell returns to Scottish Highlands.

1923
Wanderings of an Elephant Hunter is published by *Country Life* magazine in London.

1923–1924 (Winter)
Takes a trip from Kano in Nigeria to Khartoum in Sudan with Gerrit and J. Malcolm Forbes; the expedition travels with four combustion-engine vehicles, one a half track.

1932–1939
The Bells commission a steel-hulled sailing boat, which they name the *Trenchemer*, designed by Olin Stephens. She is a racing yacht and a sailing boat. In 1934 the *Trenchemer* comes in second on the Fastnet Race. The Bells sail the *Trenchemer* till 1939 when she is put up in Inverness. WW II breaks out and the *Trenchemer's* diesel engine is requisitioned for the war effort.

1940–1945
Bell serves in the Home Guard.

Post 1945
Spends time shooting and fishing in the Highlands, also writes and paints.

1950 circa
Contacts Townsend Whelen about publishing his autobiography.

1954 (30 June)
Walter Dalrymple Maitland Bell dies from a heart attack. Katie and W. D. M. Bell have no children.

1954 (18 December)
Bell's will is recorded. Estate has total value of £3,608 (sterling), which in 2017 reckons at £89,090 ($115,000 USD). This includes Corriemoillie and the surrounding land, shares in English and North American companies, 4 rifles and 3 "guns," presumably shotguns. His shareholdings upon his death include Hudson Bay Company, Anglo American Corp. of South Africa, and British American Oil Company.

1956
Pyjalé dies.

1957 (5 August)
Katie Rose Mary Soares Bell dies of uterine cancer.

1960
Bell of Africa is published in London by Neville Spearman.

References:
Bell of Africa, Neville Spearman, London, 1960.
Bell's last will and Bell's, his parents, and his wife's registry of birth, registry of death, and 1901 census on file at ScotlandsPeople Centre/ 2 Princes St. / Edinburgh EH2 / United Kingdom.
Correspondence, papers, diaries, photos, and illustrations by Walter Bell from his estate circa 1910–1954.
Incidents from an Elephant Hunter's Diary, Safari Press, Long Beach, 2017.
Karamojo Safari, Harcourt Brace, New York, 1949.
Wanderings of an Elephant Hunter, Country Life Publications, London, 1923.

In Pursuit of Elephants—A Life's Ambition

It being my sole ambition to hunt elephants, it was with some impatience that I received such interruptions as wars. In the first one in which I took part, I had my pony shot from under me, but in the second one, I managed to turn the tables on my opponent—a German Albatross—at 10,000 feet, and so satisfied a long-held ambition. Other obstructions, if less belligerent, were forthcoming from such sources as my guardians. I had to fight like fury against all this opposition, and so it was not until I had reached the age of seventeen that I really got going.

W. D. M. BELL

The Life and Times of W. D. M Bell

Part I

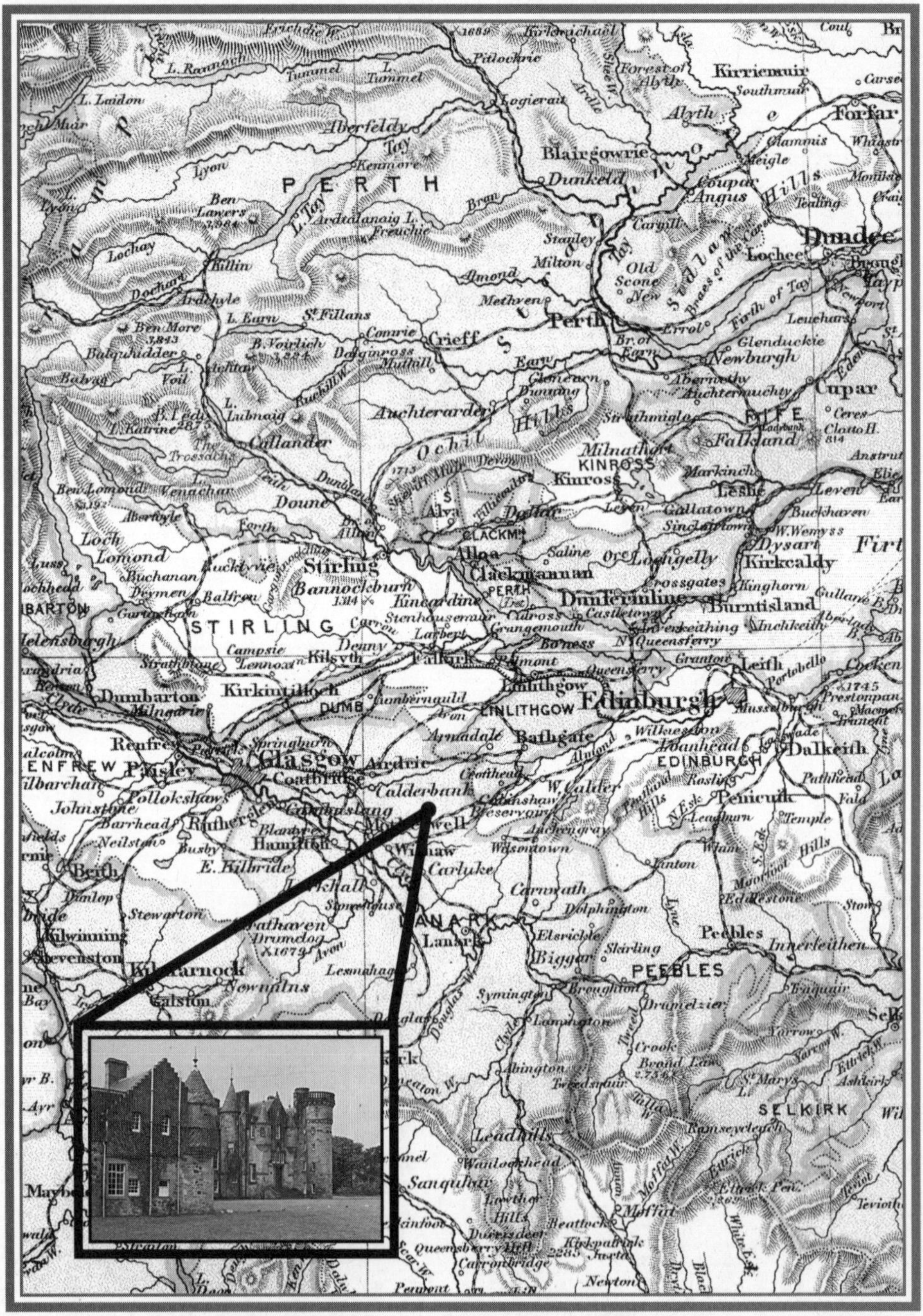
PERTH
Pitlochrie
Kirriemuir
Forfar
Alyth
Blairgowrie
Dunkeld
Coupar Angus
Dundee
Aberfeldy
Kenmore
Ben Lawers
Killin
Perth
Crieff
Comrie
St Fillans
Methven
Newburgh
Cupar
FIFE
Auchterarder
Ochil
Milnathort
KINROSS
Kinross
Falkland
Callander
Doune
Dunblane
Alva
Dollar
Loch Lomond
Stirling
Bannockburn
Alloa
Clackmannan
Dunfermline
Burntisland
Kirkcaldy
Dysart
Kinghorn
Leven
STIRLING
Kilsyth
Falkirk
Linlithgow
Edinburgh
Leith
Dalkeith
Musselburgh
Kirkintilloch
Dumbarton
Helensburgh
Renfrew
Paisley
Glasgow
Airdrie
Coatbridge
Calderbank
Bathgate
LINLITHGOW
EDINBURGH
Penicuik
Hamilton
Rutherglen
Motherwell
Wishaw
Carluke
Lanark
Carnwath
Biggar
PEEBLES
Peebles
Innerleithen
Kilmarnock
Kilwinning
Galston
Leadhills
Sanquhar
Moffat
SELKIRK

Early Misadventures

CHAPTER 1

I was born on 8 September 1880 in Uphall, Linlithgowshire (now West Lothian) of mixed Scots and Manx parentage and burdened, without consultation, with the resounding names Walter Dalrymple Maitland Bell. I have never attempted to live up to the implicit respectability of this imposing array; that would have been too much. On one occasion in my life these cumbersome initials stood me in good stead and brought me a sum of money that, but for their singularity, would never have come my way. Here is what happened:

I once met an ancient and footsore prospector padding wearily along a hot and dusty Central African trail, and, acting the Good Samaritan, I gave him supplies and a riding donkey equipped with a saddle from my own bountiful store. Sometime later a mysterious sum of money was deposited in my name in a Nairobi bank, where for a long time it lay unclaimed. Years later, the bank placed a claim notice in the local paper, and a good friend drew my attention to it. Because no two people could possibly have a name like mine, the bank accepted my identification and handed over the sum.

******

I was one of ten children, and it is understandable that my father looked upon me as just one more of a pestilent brood. My mother died when I was two years old, and because I missed the early maternal influence, this may in part have accounted for my premature and insistent urge to get away from home. I have no endearing memories of Papa, but I can dimly remember sitting silently and awe-stricken on a high chair in my father's room while my sister, one year younger than myself, was dangled on the parental knee.

My father was a bold and courageous businessman who did well in his ventures.[1] Starting in life as a timber merchant, he had by courage

---

[1] Robert Bell was a pioneer in the coal and shale oil industries and, according to his obituary in *The Scotsman*, "Mr. Bell not only exploited the shale, but to him is due the further credit of having discovered the ammonia that it contains, and which, until he led the way in erecting a plant for its recovery from the watery product of distillation had constituted one of the nuisances of a paraffin manufactory. It is now one of the most important products of the Scottish oil companies."

Clifton Hall, W. D. M. Bell's childhood home, today.

and acumen accumulated a goodly portion of worldly possessions. He had bought himself a country estate where he proceeded to enjoy the privileges and pursuits then considered to be the normal way of life, and in due course he acquired a grouse moor and even began to raise pheasants. He was by no means a poor performer at driven birds, but he was far outshone in this department by his younger brother, "Uncle Tom."

To us, Uncle Tom was a character. He had gone to Australia during the gold rush—where, by the way, he had done no good—and had now retired to share somewhat in his brother's prosperity. He was always at the shoots at Clifton Hall, where he would appear with a most frightfully dangerous gun that he loved beyond measure. He had bought it second-hand at some auction and insisted on loading his own cartridges.

Whether from previous experience of blasting powder or for reasons of economy, he always used it for his hand-loaded cartridges. There were several holes in the barrels of his gun, and at each discharge smoke would appear in the most unexpected places. We children would always try to secure a position near Uncle Tom's stance. He was our hero all right.

These sentiments were hardly reciprocated by the guns on either hand, however, and these were sometimes quite famous shots. For Uncle Tom was no respecter of persons, famous or otherwise, and he would poach their birds and wipe their eyes right and left, to their unspeakable indignation and the

EARLY MISADVENTURES

delight of his juvenile audience. He was a brilliant natural shot, always in form in spite of an extraordinary capacity for strong waters.

Undoubtedly during this period my number one enemy was my father. Not only did he begrudge his cigars, but he also strongly resented his children playing on his new billiard table. One would have thought from his attitude that his family went to the table with the express purpose of cutting the cloth rather than of merely wishing to learn the game. My only other memories of contact with my father seem to have been made through the medium of a large, highly polished walking stick.

Next on my list of enemies was my oldest brother, a strong, tough, big man. Happily he was vulnerable to distantly shouted insinuations about nasty goings-on with our pretty governess. But could he run, which I found to my dismay! Perhaps more fun, and certainly with far less danger to myself, could be got from twitting the female partner of this purely imaginary intrigue by publicly parading round a pair of size ten shoes supposedly found in her bedroom.

Yet home was quite a jolly place. Papa seemed determined to squeeze the orange of life before it became a lemon, and my recollections of that time conjure forth visions of a palatial house, elder brothers and sisters on hunters [horses], a butler in various stages of intoxication, two grand cellars stuffed with bottles, larders full of game, and the lower story overflowing with great, red, lusty Scots maids.

On the outdoors two stalwart gamekeepers—one with a magnificent black beard—kept everyone amused or apprehensive as the case—and sex—might be. There was no necessity to exercise inventiveness in the case of these sex-driven men; more was it a case of uncovering actual affairs. How that scene kept changing! Philandry in those virile days was no joke: Fertility was too high.

Another view of Clifton Hall in recent times.

I loved solitude. By the time I had learned to read, I showed a quite normal boy's taste for hunting literature. I easily acquired my favorite penny dreadfuls in all their variety and sameness. Where I showed some abnormality was in straightway proceeding to carry out such maneuvers as would instantly land me among the scenes of enchantment illustrated in my current adventure.

At the age of seven I decided my immediate aim was to kill North American buffaloes; after all, my rivalry with Dead Shot Dick and some of my other heroes preordained the course of my first safari: its destination North America and its object bison. I was quite oblivious to the fact that these buffaloes, or bison, had long ceased to exist outside any artificial sanctuary, at any rate.

At this time I had one intimate, my younger sister Florence. With her I discussed a project that had somehow formed itself in my mind, and that was to go to Monte Carlo to shoot pigeons. The main point in favour of this scheme seems to have been that Florrie could go, too. Our only means of subsistence would be the pigeons I shot. For some inscrutable reason that I cannot quite recall, I discarded this scheme in favour of the bison project. It may have been my discovery of the barrels of a dueling pistol without its locks or stock, a hunting knife, string, a pocket watch, and some pennies in my eldest brother's bedroom that had something to do with my change of plans.

My rivalry with Dead Shot Dick and some of my other literary heroes preordained the course of my first safari: its destination North America and its object bison.

Being country bred, I got no farther than my proper embarkation point, Glasgow. Once there, frustration overhauled me. In tendering the watch to Uncle Three-Balls across the counter of the cubicle so considerately provided to spare the susceptibilities of his clients—of which I was at eye level—I evidently aroused his suspicion. Whether it was on account of my youth or whether that particular type of watch should not have been in the possession of a child remains unknown. What there is no doubt about is the sudden return of "Uncle" with a large and very real policeman.

On demand of this very frightening official, out came the barrels of the dueling pistol, the hunting knife, the pieces of string, and what remained of the pennies. Thoroughly scared by that point, I easily gave up my home address. There followed a long wait by a warm fire in the police station, and then, to crown it all, who should appear but none other than my enemy Number One—my eldest brother. (See note at end of chapter.)

It was an ignominious end to a glorious project. I knew then that Dead Shot Dick would continue his devastating career forever ignorant of the danger to his reputation so narrowly averted when his seven-year-old rival was so opportunely arrested. Dead Shot would never have to fear those terrible double barrels of my brother's dueling pistol.

I continued my poisonous career at home, and it was not long before my guardians decided that they could look forward with relief to the time when "that horrible brat"—they meant me—could be sent off to boarding school. They little knew what lay in store for them.

I had now extended my reading, and Sir William Gordon-Cumming's tales of elephant hunting had finally canalized my thoughts and aspirations. Had my guardians realized what Gordon-Cumming's writings would do to me, they would have bought and destroyed every available copy of his works in a hundred-mile radius. Elephants now displaced bison in my murky brain. An obsession similar to that which was much later to seize upon one Paul Rainey,[2] whose only thought expressible in speech was, "I sees you, I sees you, sons-of-bitches," as he rode earnestly blood lusting behind his pack of dogs on his everlasting lion killings.

---

[2] Scion of a wealthy family whose fortune came from coal and coke production, Rainey (1877–1923) was active with the American Geographical Society, the American Museum of Natural History, the New York Zoological Society, and the Smithsonian Institution. In 1912, a six-reel documentary film Paul J. Rainey's African Hunt was released. Rejected by the military for health reasons, Rainey purchased an ambulance and drove it on the Western Front during World War I. After the war, Rainey hunted big game in Africa and shot some of the earliest film footage of African animals in the wild. He died in 1923 of a cerebral hemorrhage on his forty-sixth birthday.

Once a scholastic career was ordained by the higher ranks, I was irretrievably committed to boarding school. At first it did not seem such a hopeless case as was feared, and my guardians—father was now dead—[3] breathed a sigh of communal relief. In the beginning I was a bit over-awed. Soon, however, the trouble began. I was told that I had "an ingrained hatred of class privilege" or some such nonsense; actually, I was rather proud of my attitude.

There was a particular boy on whom I vented my peculiar brand of envy and malice. This boy was a first-rate man at games, and he stood very high in the esteem of masters and boys alike. He was, in fact, a leader. That he was inclined to be a bully could not be denied, perhaps, but then he came of such a high-spirited line, such ancient if robber stock, that much could be forgiven him or overlooked . . . and was. But not by the hero of this tale. Oh, no! The bigger the game, the higher the fury of my bitter enmity.

It was a cricket match between the junior teams that provided the occasion for my undoing. As it happened, my greatest enemy had condescended to act as umpire. Now this man of fifteen or sixteen years had not the faintest glimmering of any feeling among the kids of eight or nine other than that of a proper deference and fear. This was due to his attainments in the field of sport—but not to those in the academic sphere where, indeed, he was a bit of a dead-head. So when he declared me out—that "unruly, sulky, and undisciplined brat"—I retaliated. I whacked him on the head with my cricket bat. All these years later, I still shudder when I think of the sensation caused by this unspeakable sin.

All hell was let loose. An umpire had been assaulted in broad daylight during the execution of his duty . . . and in Great Britain! Had it occurred twenty miles across the Channel, one might have shrugged it off. But here! It completely flummoxed the field. No one knew what to do or say. Silence and a great fear held the multitude. The school's Number One prize at games was seen in earnest colloquy with the masters, while whispering groups of pale boys could be seen to shudder and totter on impact of such exclamations as, "What! Biffed the umpire on the boko?"

Meanwhile the cause of all this flurry stood irresolutely but alone on the battlefield until ordered off by one of the masters. For the rest of that day and

---

[3] According to Bell's own timeline, he would have been either seven or eight years old when his father died. See the note at the end of the chapter for more details. According to the obituary we found for Robert Bell in The Scotsman, Bell's father died in 1894.

whenever I came within speaking distance of one of these dignified creatures, I was greeted with horrifying details of what would happen to me. Apparently, the Head had to be consulted, and it was not until that night that I got notice that I was to appear before his august presence. It was very evident that this frightful meeting was to receive the proper and weighty consideration due to its empire-shaking importance.

By this time I was more than a bit shaken. Remember I was but eight years old. When I was confronted by a tall man with a stoop and a very large head, garnished with an outsize nose, who showed the utmost hostility by execrating the deed itself and its perpetrator not only in flowing scholarly periods but also with nasty vicious cuts in the air with a cane, there formed itself in my stupid, obstinate head the thought: *I definitely dislike school and this man.*

Whether this thought manifested itself in the increased steadiness of my eye and so quelled my opponent, as I would like to believe, or whether the Head had a sudden accession of pity, as would seem more probable, must remain conjecturable. What is known is that those vicious cuts remained in the air and found no target on my anatomy, which they certainly should have as no right-thinking Briton will deny. Instead of a sound caning by the Head, I was to be tried by the boys themselves and punished by them.

Perhaps the Head thought I would thus receive a hotter licking than anything he himself could hand out. If so, he made an acute psychological miscalculation. A committee of the older boys tried the case, presided over by the erstwhile umpire's rival, and nothing came of it. Mine became a sad case of thwarted justice.

As time rolled on, I became more and more convinced that I had somehow got onto the wrong road. School seemed to my muddled brain to lead nowhere near to the dazzling visions of sunlit prairies filled with pasturing herds of elephants waiting for my deadly rifle to lay them out. The best method of dealing with man-eating lions or leopards or crocodiles formed no part of the school curriculum. *What a waste!* I thought. My single-track mind determined to end it all and to get out.

To Africa! became my battle cry.

My next procedure was simple: I simply left for home. When my guardians demanded to know what I intended to do, I said I was going to Africa to hunt elephants. They told me there were no elephants left in Africa, and that anyhow I was not old enough. They, of course, were thinking in terms of South Africa

9

where, truly enough, all big game had been nearly exterminated by Dutch and British hunters, aided by the advent of the .450 Martini breach-loading rifle.

My guardians lightly dismissed the remainder of that enormous continent, of which South Africa formed so small a part. Their attitude was not entirely spurious because in those days not much was known about Africa outside the old Bristol and Liverpool trading firms whose past, so deeply rooted in the good old days of ivory and slave trading, was kept shrouded as these merchants had little wish to advertise their trading territories.

That the guardians were wrong we now know, but how wrong they were in their airy declaration that there were no elephants left in Africa will be evident by looking at "Elephant Control" in the latest *Uganda* or *Tanganyika Year Book*. There we can find that, instead of being extinct or nearly so, elephants are actually on the increase—in spite of a yearly destruction of some one to two thousand head by the control officers.

How I knew there were still elephants to be hunted is unknown. The fact remains that nothing could shake me in my determination. From the advantage of hindsight, I now cannot help sympathizing with my poor guardians. I was a puzzle all right. It had been made clear by the headmaster of the school I had so recently left that he could not recommend me as a suitable candidate for a further scholastic career; in fact, the headmaster had shown a rather surprising warmth in his denunciation when he referred to me as "that nine-year-old delinquent."

What were they to do? That I was a troublesome brat was not in dispute. My proposal that they should outfit me for an expedition into darkest Africa to hunt non-existent elephants fell on deaf ears.

"At the age of nine or ten?" they exclaimed. "Preposterous!" they shouted in unison.

Thus, my guardians determined to resort to the time-honoured expedient of getting out of a difficulty. They would send me to sea. In their opinion some sense would inevitably be knocked into me by the simple process of knocking nonsense out of me. In any case, I would not be able to run away while at sea nor could I avoid growing older. So it was decided to apprentice me to a firm of sailing-ship owners. When I was told of their decision, my reaction was not immediately negative, for it gave me pause to think. Deciding that it would bring me nearer my objective, Africa, I determined to fall in with their scheme.

Endnote:

This chapter raises some interesting thoughts. The first concerns when Bell's father actually died and when his siblings became his guardians. Bell wrote two versions of his autobiography. In one, he said his father had already died when he, Bell, made his abortive trip to hunt bison in North America (age seven); in the other version, he states that his father died before he was sent to boarding school (age eight). As you can see from the obituary in The Scotsman *(below), Robert Bell actually died in 1894 when W.D.M. was fourteen.*

Another bit of mystery is the number of siblings Bell had. Bell said he was one of ten children, but the records we found at the ScotlandsPeople Centre in Edinburgh list Robert and Agnes Bell as having only nine children. Perhaps Bell was counting a stillbirth? Perhaps there was an error in the records? Perhaps Bell's father had another child after Bell's mother died? It's impossible to know.

We have no idea how Bell could have confused the date of his father's death, the ascendancy of his older siblings as his guardians, and how many children were in his family. We can only surmise that Bell wrote these versions of his autobiography at the very end of his life—sometime after WWII—and simply became confused as to what happened when. Time has a way of making the memory of events hazy, so we'll leave it at that. The reader will find similar lapses throughout this book.

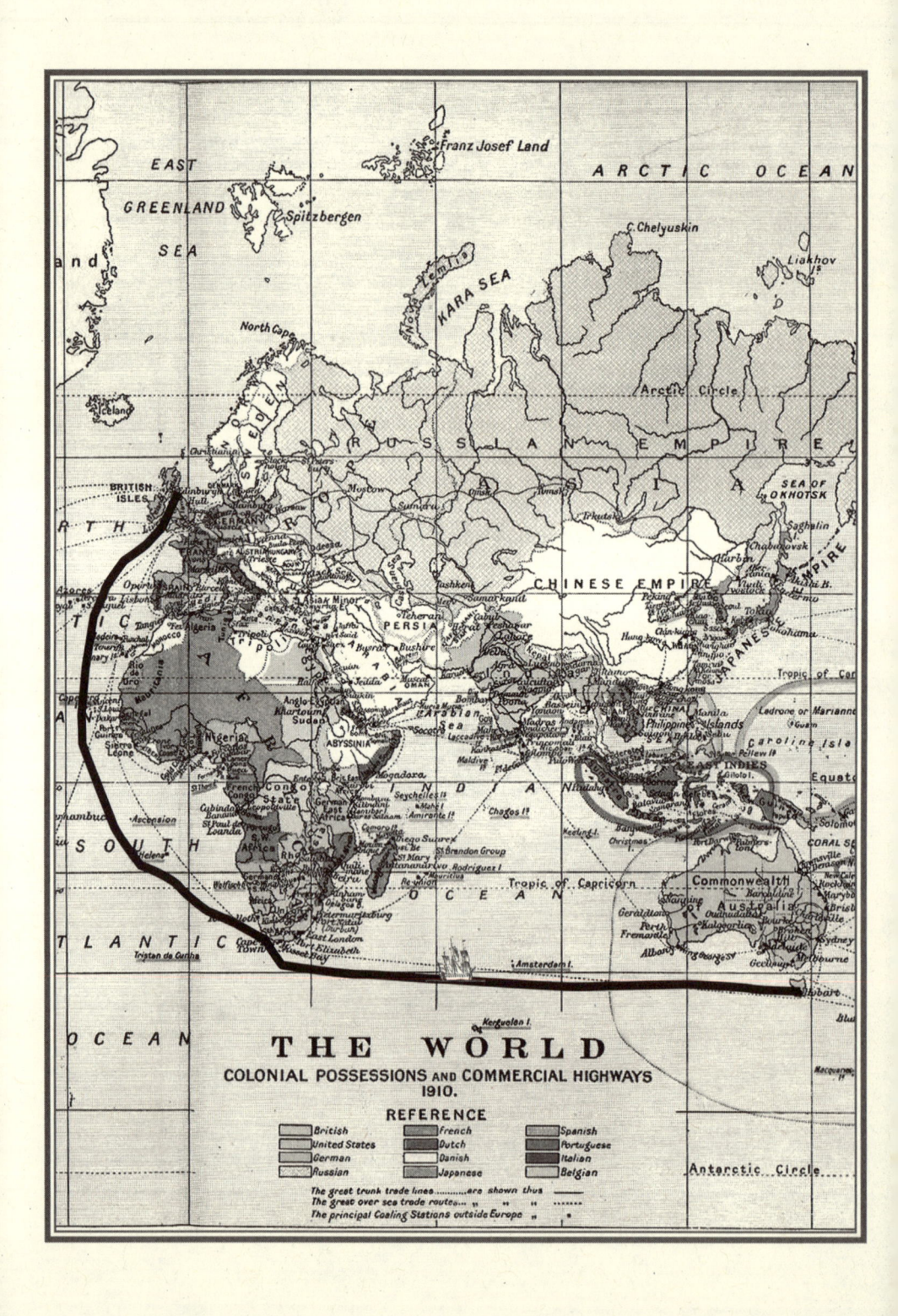

THE WORLD
COLONIAL POSSESSIONS AND COMMERCIAL HIGHWAYS
1910.

REFERENCE

British	French	Spanish
United States	Dutch	Portuguese
German	Danish	Italian
Russian	Japanese	Belgian

The great trunk trade lines .... are shown thus
The great over sea trade routes .... " "   ......
The principal Coaling Stations outside Europe " "   ......

I Take a Sailing Ship to the Other Side of the World

CHAPTER 2

In due course articles were signed and a fine outfit acquired. The outfit included a complete sea-going kit, all contained in a formidable wooden sea chest—sea boots, oilskins, jerseys, dungarees, and a magnificent blue uniform. The latter came with a brass-bound, cheese-cutter cap mounting the firm's flag in blue and white enamel and surrounded by a prodigious amount of gold braid.

So one fine morning there issued from the precincts of a very posh hotel in Barrow-in-Furness a horse-drawn "growler" cab containing in its capacious interior my eldest brother, his good Friend with Nautical Experience, and I—our hero or miscreant, depending on whether you are a cricketer or not. Stoutly displayed on the roof was the sea chest, plastered with the imposing initials W. D. M. B., flanked by two enormous glass jars of pickled onions. The pickled onions owed their presence to the Friend with Nautical Experience who considered no one adequately equipped for the sea without a supply of those spirited vegetables.

All were well and darkly dressed, even the cabby. All wore gloves—people did in those days—and the cortège might reasonably have been mistaken by an idle onlooker for a funeral party with a coffin, perhaps of a child, represented by the darkly painted sea chest, had it not been for those great glass jars of pickled onions, their occupants dancing gaily in and out of their bath of dark brown vinegar.

Had the idle onlooker been made acquainted with the real object of the "growler"-contained expedition, he would have been amazed. I can't believe a less suitably clad party ever sallied forth for the purpose of introducing the junior member to the workings of a sailing ship loading steel rails in the Barrow docks.

When we arrived at the docks, enquiries were made for the barque *Jupiter*, destination Tasmania by way of the Cape of Good Hope. Luckily, she could still be reached by wheeled vehicle, and in due course we drew alongside a racy-looking iron barque of some eight hundred tons burthen. [Archaic nautical term denoting tonnage of a ship.] The Friend with Nautical Experience began to lay off about her beauty in no uncertain fashion while my gear was seen aboard by a couple of hitherto idle lookers-on. Indeed, to such an extent did the Nautical Friend go in his rhapsodizing that I began to wonder why he, too, did not join the lovely ship.

Reminiscences of an Elephant Hunter

I set sail on the barque Jupiter, *destination Tasmania by way of the Cape of Good Hope.*

I Take a Sailing Ship to the Other Side of the World

The tide being in, the *Jupiter* had so far only presented her top-sides, spars, rigging, and masts, all newly painted or varnished, to the appraising eyes of her critics. What a different scene presented itself when, warned by a raucous voice that the ship was about to warp out into the stream, we climbed the gangway and for the first time could see her decks.

What a scene of confusion and filth! Dazed-looking men of different skin colours stumbled about as if their hangovers would trip them up, all pursued by oaths and blasphemies from a vicious-looking, Liverpool-Irish chief mate, ably seconded by a burly bosun with a broken nose. The decks aft were covered in flakes of red rust from the recently embowelled cargo. The forward was full of filthy, stinking mud from the dock bottom that had been brought aboard by the links of the cable when the slack was shortened in preparation to warping out to the anchor, catching in it an obscene load of dead cats and indescribable muck. In short, everything and everybody were filthy.

After a glance or two about the ship, my brother and his friend suddenly seemed anxious to leave the uninviting scene. Beauties of line and rigging had lost their attraction. They hastily got over my introduction to the skipper, we said good-bye, and my last bowler-hatted link with shore sped down the gangway.

There I stood, a green lad of twelve,[1] complete with gloves and boiled collar and, yes, a dickey,[2] the only person not busy at something. A burly and very dirty man went to the captain, was told something, then glanced at me.

"Hey, you!" he bellowed.

Although he was fixing me with a steady glare, I could not really believe he was addressing me. That gorgeous uniform in my sea chest and the considerable sum that had been paid for my articles somehow had led me to think I was some sort of officer. How wrong I was. In three strides the burly and dirty man—he was the first mate—had me by the ear. My bowler flew off into the scuppers as I was propelled by an irresistible force, only to be

---

[1] Bell wrote two accounts of this story, and in one he said he was twelve when he left on the *Jupiter,* and in another he said he was fourteen. Given the problems he gave his guardians, a three-year sojourn at home after being expelled from boarding school is more likely than a five-year stay. Also, in Townsend Whelen's *Bell of Africa*, Bell says on page six that he was fourteen when he returned home from New Zealand via Tasmania. Departing for sea at age twelve, therefore, seems the more likely age.

[2] A false shirt front.

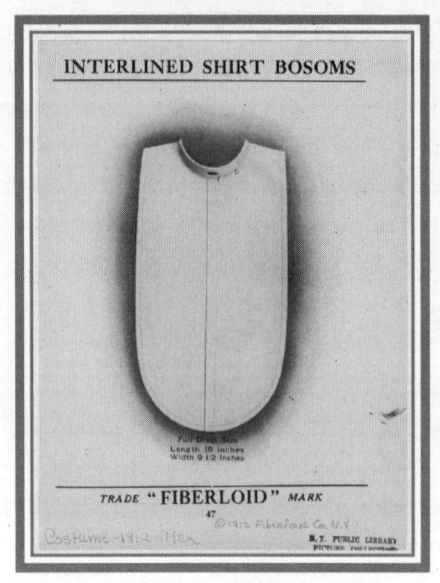

Advertisement for a false shirt front or "dickey," 1912.

brought up by the iron combing of a hatch, down which I was thrust as the first mate yelled, "Stand from under, Chips!"

A cheery "Aye, aye, sir!" sounded as I found myself shoved down a narrow vertical iron ladder in summary fashion. Into a dark hole dimly lit by a candle stub standing on one of the bulkhead frames I went. I was met by the astonished gaze of an oldish man stripped to shirt and dungaree pants and covered from head to foot in what looked like, and was, rusty mud. The stink from the cable with its obscene load from the dock bottom was gagging . . . as was the smell emanating from the man called Chips.

For an instant Chips stood silently gazing at me in my smart shore togs—overcoat, boiled collar, and gloves—as if he were dreaming. Suddenly there issued from his sweaty face the most tremendous burst of laughter as he doubled up over the coiled cable. Simultaneously a fearful clatter started up overhead. The crew was walking in the cable on the capstan in the good old-fashioned way—round and round, pushing on bars stuck into the capstan head.

"Lay hold! Lay hold!" shouted Chips to me, although I could not have been three feet away. "Here she comes!" he bellowed with some anger in his voice, making it clear what he, Chips, expected of his companion. So, with as good as grace as possible, I "laid hold."

At first the cable was dry, consisting of that part of it borne by the deck, but presently it came in good and strong straight from the dock bottom. Since no attempt was made by those on deck to wash it as it came up, we both were soon foul. In short time the shore-going gloves were reduced to slippery dangles and were thrown down among the stinking coils. The work was heavy, even for Chips, a seasoned toiler, and the heat considerable, so off came the beautiful overcoat, now a muddy mess, and weighing half a hundredweight, followed soon after by my—dare I say it?—dicky and cuffs. Well, there it is. The truth must out. I expect most of my right-thinking readers will now throw this book into the waste-paper baskets for salvage. Fancy! I wore a dicky!

I now entered into the thing with gusto and began to enjoy myself. If the others wanted to see me all mucked up, they should do so, and they should see that I enjoyed it more so than even they did. I proceeded to become utterly foul. I got it in my hair, I plastered my body with it, and I filled my handsome shore-going togs with it until I looked like one big, drowned dock rat. I laughed for the sheer joy of it, completely enjoying myself. This attitude to misfortune seemed to quite captivate the clothes-conscious Chips.

"Waal, A'll say you're the damnedest son-of-a-bitch for muck A've ever seed. Seems kind of natural like!" said Chips.

No reference to the abominable dicky, you'll notice. But, of course, there wouldn't be. A low-down, son-of-a-gun like Chips wouldn't know with what horror that humble article was so rightly viewed by the well-bred.

When the cable ceased to come in with the catting of the anchor, I was allowed on deck, and thankful I was for the fresh air. The ship was already at sea, albeit still in charge of a tug. The dismal-looking, soberized drunks were sloshing water about with brooms in a desperate effort to clean the ship. It appeared that *Jupiter* had no steam, and water was got by the simple process of putting a bucket on a line over the side and hauling the water back up.

As soon as I appeared on deck, I was accosted by a stocky boy of perhaps sixteen or seventeen years of age. Geordie was the senior apprentice on his last voyage before taking his mate's ticket—in those days B.O.A. regulations still insisted on four years in sail—and as such was about the best sailor man on board. He exclaimed, "Oh, Christ! What is that?"

Everyone stopped work and stood leaning on their brooms while grinning at the spectacle of a misery even greater than their own.

I asked Geordie where I could find a bath. For some reason I could not immediately understand, this raised a storm of jeers and cat calls. The idea of a bath on *Jupiter* seemed to tickle them immensely.

"Here y'are!" said the man with the bucket, slinging its contents over me. Geordie then seized me and laid me flat on the deck with astonishing ease considering my not unnatural reaction to these summary proceedings. With a whoop of merriment, the whole pack now set to work brooming me with far more industry than they ever showed when washing down the ship. The most amusing part seemed to consist in sweeping my hands from under me whenever I tried to get up.

Luckily for me, the chief mate now intervened in a most effective fashion, blasting and damning his mixed crew of Scandinavians, Irish, and Jamaican, and at the same time giving me a push that sent me reeling along the slippery deck, until, clutching wildly for something to steady himself, I made contact with the naked forearm of perhaps the only man aboard ship who could afford the luxury of displaying those feelings of ordinary humanity possessed by all—the ship's cook.

It would seem that every member of a sailing ship's company, from the captain downward, must appear tough, however soft-hearted he might be by nature. At least every second word must be an oath and no sentence adequate without some reference to the Almighty or Christ. Each vied with the other in spicy references to particular parts of the female anatomy, to the lowest vices as practiced in Sodom and Gomorrah, or to the fantastically unlikely union of dog and woman referred to in "son-of-a-bitch."

In the case of sea cooks, however, it seemed to be considered unnecessary that they should be tough in body, foul of mouth, blasphemous, or cruel in order to do their jobs. Perhaps it was subconsciously admitted that quite enough toughness would be provided by their cuisine, in any case, and that the partaking thereof would provide sufficient blasphemy and cruelty. Be that as it may, there is no doubt that sea cooks occupied a privileged position in sailing-ship society, at any rate. I, in my mad career along the deck, had come up against the only man aboard ship who could, if he chose, show kindness without losing face, and possibly his job. Luckily for me he chose to be kind.

Hauling me like a dithering drowned rat right into the galley, he plonked me down on a locker almost fully exposed to the full glare of the nearly red-hot range. There I was left to steam and scorch and smell as if I'd been a woolly sheep in hell. Meanwhile the kind Mr. Grubbs—that was not the poor man's true name, it afterwards transpired, but only his nickname—set about making me a large tin mug of well-boiled, well-sugared, and well-condensed-milked tea, one mouthful of which was calculated to revive the spirits of the most daunted and at the same time to remove most of the skin of one's mouth. But for Mr. Grubbs I don't know how I should have fared.

I Take a Sailing Ship to the Other Side of the World

The excessive activity, from the scene of which I had been so summarily ejected, had by this time resolved itself into a sound of industrious brooming undisturbed by the resounding and sometimes overloaded oaths that had enlivened the arrival of the chief mate. True, there was some raucous shouting going on somewhere, but it seemed to have no connection with the washing-down gang.

Feeling greatly restored in body and spirit by the kind ministrations of Grubbs—and, indeed, finding the heat from the range somewhat scorching now that my clothes had nearly dried—I ventured to look out upon my surroundings.

I found the ship still under tow of the steam tug and the land already gone from sight. The captain, a small white-haired figure, was talking to the pilot on the poop deck; there was a small boat from the tug alongside; and the chief was bawling away as a swarm of men threw off the confining gaskets on some of the sails aloft while others hove in that part of the tow line that belonged to the *Jupiter*. Evidently the tug and she were about to part company. From now on the good ship *Jupiter* would have to rely entirely on her sails for her sole motive power.

Presently there arose a perfect uproar on deck. As the captain shook hands with the pilot and that great dignitary prepared to lower his august bulk over-side, pandemonium broke loose. Everybody seemed to be bawling out in the toughest-sounding manner quite unintelligible orders to some unspecified members of the crew.

"Lee braces! Lee braces! Heave away, you sons-of-bitches! 'Varst heaving! Belay that! Sheet home! Chock-a-block, you bastard! Le' go, bugger you!" filled the air, interspersed with such expressions delivered in a pointedly critical manner from the break of the poop, as, "Of all the lousy, God-damned, sons-of-bitches! God strike me pink if you buggers ain't the lousiest set of whorehouse pimps as ever went to sea, and I've seen some." And so on and on. Apparently this was sailorizing.

"Better lend a hand," said Grubbs. "The mate will kill you if he sees you in here."

So I joined the rabble on deck, laid hold of the wrong ropes, and pulled when required to "come-up"; in fact, I made a perfect nuisance of myself. Everyone cursed everyone else, and all cursed me.

We were casting off our tug and making sail. I was about to witness that mysterious process by which a ship depending solely on wind, supplemented by such auxiliary power as could be generated by the liberal use of marlin spikes, belaying pins, fists, oaths, and sea-boots sailed from one part of the globe to another.

The gallant barque *Jupiter* had now come to life, and under her own wings she was heeling gently to a quartering breeze under plain sail. Apparently everything had been made snug, alow and aloft.

The mate said: "Muster all hands."

Everyone assembled at the break of the poop except Grubbs, Chips, and the captain's steward. The captain had disappeared below. I was not to see him again until he reappeared only when the hills of Tasmania rose from the sea—after some hundred and twenty days at sea. This was the more surprising, as it was part of his duties to take the time from the large clock in the skipper's saloon so as to strike the ship's bell at the proper time. Once or twice, indeed, I thought I could see dimly, through the spice and grog-laden fog, the outline of him, the person upon whom the safety of the ship and ship's company were supposed to depend.

If the captain had retired, the mate was much in evidence. He had beside him the second mate. Geordie, the chief apprentice, acted apparently as third mate, an arrangement very satisfactory to the owners as he was unpaid. Indeed, he had paid a very nice premium for the privilege of working harder than two able seamen.

Watches were picked, port and starboard. When there were but two left, I wondered who would pick me. I hoped the second mate would as he seemed a milder-looking man than the first mate, whose earlier exhibition had made a somewhat mixed impression on me. The choice now lay between myself and a smaller, paler urchin. Inches told, and the first mate chose me. The party broke up, the sailors to their fo'c's'le [forecastle] forward, while the apprentices had quarters under the poop deck, a narrow strip boarded off from those of the after guard that comprised the captain, mates, and steward.

This was the first time I had seen my quarters and candidly they did not impress me very much. They were high enough but only about five feet wide. So that by the time four bunks and four sea chests had been accommodated, there was precious little room left for even a table. Two of the chests lashed to the deck took the part of that useful piece of furniture. Geordie, as the old hand of the party, set about putting things ship-shape and Bristol fashion. The other chests were got down and lashed in position. The only remaining jar of pickled onions was brought in and stowed in a locker. When I ventured to say

I Take a Sailing Ship to the Other Side of the World

I was not to see the captain again until he reappeared only when the hills of Tasmania rose from the sea—after some hundred and twenty days at sea.

there had been two jars, Geordie said, "Never you mind about that! I'll look after it." And that was the last I heard of it.

Geordie now handed out a large tin dixie[3] and a sort of bucket with a lid on it to a lad he called Jim; Geordie told him to take them along to the galley and fetch the "skouse." At the same time he told me to put on some decent togs. This apparently meant blue serge pants over heavy underclothes and a jersey with dungarees over the lot. Never had I felt so much dressed, especially as our narrow quarters began to heat up with our bodies, aided by a hurricane lamp that now burned. But I was glad enough of them, and of a thick pilot coat on top of them all, when later it was my turn to keep watch on deck.

Meanwhile tea had arrived. A dixie-full of well-stewed tea sweetened with condensed milk, a bundle of hard tack, and a hash made with pickled beef, broken biscuit, and potatoes became an excellent "skouse," at any rate to hungry lads who had been working hard in good sea air. The ship was fairly steady, being heavily laden to her marks, and the wind still fair though freshening, so there was nothing yet to interfere with our appetites.

I felt considerably refreshed by my first meal aboard, and I began to take some interest in my surroundings. It must be confessed that hitherto I had looked upon everything with a bitter and jaundiced eye. It was my sudden realization that, though an apprentice was in theory something that might one day become an officer, in practice he was just a common "roust-about" at the beck and call of anyone. This realization had sadly shaken me. In fact, had I been able to do so, I would probably have performed one of my notorious disappearing tricks.

Life aboard sailing ships has been so often and so well described that it will suffice to say that for the next hundred and twenty days or so it flowed on in the usual somewhat monotonous fashion. For days on end the *Jupiter* sailed in company of a full-rigged ship whose name was not known. In the night the stranger would sail past *Jupiter* with the fresher breeze, only to be overhauled by *Jupiter* in the lighter airs of the day time. Tristan da Cunha was sighted, but a long way off.

The Jamaican developed homosexual tendencies. The potatoes got mixed up with paraffin oil. The three decks of iron rails had to be wedged tighter every watch after we rounded the Cape. When we ran in the "roaring forties," the

---

[3] A metal pot for cooking and making tea.

I TAKE A SAILING SHIP TO THE OTHER SIDE OF THE WORLD

decks were not dry for six weeks and grew a slippery scum. The weevils from our biscuit ration were exchangeable in the fo'castle for marmalade. A Swede had bladder weakness and was hove out of the fo'castle with some regularity. I noticed that in cold weather some men emptied their sea-boots of water, after doing their trick at the wheel. I found out that it wasn't water they were emptying. They peed in their boots to keep their feet warm.

In fine weather I was given the wheel and told to steer a specified compass course. I did so meticulously—only to be bawled out and cursed. The order should have been "full and by." For hours on endless hours in the night watches, I was pinned to the mizzen lower-shrouds while the mate poured into my reluctant ears the most boresome slush about some girl he was engaged to.

Once, when "four hours on, four hours off" became unbearable, I retired to the lazaret and slept the clock round. The ship's crowd were so convinced that I had fallen overboard that when I was finally discovered, everyone was so relieved that nothing was done about it.

As soon as the fine weather regions were reached, all the good heavy canvas came off and old sails bent in their places. Then, when the stronger weather south of the line was met, all these old sails were again replaced with stronger ones.

Constant work so that no-one should have an idle moment was the daily life of the ship. Never was man so enslaved as were these poor devils of a crew. For a miserable pittance of two or three pounds sterling per month, they were harassed and humbugged from one job to another. Sometimes it was setting up the rigging, or smearing down the rigging, or tarring it, or holystoning the decks. The jobs were endless and many of them unnecessary. It seemed that nobody was to be allowed to relax, ever. How I longed for a mutiny.

There is a belt of permanent westerly winds running right round the earth about forty degrees, south latitude. These winds are of almost gale force and as there are no land masses to break the seas, a hellish commotion is set up. Into this infernal turmoil all sailing-ships strived to insert themselves.

Once well in, the keel-less tubs simply rolled along with very little canvas set, but the steering was appalling, on the *Jupiter* at any rate. Only the most experienced helmsmen were used and most of the time there would be two men on at a time. Sometimes they would be lashed to the wheel housing to prevent them being washed away by the seas that might break over the poop. At any rate, that was the theory. Actually this lashing was to prevent the helmsmen from doing a bunk when they saw a particularly big one hovering high over their heads. To abandon the wheel when running is to risk the ship "broaching to" or getting broadside on to wind and water. Once the *Jupiter* logged one hundred and eighty miles under bare poles.

At long last land hove in sight, and so did the ship's captain. Pale and wan from his hundred-and-twenty days' binge, he now appeared on the poop bleary eyed as he blinked and peered over the roaring gray seas. I had not seen him since he shook hands with the pilot in the Irish Sea. In spite of this, we had somehow reached Tasmania, but it was another eight days before we tied up.

On the morrow sail was made, and in due course a wide estuary revealed itself. We now began that appalling maneuver known as "wearing ship." All hands are required for it. When the boards are short—as in an estuary such as this—the labour of coiling down all the braces and running gear each time the ship puts about becomes a heart-breaking task.

For five mortal days we beat to and fro across that wretched stretch of water, losing every yard we made on one board when putting about at the end of it. It was too rough for a pilot to come out. When the wind moderated, and one finally did so, the pilot was overheard to say that he had watched the *Jupiter* sailing right over a sunken rock time after time, a fact that he seemed to find highly amusing, judging by his gales of laughter.

There is one advantage about a head wind when approaching land and that is that the nearer one gets, the smoother the water becomes. The land warms the breeze, and, if the sun comes out, the effect on storm-raddled sailors after three months of exposure on a sailing ship's decks can hardly be understood today. In these days of steam even the helmsman is encased in glass and steel and the officer of the watch exposes only his nose to the elements. Therefore, an almost genial atmosphere might have been detected about the good ship *Jupiter* as she approached her goal of Hobart Town.

People began to look to their hands and shore-going togs, the latter only requiring airing, but the former being found in very poor shape. The constant pulling on ropes and the more constant wetting with salt water causes every fold and line of the skin of the palm to become a deep and very sore fissure. Sailors have a very terse but inelegant name for these cuts or cracks, and their

I TAKE A SAILING SHIP TO THE OTHER SIDE OF THE WORLD

remedy for them is little better than their name. They douse them with grease from the galley mixed with Stockholm tar, hardly a shore-going cosmetic.

Once safely berthed at a wharf, astern of a locally owned whaler, the thoughts of everyone turned to the delights ashore. Those with money already earned tried to get as much as possible from the skipper—a hard enough job—while the apprentices, who of course receive no pay, tried to get as much goods as they could from the slop-chest in the hope that it would be exchangeable ashore.

At that time there was still a considerable amount of whaling done out of Hobart, the old hand-harpoon type of whaling, of course. There were two whalers in port, so there gathered a pretty tough crowd at the two wharf-side pubs.

Geordie was our natural guide, philosopher, and friend, of course. He had almost completed his four years on square-rigged ships, and his knowledge of whoring, drinking, and gambling was only equaled by his sailorizing. He showed us greenhorns the ropes, all right.

Besides the professional barrel-bodied beauties more or less attached to these pubs, whose job it was to induce, or otherwise secure, custom for their house, there was a very pretty line of town girls, whose idea of fun seemed to be to see just how close to the wind they could sail without actually being taken aback.

The French term *cocotte* does not quite describe them, being in fact too polite a term. They made a dead set at the apprentices, who, in their nice blue uniforms and brass-bound hats, looked almost like naval officers. And as they required no money, doing all for love, they were fair game for Geordie and his pupils. Great fun was had by all.

I soon discovered the delights of this mild form of poodle-faking and rapidly became enamoured of a sweet, little semi-tart or tartlet. Just so far and no further was the order of their canoodlings, until one salubrious night, on a dark and fragrant bank of the park, I was apparently overheard to give expression to the exasperation of frustration, for, having parted from my inamorata with some coolness, I was greeted from the darkness by a deep and friendly voice saying, "Why don't you bat her over the head and take what you want? It was the park policeman!

Both the pubs had chuckers-out, and, of course, they were real men. They had to be. Inevitably, they were heroes in the eyes of the youngsters. Indeed, their jobs were not easy. They had to quell, without injuring, men who would

25

knife, bite, maim, and use every imaginable dirty trick against them. They also had to remain sober enough to merely convey their enemy out of the precincts and to leave him in such shape as to be able to return on the morrow more or less in one piece.

One of these chuckers-out was an Irishman. He was not so terrible to look at, albeit he had a tremendous reputation. He would be about five feet, ten inches tall, fairly burly, but very loose knit. Legs and arms seemed to be all over the place. He had a broken nose, one ear that was half-chewed off, and one eye almost closed, but he always had a joke for everyone and a smile on his good-humoured face. Well, Geordie, our know-it-all Geordie, came a frightful cropper over this Irishman. So sharp he cut himself, no one would have minded this—rather the contrary—but he involved others in his ruin. It transpired thus:

Perhaps you will remember that a Jamaican member of the crew was mentioned previously in this narrative. It will be necessary to examine this man more minutely, for, improbable as it may seem, he became the chosen vehicle of an all-providing Providence for the undoing of know-it-all Geordie.

This coloured man, or half-caste Jamaican, was a magnificent specimen physically. You would not see another such in three tours round the world. He was six feet, one-and-a-half inches tall, lithe, graceful, fine-boned, long-muscled, weighing fourteen stone, having no fat, always in the pink of condition, digestion undeniable, teeth perfect, and young. Why was such a paragon on a sailing ship? Why not on the stage? For the simple reason that had he not been at sea, he would have been in jail. He was an incorrigible and aggressive homosexual, and being of a naturally roving and enterprising nature, no one was safe from him.

Now, poor Geordie conceived, in an evil moment, the idea of pitting our Jamaican against the Irish chucker-out. Everyone was dazzled with the prowess on the yard-arm of the *Jupiter* candidate, and a purse was soon made up among the crew. Geordie at once became trainer and general manager. The Jamaican was put into training; that is, he was not allowed to get drunk more than once a day and he could have no liquor on board.

When the fight was first mentioned to him, he laughed and said he could, "Eat that man." We devoutly hoped his little weakness would not show itself in the moment of combat.

It was agreed that no formal challenge need be issued. Obviously a chucker-out has to accept any challenge or lose his job. All that would be necessary

I Take a Sailing Ship to the Other Side of the World

would be for someone to say: "Bet you so much you can't throw so and so out," book the bets, and let her go.

The great moment arrived, and no sooner had the bets been made than the room was cleared. A silence fell on the gathering, ripe as most of them were. Even the whores were quiet. Geordie was hovering on the outskirts of the light from the paraffin lamps and seemed to be arguing with someone. The Irishman appeared at the bar-end of the room in his usual get-up of sloppy trousers with belt at waist and shirt sleeves. Certainly, he looked no match for our man. We felt pretty sure of our money.

Meanwhile Geordie appeared to be having some difficulty with the *Jupiter* candidate. When he finally arrived within the circle of light, he came not as a conquering hero, but as if propelled from behind. That something was wrong was quite apparent from the silly grin on our man's face.

Soon there were yells of "Come on!" "Hold me back in case I kill him!" and suchlike, amidst roars of laughter from the audience.

The Irishman folded his arms and waited with a smile on his face.

Losing all patience, Geordie and his gang gave our man such a shove as to propel him into the middle of the arena where he finally pulled up and started to smile, vaguely and foolishly. Instantly the Irishman went into action, and it was a revelation. From a slovenly drooping figure he became a lithe, slinky, crouching demon, moving here, there, and everywhere. As he made a pass at our man, the Jamaican extended his arm, as if to shake hands with him. At once the Irishman was under his arm and lifted him bodily off his feet with consummate ease, carried him forth, and deposited him gently enough outside, thereby winning his bet. Those cunning men had doped our Jamaican!

Such was my introduction to sea-going life. As an apprentice, I was supposed to learn all the rudiments, and in four years would be in line for a mate's berth. Instead of following this course, I found our stay on Hobart, Tasmania, was far too short, and I started to think what I really wanted to do. Apart from being now rather farther from Africa than when I started, I was thoroughly disgusted with sea-faring. Shore leave over, we were recalled to the *Jupiter* in preparation for sailing. I broke my articles, forfeiting the premium my guardians had paid, and got myself ashore.

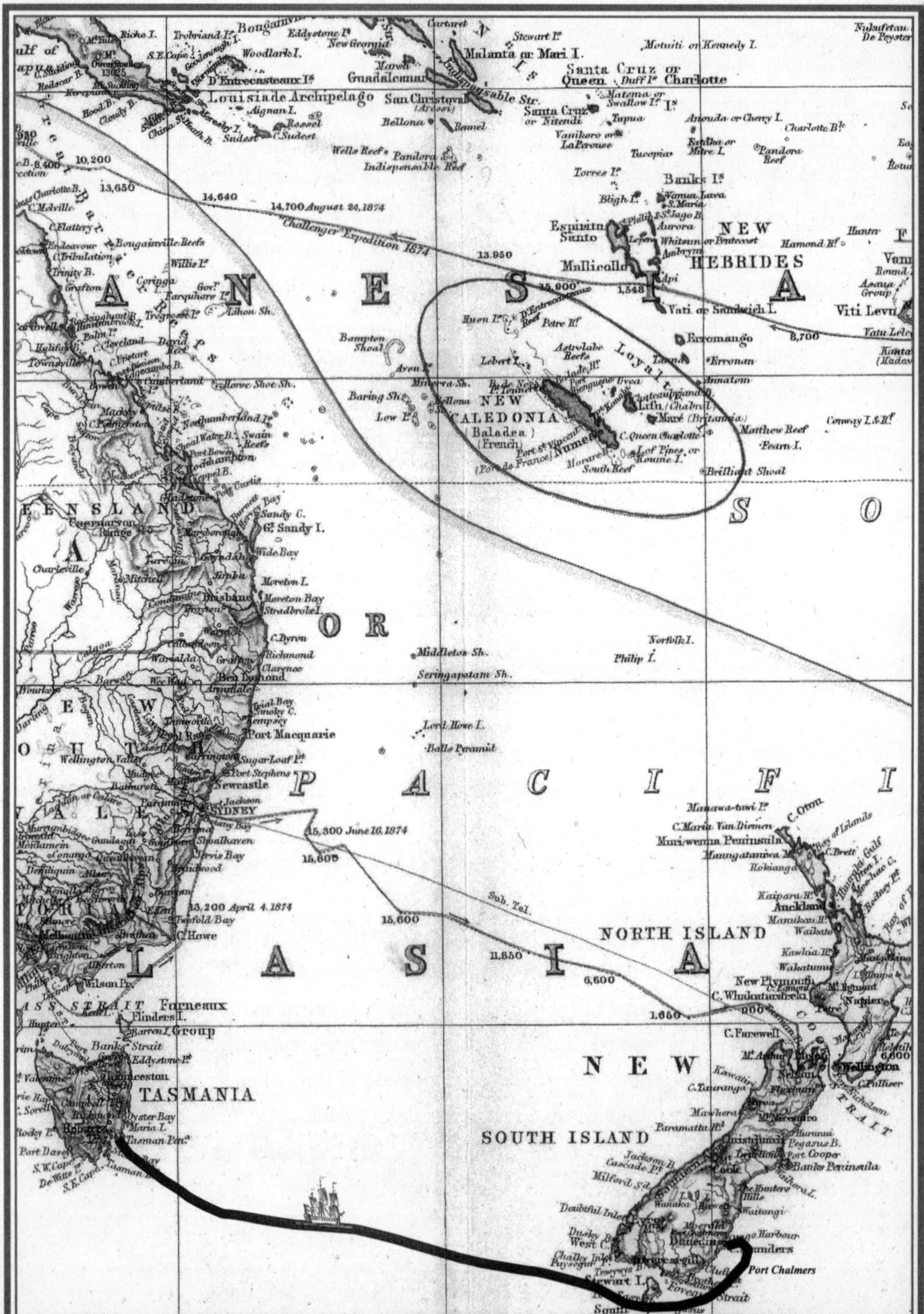
Louisiade Archipelago
D'Entrecasteaux Is
Woodlark I.
Trobriand Is
Eddystone I.
New Georgia
Malanta or Mari I.
Guadalcanar
San Christoval
Stewart Is
Santa Cruz or Queen Charlotte Is
Santa Cruz or Nitendi
Vanikoro or La Perouse
Tucopia
Torres Is
Banks Is
Bligh I.
Espiritu Santo
Mallicollo
NEW HEBRIDES
Vati or Sandwich I.
Erromango
Annatom
Viti Levu
14,640
14,700 August 24, 1874
Challenger Expedition 1874
13,950
15,900
1,548
8,700
10,200
13,650
Huon Is
Bampton Shoal
NEW CALEDONIA
(Baladea)
(French)
Noumea
Lifu
Maré
Matthew Reef
Brilliant Shoal
Loyalty
Middleton Sh.
Seringapatam Sh.
Norfolk I.
Philip I.
Lord Howe I.
Balls Pyramid
QUEENSLAND
Rockhampton
Sandy C.
Gt Sandy I.
Wide Bay
Moreton I.
Moreton Bay
Brisbane
C. Byron
Richmond
Clarence
Ben Lomond
Port Macquarie
Sugar Loaf Pt
Port Stephens
Newcastle
Port Jackson
SYDNEY
Botany Bay
Shoalhaven
Jervis Bay
Braidwood
Twofold Bay
C. Howe
Melbourne
Wilson Pr.
15,300 June 16, 1874
15,600
13,200 April 4, 1874
Sub. Tel.
11,850
6,600
1,650
Furneaux Group
Flinders I.
Banks Strait
Eddystone Pt
Launceston
TASMANIA
Hobart
Oyster Bay
Maria I.
Tasman Pen.
S. E. Cape
NORTH ISLAND
C. Maria Van Diemen
Bay of Islands
Auckland
New Plymouth
Mt Egmont
Napier
Wellington
C. Palliser
C. Farewell
Nelson
SOUTH ISLAND
Christchurch
Pegasus B.
Port Cooper
Banks Peninsula
Paramatta Hd
Jackson B.
Cascade Pt
Milford Sd
Doubtful Inlet
Dusky B.
West C.
Dunedin
Otago Harbour
Port Chalmers
Stewart I.
Foveaux Strait
Invercargill
A N E S I A
O R
P A C I F I
A S I A
N E W
S O

New Zealand in the 1890s

CHAPTER 3

Enquiries seemed to promise some hope of getting a ship to Africa from New Zealand. I had to work, of course, for I was entirely without resources. I soon found that if you listen to other people, you could get anywhere. I discovered that next to being a genius, it was best to be a tireless listener to other people's tales. It is a wearing and arduous business and requires great concentration, but it pays munificent dividends. I don't suppose I did one hour's honest work in return for my food and passage to New Zealand.

A very decent passage was had, too. There was plenty of good grub and very little work—it consisted of cleaning the carpenter's tools. "Chips" was an amiable man and seemed content to have a listener to his interminable tales. Since most people are themselves seeking for listeners, I recommend all young people to cultivate the art of listening if they have their way to make and nothing to make it with.

This working your passage is all very well, and most useful, but when the ship arrives at its destination, you are just hove out. This is not so pleasant and can be damnable—strange place, strange faces, no friends, and no money for hotels or even food. You wander round until tired out. Hungry, you drift back toward the docks, wishing now you could get some of that good food you had while still on passage. But there are still good people on this earth, or were then, and you finally find food and shelter at the Sailors' Home, bless the kind folk who run such institutions.

Here they soon size you up. "Pretty useless," they conclude. However, so long as you are young and not too obviously of criminal stamp, kindly help is soon forthcoming. For me in this case, it meant a job in a starch factory. True, the pay might be judged to be somewhat meagre. Ten shillings for a five-and-a-half day week is no great wage, especially when it costs exactly that sum for a week's board and lodging at the small lodging house where your kind friends deposit you.

What a jolly Irish widow kept that lodging house! She was free and easy and young in spirit, if not in age. She was quite good looking, if somewhat dirty, and all life was one huge joke to her. She fed you well, too, for, of course, in those days food was abundant. Her only help was another lass, also Irish, and I was allocated to her, as it were. Unfortunately, she had a most overpowering squint, although otherwise she was quite decent-looking. She was also ever so much younger than her mistress.

Nothing can prevail against a pronounced squint. Dress as you may, make up ever so carefully, nothing that you can do has any chance against that devastating catastrophe, in daylight, at any rate. And so it proved to be.

The Irish widow, on the other hand, had few reticences, and her mature charms appealed enormously to my youthful yearnings. Mistress and maid slept in separate beds in the same room. It was nothing for me to be invited to come in for a late cup of tea, and when that would happen, I would find my hostesses in their nighties, playing around. I was extremely young, it is true, but if the ladies had known my thoughts, they might not have been so forthcoming . . . or might they?

Anyhow, these thoughts received an abrupt check one evening. I had returned from work at the factory, and, after supper, had as usual been invited to tea in the bedroom. There I received the shock of my short life: A man's ugly face was beside the mistress in her bed. That man was a German and the captain of a small trading schooner. Every line and contour of that man's face was indelibly impressed on my memory, and twenty-five years later, when traveling on a steamer of which he was captain, I recognized him easily.

So, not wishing to spoil the party, I beat a hasty retreat, tealess, to my own room.

The work at the starch factory consisted in shoveling rice into large vats, where, on mixing with water, fermentation soon rendered it into sludge. This process produced the most awful stench in the surrounding area. It was hard work, any way you looked at it, and, as its reward exactly equaled the cost of lodging, it was not long before it dawned on me that there was no future in it. In fact, it appeared to me that Africa seemed a mighty long way off and that somehow I had passed it by. Therefore, it behooved me to get myself to the sea.

People told me I might get a ship to Africa at Port Chalmers, which was about ten miles away. Once there I found a cheap boarding house willing to take me in until I found a job. As a matter of fact, the landlady already had a job in prospect for me. The skipper of a fishing boat had commissioned her to find him a hand, and *Here he is,* she must have thought. Instead of a ship to Africa, I got a fishing smack to the surrounding seas.

Besides herself, the place was run by her two daughters, of some eight and ten years of age. The ten-year-old was extremely pretty, with that marvelous pink-and-white complexion so often and so sadly associated with consumption, while her disposition showed the symptoms of that fatal malady also. In fact, she was a confirmed flirt.

I was very wary of this little imp, looking upon her as a mere child, and her carryings-on as the pranks of a silly kid. What was my astonishment one evening to find her, not only sitting on the knees of sundry Jack Tars from a visiting war ship, but swilling beer with the best of them. But what fairly astounded me was what took place on the other side of an extremely thin partition that separated my cubicle from the next one.

Soon I was introduced by the landlady to the captain of the fishing smack, a tall, weather-beaten sailor if ever there was one. While he looked mighty tough, he sounded mild enough and pleasant. Little did I know what lay under that mild and even fatherly manner. I engaged myself to help this man and his fishing smack for ten shillings per week, grub found, and a share in the profits. Sounded all right to this innocent hero.

Sealing the bargain with a glass of beer, and promising the landlady to come back next time the boat put in, Skipper led the way down through some railway yards to where a stout rowing boat lay. Lolling in the stern, Skipper directed the rowing and presently the boat lay alongside a ketch-rigged, fully decked smack of some thirty tons. She looked and was a fine sea-going packet, having been sailed out from England under her own sails.

Right aft was a companion hatch giving into a snug cabin. This was the galley, crew's quarters, and skipper's quarters combined. There were three comfortable berths, a hot iron stove, cooking pots, oil-skins, sea boots, and a mass of sea-fishing gear and tackle. It was all very strange to me.

A man of few words, and no blandishments, Skipper set about preparing a meal. From a parcel he had been carrying he produced a great wadge [slab] of beef steak, throwing three or four pounds of it into a frying pan. Onions, a huge hunk of butter, pepper, and salt soon followed. Presently the little cabin was filled with blue smoke and a delicious smell, fortified with the aroma of strong coffee. Certainly he showed a practiced hand, did that skipper. Since feeding seemed to be on a lavish scale, and Skipper appeared to be such a nice, mild man, I thought I might have struck it lucky.

Two of the bunks showed signs of occupation, and I could not help speculating on the third member of the crew. But since Skipper volunteered no

31

information and since I was still over-awed by this man's silence and formidable appearance, I asked no questions but applied myself lustily to the good fare. As simplicity was the key-note, it simply entailed cutting a thick slice of bread and forking a large slab of steak on to it.

As there was no washing-up to do, beyond the swilling out by each diner of his own coffee cup, the whole repast was soon over. I then took a look-over of the boat. Right amidships was a huge well, bulkheaded off fore and aft from the rest of the ship. I was at a loss to understand what this might be for. Down through the clear water I could see small holes through the ship's skin; thus, the water could freely enter and leave as the case might be.

As I was thus occupied in speculation, I heard a hail from the shore. Up came Skipper, and, beckoning me to follow, we got into the small boat once more. On making the shore, I saw a seedy-looking man waiting, and I realized that this must be the third member of the crew. He seemed rather the worse for liquor as he smelled strongly of beer. He was about to enter the boat when Skipper sprang ashore, preventing his entry. Telling me to make the boat fast, Skipper sauntered over to some piles of iron rails with which the area was liberally covered.

Hardly had the newcomer and I had time to exchange names when we were hailed over to where Skipper stood chewing a piece of grass and contemplating an adjoining pile of rails. "Yo'll fetch two of these to-night," was all he said to us.

One is inclined to dismiss the rails in question as insignificant objects, but when an almost imbecile youth and his wholly alcoholic partner and a small dinghy are the sole means of subtracting from a neat pile and thereafter conveying over a harbour a fifty-foot-length of rail, you will realize the formidable task set us by our skipper. And there was always the fact at the back of our minds that we would be stealing.

Poor dumb creatures that we were, we received this in silence, not knowing what to say. So back to the boat we went, and there, as night fell, Skipper produced sundry pieces of tackle, including wedges, ropes, levers, and some wooden rollers. Evidently these were for our use in "fetching" the rails. At two A.M. Skipper had coffee ready and sent us off.

Two greater greenhorns can never have been faced with a more difficult job. Our qualifications for the task were absolutely nil. It transpired that my opposite number was, or had been, a publican. It was easy to see what had happened: This broken-down publican had floated himself out of the pub and home on a flood of alcohol. Beyond having made a week's fishing with Skipper, he had no sea experience whatever.

It was easy for Skipper to say "fetch" two rails, but to do it with two pairs of hands is a very different story. Say the rails are fifty feet long and happen to be fifty pounds to the yard; that's a very good third of a ton (long ton) to carry. Try lifting one of that weight, and, as we in our ignorance did, you'll soon find out. When laying track on railways, you will see a gang of twenty men walking them into position with carrying hooks conveniently spaced along their length, not two. We had no convenient long-handled hook with which to grapple the task; moreover, Skipper wanted us to get these rails aboard with only a small boat to help.

When we got down to the task, it began to dawn on us what all these wedges, rollers, ropes, and levers were for. But were they awkward, and did we waste effort and time! Between spasms of quite unnecessary and futile struggles, the publican let fall in no uncertain terms his opinion of our skipper.

Among other things he was, in the publican's considered opinion, "a blue-nosed bastard." This reference to the particular colour of Skipper's nasal organ had nothing in fact to do with it, being merely the customary designation of all Nova Scotiamen. The publican accused Skipper of handing the work off to us and not coming himself for his bloody rails because it was stealing. If we were caught, Skipper was not going to be in the soup. Here the publican fell into such a welter of commiseration on the hard lot of us two "poor buggers" that he rapidly reduced himself, and his listener—me—to a state bordering on tears.

Time, meanwhile, was passing, and fears of being discovered in daylight with two rails withdrawn from the pile and laboriously conveyed from their rightful position to the beach induced us, heroes that we were, to redouble our efforts. After infinite pains and labours, we got one rail finally set across the proper props, so thoughtfully provided by Skipper. It was then easy to float the boat over to the prop. After a good deal of bitter argument as to where the point of balance might lay in the boat, we eventually got the rail slung over the boat. Her trim certainly was not too good, but the sea was calm and off we set, mighty gingerly, to deliver our cargo to the waiting Skipper.

Meanwhile the publican was in quite good humour. He seemed rather surprised and a little proud of our exploit. Unfortunately, this manifested itself in some shattering rowing on his part that nearly upset the whole caboose into the drink. The gunwales were almost submerged, and it would have been difficult for even an expert, which we were not. So having shipped some water, I induced the publican to lay his oar inboard with some difficulty for he was feeling pretty good, and then I paddled our craft slowly over the placid water.

Once alongside we saw some real sailorizing. What a seaman that Skipper was! In a trice that blue-nose had the rail aboard by himself. He would not have us aboard. No sooner done, than his orders to us were, "Fetch t'other."

In spite of the threats, the publican swore while still distant from the ship to tell Skipper to "fetch his own bloody rails" . . . and in spite of the undeniable fact that dawn was upon us, we meekly returned to the yard and in broad daylight stole another rail. Such is the force of natural born character. Yes, there it is. Some men have that power . . . and, what is more, we got that other rail. And, what is still more, we set sail for sea the instant the rail and boat were hove aboard.

It is true that ship was snug-rigged,[1] but even then there were times when a reef[2] would have been prudent, to say the least of it. But never would that blue-nose even consider such a maneuver. Unlike most men who have experience of the sea and have learnt through bitter lessons that the sea cannot be played with, our skipper would be seized with a kind of happy thrusting fever the moment the sails were set. Always he took the wheel himself, completely ignoring us, whenever it was a case of any kind of real sailorizing. He would even sing when at the wheel. So now we found ourselves tearing along at a rate of knots with our stolen cargo neatly lashed but protruding over the rail.

We soon came to the point where we left the nice smooth water and met the kind of sea you get on our coasts where the Atlantic has a clear run in on the shore. This point is called a "heads." New Zealand's South Island lies pretty far south, and lying athwart the "roaring forties," her west coast piles up a very nasty sea, indeed. Straight into this inferno drove our blue-nose with his tired and pallid crew. Of where we were going or of what we were about to do, there was no word.

"Wonder what that crazy bugger is up to," remarked the publican, as we brewed ourselves some strong coffee in the snug little cabin. Skipper did not

---

[1] Carrying but one jib.

[2] The shortening of a sail by securing the lower portion of its reef points, thereby reducing the power of the sail.

like tea; always it was coffee, well boiled with egg shells whenever there were any. Once I got a severe cursing when I was about to dump some egg shells overboard that had not undergone a boiling in coffee.

No sooner had we made an offing than we turned north along the rocky coast for some miles, gaining some shelter as we did so. Then we sheared into a small bay, dropping our anchor in sheltered water.

"Boat overboard," muttered Skipper.

He then began to pile into the boat an assortment of nets, floats, lines, and anchors, carefully coiling down everything in a meticulous manner so that everything would run out cleanly when we set it all in place. Then beckoning me to take the oars, we pushed off.

The nets, of pretty fine mesh, were set close to the rocky shores. In spite of the shelter the bay enjoyed, there was considerable swell and "back-wash" off the rocks. When everything had been set to Skipper's satisfaction, the boat returned to the ship.

"Up anchor," was now the order.

Off sailed the ship farther north. Reaching another bay, considerably less sheltered than the one we had left, Skipper ordered soundings to be taken. It was the publican who deemed himself capable of doing so—perhaps on the strength of his one week's experience of fishing. Anyway, he started to measure out the fathoms that he had got when the lead reached bottom.

"Oh, hell!" shouted Skipper. "Give it here!"

Throwing the vessel head to wind, he soon took a sounding, threw down the lead line, and backed the foresail, all the while shouting to us to harden in the main and mizzen sheets. There we rode, head to wind, quiet and forging ahead scarcely at all, a lovely maneuver.

"Look lively and get the lashings off," shouted Skipper as he set to bringing up some chain attached to a piece of wire rope.

Now he, with us in tow, with some difficulty got one rail on top of the other at a 90-degree angle. Apparently at least the centres had to cross. Now the chain was wound round and round the point where the rails rode on each other. Then the top rail had to be swung off so that a counter-lashing of chain could be wound around. During this operation the publican and I were nearly slung overboard by the surge of the heavy iron, but were luckily saved by Skipper, all the while shouting, "Steady, blast you!"

Now came the steel cable to be shackled to the chain lashing, in its turn to receive in its spliced eye a further light chain attached to a buoy of Skipper's own manufacture. Everything was piled atop the rails in proper order and everything rode on two wooden levers, resting on the bulwark rail, their ends made fast to cleats by short ropes.

So far so clear to the ignorant brains of the crew.

But what about the inboard end of the top rail? It came right in and almost across the ship. Obviously, if the levers were allowed to tip up and spill their cargo overboard, the inboard end of the rail would capsize the whole contraption. We were about to see.

With orders to stand by the cleats and to let go smartly at the words "Le' go," Skipper seized a gantline, throwing into it a bowline and slipping this over the inboard end of the upper rail. Next he took his weight on it; then we heard, "Le' go!" Up came the levers, out slid the heavy contraption, the gantline causing the rail end to just miss the boat's side by a fraction. Down plunged the whole affair, while a line, previously fastened to the buoy, was brought in. There we lay, moored.

Skipper was unusually talkative as we made supper, pleased that everything had gone so well, perhaps. At any rate he finally told us why he needed the rails. He said that the bottom here was rock and, consequently, lost your anchors, so no one could fish in these waters except in fine weather. Now, anchored among rocks where real anchors would have been lost, we could, if we liked, ride out a gale. Once caught up in rocks and sea-tangle, nothing would or could move those two crossed rails, he said. Altogether a mighty fine piece of seamanship on Skipper's part, one must admit, especially in light of the inexperienced and not-too-strong crew he had to assist him.

Getting the buoy and chain aboard was easy, and once the good ship *Mary* was fast to the wire cable of our new mooring, the nets had to be visited once more. This was interesting and even thrilling. There is something exciting to the human breast, this hauling in of a net. And what queer-looking fish came in. I gathered that the rock cod were the most profitable. Skipper, as I said, was a tight-lipped man and seldom spoke. It was a pity, as obviously he must have been a mine rich in fish-and-sea lore of every sort. Even so I learned a lot from him.

He kept the fish alive by half filling the small boat with water. We would then row them rapidly back to the parent ship where they were immediately put into the aforementioned well filled with fresh sea water. The fish would remain alive for days in this manner. The *Mary* remained at her new moorings all that night. Although secure enough, the motion was pretty lively and seemed not at all what the publican liked.

Next morning the nets were visited but not returned to the sea as they had been on the previous evening. They were now coiled down in the dinghy in the same careful way as before. We were evidently going to move. And move we did.

Now we saw Skipper busy with banditries. He did everything himself, this man, all the while wearing the most bitter and morose expression on his face, as if to say: "Those two bloody louts can't do anything."

This attitude began to be silly, and foolish, too, for, although the publican was no seaman and pretty maladroit at sea-going affairs, he could use his hands and, moreover, boasted two well-developed biceps, whether derived from the drawing of beer or not is no matter. Undoubtedly, he could have been of very much more use than he was afforded the chance of proving. The same could be said of the junior member of the crew to an even greater degree. After all, I surmised, one cannot live and work aboard a sailing ship for one hundred and twenty-eight days without learning something. Well, at least that is what we thought, the publican and I.

We now reached the wide open bay where the entrance to our home port lay. The bottom being sandy, we prepared to anchor. Before doing so, Skipper tried a couple of hand-lines over the side, each with three hooks, baited with squid we had taken in the nets previously.

No sooner down than he yelled, "Let go the anchor!" with some urgency.

An order from this man simply electrified us. Even the publican, who was a confirmed "Ca-Canny" and obstructionist leapt to do his bidding. Perhaps it was his taciturnity or maybe his undoubted knowledge of his craft, or his complete confidence in himself, or a combination of all three, that produced this alacrity. He had and was a character, our skipper.

There he was now madly hauling in his lines, shouting to us to get ours going, too, all the while heaving in huge fish, two or three at a time, re-baiting, chucking over the line, feeling another line, and even finding time to bait three more lines. He was now attending to five lines, each with three hooks, and bringing up from a depth of eight or ten fathoms two or more reluctant fish of any weight between forty and seventy pounds. The wear and tear on the hands was terrific, as the landlubbers soon found out.

37

It is a strange thing, this hand-lining. It can be observed that one man will take in as many fish as he can bait and return the hooks to water, while the next man, with identical gear and bait, will apparently be completely ignored by fish only a few feet away. It was almost invariably so in the case of the *Mary*. Only Skipper took fish in quantity. Whether it was insensitivity of touch, resulting in too late striking, or whether the accomplished fisherman has acquired some way of presenting the bait to the fish that the tyro has not, remains in doubt. The fact is that while Skipper would take in a score of groper,[3] the crew might laboriously land five or six on the deck, a matter that by no means escaped the notice of the irate blue-nose. If language is any criterion, it would certainly have appeared to an impartial observer that this particular short-coming of his crew had very high priority in his list of life's worries.

Over the glassy sea was a boat with a single occupant, busily hauling in fish. Suddenly there was a silvery gleam shooting up beside the figure standing in the boat. On that instant, the figure collapsed into the boat. Next thing the figure reappeared frantically hauling in the anchor and then as frantically rowing for home. This maneuver was greeted by Skipper with a loud guffaw. We got the explanation of these queer happenings from Skipper only with difficulty. It appeared that the lone fisherman was a French-Canadian named Joe and that the flash was a shark, and Joe, being of a superstitious nature, could not take it.

The deck of the *Mary* was by this time so packed with huge slippery groper that any further addition to the pile would have simply slid into the sea over the low bulwarks. The rope by means of which the *Mary* had been riding to her anchor was pulled in. Skipper, meanwhile, took a basinful of small triangular pieces out from the gullets of the groper. It was apparently a sort of gland and when fried it was most appetizing. It was the only fish ever eaten by the crew of the *Mary;* always it had to be beef steak or mutton.

Because the *Mary* now had a good lot of fish on board, the publican and I had visions of going to town with our pay roll. But life, the humorist, had other ideas on the subject.

No sooner had the anchor been got and the sails set than Skipper's eagle-eye spotted something in the water. Backing the foresail and hardening in

---

[3] Eastern blue groper or wrasse.

the main and mizzen sheets, the *Mary* now rode the sea close-hauled, forging slowly ahead. The dinghy was got overboard, while Skipper appeared with a bundle of short sticks, each with a wire trace and short line attached to one end. These were short rods. At the end of the wire cast, a small piece of whitewood with a large hook through it was attached. The hook had no barbs, and a piece of red or white flannel seemed to be the bait. Leaving the publican to tend ship and frying pan, I rowed away with Skipper directing. As the dinghy moved over the sea, Skipper kept flogging away, a rod in each hand.

Presently he was into something. With a dexterous flick of the rod, there flew through the air a long, dark-coloured, very slim fish to land with a bang in the dinghy alongside my legs. The flick that had brought the fish from its native element had also disengaged the barbless hook from its jaws. That meant there was now nothing to prevent the fish from sinking its frightful-looking teeth in my calves.

Before avoiding action could be taken, however, a perfect rain of wriggling, snapping bonito came pouring into the boat from every angle. Maybe Skipper intentionally landed a few on my squirming body; he was that kind of man. But I soon got to work with his rod, and once I had mastered the trick of getting the fish off the hook and into the boat and not back into the sea again, I soon forgot my legs in the exalting business of seeing who could get the most fish into the other man's part of the boat. Presently the dinghy was so full that rowing became difficult. Then back to the *Mary* we went, where a rope was attached to the dinghy so that it trailed astern.

Now the problem was what to do with the load of bonitos. The well was full of living fish, the decks piled with dead groper, and the dinghy was in a similar state. It was decided that we would sail and tow the dinghy.

Luckily, there was not much wind, so all went well. Smooth water was reached without any serious swamping of the heavily laden dinghy. Now just inside the "heads" there was a signal station, evidently connected by telephone or telegraph with the town. Skipper was often in the habit of using it for getting orders from his owners. He had an arrangement with the people in the signal station whereby in return for various favours conferred, various favours were received.

Hence, in this case as the *Mary* stood slowly past, a signal was made from the shore and Skipper steered in for a sheltered cove and dropped the hook. The dinghy being laden deep, Skipper beckoned to the shore and soon a small boat came alongside. It took him ashore, and finally the publican and I had at long last an opportunity to compare notes, curse Skipper, and make a fine brew of hot, strong, sweet coffee.

Just as we were relaxed and enjoying life once more, that all-pervading pest arrived back from the shore, his face black with rage, his nose appearing pale by contrast. Dismissing the small boat without so much as a nod or wave, he continued to glower about him, much to the discomfort of his crew, who could only speculate on the reason for all the "stramash." When night fell, the tale of woe unfolded itself.

"Turn out and dump them groper," was the gruff order just as we two hobos had made ourselves comfortable in our bunks.

Hardly believing our ears, it was not until we saw Skipper actually begin to throw those lovely fish overboard that we realized we had heard aright. Away streamed the silvery bellies on the tide. All the time and strain of catching them—the blistered hands, the sea-outs—all gone for nothing.

It appeared that as everyone had caught groper, there was a fear of prices coming down. So our lot was to be dumped. He had received all this on the telephone from the owners. No wonder Skipper was black with rage, for overside had gone his, and our, shares of the catch.

This was bad enough in all conscience, but further trials awaited Skipper, poor man. By this time, he simply loathed the sight of us. In his eyes we could not fish; we could do little right. What put the final touch to his smouldering resentment was largely his own fault, which probably only added to his fury.

This is what happened: Anchored as the *Mary* was, ten miles from her port, Skipper decided to remain on board and to send the bonito and the netted fish by dinghy in charge of the publican and me.

Knowing our limitations, Skipper's decision was courageous but, as the sequel showed, somewhat rash. He had seen the laden state of the dinghy because he and I had caught the bonito. And now he proposed to add the considerable weight of the fish in the well to the load, on the argument that the water was smooth . . . and as for the distance to be rowed . . . why the tide would be with us.

And so it proceeded as with all dictators. Not one fish would he allow to be jettisoned. We were so grossly overloaded that down went the dinghy until it had no more than about three inches of free-board once the crew was on board. Off went the boat, gingerly rowed between those nausea-causing rolls peculiar to over-laden craft. There was about the publican's a sickly pallor, for the poor man could not swim.

New Zealand in the 1890s

Our unanimous inclination was to hug the shores of the sand banks, but after grounding a few times, we decided on a different tack. By that time, too, we had gained confidence with the miles covered, so on observing a roaring fair tide way out in the channel, the two of us decided to take the middle course.

No sooner had we reached a position midway between the shores than we sensed we were now fairly shooting past the banks. It was easy on the oars, all right. As we sped along, we idly glanced at the increasing bulk of an approaching steamer. "It is one of those refrigerating meat boats, isn't it?" I asked.

"Oh, ten to fifteen thousand tons!" The publican answered. "These boats are fairly fast, too, and some of them carry one hundred and fifty thousand mutton carcasses as well as a few passengers," he said.

What we didn't think about in those indolent moments as we sped idly along was the wash from the steamer.... Finally, we both looked up and with a horrified glance, we caught sight of a high wall of water streaming out at an angle from the side of the mountainous wall of the imminent steamer.

Over the glassy sea was a boat with a single occupant.

41

"Christ! Pull like hell!" roared the publican.

We were too late, of course. No hellish or other kind of pulling could extricate us from our predicament. What was coming was coming. Before we could react, that inescapable wash was upon us. Certainly we knew enough to keep our boat bow-on to the advancing wall, but that was not enough. The small boat could not lift to the wave: Insufficient buoyancy undid us, and instantly we were swamped.

For a moment we remained seated, up to our middles in water, while gazing stupidly at our fish floating gaily away on all sides. Had we remained so, all might have been well. But the publican being a non-swimmer now panicked. Clutching at the higher gunwale as the foundering dinghy lurched, he fairly upset the whole shebang.

Over she rolled, spewing forth the silvery cargo. Down went the publican spluttering and trying to cling to the underside of the dinghy, which, of course, kept rolling over as he tried to climb on to it. In the process, he abandoned his surest life-saver, the oar he had in his hand when catastrophe overtook him.

When I saw the oar floating away among the fish, I had the sense to grasp the notion that without oars we would be in a pretty fix. I therefore swam off with my own oar and soon retrieved the escaping one. Returning to the dinghy where the publican was still struggling to mount it, I shouted to him to keep still and not swallow so much water. I yelled to him that I would soon propel the boat into shallow water, which is what I did. Once there it was easy to keep the boat right side up and to empty her of some of her load of water by surging her to and fro. The bailer, of course, had gone the way of the cargo.

Sitting on a sandbank, we took stock of our position. It began to dawn on us that things certainly did not look too good. What was that blasted Skipper going to do when we returned to the ship? It seemed to us that such an ending to our expedition could, at the best, produce a storm of blasphemy and abuse and, at the worst, actual violence might be directed against the perpetrators of such a gaff. Wet and cold, for a shrewd wind was blowing, we two miscreants—for that is how we saw ourselves—embarked once more and pulled wearily over the tide toward the *Mary*, our minds uneasy about our reception.

It was the publican's suggestion that we should brazen it out with Skipper. Believing attack to be the best form of defense, he proposed that instead of meekly awaiting the inevitable storm of abuse that we should get in first with an accusation of gross overloading of the boat. We hoped, thereby, to steal Skipper's thunder. After some discussion, during which we both began to feel some considerable indignation at the way we had been treated, it was finally decided to adopt the suggestion. Our resolution thus buttressed, the rowing became more determined in spite of some inward trepidation both of us were feeling.

All worked out well for our scheme. Skipper was not on deck as we approached. He was mending gear in the cabin as we came aboard with a quite unnecessary amount of noise. The boat being made fast, we advanced with great determination upon our fate.

"We've lost the bloody lot and nearly lost our lives," bawled the publican at the head of the ladder, peering down at the grim face below.

A great wonder seemed to spread over Skipper's rugged, weather-beaten features. Stillness reigned as I peeked under the publican's arm at the sight below. It was as if this man had been used all his life to telling one great big lie and suddenly the lie had become the truth. Without doubt, he had called us many things that he would freely admit were exaggerations, to say the least of it. And now all his exaggerations were shown to be true, by the living heck! No wonder the poor man was struck dumb.

Skipper never recovered from this blow, at least while I remained with him. He became even more bitter and taciturn than before, if that were possible. He seemed to find relief for his feelings in reckless sailing. He would see an approaching steamer, cram on, and steer directly at her when she would be mid-channel in a narrow part. Grazing her stem, he would engage her bridge in an exchange of torrents of blasphemous curses that were quite ably returned with the aid of a megaphone.

We still got our basic wage, which was ten shillings, and sometimes our individual share would amount to three or four pounds, but after this last disaster, not much more than our basic wage would be forthcoming.

By this time I also realized that I was getting no nearer to the happy hunting grounds of Africa, so I decided that it was time to move on. My plan was to relocate to Invercargill at the southern end of the island because homeward-bound steamers could be found there. Needing the resources to get to Invercargill, I turned to "swagging."

NEW PLYMOUTH
NAPIER
Cook Strait
NELSON
WELLINGTON
BLENHEIM
OCEAN
HOKITIKA
WESTLAND
CANTERBURY
CHRISTCHURCH
SOUTH ISLAND
OTAGO
DUNEDIN
STEWART I.
C. Egmont
Opunake
SOUTH TARANAKI BIGHT
Sydney to Wellington 1160 m.
Melbourne to Nelson 1340 m.
PACIFIC
from Melbourne 1266 m.
C. Farewell
Farewell Spit
West Wanganui Inlet
Golden Bay
D'Urville I.
Collingwood
TASMAN BAY
COLLINGWOOD
Heaphy R.
Karamea R.
NELSON
Havelock
Picton
WAIMEA
Mokihinui R.
Rockford
C. Foulwind
Westport
MARLBOROUGH
Charlestown
Brighton
Clarence R.
Cobden
Greymouth
Whitcombe
Staffordtown
GREY
AMURI
Kaikoura
Amuri Bluff
Conway R.
Dillon R.
Cheviot
Hurunui R.
HOKITIKA
Ross
Waitaha
Table I.
ASHLEY
PEGASUS BAY
Abut Hd.
Okarito
WESTLAND
Raleigh
Ashley R.
Waimakariri R.
CHRISTCHURCH & R. Avon
Lyttelton Tn. & Port
Banks Peninsula
ASHBURTON
Haast R.
Jackson B.
Cascade Pt.
Barn B.
Akaroa Harb. & Tn.
MACKENZIE
Hollyford R. & Martin B.
Milford Sound
Pareora
Rangitata R.
Timaru
Omarama
WAIMATE
Bligh Sound
George Sd.
Upper Ferry
Waimate
Waihoa R.
Charles Sd.
Pembroke
Arrowtown
Wakefield
Waitaki R.
SOUTH ISLAN
Thompson Sd.
Doubtful Sd.
Daggs Sd.
Queenstown
Cromwell
Ophir
Alexandra
Oamaru
Herbert
Hampden
Breaksea S.
Resolution I.
Palmerston
Hawkesbury
Waikouaiti Bay
Port Chalmers (Otago Harb.)
TUAPEKA
WALLACE
DUNEDIN
C. Saunders
PENINSULA COY.
Dusky B.
West C.
Lawrence
Tapanui
Chalky I.
Preservation Inlet
Windsor Pt.
Winton
Clinton
Gore
Tewaewae Bay
Riverton
Invercargill
Molyneux Tn. & Bay
Solander I.
FOVEAUX STRAIT
Codfish I.
Mason Bay
Toitoes Bay
Waikawa R.
Paterson Inlet
STEWART I. & COUNTY
Breaksea Pt.
CANTERBURY BIGHT
Steam Routes
Railways
Roads
Heights in English Feet

Swagging and Other Adventures

CHAPTER 4

New Zealanders call the gentle art of getting along without working "swagging." It is an art, be it said, brought to a high state of perfection in this land of cheap and abundant food. There were many men who lived by swagging in the 1890s. Pretending it was work they were looking for, they would almost always be invited to have some grub. (So far as my experience went, women took no part in this system.) As long as they were not asked to do any work, they were happy, roaming from place to place, year in, year out.

It was an inverted sort of hunting where the bag consisted of jobs dodged instead of trophies captured. No responsibilities, no ties, no money, no property, this life seemed to offer these men a freedom from worry and a system for living that could be obtained by no other organized means. Since I had some hundred-odd miles to tramp to get myself to Invercargill at the southern end of the island, I decided to try a bit of swagging on my own.

At one sheep station, I was offered a temporary job as "rabbiter," the real one having fallen ill. A rabbiter's duties consisted of killing off by all legitimate means as many rabbits as he could. To accomplish this, he had a pack of dogs of all kinds and sizes. He rode a pony to this pack and carried a gun, not for shooting rabbits, but for shooting any dog that might take to sheep-worrying. He also carried a stock whip for disciplining his dogs.

About one third of the pack consisted of terriers of every breed. These were the tufters. Their job was to chase out any rabbits lurking in the tussocky grass. The other seventy- or eighty-strong dogs in the pack were speedier, mostly collies and greyhounds. It was a sight to see these chasers surround a patch of heavy tussock, all the while waiting to rush in on any rabbit displaced by the tufters. Some rabbits escaped, of course, but many were killed. No dog was allowed to eat a rabbit, as surfeit would soon have brought operations to a close had they been allowed to do so.

There were no kennels for these dogs; they were all simply pegged out, that is, chained to pegs driven into the ground. It was a major operation to feed this multitude. Enough rabbits would have to be brought in, skinned, gutted, and cooked for the whole lot. The fleas about the rabbiter's camp had to be seen to be believed. As I got little more than grub in return for working ten or twelve hours a day, I tarried not long on this job.

After my turn at swagging and being a rabbiter, I was introduced to another equally free and enterprising method of earning a living, that of "egg-snatching." The unsympathetic call it stealing. Here's how it came about:

Arriving somewhat weary and footsore at a small country railway station, I was resting my weary bones on one of those shapely but hard seats, so universally provided by railway companies for their passengers' convenience, when I was accosted by a lad of much about my own age but vastly more experienced in worldly affairs. After a little give and take, the stranger invited me to doss down with him that night.

When we came to a stranger's shack, I was relieved to find that there were no other inmates, neither of the human nor of the Norfolk Howard[1] variety. In fact, all was decent, clean, and homey. After asking me if I was hungry, the stranger took from a box a couple of dozen eggs and began to fry them with a plentiful supply of butter. Lots of bread was forthcoming as well. We had a grand supper.

The stranger asked where I was bound for. When he heard that it was Invercargill, he immediately said there would be a train leaving about two A.M. for that destination. That sounded fine to me, but there was one little fly in the ointment—I had no money. As the stranger seemed so well off, so comfortably housed, so affluent in fact, I was a little diffident about mentioning this awkward deficiency.

In the afterglow produced by a dozen eggs and lashings of tea, the stranger told me that he merely wintered in this "caboose," that his job was with a gang of sheep shearers, and that he fed himself by a system of robbing hen roosts by night. "Dead easy," he said. What other accomplishment he might have had in his repertoire he did not disclose.

Somewhat relieved and emboldened by these confessions, I now disclosed to my companion that I had not a bean to my name, so how would I be able to go by train. My disclosure produced a roar of laughter from the stranger. He promised to show me how it could be managed when the time came. "Meanwhile," said he, "we must to business."

The so-called "business" meant first a walk in pitch darkness of two or three miles before we came to what seemed to be the outbuildings of a farm. I was stationed by the road we had been following, and the stranger disappeared. In an incredibly short time he reappeared with quite a haul of eggs. Not a sound was to be heard.

---

[1] Slang for bedbug.

At one sheep station, I was offered a temporary job as "rabbiter," the real one having fallen ill. A rabbiter's duties consisted of killing off by all legitimate means as many rabbits as he could.

In all, we visited three places that night, and all of them produced something. I had some score of eggs disposed about my person, while my companion, being more expert, had a good many more. Thus provisioned, we returned to the shack. I now discovered that it was but a step from egg snatching to train jumping.

It was soon time to go to the station, to which we now proceeded. A long goods train drew into the platform. With practiced eye, my friend selected a truck carrying large diameter pipes, for culverts probably, and then told me to mount the truck and conceal myself inside one of them. He warned me not to move until I had reached my destination. Wishing me a cheery farewell, the hospitable and kindly stranger betook himself to his shack full of eggs, while I tried to make myself as comfortable as I might be under the circumstances.

So long as the train was stationary, all was well. But as soon as it set off, the open pipe produced a howling gale, which pierced me to the very marrow. It was so wretchedly cold as to be quite insupportable. I was obliged to come out and crouch in the lee of the forward end of the truck, thinking I would dodge back into my bolt hole the moment there was any sign of another stop.

All went well in this manner, and I successfully negotiated several stops. But goods trains are proverbially slow and I became mighty sleepy toward dawn, besides being petrified by cold. Hence it was that the arrival at Invercargill found me crouched in my forward berth completely void of cover and passing in full daylight slowly through a main station with railway officials in uniform staring from under their cheese-cutter hats mighty grimly and straight at me. At least it seemed that way to me.

Too late to do anything about it, I awaited my doom with lively—and shivering—apprehension. Thoughts of prison horrified me as the train continued to trundle along through the station to finally pull up alongside some wharfs where sundry steamers lay loading cargo. While I had landed at the important harbour of Invercargill where many steamers called, I believed that it was now farther than ever from my reach. Instead of finding a steamer to take me to my destination, I was apprehensive as anything over the incipient encounter to come.

Instead of a menacing policeman brandishing handcuffs, however, there appeared a large but kindly looking man in overalls. "Come on," said he.

I uncoiled my stiffened bones and stepped onto the platform.

The large man smiled at me. "'Spect you could do with some breakfast?" queried he.

I told him that nothing would suit me better. We proceeded on our way, whither to only the large man knew.

Presently we arrived at a nice, clean, little house, one of a row of similar buildings. We entered and the large man introduced his wife and daughter to me. With true tact, the large man had not enquired my name; he referred to himself as Bill. No questions were asked either then or later. He seemed content to help a fellow human being whose need was obvious.

Over an ample breakfast, the large man disclosed that he was the driver of the train that had brought me so far and so cheaply, if not in any great luxury. He said they had spotted my presence on the truck long before we had arrived, and he hoped that I would keep well hidden, as some of the railway people were against hobos jumping rides.

No sooner was my inner man satisfied than the hospitable host turned to that of my outer man. There is no denying there was reason for this. You cannot live and sleep in the same clothes for weeks without some loss of polish, to put it mildly. Soon I was completely bathed and, clad in my host's clothes, looked a great deal cleaner. It is true the fit might be criticized in less kindly circles, but here it only evoked some good-natured laughter, and even seemed to endear me to my benefactors, including the daughter.

This studious and bespectacled young lady had not been too forthcoming, it must be confessed, while I had been grubby and covered with ash and coal smuts from the engine. But now I was so nobly and amply covered in borrowed plumes, her serious face was wreathed in smiles. She even suggested I should accompany her on a visit to town. Her father, Bill, now retired for some well-earned sleep.

Before we left, she placed on my head one of her father's soft felt hats. The effect was to completely extinguish that part of my countenance not already engulfed by her father's boiled collar. This reduced her and her mother to such fits of helpless laughter that the hat was instantly abandoned. A cap of the same generous proportions had an equally startling effect, albeit the element of surprise was no longer there. This, too, had to be abandoned; the ladies contented themselves with dosing my hair with some of Bill's brilliantine and brushing it into a truly magnificent cow-lick.

Thus furbished up and smoothed down, we sallied forth on the town. Little did I know what lay ahead of me until a glimmering of what it might be came with the ringing of church bells. You see, I had not known it was Sunday. Almost certainly we were bound for a service to be followed almost as certainly by Sunday school classes.

Now I had had some painful experiences of church services, experiences that remained very fresh in my memory. Long, deadly, dull drives in a two-horse shay, to longer, deadlier and duller sermons on noxious, hard-wood seats, constantly under the stern and forbidding presence of an embittered guardian. These then were my memories as I eagerly sought for some pretext to return whence I came.

As I walked along beside my new-found friend, I was considerably obstructed by the excessive length of my benefactor's pants. So much so, indeed, that I had felt obliged to put my hands into the pockets and so surreptitiously to hold them up. This gave me an idea. Releasing the too-generous garments, I stopped short and when my lady friend asked what the matter was, I drew her attention to my feet, which were certainly hidden by the ample folds. I said that I was afraid I would have to go home as I thought my braces had given way. Cunning rascal that I was, I got away with it. She let me go and my escape was consummated.

Whether she had a suspicion that I had played a trick on her never became known. What was apparent, though, was a certain coolness on her part toward me after this episode. It certainly didn't help for her to see the alacrity with which I accepted her father's invitation to go with him up the hill to where an old ship's captain lived. She must have thought it odd that my braces were sufficiently in order to venture on such an expedition, for it entailed a climb up a hill that might be expected to try out the stoutest suspenders.

All went well, and we duly arrived at quite an imposing house. It had a well-kept lawn sporting in its middle the usual sea-faring appliances. Ancient mariners all seemed to like to surround themselves with these types of outdoor ornaments, just to remind themselves that they no longer had to embark on that unruly element, the sea.

How they play the part, these old shell-backs. No sooner were we through the gate than the captain appeared on the bridge—that is the veranda—and bellowed a greeting as if he were contending with a full gale and had at all costs to make himself heard by deaf men above the frantic flapping of shredded canvas and thundering seas. Never mind that it was a calm Sunday afternoon in a slumberous town. Hearty were his greetings and hearty his appearance.

In reply to his discreet enquiries, I had confided to my benefactor that my object in life was to reach Africa. Hence this visit to the sea captain. If anyone knew the way of ships at sea, it was the aforesaid sea captain. He would surely know.

"Africa! Africa! Big place, Africa!" growled the old sea-dog, "What part of Africa?" enquired he.

"Well, Zanzibar," I ventured.

"Zanzibar! Zanzibar!" ruminated the captain. "Might get you a ship to Mauritius. A sugar ship."

"How far would that be from Zanzibar?" I asked.

"How far from Zanzibar?" considered the captain. "Might be a couple of thousand miles."

I found this a rather daunting prospect, but I thought I might learn something, so I asked if there were any steamers plying between Mauritius and Zanzibar.

"Might be an occasional one," said the captain, "but if you take my advice, you'll go straight home and start from there. Plenty steamers from there to any part of Africa. Plenty ships going home," said he as he walked over to the edge of the veranda in order to point down at the well-filled berths in the port.

In reply to a query as to how I could get a passage on one of them, the captain asked if I would pay for or work a passage.

"Work," I replied.

"Well, that's easy," said the captain.

We arranged to meet on the morrow and were about to leave when the captain announced that we would take tea with him before doing so. Over tea he suggested I might like to do a trip to the Macquarie Islands. It appeared he had a friend who owned a schooner and who had a concession for the seals and penguins on the islands. This friend was now fitting out and was to take forty men who were to be left on the islands for several months to garner the harvest of seal and penguin oil.

"Tons of grub and good money too," said the captain.

He probably has shares in the venture, I thought to myself, judging by the way he painted, in glowing colours, the romance and all that of this adventurous expedition. Although attracted, I withstood the captain's blandishments. For one thing I had learnt in Hobart that seals were killed with clubs, and this did not appeal to me at all.

No, I decided I would go home and start out all afresh for Africa. Maybe my people would now see that I was determined to get there and might think that I was now old enough to be properly launched on my irrevocable career.

******

The ship chosen by the ancient mariner for my conveyance was the *Destiny*, and it proved to be a large and very modern refrigerator steamer that was carrying frozen meat to England. Since I had had enough of sailing ships, I decided that this would do me fine. I signed on as a "frost jack," sweeping snow out of the cold-air trunks running around the sides of the holds containing the thousands of frozen carcasses, each in its spotless muslin wrapping.

These air trunks were of a size to accommodate a boy, or a very small man, in a kneeling position. The idea of the designers was that a boy would brush off the snow and hoar frost from the sides and top of the passage. What they had forgotten was to provide any means of getting rid of the resultant mass of snow. Perhaps they thought that the acute discomfort aroused by the penetration of the frozen particles to all parts of the boy's anatomy would provide the solution to the problem. However that may be—and was—the homeward voyage was achieved in comfort and ease.

Cape Horn was rounded in calm waters and in due time the Thames was reached.

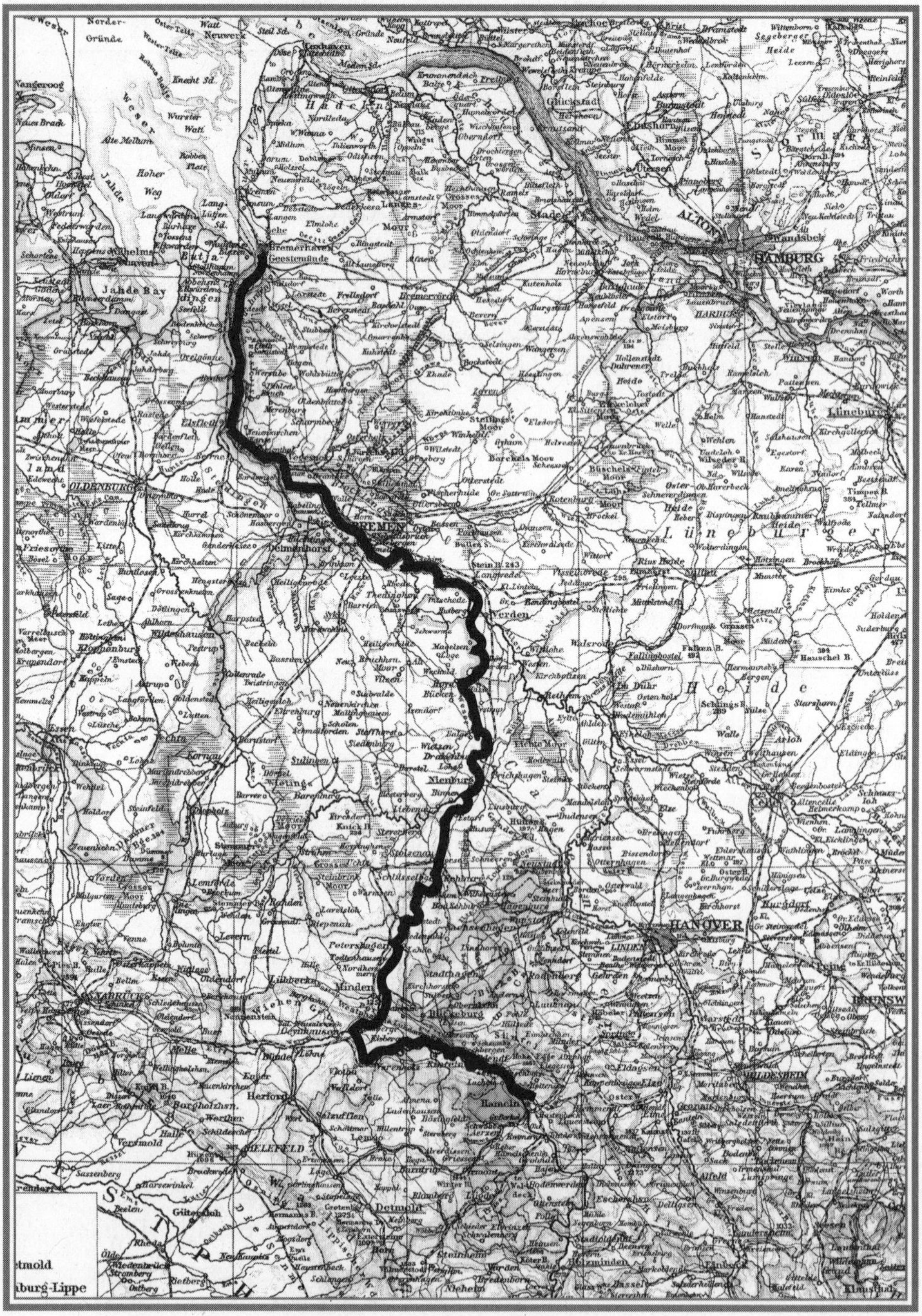

HAMBURG
BREMEN
HANOVER
OLDENBURG
Bremerhaven
Geestemünde
Jahde Bay
Lüneburger
Heide
Stade
Glückstadt
Verden
Nienburg
Minden
Hameln
BIELEFELD
Detmold
HILDESHEIM
Delmenhorst
Elsfleth
Bremervörde
Cuxhaven
Herford
Lemgo
Celle
Rotenburg
Soltau
Stolzenau
Weser
Sulingen
Vechta
Diepholz
Steinhuder Meer
etmold
nburg-Lippe

My Escape from Germany

CHAPTER 5

Arriving home, I once more put up the eternal cry: "To Africa! To Africa!"

My exasperated guardians brought out once more the same old arguments. Too young—I was fourteen—no elephants left in Africa; they are extinct. They really believed this, poor things. Again, they were thinking only of the white-colonized South Africa, airily pooh-poohing the rest of that vast continent. My people also thought it was about time for me to settle down, choose a profession, and get some education. They just laughed when I begged them to fit me out for Africa.

"Preposterous idea!" they all agreed.

"To Africa! To Africa!" I insisted. My cry fell on deaf ears.

"No, no," they said, "you will be a soldier." And so off they sent me to a place that called itself the Oxford Military College.

I soon tired of this place and announced my intention of leaving at the end of term. I had no wish to become a soldier. On confronting the principal, I listened to that gentleman produce various and weighty reasons why I should continue my studies for an army career. I was, however, quite determined and steadily refused all arguments. Finally, seeing that anything further was breath wasted, the principal said how sorry he was—to lose one hundred and fifty pounds a year, probably—but that should I ever be in trouble, to be sure to write to him. He added, rather too hastily I thought, "But do not ask me for money. I couldn't do that, but advice I will always be delighted to give."

Now I had certain expectations from my father's will. It was also quite clear that my guardians did not see eye to eye with me on the matter that some part of these expectations be made available for the purpose of fitting out an expedition against the African elephant. Since they were also the trustees of my father's estate, I had not a sliver of hope that I could change their minds.

Not to be easily dissuaded, however, I thought that something might be done in anticipation of the happy time when I should come of age. I had gleaned from various writings that there were benevolent gentlemen in the world who would "advance on security." And with this in view, I wrote a letter to the man who had been my father's factor and who still continued to serve the trustees, my guardians, in the same capacity. This poor man, on receiving the letter, showed it straightway to his employers, who had a good laugh at my diplomacy.

The net result was as before. The same old arguments were once more brought out: "There were no more elephants left in Africa. The Dutch had killed them all." And so they had—in South Africa. What my worthy and well-meaning trustees forgot was that Africa is a mighty big continent.

Thereafter, my guardians made several abortive attempts to get me—that "obstinate young brat" as they called me—educated. It was all to the naught. During this process of moving from one school to another, my young sister, to whom I was greatly attached, kept a more or less constant watch from a window overlooking the drive . . . in daily expectation of seeing a familiar figure once more returning home. So it went for a while, but I was recalcitrant and refused to give up my dream.

Then my guardians came up with a new idea: "You must get some schooling, and if you won't do it here, you will get it in Germany. When you are old enough, you can go to hell." Or words to that effect. So off to Germany I was sent, to a crammer who had been a master of languages at one of our public schools, and who had there imbibed a lasting hatred of the British and all things British. Rumour had it that this feeling had been reciprocated by his pupils.

This Herr was an imposing-looking creature and cultivated a fancied resemblance to Bismarck, on the slenderest foundations as far as any of his pupils could see. Warned possibly by my guardians of my propensities, he now set about to combat my desire to escape an education. With some cunning, he persuaded my guardians to provide me with some shooting recreation, which he felt would off-set the attractions of wanderlust.

With this idea in view, he took me to a nearby village that held a yearly auction and shooting match in the communal woods and forests. For five pounds sterling, the Herr procured a cheap twelve-bore, and I was turned loose to see what I could lay low.

I shot a few hares, an occasional partridge, and some wood pigeon. There were also roe deer, but these were rare and very much sought-after. One day, however, I managed to get one. I was not too sure if I was entitled to kill a roe deer; the Herr had not been very explicit when translating the regulations. So I thought it wiser to hide it and return to consult the Herr.

The Herr, who was given to starving his pupils, especially of meat, was delighted when I told him of my exploit. He wanted to know if I had hidden the meat well and if I could find the place in the dark. Then, said he, "You will take a bicycle lamp and this sack and bring in every bit to-night."

I concluded from all these precautions that I was not entitled to kill roe. Indeed, I learnt later that it had been the closed season for deer. But, of course, this fact only added excitement to the affair. So, as soon as darkness fell, I went back to where I had hidden the carcass and brought in the entire roe, much to the delight of the Herr, who fed the whole school on it for a week.

About this time I came upon a lovely book by Fridtjof Nansen[1] called *Farthest North*.[2] Profusely illustrated, it contained complete working drawings for the construction of his kayaks, which had contributed so much to the success of his journeys.

Also, by this time I was not only somewhat tired of the Herr and his doings. I had also conceived an active dislike of that gentleman . . . ever since the Herr had dashed to pieces on the cement floor of the salon a new meerschaum pipe that I was colouring. When I threatened him—a boy half his size but infuriated—he had screamed for his ancient grandmother to protect him. This good woman had immediately arrived on the scene, which robbed me of my revenge. I decided then and there it was time to move on.

I now conceived a project to build a kayak as per Nansen's directions that would take me away from this place. It seemed to me that with such a craft and my gun, the world lay before me like an open book.

I patched up my quarrel with the Herr after an appeal from Grandma who said that the Herr had a weak heart and must on no account be excited. Once again at peace with the Herr, I proposed a journey to Hanover, which the Herr

---

[1] Fridtjof Nansen (10 October 1861–13 May 1930) was a Norwegian explorer, scientist, diplomat, humanitarian, and Nobel Peace Prize laureate. He led the team that made the first crossing of Greenland's interior in 1888, traversing the island on cross-country skis. He won international fame after reaching a record northern latitude of 86°14—during his North Pole expedition of 1893–96. Although he retired from exploration after his return to Norway, his techniques of polar travel and his innovations in equipment and clothing influenced a generation of subsequent Arctic and Antarctic expeditions.

[2] *Farthest North* is a brilliant, first-person account, originally published in 1897, of Nansen's dangerous voyage to the North Pole by sledge. Nansen's expedition is said to mark the beginning of the modern age of exploration. Since this book was published about the time Bell left for Africa, it's doubtful whether this was the source of Bell's inspiration. It's more likely that the wellspring was a similar, adventure-laden book that offered tips on canoe building.

accepted with some alacrity. Since on these occasions all expenses were paid by the pupil's parents, the Herr had a very good idea what was his due in the way of hotel accommodation, cigars, wines, etc. The object was educational, of course, "for were there not museums and monuments calculated to broaden the outlook of any boy?"

As far as I was concerned, however, the real object of the Hanover expedition was the acquiring of various materials for the building of a kayak. One would not have chosen Hanover as being particularly suitable for the provision of bamboo, yet so it was. It required some searching, certainly, but finally some suitable bamboo was discovered in a dingy warehouse. This was unfortunately of the female variety, which means it was hollow and much given to splitting. But, as Nansen had not mentioned the sex of his bamboo, I took what I could get without misgiving. Canvas, sail, needles, palm, copper wire, and thread were easy; paint was obtainable locally. The Herr paid for all this paraphernalia without suspicion.

Fridtjof Nansen's bamboo-framed kayak.

About this time the Herr engaged a master for the boys, and he was a queer fish, indeed. He was a stocky little man of twenty-five years or so and he had some peculiarities. One was that he ate only bread and raw carrots. He had also a very red face. Of course, the boys were in fits over the new master, and they suggested that the Herr had engaged him solely due to the economy in feeding him. They loved to draw attention to the fiery countenance of the poor little man, hinting that more than raw carrots lay behind it. He utterly failed to keep any sort of discipline until one day he challenged any meat-eater to walk against him for fifty miles.

Now, none of the boys had ever attempted to walk such a distance, or anything like it, but so convinced were they of the superiority of a meat diet over that of a vegetarian one that they light-heartedly accepted the challenge. The boys merely stipulated that one or two umpires, mounted on bicycles, should accompany the contestants to see that the "cow," as they called the little man, did not bolt into some wayside inn and there to engulf a large beef steak. The race took place and the "cow" came in alone—no meat-eater even completed the course.

Rather to my surprise, the Herr seemed to have no objection to my project of building a kayak. On the contrary, he seemed to encourage it in every way. Perhaps he thought it would allay the wanderlust and would come to nothing, anyway.

It was not long before the kayak took shape. So engrossing became the construction by the time the craft was in frame and so sporting did it look, with its sharp double ends, that I was determined to let loose all my tame wild birds as their care and feeding interfered too much with the work in the shipyard. My avifauna contingent included redstarts and common tits, but the pride of my heart was a family of bearded tits now grown to the flying stage, a feat of rearing commonly regarded as almost impossible. So off the birds had to go to fend for themselves, although they continued to fly in and out of their rearing place and to take food from my hand for a considerable time.

Even the release of the birds conveyed no suspicion to the brain of the Herr. Work in the shipyard continued at a rising tempo until one day there only remained the transport of the completed craft from the building site to the river. This was effected by the hiring of a horse and cart from the neighbouring village. No one smelled a rat in these proceedings, mainly I suppose because the river that ran near at hand was not navigable. It was a tributary of the mighty Weser, debouching at Bremerhaven.

I had one little interruption to my plans. The Herr required an occasional trip to the fleshpots of Berlin and decided that now was the time. He arranged the trip with the usual focus on an educational tour for his boys. The Herr took a few of the pupils, of sufficient parental affluence, to one of the lesser Berlin hotels. It was there that I discovered what world beaters the Germans considered themselves to be, what a good zoo looked like, and how the beer-swilling German can unashamedly weep over music.

Back at the school once again, I concentrated on the shaping of the paddles; these gave me more trouble than the building of the kayak. The first one broke. Evidently, the wood required was ash and it was not so easily got. Finally, at a cost of a few marks I got the village carpenter to fashion one that would work. I then made a few tentative voyages on the river. All seemed well, and still the Herr seemed quite indifferent. It remained now to gather some provisions; cartridges I already had.

The river upon which the kayak operated joined the Weser some forty miles down its course. The idea underlying all these activities was to simply paddle down these forty miles. On reaching the Weser, it was easy to see from any map that nothing lay between one and all the seas of the world. It was these forty miles that might be troublesome, however. There were rapids marked; indeed, it was all marked as not navigable. I reasoned to myself that, after all, kayaks were supposed to be able to go anywhere and that they could simply be carried round any place they could not navigate, such as rapids or falls.

I stocked my kayak with provisions and a shotgun without a soul suspecting my intention, and one fine day I took my departure. Apparently, I hadn't thought out carefully the idea of navigating rapids. Had I been going up against the stream instead of down with it, I might have learnt to discriminate between the possible and the impossible. I would also have had more time for choice. As it was, I shot off in my heavily laden canoe and went downstream at a most inspiring rate of knots.

All went well and speedily for a while. In the beginning my progress was uneventful, for I had traversed this part before. I managed to negotiate weir and falls safely by portaging around them. Success routed caution. Because I had successfully shot through some quite nasty-looking rapids, when I came upon a mild-enough-looking mill weir under a considerable depth of water, I thought I would chance it. The result was a complete wreck.

It was a spike or projection on the weir that had caught my fast-moving craft and quite simply ripped her open. Instantly she filled but did not quite sink, probably because the hollow bamboos gave her enough buoyancy. Anyhow, being a fair waterman, I soon had the nearly submerged wreck towed to the bank.

The weir was overlooked by a mill, some little way downstream, and it was not long before someone saw my predicament. As any sort of a craft was totally unknown on this river, the sight of a kayak scooting downstream brought no little surprise to the country mind. When the fast-moving apparition was seen to charge the weir barrier and then to almost leave the water as it shot over, it can be imagined just how astonished the natives were.

Rushing to the rescue, the good millers soon had the wreck and its crew high and dry on the bank. Most of the cargo had gone through the open bottom, but the gun had luckily been lashed to the cockpit. It was wet but undamaged.

All hands now repaired to the mill where a scene of great hospitality unfolded itself. Some strong, rough brandy appeared and some equally strong coffee. The jolly millers, male and female, partook of everything as if they, too, had need of reviving. My clothing was soon sizzling and steaming round an enormous wood-burning iron stove, while the head miller wiped down with loving hand the twelve-bore shotgun.

While all these jolly proceedings were in hand, I had time to review my situation. At first sight this seemed somewhat grim, for the boat was a total wreck and the provisions had gone to the bottom of a pretty deep pool. But the worst aspect of the case was undoubtedly my total lack of funds. The Herr was not such a fool as he looked. He had always carefully withheld from his boys any petty monies that normally would have been allowed.

Meanwhile a meal of rye bread and sausage appeared. All partook of it in the hearty German manner, and the atmosphere of the party became even jollier, if that were possible. The head miller continued to fondle the twelve-bore gun lovingly.

When asked where I had been going when disaster overtook me, I disclosed to my astonished hearers that Bremerhaven had been my destination, at the mouth of the Weser, and from that port I intended to take ship for England. This announcement seemed to fill my hearers with great surprise. My female listeners seemed filled with pity, too, for the wreaking of such a promising expedition. The head miller assumed a thoughtful look and presently drew from me the admission that I was

Reminiscences of an Elephant Hunter

My escape from Germany in my home-built kayak. (Sketch by W. D. M. Bell)

without funds and that at all costs a return whence I came was completely out of the question.

After pondering weightily these matters, the miller called for a railway timetable. He set aside the gun while he laboriously studied that complicated-looking volume and then began jotting down some figures with a short pencil stub. Suddenly his brooding, weather-beaten features broke into a jolly smile as he announced with a huge laugh that "It could be done."

"Look," said he, with kindness shining brightly from every line and wrinkle of his strong peasant face. It will cost you so much by train from here to Bremerhaven. So much you will require for food. And I will buy your gun for that amount."

This announcement came as a great relief. It resolved my difficulty, and I was overwhelmed by the kindness of my host, assisted as I was quite possibly by the potency of the brandy. It was only later that this feeling was somewhat qualified when I found how nearly the calculations had been made on the costs of travel and commissariat. The price given for a perfectly good shotgun just covered, by the barest margin, the cheapest class and the simplest food for the journey, leaving hardly a pfennig over. Luckily, a ship was easily found and I was quickly home.[3]

In looking back on those days, how surprising it seems that there were no passports required, even in Germany. Apparently, one could circulate all over the world without let or hindrance. How very different it is now, with permits for this and that, restrictions on everything and immigration officers on the look-out at every port. It hardly seems an advance on those spacious times.

******

Once home, I immediately again began to pester my harassed guardians with the eternal cry: "To Africa! To Africa!"

Humbugged to death by my persistence and giving up all hope that I would ever make good, my guardians finally yielded to the inevitable. To Africa I should go.

With a rifle, a second-class ticket, and a few sovereigns, I was at long last headed in the right direction: Mombasa, East Africa.

---

[3] In Bell's escape from Germany (1896), he launched his kayak on a tributary to the Weser River. Bell states that this tributary was 40 miles from the Weser, and the Weser is 431 km (268 miles) from its source to Bremerhaven. Bell doesn't state exactly where his boarding school was located, but if it was situated at even half the distance along the Weser to Bremerhaven, this intrepid young man was facing quite the adventure!

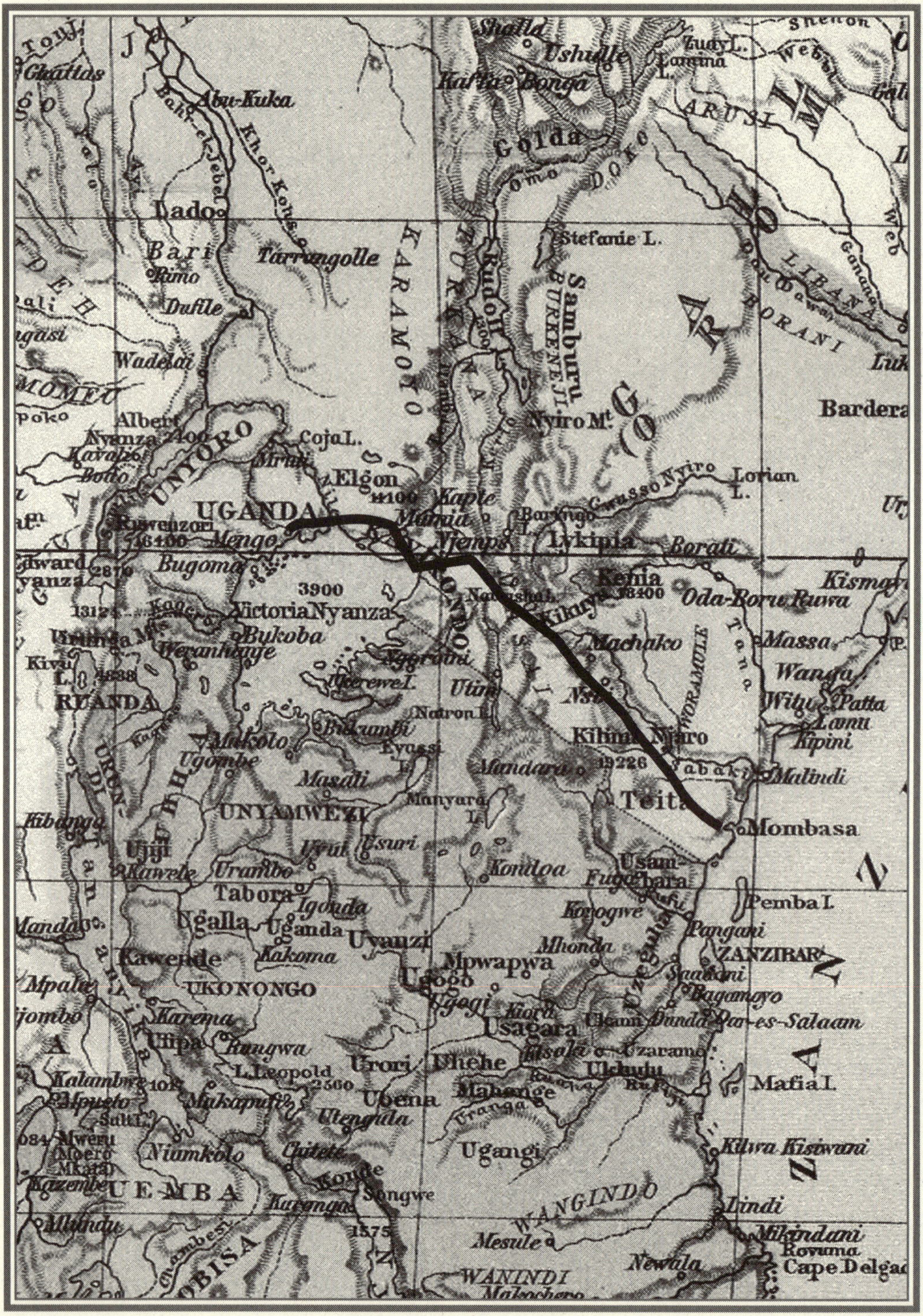

Abu-Kuka
Kaffa
Bonga
Golda
ARUSI
Lado
Bari
Dufile
Tarrangolle
Wadelai
Stefanie L.
Samburu
Bardera
Albert Nyanza
UNYORO
Coja L.
Elgon
UGANDA
Mengo
Bugoma
Nyiro Mt.
Lorian L.
Kapte
Baringo
Lykipia
Borati
Kenia
Kismayu
3900
Victoria Nyanza
Bukoba
Oda-Boru-Ruwa
Machako
Massa
Kikuyu
Natron L.
Ukerewe I.
RUANDA
Wanga
Witu
Patta
Lamu
Kipini
Malindi
Kilima Njaro
Mandara
Teita
Mombasa
Masai
UNYAMWEZI
Manyara L.
Ujiji
Kawele
Urambo
Tabora
Igonda
Kondoa
Pemba I.
Pangani
ZANZIBAR
Ngalla
Uganda
Kakoma
Kawende
Uvanzi
Mpwapwa
Mhonda
UKONONGO
Karema
Usagara
Bagamoyo
Dar-es-Salaam
Rungwa
L. Leopold
Urori
Uhehe
Mafia I.
Ubena
Mahenge
Ugangi
Kilwa Kisiwani
Niumkolo
UEMBA
Songwe
WANGINDO
Lindi
Mesule
Mikindani
Newala
WANINDI
Rovuma
Cape Delgado

One Foot in Africa, 1897

CHAPTER 6

I was close on seventeen years old when my eldest brother conveyed me to a gunmaker's for the choice of a suitable rifle to take with me to Africa. This part of the adventure was, of course, the mainspring on which all depended, in my estimation at any rate. A beautiful single-shot .303 was produced at an attractive price—it was second-hand—and my brother soon concluded the bargain. For me, this process was akin to knocking on the Gates of Paradise. Next, a second-class passage was secured on a small German passenger steamer to Mombasa, East Africa, among many other ports of call.

Ever since I could remember, my sole ambition in life had been to hunt first bison then elephants. This inexplicable obsession had never left me, but there would be still many obstacles to overcome before I could realise my ambition. Thinking back over the years, I would say that ignorance was by far the greatest of these obstacles. Ignorance of an African language perhaps the greatest of them all.

In those days, there were no other preparations for the cracking open of what was still to most people the Dark Continent. No particular medical supplies, mosquito nets, tropical headgear, or other paraphernalia seemed to be considered necessary, or for that matter, not even a tent, or a camp bed, or cooking equipment was considered essential. Simplicity was certainly the keynote of my first expedition. I set off with one rifle, a few cartridges, a steamship ticket, plus a few golden sovereigns in my pocket. How few these were would soon transpire.

Among the passengers on the good ship *Somali* was a large burly South African, much versed in African ways, and possessing a revolver and an apparently insatiable thirst. He was my cabin mate and the only English-speaking person aboard.

The voyage was uneventful until, in due course, some Portuguese soldiers were embarked at Lisbon. Now the South African had been in some obscure military organization and, of course, was of an extremely critical nature on all matters to do with soldiering. This was especially the case when he was in liquor, and that state occupied a large part of each day.

He and I used to watch the poor little Portuguese soldiers drilling down on the cargo deck from the vantage point of the boat deck, all the while the South

African would satisfy himself with a running commentary full of scathing remarks on the show below, interspersed with shouts of scorn and laughter.

Now, although the Portuguese understood no English, they could hardly misapprehend the meaning of these remarks, and so, when one day the South African jumped down among them and snatched a rifle from a scared-looking youth and began to show them how they ought to drill, they could stand it no longer. One of them picked up a large piece of timber and straightway felled the South African to the deck with a shrewd whack on the head. At that point, the whole crowd poured straight down the hatch to the 'tween-decks, leaving their prostrate enemy in solitary possession of the field.

These jolly doings had not gone unobserved, however. The ever-vigilant first mate landed on the battlefield almost as soon as I did myself and took charge of the situation. The South African had meanwhile come to and showed some annoyance to find the mate abstracting his revolver from his clothing. With some difficulty I succeeded in getting my cabin mate to quieten down, while the mate carried off the pistol after being assured by me that the "Afrikaner had no further firearms."

Having now been relieved of any danger of having to make good his boasts, the "Afrikaner," as the Germans called him, proceeded to vow vengeance on the "dirty bastards"; he was, however, easily persuaded that a tot of brandy would do him good. Needless to say, nothing came of the affair, but the pistol remained in custody of the ship until we arrived at Mombasa.

******

That romantic town received the arrival of the ship with no little excitement but, strangely enough, the South African's and my arrival passed unnoticed. We repaired to the only house that pretended to be a hotel, the "Africa," which was an Arab house kept by a Greek oozing with the oil of prosperity.

When we arrived in Mombasa it was 1897, the construction of the Uganda Railway had just begun, and soon we would learn that there was a scare on. Although the surveying parties had already penetrated well into the interior, the actual construction work was being retarded by marauding lions. More later on all this, but just let me say that Providence had landed me and my rifle on the right spot. Lions were all anyone talked of.

Now the South African was booked through to a South African port and I had been looking forward with some pleasure to the departure of the ship with my cabin mate on board. Truth to tell, I felt I would be well rid of him and his embarrassing ways. When, then, I heard the Greek hotelier telling my companion that there was a good job offering in the stores department[1] of the imminent Uganda Railway project and how jubilantly this news was received, my face fell the proverbial mile.

Still worse was to come, however. When the South African paid a visit to the person in charge, he immediately secured the job. To be in charge of stores! That seemed to open up a vista of pure delight—to the gaze of that old soldier at any rate.

Now it was necessary for the South African to get his luggage ashore. I was enlisted to help, so back to the ship we went. When the purser was told that the South African was leaving the ship, the officer presented—with some promptitude, I might add—the South African with his liquor bill. Unfortunately, this was before the latter had succeeded in getting his baggage transferred to the waiting shore boat. The bill was of formidable size, in spite of prices then prevailing being so low for spirits out of bond. It was something like three and sixpence for an entire bottle of whisky. More disturbing still was the reluctance of the South African to pay it. Quite an altercation, indeed, arose over the affair. Many and ingenious were the reasons given why he should not pay it. Everything except the truth, that being, of course, that he had not got the money . . . or had he?

My status as a would-be explorer meant that I did not have the funds to spare to help the South African pay his bill. Amidst assurances that I would be re-paid as soon as an advance could be secured from his new employer, the South African finally prevailed on me to take from my meagre stock of money the funds necessary to bail him out. Although I had been round the world and had knocked about all over the place, I was apparently of the stuff that mugs are made, for, of course, I never saw a stuiver[2] of my money again.

After clearing my friend from the shackles of his liquor bill, I found that what remained of my slender stock would barely pay my hotel bill. Something would have to be done about it.

---

[1] A stores department receives goods and acts as a caretaker of materials. As demands for materials come in, the stores department officer procures the materials and then issues the goods to the specific area of the company that has requested them.

[2] A stuiver is a small coin formerly used in the Netherlands, equal to five cents or one-twentieth of a guilder. Last conversion rate available was two guilders for each dollar. (The Netherlands currently uses the euro.)

Mombasa in those days was still the headquarters for some fairly important trading caravans. Safaris to and from Uganda and beyond frequently left for or arrived from the mysterious interior. The trade was still a system of barter. American and Manchester cotton goods, iron and brass wire, iron chain, Venetian glass beads, Dutch shag tobacco, and kauri [cowry] shells were traded for ivory and a few slaves.

As this latter trade was beginning to be frowned upon by the authorities, especially so by the naval people, it had to be carried on under the elaborate camouflage so dear to the African mind. Perhaps the commonest form was the conversion of savages to Mohammedanism by circumcision and the bestowing on the convert the name "Son of So-and-So."

This was a grand game as it legalized everything and enabled the "father" to use his "sons" in any way he might think fit. For years white men employed "boys" at the current rate of wages, only to find eventually that every cent of it was carried to "father," who might or might not allow the "son" a small portion of his earnings as a gift.

It had always been my intention to join one of these trading caravans. I wanted to live as they lived and, thus, to penetrate parts of the vast continent that would otherwise be unattainable to anyone of such slender resources such as mine. The idea was that in return for the protection afforded by the guns of the safari, I would kill meat with my rifle for them. The ivory I would keep.

It must be remembered that most tribes were still a law unto themselves, and some were actively hostile to all travelers. Permission to traverse their country had to be paid for in *hongo* (tribute) if the tribe was warlike and numerous; if otherwise, a few shots from the safari guns smoothed the passage.

With this end in view, I set some enquiries on foot but met with scant encouragement, to say the least of it. It appeared that the very last thing these safaris wanted was the company of a white youth. To them I could only be a spy. They had no knowledge then of what a capable hunter, armed with a modern rifle, could do among the countless herds of elephants roaming the equatorial bush. Even the one or two experienced whites I consulted seemed dead set against the idea, pointing out that, even if the safari leaders consented to the joining up of a white, which in itself was almost inconceivable as they were all more or less involved in the illicit trade of "black ivory," a white man could not possibly stand the "racket."

ONE FOOT IN AFRICA, 1897

UGANDA RAILWAY.

THE HIGHLANDS OF
BRITISH EAST AFRICA
AS A
WINTER HOME FOR ARISTOCRATS
HAS BECOME A FASHION.

SPORTSMEN in search of **BIG GAME** make it a hobby.

STUDENTS of **NATURAL HISTORY** revel in this **FIELD** of **NATURE'S** own **MAKING**.

UGANDA RAILWAY Observation Cars pass through the Greatest Natural **GAME PRESERVE** in the **WORLD**.

For reliable information, etc., address:
PUBLICITY DEPT., UGANDA RAILWAY.
DEWAR HOUSE, HAYMARKET, S.W.

67

Reminiscences of an Elephant Hunter

For one thing, they pointed out, these caravans did not work to any time schedule. These expeditions spent months in preparation and years on the expedition itself before settling down in remote parts and in permanent camps to trade. There they would join forces with one tribe to raid a neighbouring one. Centuries of battling one another had reduced the tribes to a common degree of strength, so when there was a sudden accession of a force of two or three hundred guns to one of the sides, it made the issue of the struggle a dead cert. Then there were the little goings-on in these raids that had to be taken into account: for example, the massacres and the disembowelling of pregnant women with a single knife slash across the tautened belly.

"No! Decidedly no!" I was told. "It would not do. A white man could not stand the racket."

Obviously, I had to come up with a new plan.

Visiting the South African one day at his new job, more in search of company than with any hope of being repaid by that worthy, I found him in liquor as usual but also highly delighted with his new job. He was in complete charge of the stores for the survey parties of the newly projected Uganda Railway, his predecessor having been laid low by fever. The job seemed to have

A Ringling Bros. and Barnum & Bailey advertisement featuring Frank Buck in a solar topi (1938).

been made for him. How the survey parties came off from the connection was another matter. They must have wondered why their whisky ration was suddenly so meagre. But those were spacious days and I daresay that even the South African's consumption passed unnoticed.

He said that the survey wanted white men. It appeared that the transport for these parties consisted of mules, American backboard wagons, and Indian muleteers. The latter had been on strike and had refused to circulate unless they were given the protection of a white man on each safari. Native spearmen had been active in opposing one or two of these expeditions and lions had succeeded in killing several Indians, besides stampeding mule trains.

This news came like a foresniff of paradise to me, for I was by that time itching to let off my precious .303 at something bigger than a rabbit. I resolved to look into the matter forthwith.

Accordingly, my companion led me to a large, new office building quite recently arrived in sections and erected under the mango trees and coconut palms of Kilindini, a gharry[3] ride out of Mombasa. Here I was introduced to a stout, important-looking man. The only questions he asked were whether I had a rifle and did that rifle have ammunition. I was instantly engaged as a hunter and ordered forthwith to proceed up-country immediately to Voi, the then headquarters of the transport.

After I was duly enrolled, I was handed a letter to deliver to one Brittlebank at Voi, who, apparently, would be my boss and do everything necessary to get me kitted out. Included was a railway voucher that entitled me to cover the few miles of newly constructed railroad.

Bidding my friend adieu, I embarked on my journey the next day. The train, filled to capacity with material, went off in great style and a shower of sparks from the wood-fired boiler, while excited *baboo*s in turbans and frock coats and tight-fitting pants blew whistles and waved flags. All very inspiring and jolly.

******

It was the time in world history when the solar topi [also known as a pith helmet] was at the zenith of its power. That outrageous dictatorship had not yet been debunked, and it was still considered suicidal to be caught by

---

[3] A gharry is a horse-drawn cab.

REMINISCENCES OF AN ELEPHANT HUNTER

The Uganda Railway, known as the Lunatic Express, near Mombasa, about 1899.

the sun outside its enveloping shade. Very often it was so—when sun-heat from without met alcoholic-heat from within. I was no subscriber to this fetish, however. For one thing I had been through the tropics twice, once slowly on a sailing ship and once less slowly on a cargo steamer, and no one had worn a topi. Indeed, some wore no headgear at all. So I wore my single-felt hat without suffering any inconvenience from the sun.

The same could not be said of my traveling companions, nor of the locomotive. The former pestered me with warnings of the dire consequences of neglecting the topi, the latter by landing burning sparks on my hat and burning holes in it. This allowed for increased ventilation and was more of an advantage than otherwise.

Liquor was much in evidence. I thought it a somewhat curious way of reducing the external temperature by adding to the interior one, all done with libations of alcoholic strength unknown to present generations. Concluding that much of the sun's destructive power could safely be more truly attributed to that of the bottle, I contentedly munched on delicious fruit while I watched as my companions opened tins of such deadly delicacies as pork pie, camp pie, etc., and washed them down with bottled beer or whisky and soda. I had bought a huge basket of bananas and mangoes for one rupee, basket included, and I was quite happy with my far more healthy fare.

******

At one of the wooding stations—our locomotive burned nothing else—the news came through that a white man, one of the construction engineers, had been taken from his tent at Voi by a lion and killed. This set my ears a-pricking. *At long last we are getting places,* I thought. *This is the stuff.* Searching for more details of the happening, I questioned the bearer of the news more closely, but without success.

Sooner or later Voi was achieved as the road was very, very new and the speed was less than ten miles per hour. Delivering my letter to Brittlebank, I was fascinated by my first view of what was to be my job. Imagine a large clearing in African thorn bush where all the larger trees had been left standing, only the low stuff cleared away. Among the trees numerous tents were pitched. Long rows of mules stood tethered to lines by head ropes while heel ropes attached to pegs lay idly on the ground behind them, to be used only at night as a precaution against stampedes caused by lions.

As I looked around, I saw there were huge camps of bell tents occupied by Indian coolies—the construction gangs—on every side, but the odd thing about the whole show was the enormously thick thorn fences, fifteen feet high and twenty feet thick, that surrounded and sub-divided these camps. Most of the largest trees had platforms twenty or thirty feet from the ground.

Brittlebank, my boss, was an eagle-faced man of some forty-five years. He, too, wore a single-felt hat. He had a peculiar gait when walking due to a canoe accident in Canada when both his ankles had been broken. He had prospected for years in every country of the world, spoke many languages, among them Persian, and still had with him a devoted Persian boy. Over a cup of tea, Brittlebank disclosed what my job was to be.

Briefly the plan of operations was this: The mule trains took over stores at the rail head for the advanced survey parties. Roughly speaking, the new railway followed the old caravan route to Uganda; thus, the mule convoys for the most part followed that ancient trail, with only minor digressions to survey camps in the bush. This good plan had recently been put in jeopardy, which is where I came in.

Apparently the whole organization was in the grip of fear because some forty coolies had been eaten and a white man had just been taken from his tent.[4] The Indian coolies were on strike, the precious whites were sleeping up in trees, and the Indian muleteers of the supply trains were refusing to go on with their trek without protection. Every tent of ten men had been issued with a rifle. Everyone was to be within the camp zarebas by sundown. All gates were closed by sundown and still the marauding lions claimed their nightly toll in spite of fires, lanterns, shots, and firebrands.

Parties of white men tracked the beasts as far back into the surrounding bush as they could hold the trail. No one could understand how a lion could possibly escape through or over those immense thorny fences and carry a man, but they did. Of course, no one then knew the capabilities of lions. We now know that a lion can get over such obstacles carrying a cow weighing six or seven hundred pounds, so an average coolie of one hundred and thirty to one hundred and forty pounds would present little difficulty to these active cats.

So long as the lions confined their attentions to coolies, the matter was treated with some calmness by the authorities. But, as Brittlebank reported to me, when the white man had been taken from his tent—dragged from it by the head in spite of spirited resistance on the part of his boy—things were brought to a boiling point. The whole camp was in a ferment. Something must be done about it to keep the railroad on schedule.

Among many other attempts to outwit the cunning rascals, an elaborate steel cage had been built. This contained within it a small inner cage. The idea

---

[4] This episode in East Africa's history was made famous by Col. John Patterson in his book, *The Man-Eaters of Tsavo*.

was to leave the door of the outer cage open for the lion to enter while the inner one was to contain human bait consisting of armed Sikh police. Once the lion was in, the policemen were to pull the door of the outer cage shut and then proceed to dispatch the lion, or lions, at their leisure.

Everything went to plan. The lion came, walked around the outer cage, entered, and the door clanged to. He was trapped at last. Unfortunately, however, the bullet meant for the man-eater missed him and shattered the locking device on the outer door. Once more the terror was at large.

The next episode in this saga concerns a plucky white man who stationed himself on a small bridge much used by the marauders. He knew his stuff and armed himself with a shotgun and buckshot. Sure enough, along came a beast. At point-blank range he fired, and the buckshot . . . flattened a donkey! The beast had somehow been let out and the plucky white man had been on alert to shoot anything that moved and looked like an animal.

The crisis continued.

Something had to be done about the lions to keep the railroad on schedule.

Of course, I was tremendously excited by all these doings. By the look of things, Africa was going to live up to my expectations. I hastened to try out my single-shot, falling-block .303 and to familiarize myself with the bush. I was thrilled with the idea of coming on a man-eater all by myself, and of laying it out, of course. Although I had not yet sighted a lion at that point, there is one thing I did find out: That was the poor extraction of these falling-block actions.

Under the African sun, cartridges that had presented no extraction difficulties in temperate climes now almost refused to leave the chamber. Indeed, it was only by the vigorous use of a ramrod that they could be induced to do so. I thought I would have to shoot mighty close and carefully since I could not count on a second shot in a hurry. It is to this early training that much of my later success is probably due.

My job was to guard the mule convoy from anything and everything—lions, hyaenas, rhinos, elephants, or native Africans. The whole convoy that carried supplies to the surveyors was under my command. I could ride on mule back, walk, or sit on the buckboard wagons. I could call a halt or demand absolute silence if it would enable me to get a shot at a prowling lion. As there were no game laws in those days and as part of my job as convoy leader was to provide meat for all hands, I enjoyed much good fun.

Between bouts of trying to track the man-eaters in their thorny cover, which I found extremely difficult to do because of the hard, dry ground, I soon became instructed in my job. Besides accompanying a mule convoy, thereby instilling confidence in the Indian muleteers—poor things—I was also to see that the mules were properly fed, watered, harnessed, and vetted.

While it seemed quite a list of requirements—for a boy at any rate—I found the work extremely interesting. The mules were lovely animals from Cyprus, the harnesses and fittings of the best, the American backboard wagons just right for the job, and the Indian muleteers a quiet, docile lot and, on the whole, not unkind to their charges.

Those being the hey-days of the white man, I had Indians that barbered, cooked for, and manicured me, all in a most efficient way and from among the muleteers on a quite voluntary basis. The truth was that these people were in a far land and in a blue funk[5] of native Africans and, with some reason, of the

---

[5] A blue funk is a state of great terror or loss of nerve.

lions. Poor creatures, they thought that all lions were man-eaters like those at Tsavo. They even had confidence in the white convoy leader . . . little did they know upon what slender grounds that hope rested.

At this time there was a handsome general bounty paid on any lion killed within a mile of the projected railway route. Now, a two-mile-wide strip defined merely by a row of wooden pegs is a very arbitrary limitation to an enthusiastic young hunter, and some of my bounty skins may have come from areas a little wide of the mark. I need not have worried, however, for upon claiming bounty, I was curtly reminded that lion killing was my job, wasn't it, and that I was being paid for that job, wasn't I? Thereafter, I stayed inside the limits.

As much of our marching was done by moonlight so as to save the mules from the heat of the day, it was quite common to mistake almost every moving object for a lion. To kill by moonlight is quite a difficult matter, I soon discovered. Lions, or any animal, are almost invisible to the human eye unless silhouetted against water, a flood-lit trail, or the horizon. Often all I could see was a shadow, and it required nice judgment to guess from the shadow where exactly the vital spot of the animal lay. I found the most effective method was to lie down so as to glimpse the animal against the star-filled heavens.

Whenever I fired at a lion, the Indian muleteers became petrified, coming as they did from the Tsavo camps where so many of their mates had been eaten. At any shot I made, the whole convoy would be thrown into such complete disorder that I found I had to work well out ahead of them to get any chance at all.

Anything more calculated to intoxicate a boy like me than this job could hardly be imagined.

Soon we began to operate in the great game plains, where Nairobi is now located. The herds of zebras, hartebeests, brindled gnus, impalas, Grant's gazelles, and Thompson's gazelles were unbelievable. By day we would wend our way through miles upon miles of game beasts, the whole landscape shrouded in the dust from their traffic. There would be giraffes swaying along the horizons; the dark forms of obstinate rhinos crashing about here and there; wild dogs panting in the shimmering heat with full bellies and lolling tongues; and lions passing the mid-day heat in the reed beds that lined the rivers, only to come out later on, to roll and play before the night's hunt began.

At sundown Africa would come alive. Roars and grunts would fill the air while the thunder of countless hoofs told of the nightly crop being harvested, and yet the impression I gathered was not of tragedy but of supreme enjoyment of life as these superb herds frolicked and hunted and raced in a perfect balance of nature.

At first I treated every lion as a potential man-eater. They were nothing of the sort. In fact, they would have scorned to eat one of our tough mules. Apart from the few real man-killers of Tsavo, I doubt if any of these lions, had he been asked to eat one of our muleteers, but would have vomited.

So it gradually dawned on me, and in time on the Indians too, that we had little to fear from the well-fed lions of the game plains. These lions could scarcely fail to kill something from among the abundance of wild life around them. Doubtless all those roarings and ventriloquial gruntings and whoofings had the effect of stirring up the herds, stampeding them, and thus driving them within range of the killers' mates lying flat and motionless in ambush.

It took time because of their experiences at Tsavo, but eventually, everyone realized that only under exceptional circumstances does the African lion become a man-eater. They also gradually began to understand that they were as likely to be attacked by the lion living among the vast herds of game that lined their route on all sides as they were to be tackled by domestic cats.

Rhinos were another matter altogether. They do not see very well, are exceedingly pugnacious, and are just as likely as not to go straight for the middle of a long line of men or wagons. They cannot be depended on to run away. Any efforts to scare them off, such as shouting or firing shots, only serve to get them all excited. Once agitated, they whirl around as if on a pivot with ears and horns aggressively cocked. It is a toss-up if an aggrieved rhino will trot away or rush you.

Should it be the latter, you must at once deal firmly and decisively with the menace. As he nears you and sees the long line of men apparently stretching away on either side, he seems to think he is surrounded. The next thing you know, he has launched himself into an incredibly swift gallop and is on or through you in a split second.

We had this experience, and it did us no good at all. The mules bolted, legs were broken when men were bucked off the wagons, harnesses got tangled up, whisky cases got smashed, and panic reigned. Thereafter, I simply shot any rhino that refused to get out of the road.

In the cool of the night the .303 extracted reasonably well, especially if a tree trunk was handy on which to thump the lever. The first time I drew a bead on an object that could be really distinguishable as a lion in the shimmering moon-light was one night when I was again out ahead and on foot with my single-shot .303 in hand. For some time a gray shape had been noticeable flitting along in front, but on the borders of the trail. Suddenly this hitherto shapeless object stood clearly silhouetted dark against the flood-lit trail beyond, undoubtedly a lion or lioness.

The distance was, perhaps, thirty to forty yards, too far for a sure kill. Advancing slowly toward the lion, I kept trying my sights on him with but little success as the moon was beyond the target and did not, therefore, light up the sights. To my astonishment, the lion sat down in the middle of the road and looked now so uncommonly like a large dog that I paused. I immediately began to doubt myself. *Is it really a lion or lioness?* I wondered. In the next breath, I said to myself that I certainly wasn't going to bring off a repetition of that Tsavo episode when someone mistook a donkey for a lion.

Meanwhile the jingling of the approaching convoy smote my ear and just as I was about to give the beggar fire, whether lion or dog, a frantic shout from the leading muleteer made me look round.

"Sahib! Sahib! No good! No good!" cried his and a dozen voices, all calculated to scare away the lion.

On demanding of the interpreter what all the fuss was about, it appeared that in the unanimous opinion of the muleteers it was crazy to shoot at lions because it would inevitably result in a charge and the stampede of the mules. By this time, of course, the lion had moved off. He had not minded a khaki-clad stripling but an advancing horde of shouting men, rumbling wagons, and jingling mules was just too much for him.

******

The camp at Stony Athi was perhaps the most rewarding in lion scenes. It was not an uncommon sight to see ten or fifteen lions entering or leaving the extensive reed beds or just playing about. If you, a khaki-clad figure, walked toward them, they would certainly retreat but only at their own pace. If you ran toward them, one or other would stop and sometimes advance to meet you. They seemed uncertain as to what the queer-coloured figure meant. They were eager to avoid trouble, but if they suspected attack, they were quite willing to have a show-down.

As I said, our mules were always tied by the head to ropes stretched between the wagons, and as further security every mule was heel-roped to stout pegs. Even so they would sometimes break loose when panic-stricken zebras or wildebeests driven mad with excitement in some lion drive would stampede close to or even through our camp. Strange to say, I do not think we ever lost any mules. All would come back or be caught the next morning. Lions apparently had no use for our tough, four-legged companions.

Buffaloes were fairly numerous but shy. Not that they were much hunted, but they were recovering from one of the periodical plagues of rinderpest. It is extraordinary how nature instills a new sense into animals to meet just such a crisis. When they are numerous, they crowd the open landscape forming perfect targets for man and lion alike. When the herds are decimated, the survivors retreat to cover in the daytime, whether bush or reed bed.

As the survey progressed, we began to see elephant sign, but without the native African to assist us, it was difficult to come up to them. I was most keen to get on with my lifelong ambition to hunt elephants, yet I could do nothing without native help, and that was not forthcoming because no Africans worked at the construction. The builders of the railway employed Indian labour exclusively; the coolies were recruited in India and shipped over by steamer.

In 1897 native Africans were still gentlemen at large, raiding, woman-snatching, and carrying on as from time immemorial. They seldom came near our camps. The white invaders of their land had not yet invented the taxes that were soon to compel the native to work at least some part of the year. All this meant I had no native resource to help me in my goal of becoming an elephant hunter.

I now focused on my armament with somewhat critical attention. The rifle that had to begin with seemed the most perfect one in the world began to assume a different aspect in light of the recurrent extracting difficulties. Meeting a Greek trader one day at a common camp, we compared rifles. That of the Greek was a Winchester single-shot, black-powder .450 falling-block with a long taper cartridge. Not nearly so modern a weapon as my beautiful Fraser .303, but it was still an accurate, hard-hitting gun and, above all, a sure extractor.

I offered to exchange rifles after ascertaining that the count of ammunition was roughly that of the .303's. Unfortunately, all his cartridges were of that abomination—the hollow, copper-point variety of bullet. I knew nothing of this at the time, however, and, as the Greek seemed dazzled with the .303, a trade was soon effected.

On buck the .450 performed quite well, although it spoilt much meat. As antelope were in their thousands, this did not matter much. But on rhino I soon realized the shortcomings of that soft-lead, hollow shell. Had there only been some of the solid variety of bullet, I would have been all right. As it was, I soon found I could kill buffaloes by keeping my bullet well away from big bones. The story of how those wretched bullets very nearly put me in queer street appears in *Karamojo Safari,* so I will briefly summarize what happened:

> One morning the boys came rushing into camp at sunrise in great excitement to say that a lion was drinking at the water hole. Clumps of high bush studded the hillside. *Now I can put the .450 to good use,* I thought. An African with a muzzle-loader joined me and we set off.
>
> We soon spotted the lion in a patch of grass, and only his head showed. I fired for his head at some thirty yards, expecting to blow it clean off. Instead, there started up a most unholy to-do, and then silence. The African and I snooped around that patch of bush but could neither see nor hear anything. At last the African declared that the lion must be dead,
>
> *I devoutly hope so,* thought I. Unfortunately, I was not too sure.
>
> I was right. With a whoosh and a roar, there came Leo in a split-arse charge not feet away. The African took off with Leo on his heels. Just when I thought Leo had him, the African fell and that lion shot clean over him. I instantly got the lion in my sights, and as he came broadside on, I got in a shot on his shoulder, which obviously shook him, but did not knock him down.
>
> Luckily my last shot at Leo's shoulder had sickened him considerably, although even now he was full of fight when the boys came on him at a three- or four-yard range. It was with difficulty that I got in a finisher because the boys had so mobbed the lion with their sticks and knives that I did not have a clear line of shot.
>
> Examination showed that the first shot in the head had broken the lion's lower jaw. That was probably why no one had been bitten. The second shot had caught him fair on the shoulder. Both bullets had simply blown up and caused only surface wounds. This gave me pause to think.

Out of this episode and other doings with agitated rhinos, it became obvious to me that at all cost a bullet must not break up. It was a lesson that served me well in my later career as an elephant hunter. I soon acquired a .303 Lee-Metford, which was then the latest army rifle. It used a nickel-jacketed bullet weighing 215 grains and, although soft-nose bullets were being made for it, I would have none of them.

Admittedly these so-called solids had to be accurately placed. But why should they not be so? The barrel was straight and the bullet flew truly. So it was merely a case of placing it properly on the animal so as to reach a vital spot. I learnt this lesson well, and I thus began my life-long study in the necessity of nerve control and the knowledge of anatomy that was to serve me so well in later years.

******

The months passed with the rail-head gradually creeping inland. What is now Nairobi was passed as just one of the many camping grounds. The lovely country of Naivasha was passed with no thought of the great changes that were to transform it in a few years. Donkey transport was coming more and more to the fore, and a large camp was established on the shores of Lake Naivasha for the resting and recuperation of transport animals.

It was here that I woke up one morning to see the plains literally covered with thousands of head of cattle and sheep. They were of a breed strange to that part of the country. In reply to questions, I was told they belonged to three white men who were camped down by the lake shore. I went off to see who they were.

I was welcomed by two white men—the third man had gone elsewhere. They were two hard-bitten characters if ever there was. One had a pronounced limp, the other a beard, and it transpired the former had fallen foul of a leopard. The other was distinguished by the use of a brand of blasphemy that reminded me of my sailing-ship days. Both had *kiboko*s dangling from their wrists. Judging by the service they got from their boys, I judged they were not backward in using them.

Over the inevitable liquor they told me that they came from the north and that they had had some differences with the tribes up there. From the look of the large flocks and herds that literally covered the country in every direction, I could surmise what the trouble had been. A huge double-barrel gun stood in a corner of the grass hut.

"What is it?" I asked.

I was told it was the "Doctor's" eight-bore Paradox. The missing member of the trio apparently was called the "Doctor." I handled the monstrous piece of ordnance, and from what I could gather, it killed elephants. The bearded fellow had an opinion, and, picking up a .303 ten-shot rifle, he declared that this rifle was much more effective for elephants. This was an opinion that I could well believe, in spite of the formidable-looking cartridges put out by the famous house of Holland & Holland for the Paradox. Each bullet had a hand-turned steel core enveloped in lead and cost a shilling each, an unheard-of price in those days.

On the whole these men were pretty close-mouthed about where they had been, and I was then too innocent-minded and too ignorant to enquire closely into the matter.

It was sometime later that I heard all three of these gentlemen were being held in custody on a series of charges ranging from murder to dacoity,[6] so I decided to visit my acquaintances in the jail where they were installed. I found them taking this adverse turn in their affairs with some ease, not to say levity. When I told them (with some malice it must be confessed) that the talk was that they were to be scragged[7] as an example to others who might be tempted to follow in their footsteps and that a large expedition had been sent out to follow their trail and to gather evidence to be used against them, they roared with laughter. They then straightway ordered their warder to produce cold bottled beer. Whereupon they wished everyone the best of luck. Altogether they seemed extremely well pleased with themselves.

One day Mule Transport received orders to help in every way possible a certain reputed big shot who would visit us shortly. He arrived with a lot of luggage and a strong German accent. We got his stuff onto our wagons, and I was told to convey him to the lake, as we called Victoria Nyanza. He seemed a pleasant enough fellow, but what interested me most was his project. He proposed to explore the unopened country between Uganda and Abyssinia, and he said he had letters to the authorities in Uganda.

This man was undoubtedly German who, nevertheless, spoke almost perfect English. He arrived with all the recommendations possible. It was reliably stated that he bore a personal letter from Queen Victoria herself. The railway transport was ordered to help him on his way. The traders were told to supply him with anything and everything and they would be certain of payment. He proceeded to take full advantage of everything so willingly offered. He paid for nothing, but that did not come out at the time.

---

[6] Armed robbery with violence.

[7] To execute by hanging or garroting.

Contact then between railroad builder and native African was almost nil. True, the latter would come down by night and steal thousands of the little steel wedges that held the rails to the steel sleepers because their blacksmiths could easily forge from them quite good spearheads. They also appreciated the bright copper wire that began to appear as the telephone-telegraph advanced. But as for friendly, intimate hunters' talk round the campfire, it just did not exist.

In point of fact, there was considerable hostility on the African's part to the idea of having anything to do with Indians. One can hardly blame them when one considers the vast gulf between the primitive, but pure sexual basis of the African's life and that of the effete, centuries-old phallic worshipping cults of India. It was the considered opinion of most Africans that no goat, male or female, was safe from the Indians. Inevitably, this opinion was expressed in the killing of a coolie gang or two, which, of course, led to further trouble.

Thus, it was that I began to realize that I had gotten myself into the wrong camp somehow. I had found all other game standing, waiting by the roadside to be shot, yet I could find no elephants. I found the African hated the sight of me and my Indians. Without the African's help, I could not find where the elephants lived. I must shed my Indian burden, somehow get myself in with a trading caravan and trek away into the interior. This required funds, and I had none.

So, although I was now ready to embark upon my long-cherished resolve to become an elephant hunter, my finances were not such as to enable me to outfit a safari on an adequate scale, nor was my knowledge of the country sufficient. I also needed a way in with the native Africans; those living along the routes of the white men were also shy of contacting people who seemed only intent on making them work. It was, therefore, with eager anticipation that I welcomed the German explorer.

I asked him if he wanted a hunter. He said he would be delighted to have a hunter who could shoot elephants. I at once proposed myself for this role. He asked about the conditions of my employment with the Uganda Railway. I told him I had to give a month's notice. He told me to fire it in at once, and he would send for me to join him at Kampala in Uganda. I did so pronto.

Soon I found myself in Central Africa and out of a job. Worse still, I was totally without resources. I had my rifle, however, and with that I knew I would not starve. As all communication in those days was by native canoe across the lake, I had perforce to await my new boss's instructions there. Being thickly inhabited and intensively cultivated, the area did not offer much game except for hippos in the lake itself.

I soon found quarters in a native village where I was given a very decent hut. There I waited for the summons. My hosts, the Kavirondo, were a completely nude tribe. They were very kind to me. I was able to pay my way by killing hippos for them. They loved the hunting of these animals from their native canoes, and were very sorry to see me go. For go I finally had to.

For one thing the mosquitoes were very active and full of malaria. I thought of myself then of being tough, so, of course, I scorned mosquito nets. My hosts simply built up a huge fire in their huts at night and either scorched or smoked the buzzing multitude out of it. I could not stand that much smoke and thought the mosquitoes the better option. The mosquitoes won, and I began to have all the usual fever symptoms. Still there were no summons from across the lake.

The summons never did come. What I heard was that my explorer had left with his safari for new country without a word to me. I also heard he had made good use of his credentials, taking all that was offered, paying for nothing, not even his porters. A bad penny if ever there was one.

I was now in a fix; there was no doubt about that. Here I was stranded in Central Africa without a shilling to my name! However, with the resilience of youth, my thoughts now turned to finding some means of acquiring the wherewithal to fit out my own safari. Reading an old paper one day about the gold strike in the Yukon, I thought, *Here's the very thing.* I conceived the idea that if home circles should still prove unwilling to finance an African safari for me, I might strike it lucky in the gold rush.

I acted instantly and joined a native safari returning to the coast. What fever I had on that seemingly interminable foot-slog! No mules now to ride or comfortable buckboard to lie in when the fever was strong upon me. But how kind the safari people were. Many a cup of tea did they brew for me, and in return I shot meat for them.

On arriving at the coast, I sold my rifle and beat it for home. This time I traveled steerage, and mighty good it was, if somewhat crowded.

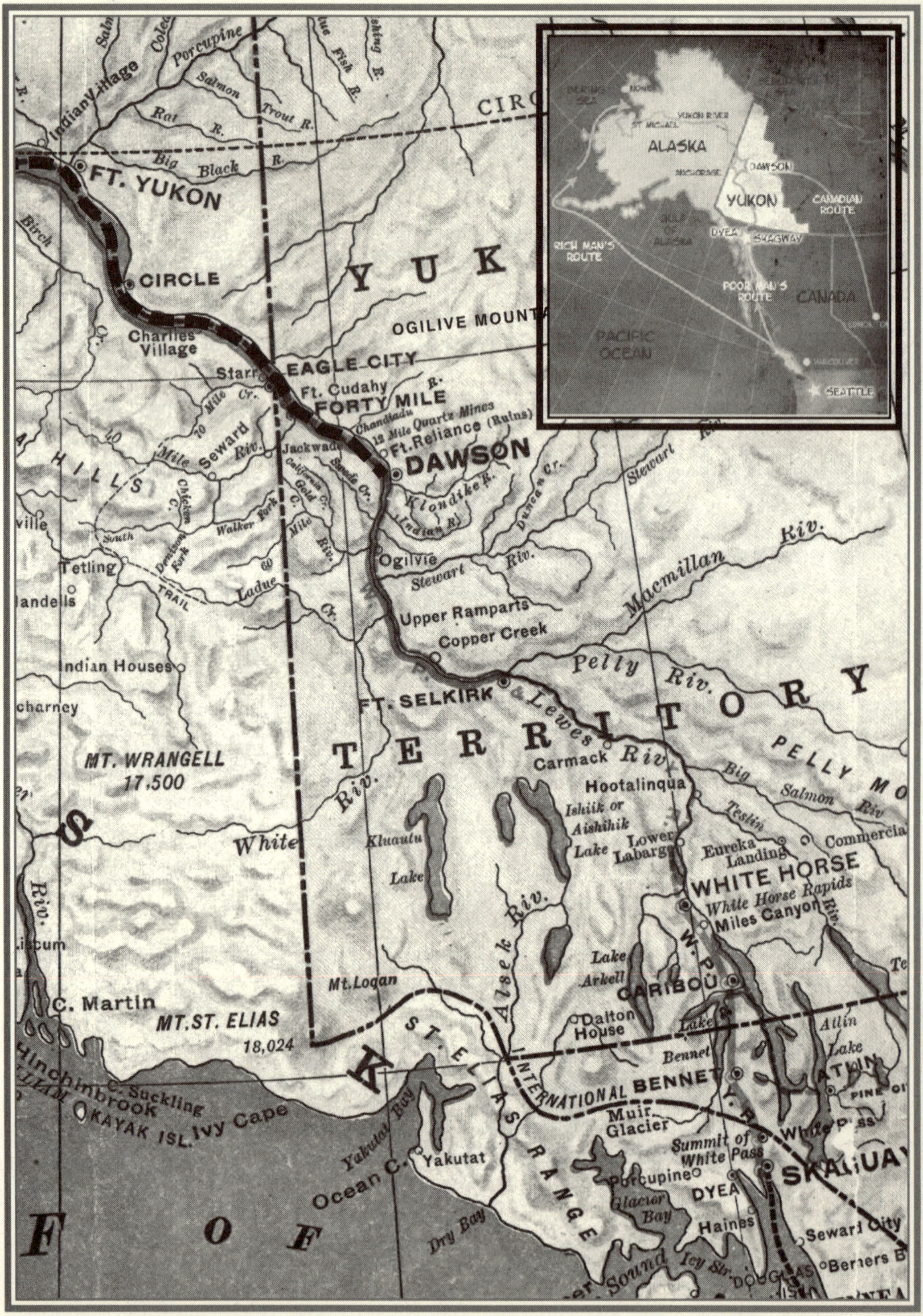

FT. YUKON
CIRCLE
Charlies Village
Starr
EAGLE CITY
Ft. Cudahy
FORTY MILE
Ft. Reliance (Ruins)
DAWSON
Klondike R.
Ogilvie
Stewart Riv.
Upper Ramparts
Copper Creek
FT. SELKIRK
Pelly Riv.
Macmillan Riv.
YUK
OGILIVE MOUNTA
TERRITORY
Carmack
Hootalinqua
Lower Labarge
WHITE HORSE
White Horse Rapids
Miles Canyon
CARIBOU
Dalton House
BENNET
Muir Glacier
Summit of White Pass
DYEA
SKAGUAY
Haines
Sewart City
Berners B
MT. WRANGELL
17,500
Mt. Logan
MT. ST. ELIAS
18,024
ST. ELIAS RANGE
C. Martin
Hinchinbrook
KAYAK ISL.
Ivy Cape
Yakutat Bay
Yakutat
Ocean C.
Dry Bay
Glacier Bay
Indian Village
Big Black R.
Tetling
Indian Houses
White
Kluautu Lake
Ishiik or Aishihik Lake
Lake Arkell
Big Salmon Riv
Eureka Landing
Commercial
Atlin Lake
ATLIN
F O F
ALASKA
BERING SEA
NOME
YUKON RIVER
ST. MICHAEL
DAWSON
YUKON
CANADIAN ROUTE
GULF OF ALASKA
DYEA
SKAGWAY
RICH MAN'S ROUTE
POOR MAN'S ROUTE
CANADA
PACIFIC OCEAN
VANCOUVER
SEATTLE

Another Foot in the Yukon

CHAPTER 7

As I said, in those spacious days one could go anywhere without papers and not be regarded as some sort of spy or felon. I cannot recall having any serious difficulty getting to any place on earth I wanted to visit, and never did I need the cumbersome, elaborate credentials of today's traveler. If you had no money—a chronic condition with me—you could work. Better still, if you had a good ear for patiently enduring the trouble of others, you could often listen your way for a large part of the journey. In those days people seemed to be genuinely helpful and quick to aid the footsore wanderer. Perhaps they still are today, but if so, the mountains of red tape discourage them.

On the ship back home, I resolved that the only way out of my difficulty was to try again for that assistance that would set me up on my own. I figured that I could now point out to my guardians that there were, indeed, elephants in Africa and that I now knew where to look for them. This information was no longer hearsay; I now had first-hand experience from my time in Africa. I also felt that I had the necessary knowledge to lead an expedition.

On arriving home, I found that my trustees remained reluctant to allow sufficient funds for an African safari, so I lost no time in making plans to go to the Yukon. Even at that young age, I found that there are many ways of getting what you want, but the only sure one is to want something bad enough. Sooner or later if you "want to" enough, you will get it no matter what it is. So, "wanting to get to the Klondike from the shores of Victoria Nyanza and wanting to do so enough," I got there via my friend, mentor, and gunsmith—Dan Fraser, of my hometown.

Did I tell him of those sticking .303 cases and their rotten extraction? Yes. When he was so conscience-stricken and sorry, I relented and told him how right he had been about the killing properties of the 215-grain bullet when placed right. I then asked him to propose a weapon to take with me, now that I was off to the Yukon.

Inset map (left) shows the possible routes to reach the Klondike, Yukon, in the late 1890s. The Klondike is a region of the Yukon territory in northwest Canada, east of the Alaska border. The Klondike River flows through the area and enters the Yukon River from the east at Dawson City.

We talked it all over in the very dim light of our combined knowledge of the North American continent. Dan had been to England, and I had been round the world as a sailor, a career in which no man has less chance to see any of the country in which his ship may visit. Dan was convinced that at all cost the firearm must be a black-powder-burning weapon so as to facilitate the reloading of expended cases. He advised that I take a .360 Farquharson with a 300-grain, solid lead bullet containing 5 percent tin. He supplied the Farquharson with gold washed locks that would work dry in winter without lubrication. It proved a knock-out for its job.

He said this weapon would let daylight thru the toughest grizzly, and he suggested providing me with a small, light-reloading outfit so that I could have perpetual daylight, I suppose. When I brought up possible extraction difficulties, he said I would never have them with the .360. He proved to be right, but all the same I cursed that action many times as it was a mean job poking out that case, loose as it was, with hands numbed from the cold. At any rate, the pressure was much lower in this cartridge than in that of the sun-baked .303.

Among the various bits of knowledge we had gleaned from newspapers was the fact that everything had to be carried in on one's own back. This included all food, clothing, tools, gun, and ammo. This information led us to weigh our proposed cartridges carefully. We estimated it would be better to carry ammo than food as we thought there would be lots of game by the wayside. Probably Africa's teeming game herds distorted the picture because, actually, there proved to be mighty little wild life along the main route to Dawson, in the Yukon itself. However, it was decided that I should be able to walk in with the Farquharson (a light rifle in itself); 160 rounds of all solid, 300-grain bullets; enough food for a few days; and the usual accessories.

What a bullet that solid 300-grain was. It was a ridiculous-looking cartridge, for it seemed all bullet. I don't know what the muzzle velocity was, but it must have been quite low. I doubt if it exceeded 1,800 f.p.s., if that. It seemed, however, to push everything it was pointed at right over and down for keeps.

Naturally, I wasn't taking long-range shots; I didn't have to then. I daresay my longest shot at moose was about fifty yards, generally less, and then it was in the neck. That slow-moving, majestic projectile seemed to be a number one-killer. The bullets didn't seem to want to expand. Of course, the bull moose's vertebrae flattened the nose a bit, but the bullet held together.

I can remember my first grizzly. There were two of them rolling about on a hill side. There was plenty of cover and the game was unsuspicious, so I got within thirty yards. I made sure of the first grizzly with a neck shot, and I put a 300-grain solid up the stern of the other as he fled downhill. I cut that bullet intact out of his chest cavity not so far from the skin, either. When I think of those old bullets and compare them with their modern counterparts, I begin to wonder. I could not repeat that stern shot safely with any of the high-velocity, expanding stuff of today. With a suitable bullet weight, a solid is a certain kill on any animal except the very largest. On African lions it is deadly, but naturally you must place the bullet precisely in a vital organ.

******

I had now re-equipped myself with but little else than my rifle and cartridges, and dreaming of the gold that would make my own African safari possible, I joined the rush to Dawson. I set off for the Klondike on a tramp steamer from Liverpool to Seattle.[1] On that ship, I found a goodly company of immigrants, mostly from Scotland, and it was a very jolly crowd.

There were two lovely Irish hunters well installed in the hold. The man who looked after them was a most amusing character, as also was the owner. The chief occupations of those onboard the rather slow passage was to lean up against the horses' stalls, yarning, flirting with the young immigrant girls, and listening to the evening sing-songs. The horses had been bought at country fairs in Ireland and were to be raced in Canada and the States where they would be leniently treated by the handicappers since their previous form was shrouded in mystery. It was quite a profitable business apparently.

There were two sisters traveling on this ship who offered a remarkable contrast. One was the typical Englishwoman of the Continental cartoons: tall, gaunt, and forbidding. The other was small, extremely pretty, and most genial. Of course, I was drawn into her net immediately, as was the race-horse owner. Anytime we two gawks were seen fussing round the honeypot with rugs or deck chairs or whatnots, Sister Grim would keep her eye on the proceedings.

---

[1] In another version, Bell said he set off from Africa to Seattle, and in yet another version, Bell said that he set off for the Klondike on a tramp steamer from Liverpool to Quebec. In *Bell of Africa*, Bell states that he set off from England to Canada.

As it happened, these two sisters had some of the largest trunks of clothes I had ever seen. Sometimes Sister Sweet would invite her two cavaliers—on the principle of safety in numbers—to her cabin, but always Sister Grim would also appear. It was then that I first became cognizant of the extent and size of their joint wardrobe as we sat about on it in the crowded cabin.

That wasn't the last I saw of their luggage, however. Oh, no, those two rascally girls used their two devoted admirers, both of us pretty muscular blokes, to pass through Customs and to tip the porters for that mass of baggage. Certainly we got a smile and a wave from the pretty one and a triumphant grin from the ugly one as their train pulled out of the station. It didn't take us long to realize we had been conned. We two rivals looked hard in each other's eye as we muttered, "Never again!" We were firm friends once more.

At Seattle I embarked for Dyea. On the jammed steamer among some five hundred other gold seekers, I met one Micky, a brother Scot. Micky was a queer-looking man of about thirty-five or forty, weighing eighteen stone (two hundred and fifty-two pounds)—all of it sheer muscle. His head was much too big for his shoulders and, apparently, too big for any known hat, for perched at the very top and violating all laws of proportion was a fine felt "trilby." Micky was proud of that hat. He had bought it as part of his outfit for trekking into the Yukon, not realizing that it would be much more suitable in the foyer of a theatre.

While Micky was of gigantic build physically, he had, as so often happens, the nature of a very mild, timid child. Micky was going to meet his brother who had struck it lucky in the gold fields and who proposed to take advantage of Micky's brawn in the development of his claim. As this entailed long and severe navvy work [manual labor], Micky was just the man for it.

We soon became friends and agreed to travel together. Micky's brother had told him what to bring in with him—bacon, flour, sugar, and coffee. It appeared, in fact, that the bare essentials at that time were worth more than gold in Dawson. All this Micky told me, so I in turn disclosed that I had almost nothing in the way of provisions, other than perhaps enough for a fortnight. I then told him that I had a rifle and a good stock of ammunition. We both thought that this was all right, that we should get lots of game along the way, and that combined we would do very well. Micky agreed with the utmost good humour. Both our heads were full of notions of grizzly bears and moose or deer waiting to be shot by the wayside.

Another Foot in the Yukon

The SS Excelsior *leaves San Francisco on 28 July 1897 for the Klondike.*

Well, when Micky and I arrived at Skagway and Dyea, we had to hump our loads to Whitehorse, for the railway was not yet completed. Micky shouldered his gigantic pack with ridiculous ease. It was remarkable to see the strength and energy of this huge man who, incidentally, was a very small eater. He was as simple as a child, had never had a woman, and was astonishingly religious. But if pushed far enough, he had a temper, had Micky, as I was soon to realize.

Once we arrived in Whitehorse, we were still some three hundred and thirty-one miles away from Dawson. (See map at the beginning of the chapter.) To reach Dawson, you had either to pack in a canoe, which some did, or you had to buy a scow. Some long-headed men in Whitehorse had thought it more profitable to fell trees, convert them into rough boards, nail them together, cover the bottom with tar, and sell these so-called scows to the milling throng of gold seekers at a fantastic price than to prospect for gold. They were onto a good thing.

No one had the means to delay in Whitehorse as their sole sustenance lay in what they carried on their backs. There was nothing that could be got to eat there except by stealing, and that was looked down upon to the extent that

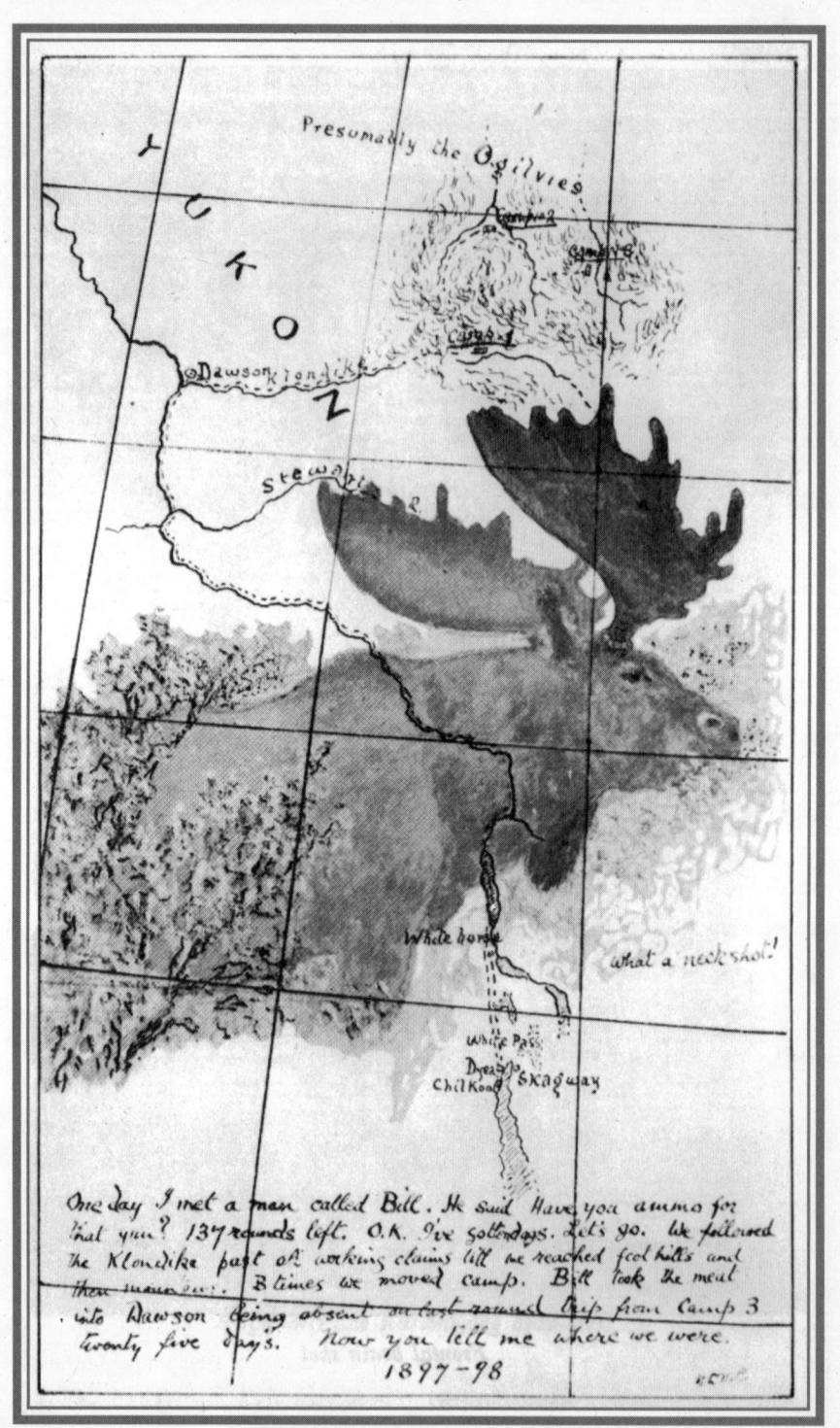

Bell's drawings of his time in the Yukon.

Another Foot in the Yukon

Wolves in numbers but ammo short.

Sometimes the humble marmot provided the only food. Excellent.

Bear plentiful.

although gold could be taken with but little trouble, the theft of foodstuffs merited shooting—pronto.

These scows were merely flat-bottomed, oblong boxes held together by their ends and a thwart or two. The front end sloped and the hind end was square. They leaked like sieves and warped all over the place. When manned by two men, one would be almost constantly bailing while the other steered by means of two young fir trees roughly shaped to faintly resemble oars. Two holes or slots out in the sides served as rowlocks.

The builders were much too canny to sell their wares afloat. You took them (or not) high and dry on the beach, launching them yourself after paying over the money. We chose our boat after much haggling over the price. Now, green fir is pretty heavy stuff, so for ordinary folk there were skids for sliding them into the river. Micky, however, ignored these aids and picked up the coffin-like affair with great ease and placed it gently afloat.

I will swear that scow must have weighed three hundred pounds. Micky was not showing off, or anything of that sort. He just did not know how strong he was. But the onlookers did and especially the man who had sold us the boat. He knew the weight of that lift. Unfortunately, the feat threw him into convulsions of laughter. I, with my slight experience of boats, promptly paid for an extra oar, for I thought Micky might so easily break an oar, especially as he said he had no boating experience.

The man who sold us the boat roared as Micky stood looking solemnly and in astonishment into the scow, rapidly filling with water through all the seams. Everyone else roared with laughter, too. Micky became annoyed. Although naturally of a girl-child-like nature, when he was rattled or seriously annoyed, he could assume a very nasty attitude, indeed.

Naturally enough he turned to the man who had taken the money, demanding in language quite unknown in those parts to have his money back. It sounded so strange to hear words from that barrel-like chest in a high falsetto voice. The crowd began to gather round scenting a "to-do" of some sort. I shall never forget how his small, close-set eyes smouldered as he fixed them on the boat-seller. Before anyone could do anything about it, Micky was after his man like some huge grizzly seeking its prey. Luckily, the man retreated smartly.

Obviously, Micky thought he had been done in by the boat-seller. I came to the rescue, however, and smoothed Micky down, assuring him that the scow leaked because it needed recaulking. I had to drag the now smouldering Micky from following the man who was now retreating somewhat nervously before the Carnera-like[2] figure of Micky.

After procuring some pitch and moss, we made repairs on the worst of the seams. Once we got the scow afloat, we soon had our gear aboard and off we set on our four-hundred-and-fifty-mile dash to Dawson. Immediately below us lay the Whitehorse Rapids, by all accounts a most deadly place. So they are when the river is in spate with chunks of ice milling around. The rapids we found, however, were more like a gentle mill-race; in fact, Micky and I continued to wonder when we were going to come on them long after we had passed safely through.

Certainly there were a few races, a little white water, and one or two whirlpools where our wretched box slewed about in an ungovernable way. With Hercules at the propulsion and me steering with the extra oar, we managed to keep out in the middle and, thus, free of all rocks. Generally, we made famous progress. With Micky being quite tireless at the oars, lifting that old box almost out of the water at every stroke, the box simply ate up the miles.

At that time of year daylight was practically continuous round the clock, and Micky had a fearful urge to lay behind the four hundred and fifty miles of river between Whitehorse and Dawson City, the mecca of the gold-seekers. Initially we had to overcome our desire to catch crabs, but almost immediately we abandoned that in our need to get to Dawson as soon as possible. Micky would not stop to let me hunt; he would hardly stop to sleep; consequently, I had little chance to contribute anything to the pot. We took only short halts to boil a kettle and battle a horde of mosquitoes, and then on again we would go.

Even so, we were being constantly passed either by bigger floating crates or by those lovely Peterborough canoes some enterprising beggars had packed in over the pass on their backs. The urge to reach gold was evident on all sides: "Ever on, on" was the cry! Hurry, hurry! Rush, rush! It was vocal, this traffic. One would think these people had already struck gold to hear the singing. Singing as they went, night and day, hell bent for Dawson.

---

[2]Primo Carnera (26 October 1906 to 29 June 1967), nicknamed the Ambling Alp, was an Italian professional boxer and the World Heavyweight Champion from 29 June 1933 to 14 June 1934.

This was not at all my idea of traveling. I could not help contrasting my present mode with the African method of a ten- or fifteen-mile tramp through a game-laden park or bush land, a comfortable meal, and then a stroll out with a rifle. There had been abundant safari-wise Indians, and later Africans, to wash clothes, carry junk, carve up game, pitch tents, and do all the chores that I now found I had to do myself. Not nearly such good fun, I concluded. However, like everyone else, I thought such acute discomfort must result in the finding of gold, so on I went with my silent, determined companion—poor sucker that I was.

Meanwhile, I kept a sharp look-out for something to shoot. There seemed a strange absence of wild life. What a gameless country it appeared to be. The land seemed clothed with everlasting pine forests right down to the water's edge, so we never saw a thing with the exception of a few ducks, and these Micky would not stop long enough for me to shoot. I suppose the constant stream of traffic going "down" (north) scared everything away.

On arrival in Dawson, what a scene met the eye. Dawson itself seemed a milling throng. Everyone busy going places or coming back, the only leisured ones were the gamblers. The water-front was its main street. The beach was lined with craft of every description. Among this swarm were older toughs, some obviously not-so-tough, and some would-be toughs. There was plenty of gold but precious little food. Plenty of six-shooters in evidence, too, but very, very few rifles.

Micky suggested we go to his brother's place first, and he proposed I should work there until I knew enough about the mining laws to launch out on my own. Faced with the proposition of how to find gold and what to do with it when found, how to stake a claim, and all the intricacies of the law in this connection, Micky's offer certainly had its points.

Food alone was a burning question. Even with money, food could not be got; there simply wasn't any. I had not seen any game on which to live, either. Consequently, this proposition now appeared to me the only thing to do, so I threw in my lot with Micky. Working alongside that human dynamo just about killed me. Just to watch him made me tired. My back still aches when I think of it.

Micky's brother's claim on the Klondike was within one day's trek, so we disposed of the scow for a dollar or two, and we then shouldered our considerably reduced packs for the final leg of our journey. Arriving at the Klondike, we found a couple of rough log huts standing on the hillside.

These cabins overlooked a large heap of gravel down in the creek bottom. Some Heath Robinson[3] flumes of lumber conveyed water along and down by the gravel heap. There was a large hole in the ground from which the pay-dirt came. As the whole ground was frozen solid to an unknown depth from six inches down, it had to be melted by some means before it could be washed and the gold recovered. They called this "placer" mining, and it entailed the hardest kind of work.

There appeared to be two methods in operation in placer mining, and the object of both was to melt pay-dirt. The most primitive consisted in heating large stones in log and brushwood fires. When extremely hot, they were dumped into the bottom of the hole to thaw what they could of the surrounding earth. This was slow and cumbrous and only the very richest stuff repaid the labour. Our arrival coincided with an improvement just coming out, and this involved the use of steam. A wood-fired boiler forced steam through perforated steel points that were driven into the frozen dirt.

Micky and I were set to work straightaway down in the hole to shovel the thawed stuff into boxes that were then hove up to the surface. It was all right for Micky—actually it was just the job for him—but it wasn't for me. The pay sounded good, ten dollars a day, paid in gold dust, but the work was much too hard.

During this time, I learned all the complicated mining laws—how to stake a claim, how to register it, and what development work had to be done before a title to it could be obtained. I began to look at the appalling work entailed in mining a claim, and I realized that things would straighten themselves out only when, and if, I found a claim sufficiently rich. As the toll on my back increased, however, the dreadful work and the unlikely rewards were always forefront in my mind.

So when the boss came to watch me miserably toiling alongside that Brutus and remarked that I "wasn't pulling my weight," I terminated my employment on the spot. I said good-bye to Micky, got what was owing to me, and departed with relief from that ghastly job—a relief, be it said, mutually shared by my employer. I was thoroughly sick of the unending navvy work.

---

[3] William Heath Robinson (31 May 1872 to 13 September 1944) was an English cartoonist and illustrator best known for drawings of ridiculously complicated machines for achieving simple objectives.

What a difference working life was in the Yukon! In Africa, no white man works. In the Yukon only whites work, and mighty hard, too. It was much too hard for me. I soon decided to join a bunch of gold seekers as ignorant as myself. Our plan was simple: We would rush from creek to creek staking claims, not developing them, but staking them. We merely erected the boundary posts, suitably inscribed, leaving the development work until some future date.

Our hope was that someone would somewhere on that particular creek dig a hole and find pay-dirt. Then, of course, all claims on that creek would automatically gain a certain value. The idea was that after such a strike it would be time enough to do the development necessary to acquire title to the claims. It did not work out that way because anyone making a strike soon brought in his friends who simply jumped the unregistered claims and set up their own stakes.

Having a rifle made me welcome with this group of gold seekers as we all thought game meat would be plentiful. Occasionally I was able to contribute to the pot, but, actually, it was hard, indeed, to meet up with anything to kill. Most game was scarce because it had been scared away by the racket of the claim stakers with their smudge fires and bush whacking.

Since food at that time was nearly unprocurable, this got me thinking. Naturally, my thoughts turned more than ever to the hunting side of the picture, especially as I was not too keen on developing a claim. I discovered that meat from the game of the country was a highly prized commodity, but when I enquired, I was told I would have to go one hundred miles into the interior to be sure of getting anything. It was obvious that all game had been shot or pushed back from the neighbourhood of such centres as Dawson.

Transport once more became the greatest difficulty to my new plan. It was still summer and dogs and sledges could not yet operate, so I needed to find a way to move the meat I would shoot. All transport in winter was, of course, by dog-sled. In summer the dogs were simply turned loose to fend for themselves, and a nasty hungry mob of starving creatures they were.

They roamed the countryside until some enterprising spirit conceived the idea of boarding and lodging them on an island in the Yukon River at five dollars per week. He got thousands of dogs. He simply tied them to pegs and fed them just that amount that enabled them to remain alive. He had a few Indians who netted the huge red king (chinook) salmon weighing up to seventy pounds, and each dog received about two ounces daily ration. His project probably paid better than any gold mine.

******

Talking of free enterprise, I found another instance of it nearby. Some long-headed character had brought down a bevy of professional "beauties," and on their arrival, another bloke correctly saw that everyone in Dawson would go on the rut and that this activity would need housing. He, therefore, built a townlet of log huts on the western bank opposite Dawson and outside the municipal limits. It was all done according to Canadian law, which does not allow prostitution within city limits.

He was content to run the ferry service between the "city"—itself a bunch of shacks—and this suburb. It was said that this entrepreneur quite simply ran the ferry, the girls taking and keeping what they could get. The girls did not stay long and were constantly replaced with fresh arrivals. A wearing business, indeed.

Some great gambling used to take place in Dawson. Once I was watching a table that literally groaned with the pile of gold heaped in the middle. Someone remarked there must be twenty thousand dollars' worth of gold in the kitty. The "raises" were fantastically high and so was the excitement.

Banking was certainly also very different from what I was accustomed to; it had a genuine flair of the Wild West to it. On arrival I changed my few remaining dollars into the local currency at a reputable bank; in exchange I was given their equivalent in gold dust, which I, like everyone else, carried on my person in a buckskin bag.

I had occasion to buy a meal at an eating place, and to pay for it, I did as others were doing: I slung down a bag of dust. The man dribbled out some of the dust on to his scales then ran his magnet through it. To my horror the magnet came out encrusted with iron filings. More dust from the little bag had to be added. Again the magnet did its full work. Appalled, I remarked that I had that dust straight from the bank. The man, who had shown no surprise during this little operation, merely smiled.

I went straight back to the bank, a log shack, thinking I had been robbed. I was told that what I had got in exchange for my precious notes was "commercial" dust, which was customary tender. I was also told that the percentage of base metal was controlled, God knows by whom, and that, in fact, everything was as it should be. Apparently even the banks were "racketeering."

******

I soon took to hunting entirely, leaving the gold seeking to those more energetic than I. I found I could live on my rifle and that meat was exchangeable for gold, not weight for weight certainly, but not so far either from that very proper basis. You can live well on meat but you can't live at all on gold. Certainly there were lean times when the humble and wrongfully despised marmot was called upon to fill the pot. There were times of great plenty, too, when it was hell's own job keeping the predators off the meat without wasting ammo.

One day I was talking to a man called Bill—nobody used his own proper surname—who proposed that we should work together in a meat partnership. Bill knew where we could get game. He only had a six-shooter, but he had a dog-team; I had a rifle and ammunition. He reckoned we would have to get one hundred and fifty miles into the interior before we could count on a more or less sure supply of game. Bill suggested we pack his dogs into good game country and establish a meat cache. He also said that we ought to be in there before the freeze up.

Bill furnished all the experience in traveling, living, and in making a log hut, which we would use as our headquarters. I would hunt from the hut and Bill would take back what I had already shot and sell it to the meat-famished miners. I would keep shooting until Bill returned for another load. Bill held out glittering prospects of not only being able to feed ourselves—a most pressing problem—but of piling up the dollars, too.

Carcass meat could be sold for as much as two dollars the pound, bones and all. A caribou would net three hundred dollars and a moose up to one thousand pounds would bring in six hundred dollars. It seemed a little gold mine . . . and sounded good to me. To hell with gold. This was better than a mine. Bill seemed a decent man, and the partnership was formed forthwith, without formality or any further to-do.

Naturally we did not want to go back any farther than was necessary to secure a fair supply of meat. We went inland about one hundred miles east of Dawson before we began to see much sign of game. It was there we saw a moose and two grizzlies. Bill said we should go for the moose because it would taste better.

Another Foot in the Yukon

One day we saw a bull moose in scrubland, while away in the distance were two grizzlies rooting about on a hillside.

It was in the fall and the rutting season was fast approaching. The old fellow showed plenty movement, thrashing the willow bush and playing up generally. This was the only time I felt undergunned, for my rifle was no great performer by modern standards, and I was none too certain of it on such an enormous animal as a moose. It looked so gigantic at thirty yards. Nothing would induce me to fire a hasty shot, and it paid off, for when he finally got that 300-grain bullet in his colossal neck, he dropped to the shot without a move, without a quiver even. While it didn't seem possible to knock out such a formidable beast, even then I knew my stuff.

Bill was delighted and so was I. I wanted to go for the grizzlies and Bill said they would do for the dogs. I got one of them after a careful stalk.

Although the nights were cold, they were not yet cold enough to freeze meat hard, so we had to smoke it. Bill was delighted that we had found game so close to Dawson. He said we should build a hut to use as our headquarters for the winter. We heard wolves, too, and this seemed to indicate game. But it proved not so. We shot nothing more as the weather was still too hot, but we scouted round a lot. Since we did not see much game, Bill decided we would have to move still farther yet. He seemed to think nothing of abandoning the log hut.

This time we moved another fifty miles east and were obviously getting higher. We saw quite a lot of moose and bear but no caribou. These Bill said would trek in later. We built hut Number Two. Here we killed just what was required to feed ourselves and the dogs. It was a unique kind of hunting.

After a few days scouting round, we realized we would have to find some country richer in game, and so we abandoned hut Number Two. When we built Hut Number Three, it must have been all of two hundred miles from Dawson. The country was more open and uncommonly like the Highlands of Scotland; it was also quite high.[4]

Above the timber line the mountains had a gray cast almost like dirty snow, and in shaded spots there were unmelted snow drifts that had become solid ice. Bill said the mountains were gray in appearance because they were mostly

---

[4] In another section of Bell's archives, he wrote, "We finally reached what I now recognize as the Ogilvie Mountains. Of course we had no maps—I doubt if any existed."

limestone. If this was so, it probably accounts for the absence of prospectors, for we never saw a living soul all the time we were up there.

Game was now abundant, and we had no difficulty in keeping ourselves in meat. Moose, cariboo, grizzlies, wolves, and wolverines were plentiful. One day we counted fourteen bull moose and we had no binoculars. Bill reiterated that what we wanted was moose, particularly good bulls that would weigh seventeen to eighteen hundred pounds. How we were to handle such enormous animals made me wonder.

Bill was a taciturn man, hardly ever speaking unless he had something to explain anent [concerning] the art of living as our forebearers must have lived thousands of years ago. We were uncommonly dirty, covered with a layer of grease-bound wood smoke that daunted even the most enterprising mosquitoes and black flies.

There now began a training in hunting that was to benefit me enormously. It would be hard to devise a better set-up for the purpose. Every shot had to kill; not one could be wasted. The Farquharson cartridge itself was nothing great judged by present-day standards. It was a .360 calibre, and I had stocked nothing but solid lead bullets since I had learnt to shun all hollow-point or otherwise expanding abominations. The bullet had no great velocity—about 1,800 feet per second. What it taught me above all else was the absolute necessity to place my first and only shot accurately in a vital spot.

I soon found that provided I did so, any bullet that would hold together did the trick. I formed an opinion then that it is not the rifle so much as the man behind it that constitutes a killer, and it's an opinion that nothing in my vast after-experience has ever altered. Certainly I came to recognize that confidence in approaching so-called "dangerous" game can be afforded the inexperienced by the use of formidable weapons of tremendous power. For myself, however, I was content with any straight-shooting gun throwing a quite small bullet that would hold together sufficiently so that I could make it reach one of the centres of vitality. For me, it became the lighter the better, so long as it fulfilled those conditions.

By this time the nights were becoming very cold and the muskeg showed signs of freezing. We had chosen the site for our latest hut near three trees that grew closely together in such a way a platform could be suspended between them. Our idea was to hang meat so that it would freeze by night without the wolves being able to get at it. When the real cold came, meat previously frozen hard would keep indefinitely.

Bill now set about the task of constructing a dog sled. A marvel with an ax, he soon had a contraption that would serve. He explained that his real sled was down in Dawson. He also said he would show me how to make snow-shoes because I would require these later on in order to hunt.

When we counted our ammunition, I had left over from my original 160 rounds but 103; Bill had 40 rounds for his six-shooter, a long-barrel Colt .45 that fired what looked like a rifle cartridge. He suggested that he would leave the Colt with me when he made his meat run to Dawson. He said if really heavy and soft snow came, I should be able to kill a moose with the .45 if I could scare it suddenly into heavy drift snow. That would work provided I was on snow-shoes. Using the .45 also meant that I could save the precious rifle ammo. Since I had never been on snow-shoes, I determined to practice the use of these terrible affairs at every chance.

As soon as everything was shipshape, Bill said it was time to pack in what meat we had. Winter was coming in fast, and everything began to freeze. Mosquitoes were at last kaput. The dogs were in great shape on moose and other guts. The time had come for the first trial.

Bill said that he would leave a couple of dogs with me to help in getting in the meat. He could not leave his ax with me, for he would need it on his return to Dawson. He promised to bring me one on his next trip back.

Bill seemed not at all daunted at abandoning his pistol. I suggested he might have trouble with wolves. There was evidence enough of these game killers on every hand. But Bill said he would be all right and left it at that. He seemed genuinely anxious I should have his gun.

When the first snow fell and the freeze-up of the country was complete, Bill left with a load for Dawson and I continued to hunt. Of course we overloaded the sled. This caused some delay while a raw-hide thong was de-frosted for the repairs to the sled. The dogs, too, were infernally frisky and hard to control in the beginning.

As Bill was at last ready to depart, he said to me that he hoped to be back in twenty-five to thirty days. He told me not to worry if he did not show up in that time. He instructed me to just keep piling the stuff into the hut and to keep the wolves and wolverines and foxes from it. Bill issued one final warning about the wolverine, saying that they are "meanest cusses in the North." With a "so-long," he left.

Now there began an experience that I never forgot. The hut that had appeared much too large at first soon began to assume the look of a Christmas butcher shop. Wherever I turned, I was confronted with carcasses. Shanks greeted me wherever I peered into the semi-darkness. Two of the pack dogs had been left behind, and the three of us were inseparable companions. I somehow managed to keep up a livable temperature in the hut until the slabs of frozen meat filled the air space and made the place easier to heat.

There were days of blinding storms when hunting was impossible. Then after the rut (mating season), the moose fell out of condition. Cariboo grew numerous in the fall, just as Bill had predicted, and I realized that our hut fronted their migrating route. I had always loved solitude and I cannot honestly say that I was anything but supremely happy. I had nothing to read and yet the time flew.

The grandest sights I ever saw in these prolific game lands were during the rut. The bellowing bull moose were simply magnificent, as might be expected from such massive animals. Curiously, they broke out just about the same date as our Scottish stags, and as in Scotland, they soon lost condition. Occasionally I saw a fight between two equally matched bulls, but as a rule one or other would give way sooner than accept a trial of strength. What a colour film of such an encounter would be like, I do not know. But I would go a long way to see it.

******

Although I had no difficulty in filling the cabin with frozen meat, much was inevitably wasted—that is, eaten by wolves. When I killed a moose, I could not possibly get it all home at once. What I could not move had to be slung up in trees. Inevitably much of it was gone when I returned for it. In spite of the difficulties, I soon had that shack piled with meat ready for Bill's return.

On examining my calendar—cuts on one of the wall logs—I found Bill had been away twenty-five days. I could shoot no more; the house was stuffed with carcasses. Some snow had fallen, but I thought it nothing that would prevent Bill's return. At least that is what I hoped. Everything was gripped in frost. Time began to seem long, but the two huskies were great fun and companionable as they gnawed on bones to their heart's content.

Every now and then the dogs would growl at the sniff-sniff of some prowling wolf as he smelled at the moss-filled cracks between the logs. No ammunition could be wasted on these gentry, of course, once I had killed enough to make a warm covering for my bunk.

I tried to dress some of the skins that were as hard as boards so as to reduce them to some sort of pliability. This I found exceedingly difficult. I only just managed to get a couple of wolf skins to lie fairly flat on the bunk instead of sliding off. How I longed for an Eskimo or Indian woman to dress the skins for me, to make skin garments, and possibly to act as a bed-warmer, too.

After the twenty-seventh cut on the log, Bill returned. I will never forget his look when he came to the door and peered in. The whole place was stuffed high to the roof with carcasses. A broad grin—about the only one I ever saw—spread over his leathery features. When he found he could hardly squeeze into the shack for the pile of carcasses, all he could say was, "Great work! Great work!"

He brought coffee and sugar and flour—things that could not then have been bought in Dawson for gold but that were forthcoming only for meat. Bill was in great spirits, telling me that he had got one dollar and seventy-five cents per pound for the whole cargo, bones and all.

Fresh meat is a pretty complete diet, it seems, especially when eaten as nearly raw as possible, and I had not missed the commodities of civilized life. The French call wine, flour, sugar, and coffee the necessities of life. They may be, but I have found that if need be, a man can live without them. Bill also brought me an ax. That was much more to the point. When he had taken our only ax with him, I had missed that humble article mightily.

When he saw the two dogs he had left with me, he burst out laughing. They were rolling fat. He remarked that he would soon take the fat off them when he got them into his team. I begged him not to take them as they were my sole companions and had now become house trained.

Bill told me of the latest Dawson rumours. All the gossip of a mining town included the latest murders, the rumoured arrival of a police force, the latest gold strikes, and so on. He told me that he had banked the money he got for the meat. He stated that he would like to leave the next day with a load so as to make room for more meat.

When we reviewed the precious store of ammo, we found there was still plenty for the rifle and the .45's had not been touched. I told him how much good meat I had lost owing to having to leave it out, and I told him what a hellish job it was to get the meat back to the cabin. Bill pondered this awhile. Then he suggested tying it as high up in a tree as I could. I told him that I thought the wolverines would still get it.

Bill then told me that he needed to take all the dogs with him because he reckoned to double-load the sled now that the trail was improved a bit. I told him that I needed the help of the dogs as well, and, in fact, I could well do with one or two more. He agreed to leave me the two I had and add another, a bitch in pup.

He asked me if I had had a chance to use his pistol, and I said I had not yet used it. When Bill heard that, he said he could well do with it; it made things more "comfortable" on the trail. I pressed him to take it along with him, pointing out I still had ample cartridges for the rifle and had, indeed, only used about thirty rounds so far.

The next morning we loaded the sled with a fearful pile of meat while the dogs consumed as much as they could hold. Bill had changed his mind about the Colt pistol and decided not to take it. He reckoned I might get a chance to use it, so he would leave it. He seemed to attach great importance to this weapon. Why, I did not understand.

"It's a mighty good gun," Bill always said, impressing on me its importance.

The start was somewhat downhill, and Bill was soon off in a smother of snow and yells to the dogs. Indeed, it was all downhill to Dawson as the camp was almost at the limit of timber growth and was possibly three thousand feet or more higher than Dawson.

With the hut almost empty again, it became much colder. I hung some skins on the walls and this helped considerably, though I wondered how it would affect the meat. I need not have worried.

I did not know what the temperature was in degrees, but I had more evidence than I cared for that it was darned cold. It began to snow steadily. There was some wind, so drifts were to be expected. After overhauling my cumbersome snow-shoes, my thoughts then turned to Bill's six-shooter.

The pistol itself had about a seven-and-a-half inch barrel, and the bullet was a solid lead affair, which I was relieved to see. Something could be done with it, I concluded. Conditions should be right whenever the snow stopped.

I decided that all I had to do was locate a moose and wait for when it would inevitably bog itself down in the nearest drift. With me on my snow-shoes, I would then move in for the kill. This is how I thought the scenario would go.

How very different the actuality. I found a bull moose all right, but instead of leaping into the nearest drift, it most carefully avoided such places and continued its flight at a much faster gait than anything I could produce on my frightful foot gear. I wished to goodness I had brought the rifle instead of the .45. Then I remembered that Bill had said something about stampeding moose so that they would plunge into a drift. I determined to try it. I thought it would please Bill as he seemed to have shown disappointment in that I had not tried it out.

Next time I saw moose I had both my rifle and the .45 with me. With a little trouble I got quite close to a good beast in a patch of fairly thick scrub. I was awfully tempted to rifle shoot the beast; in fact, I was only deterred from doing so by thoughts of Bill and the poor condition of the animal. Suddenly emerging from my cover, I gave an unearthly yell I hoped would gally[5] the beast sufficiently.

The startled beast launched into a straightaway stampede and inevitably came on heavy drift. I pounded and slithered along behind, my legs wide apart, a most exhausting business. Soon I noticed, to my astonishment, that I was actually gaining on the moose. Up to his belly in soft snow and not even then reaching anything solid, the moose was practically helpless. All the while I kept coming along slowly but surely. When I was quite close, the moose gave up the struggle to escape and seemed only anxious to defend himself. Now, of course, it remained only to pistol the beast in the brain.

Bill would be satisfied, but as far as I was concerned, I would prefer the rifle, except, perhaps, when the whole country should be so covered in deep, soft snow that no other method of hunting could be employed.

One disadvantage to this kind of hunting was that the dogs were a nuisance. When not left at home, they had to be tied up in the woods, which they resented, so they barked and howled. When left in the shack, they had to be fetched, and, in the process, much meat was destroyed by wolves. In fact, this was a two-man job or, better still, a man and native-woman job.

Although game became noticeably scarcer in the immediate vicinity, entailing longer hunts and longer hauls, I never failed to have the store full when Bill returned. On each trip back to Dawson Bill took a full cargo. I delighted him with the story of how I had killed a moose with his Colt.

Meanwhile I figured the money pile in the bank must be growing. Bill was singularly reticent on this subject, however. I should have demanded the opening of an account in my name, but I was young and trusting and thoroughly enjoying myself. Bill seemed such a good fellow and so pleased

---

[5] Scots for "to frighten."

with the way things were going. Readers of a more worldly nature than I will no doubt by this time have written me off as the complete "sucker." And so I was, of course. Even when Bill said he would have to take back the Colt .45 as wolves were troublesome on the trail, I scented no rat. As I already said, I preferred the rifle, and I thought it only right that Bill should have his pistol.

It was toward spring when Bill left on what was to be the penultimate haul-out. We reckoned that if he could make it back in good time, we would get one more cargo in before the break up. Bill took an even larger load than usual as he said he could sell some of it on the way into Dawson to miners at claims that were being worked. That was the last I ever saw of Bill . . . I just didn't know that yet.

I hunted right along until the store was once more full. Then I waited and waited. I now had leisure to look about me, to watch the game and all the various doings in this lovely land. The dogs were my great stand-by and when the puppies arrived, life was real fun. At last the winter showed signs of ending. Still no Bill. If he did not come soon, the meat would be ruined. I began to think what I should do.

I began to fancy Bill must have met up with some accident. River crossings were treacherous things when the break-up was near. I remembered a tough,

I never failed to have the store full when Bill returned. (Sketch by W. D. M. Bell)

oldish man and his dog who had visited me in camp when I was mining with Micky on the banks of the Yukon. This man had had a pack weighing one hundred and sixty pounds on his back, comprising provisions, ammo, pan, pick, shovel, and a rifle. He proposed to come out somewhere on the coast, six hundred miles away, and all unknown country.

As he sat chewing the rag over coffee, there came the ear-splitting cracks that warn of the break-up. Hurriedly he got his pack slung on, seized his rifle, called up the dog, and set off across the now cracking and splitting ice. The Yukon there, opposite the mouth of the Stewart, was quite "a ways across," in the words of the old prospector, and before he made the west bank he was having to hop from one piece of ice to another. He made it all right and made the coast, too. Never a trace of gold, though. But copper! So pure the Indians simply dug it out and hammered it into bullets for their percussion guns.[6]

Some such conditions might have overtaken my friend Bill, I thought.

At long last, there seemed to be nothing for it but to return. Spring was advancing, and the temperature in the daytime was rising. I would have to do something soon about the now-thawing meat. I decided to seal up the shack as best as I could to keep out marauders—just in case I should meet Bill close at hand—and follow Bill's trail.

As I gazed around at what had been a happy camp, I noted that all the bits of skin, horns, and bones had been conjured away as by some giant Hoover. I packed the dogs with what food they could carry, and as the pups could now all run, we set off for Dawson. I left what was then one of the best game countries I knew of outside Africa.

There was no word of Bill at the claims, and no word of Bill in Dawson itself. "Bill? Bill Who? What Bill?" Everyone knew any number of men named Bill. At the eating houses all were most guarded in their answers. I went to the two so-called banks. Again, I was met with "Bill Who? Bill What?" Not a trace could I find of him. Whether he skipped with the money or was caught in a spring break-up, I never learned.

As the politicians say, "A grave situation had arisen." Bill never told me where my share of the business was. Knowing Dawson, I could imagine that

---

[6] It is unclear how Bell would know this information because there is nothing in his notes to indicate that he ever saw this prospector again.

everything had been paid for in dust, and he would have it. I decided to look up Micky, not knowing if he was still there. I found him in considerable good form. He had slaved away at his brother's claim and was now in funds. I told him about the spot I was in, and then I suggested a little holiday in the city. Micky greeted the idea as something marvelous; it had never occurred to his one-track mind that such a thing existed in this land. We two betook ourselves to town.

At this time there were three amusements to be had in Dawson. First, you could gamble if you had gold. This was about the most costly. Closely followed in that respect was a trip across the river to the local Joy Town. Third, you could stand around and listen to the colourful waterfront lies that took the place of a press. This cost you some credulity only.

I knew that Micky would not abide the gambling halls, and I very much doubted whether Micky would care to cross the river. The two of us were mooching around in a rather lost way when Micky—the straight-laced, God-fearing Mickey—suggested the very thing. We paid our dollars and crossed the ferry.

To sex-starved men, the dames appeared perfectly lovely. Dancing was in full swing. Lack of youth, modesty, beauty, all were unseen. Most of them were drunk, if not on whisky certainly on gold. They were having the time of their lives. I urged Micky to dive in and grab a girl.

His small eyes peered from beneath his angular features with a ferret-like intensity. But that was all. That huge, bull-like body had not the heart to grab a dame where only the most determined grabbing could succeed, there being perhaps two hundred men to ten women. Poor Micky! He wanted to all right, but nothing but a pint of whisky could have made him conquer his shyness . . . and he would not touch liquor.

I now had to face up to a crisis in my affairs. I was pretty well cleaned out. I was standing around not long after Micky returned to his claim and thinking about what in the world I would do next when I heard that some war had broken out in South Africa and that Canada was said to be sending a contingent. *The very thing*, thought I. *Back to Africa!*

By selling my rifle—that went well because I still had some ammunition—and the dogs, I could just make it. I beat a hasty retreat to the recruiting booth at Calgary by way of Nome and the Aleutians.

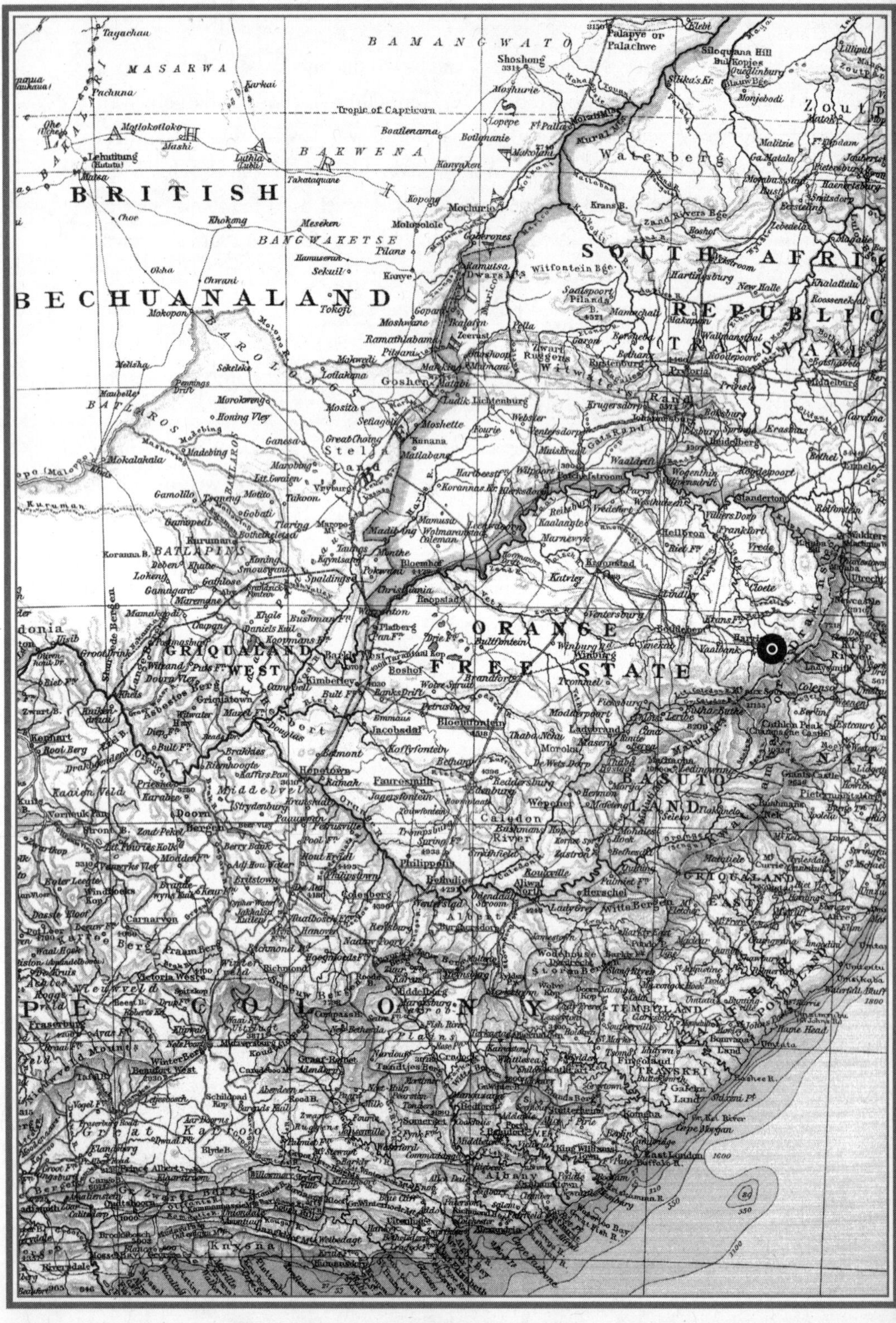

Back to Africa and the Boer War

Chapter 8

At Calgary I found about five thousand men were offering themselves for five hundred vacancies. There were severe tests. I reckoned I would get in on my previous experience of East Africa. After all who in Canada knew the difference between East Africa and South Africa? All was Africa to them.

I made the almost fatal mistake, however, of appearing bare headed at the recruiting office. Not that I was prematurely bald or anything like that. No, what the recruiters wanted for the first cut was the "appearance" of shooting proficiency—cowboy hats; Stetsons and chaps; long, high-heeled boots; large spurs; and so on. This was easily rectified, of course, by borrowing the requisite items. I scraped by for the next cut because of my shooting and medical tests, helped by my previous African experience.

There was the small matter of having to own a horse, for the outfit was the Canadian Mounted Rifles, but this, too, was easily rectified. Since the government handed a recruit forty dollars for his mount the moment he was accepted, it was easy to borrow one for the induction. That East Africa, where I wished to hunt, was several thousands of miles from the scene of the Boer War didn't bother me the slightest. I was at least headed in the right direction.

About half the contingent of volunteers came from the Northwest Mounted Police, and among them was the choicest selection of old soldiers it would be possible to meet anywhere. The sergeant-major in charge of the volunteers was a real soldier who was on loan from a Guards' regiment, and his job was to instill some sort of order in the mob, poor guy.

And what a mob it was. No one was yet in uniform. Many still wore their chaps, spurs, and their Stetsons—and carried their Mexican saddles. No one without such gear had a chance with the girls of western Canada.

The sergeant-major proved up to the task of bringing order to the chaos, and he proved to have no great difficulty in handling the queer assortment of recruits. He simply put each recruit between two Mounties, old troopers to whom nothing anent the gentle art of living in and out of battle was unknown. Soon enough the most undisciplined mob of men and horses was licked into some sort of shape, put into uniform, packed onto a train, and shipped east.

Reminiscences of an Elephant Hunter

Soon enough the most undisciplined mob of men and horses was licked into some sort of shape, put into uniform, packed onto a train, and shipped east.

There were some good cow-punchers and fine horsemen in the outfit. It was a grand sight to watch them handle the horses so recently caught up from the range. Wild as deer, these horses were carried bodily into the horse trucks, squealing, biting, and kicking, by the great lusty lads from the ranches. Before we were shipped out, watching a parade with horses bucking all over the place was as entertaining as any rodeo.

If a horse escaped, he would be instantly roped by two or three guarding cowboys. The Mounties very wisely left this job to the volunteers. It seems incredible that a horse could escape out of these high-sided trucks, but one did—straight over the top. He must have climbed out on the backs of the other horses and was over the top with one mighty bound.

The train was as usual traveling slowly, and the animal landed quite unhurt, starting off for the wide open spaces. The train stopped and the boys got off to go after him. Using nothing but their own two feet to catch a wild horse on open prairie was a sight to see. I do not suppose anyone would have risked a nickel on their catching the deserter, but they did, and they loaded him in again without the aid of anything but pure manpower. A splendid effort.

******

No one seemed to have the slightest idea of what the war was all about; even more, no one seemed to care. Had they known, maybe so many would not have volunteered. In the spirit of a great lark, men left their homes and work—some even sold valuable ranches for a mere song—just to go. I've often wondered whether it was the romantic notion of war that attracted them as much as it was an opportunity to escape the drab routine of daily life. Maybe it was simply a chance to see a bit of the world.

Whatever it was, a wave of war enthusiasm swept the country, and all along the way the people crowded to the stations to give us cigarettes, chocolate, and other time-honoured tokens traditionally showered on the departing soldier. Everyone turned out to enjoy the patriotic mood until we came to French Canada where we found not a soul on the platforms.

Somehow we finally got to Cape Town, though how the poor nags stood the ammonia-filled air of the holds for so long was a wonder, for there were no electric ventilators in those days.

In light of subsequent wars, nothing need be said of the Boer War itself except to describe it as semi-guerrilla warfare. Our small part in it was conducted amidst all the inanities and confusions that only the rank amateur can create: endless, pointless, tedious, horse-killing marches; completely disorganized camps; conflicting orders; foundering horses; occasional bursts of long-range and largely ineffectual rifle fire; and, inevitably, trigger-happy sentries. The worst aspect of this semi-guerrilla warfare was the terrible waste of horses.

The wily Boer was well mounted, knew the country, and could live off it. Most important, he had his heart in the fight because he was protecting his family, his home, and his way of life. We, on the other hand, milled around while dragging our supplies with us.

That war taught me two things: the fallibility of the horse as a means of transport and the excellence of the military small-bore rifle as exemplified in this case by the .303 Lee Enfield. With its 215-grain bullet of round-nose form and medium velocity, it seemed to me just the weapon for those countless old bull elephants I knew still existed in parts of Africa. It also taught me how infernally inaccurate rifle fire can be.

Even when delivered by supposedly good riflemen, such as the Boers, someone calculated that about 5,000 rounds had to be fired to secure a hit. The only incident that came my way was when my pony was shot in the neck when a patrol of us bumped into a flurry of Boers. They were firing their rifles, 7mm Mausers, from the saddle at full gallop, and I'm pretty certain hitting nothing, while our fellows were firing at full gallop at their pursuers with their 4½-inch-barrel Webley revolvers. They also were hitting nothing . . . except my pony.

I was on a small, somewhat fat Argentine that lacked stride when I found myself uncomfortably between the two cones of fire. A shot in the neck put my pony down for good. He turned over like a rabbit, shooting me straight out and forward and breaking my rifle stock in the process.

My comrades having disappeared over the horizon, there I was, dismounted on dead-open veld with two- or three-score Boers looking at me. I had no choice but to surrender and be marched to their camp. There I was accosted by some Boer women who stared at my Canadian Mounted Rifles badge and demanded, "Are you not a colonial too? Why are you fighting us?"

I was hard put to answer that one. I could hardly tell them I had come along for the free transportation.

I do not think these Boers really wanted to be burdened with prisoners. At any rate, there was another prisoner in the camp, an Englishman, and we two prisoners were given a whole sheep as our daily ration. Nothing else. A whole sheep. One evening instead of returning to the wagon where we were supposed to sleep, we simply kept going. Coming to a meali (corn) field, we lay doggo and waited for the dark. Then we struck across country where we vaguely knew a British column to be operating. We found it quite suddenly when a picket halted us with a rifle pointing straight at us and a finger clutching the trigger a bit too firmly.

As we had so recently arrived from among the Boers, we were expected to know a lot about them. Moreover, we were members of a Canadian outfit, and the staff officers seemed to lump all colonials in the same category as guerrilla fighters. So they promptly made us scouts attached to headquarters, mounted us, and put us on double rations. All of which was much to our liking, especially as there seemed to be no duties attached to the job other than to rustle Boer ponies wherever we could find them. These we turned over to the remount officer who made an "honest" penny by selling them to the army.

It happened that the column to which we were attached took up more or less permanent quarters in the town of Harrismith. Inevitably all sorts of sports were organized, among others horse racing. Somehow some thoroughbreds had escaped the Boers and found themselves at Harrismith, together with some

The fire got my pony and I was made prisoner. (Sketch by W. D. M. Bell)

former Johannesburg turfites.[1] It was they who organized the races and put up the prizes.

Now there was a handy half-breed mare belonging to one of the yeomanry regiments. The owner was willing to race her, and she was straightaway put into training under the care of me and my mates. This mare could gallop like the wind, but she was exceedingly excitable and hard-mouthed. In all the try-outs she simply left everything standing; the problem was that she could not be held.

The pundits pondered the problem deeply. If someone physically capable of holding her had the mount, she might be handicapped by the extra weight. On the other hand, if she had a light jockey, she would probably go all out and win too easily. That she would win, no one in the know doubted for a moment. All were prepared to stake all they had on her. You never saw such galloping quarters. At last it was decided that the light-weight jockey should have the mount.

Her race came round and she was led to the starting line in a highly excitable state. All sorts of droopy-looking thoroughbreds were there, glancing with scorn at our common mount. All the money we could scrap up—and at good prices—we put on her. Cautioning the jockey to hold her and not to win by too much, we held our breath as the flag was lowered.

Right from the start that blessed mare took the bit in her teeth and tore away. Almost instantly she was in the lead. It being rather gravelly ground, she threw up a hail of small pebbles behind her as those two magnificent hindquarters spurned the ground like two great steam pistons. Soon she was lengths ahead, with her jockey leaning back over her tail and using all his strength to control the fiery devil. It was the funniest sight. All the other riders were in the orthodox position between their mount's ears. She came in fifty lengths ahead and could not be stopped even then. Of course, it was finished as far as we were concerned.

******

In due course the Boer resistance began to dwindle. When we heard that the Canadian Mounted Rifles were to be sent home via England, I immediately

---

[1] Someone devoted to horse racing; a person likely to be found at a racetrack.

Back to Africa and the Boer War

The 2nd Regiment of the Canadian Mounted Rifles on patrol in South Africa, February–March 1902. Note the rather bedraggled appearance of some of the Stetsons, the Orndorff bandoliers, and Mark 1 Lee-Enfield rifles.

pressed hard to rejoin the unit. I took my discharge in England, and, as I was now a free man, I set out to plan my long-awaited elephant safari in earnest.

It also helped that Canada was paying her men about five times the British rate, and with that as a basis, I thought that surely I could raise the remaining funds for an expedition on my very own. Now that I was of age, nothing could stop me.

As I said, my war experience had taught me that the British .303 was quite a useful weapon, and I thought that coupled with a 215-grain, solid-jacketed bullet, the combination should serve me well for elephant hunting. For my first real venture I backed up my opinion that it was more a matter of where you placed the bullet rather than a bullet's particular striking energy, muzzle velocity, or anything else, by acquiring two sporting model .303s, each with a ten-shot magazine. In fact, these were military rifles with the barrel cut down a bit and with sporting pistol-grip stocks added. They cost eight pounds each.

I did not decide on these rifles lightly. As I said earlier, I had had a great friend in one Daniel Fraser, a gunmaker of Edinburgh. My old friend and mentor was now dead,[2] and that made my choice of weapon easier. If he had been alive, I feel pretty certain I should have been saddled at a tender age with the heavy ordnance in double-barrel form that he was so fond of getting me to shoot from his bench.

Often Fraser would take me down to the testing range where he would have me try out various rifles, single and double, in the "white" or raw stage—that is, before they were blued. It was there that I gained insight into the intricacies of making two parallel barrels shoot together. They never did so and, consequently, had to be adjusted so that their lines of fire crossed each other at the correct distance from the muzzle.

Those experiences taught me to dislike firing a .577 or .500 in a semi-prone position from a bench rest. The whole punch of those infernal artillery pieces expended itself against the leaning body of the firer—all in cold blood, mind you—so that one felt one's whole skeleton would fall asunder. I took a strong dislike to these mighty pieces, although I did admire their craftsmanship. How Dan used to curse me for bad grouping. Dan could fire them all day long, getting better and better groups from them, without turning a hair. He often berated me for flinching. But he died young, so perhaps it was meant as a warning.

In choosing those .303s, I successfully resisted the blandishments of the famous gunmakers with their wonderfully illustrated catalogues showing the effect of their marvelous wares on big game. What spectacular catalogues these old gunmaker firms used to turn out, depicting the loveliest and most exciting scenes of hunting big game. These catalogues were to be had for nothing, too, and today I think that a collection of them would be a pleasant memento of those times.

---

2   *The Times* (London)
Tuesday, 10 December 1901

The death took place suddenly, at his residence at Duddingston, near Edinburgh, on Saturday night (7 December), of Mr. DANIEL FRASER, a member of the Queen's Edinburgh Volunteer Brigade. Mr. Fraser, who was 53 years of age, was one of the best-known shots in the country. He attended the National Rifle Association meeting in 1868, and from that time never missed a meeting. He won the Duke of Cambridge's Prize in 1869 and the Queen's Prize badges eight times, his last badge being for third place in the final stage of the competition.

I remember that the "dangerous" character of the animals was much stressed in these catalogues—not enough to scare the prospective hunter into abandoning altogether the project of placing himself on the same continent even, but just enough to make him buy one—or better still two—of the firm's products. What the catalogues always stressed was that the "shock" resulting from the discharge would lay the hunter's assailant prostrate at his feet. The "shock" intended for the ravenous animal to receive was carefully measured in many foot pounds—and they ran into thousands. Curiously enough, no mention was made of what happened to the miserable human at the other end of the gun. The hitting of the animal seemed to be taken for granted.

Once I had settled the question of the battery, gathering together the rest of the equipment was easy. I made my plans, put together the rest of my kit, and once again boarded a ship for East Africa.

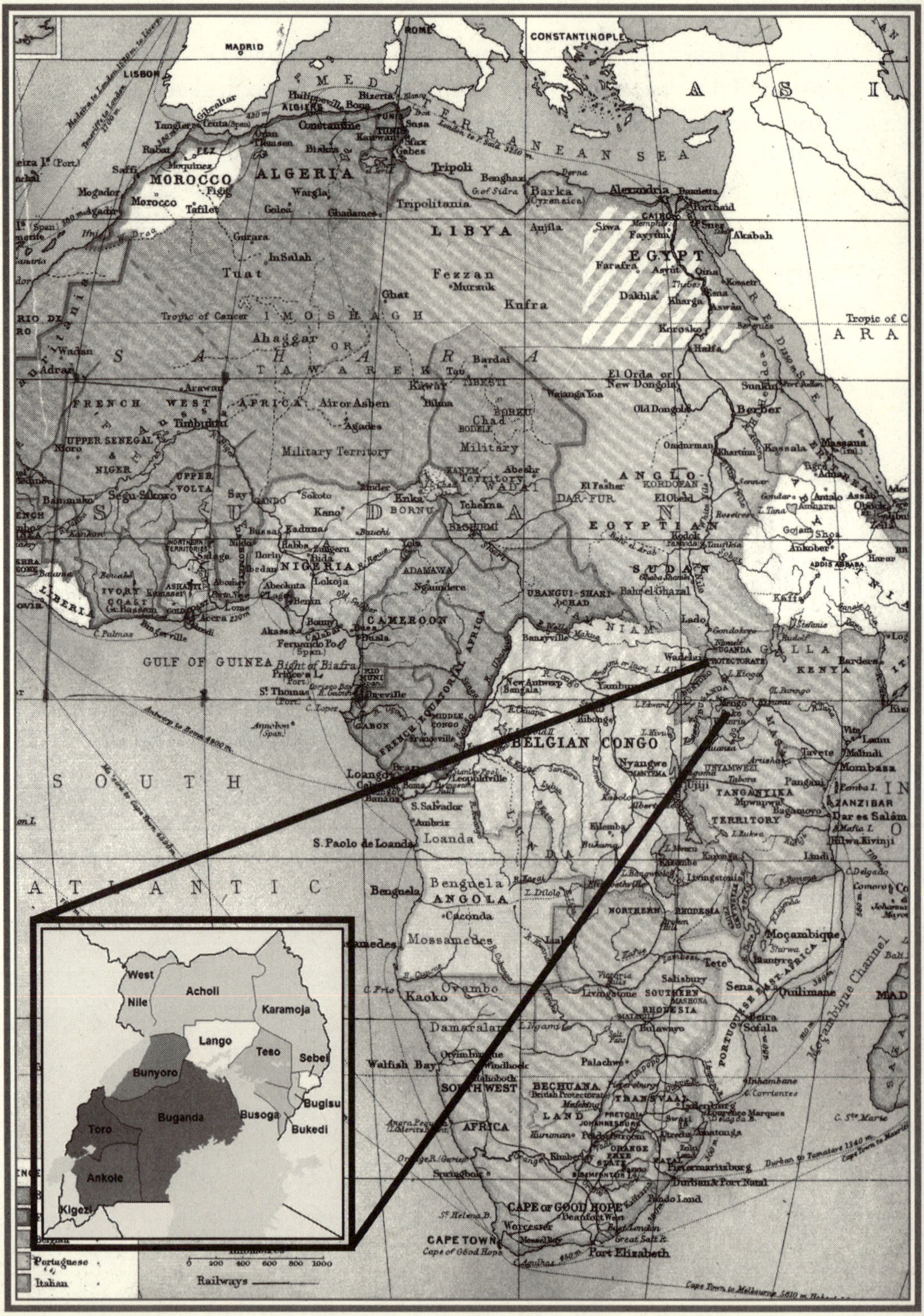
West
Nile
Acholi
Karamoja
Lango
Teso
Sebei
Bunyoro
Bugisu
Buganda
Busoga
Toro
Bukedi
Ankole
Kigezi
MADRID
ROME
CONSTANTINOPLE
LISBON
ASIA
MEDITERRANEAN SEA
MOROCCO
ALGERIA
LIBYA
EGYPT
Tripoli
Alexandria
Tropic of Cancer
FRENCH WEST AFRICA
Military Territory
NIGERIA
GULF OF GUINEA
ANGLO-EGYPTIAN SUDAN
KENYA
BELGIAN CONGO
CAMEROON
FRENCH EQUATORIAL AFRICA
TANGANYIKA TERRITORY
ANGOLA
NORTHERN RHODESIA
SOUTHERN RHODESIA
PORTUGUESE EAST AFRICA
SOUTH WEST AFRICA
BECHUANA LAND
TRANSVAAL
ORANGE FREE STATE
CAPE OF GOOD HOPE
CAPE TOWN
Port Elizabeth
Mocambique Channel
SOUTH ATLANTIC
Portuguese
Italian
Railways

INTO THE UNKNOWN

CHAPTER 9

At twenty-one life holds no terrors. Fevers, dysentery, snake bite, bilharzia, poisoned arrows or any other form of death pass one by or are highly brushed aside without a thought. Death by violence seems so remote as to be non-existent for all practical purposes. Fatigue through exertion seems almost as remote. In short life is jolly.

My discharge and subsequent pay out from the Canadian Mounted Rifles enabled me to fit out my first safari. True, it was a very humble affair, but it was my very own. I could not run to donkey transport, so I bought some bullocks and broke them to packing. Those cursed beasts nearly broke us all—they were so pig-headed.

I got among some fine old bulls and my anatomy studies carried out in Unyoro bore excellent fruit. I never turned back, and my rifle continued to keep me in style for some twenty-five years wandering over much of tropical Africa.

My .275 Mauser, which I acquired later, provided me with the wherewithal to penetrate the most remote fastnesses of those old man-shunning elephants that had finished with breeding and were due to die shortly anyhow. Many of them were found to be suffering from the most frightful liver disease.

Great cysts filled with a curry-like dry powder were found when the boys' butchering operations laid them bare and quantities of highly compressed balls of the same stuff were retrieved from the intestines, some as large as footballs. In fact, when faced up to the facts squarely, I was really doing them a great service in putting them painlessly out of their misery. Instead, I found myself being blackguarded right, left, and centre by ignorant know-alls for exterminating elephants. I killed one thousand, and a few over for full measure, of such crotchety old fellows. I never counted the few cows that simply insisted on having it. All this, however, is all in the future.

******

REMINISCENCES OF AN ELEPHANT HUNTER

When I arrived once again in Africa, I found my luck had turned at last. I found friends everywhere. I once more found myself at Kisumu[1] on Lake Victoria, but this time I reached it by rail.

Since my former visit, the Uganda Railway had been completed. At Kisumu I made friends with the naval man in charge of a small steamer that had arrived in sections and had been put together and into service for navigation on the lake. The captain advised me to try Uganda, or at least to see it, before deciding finally on my first hunting expedition. He offered to put me up at his headquarters in Entebbe, the capital of Uganda.

From there I went out on small expeditions and had my first taste of really high-grass hunting. The word grass is misleading in this connection,

---

[1]This is a good example of how Bell's two versions of his autobiography sometimes gave conflicting information. In one archive, Bell wrote that he arrived in Kisumu via the completed Uganda Railroad, and in another he wrote that he arrived in Mumias after returning home from the Boer War and then proceeding to East Africa. In researching the history of the Uganda Railroad, we found that the track went to Kisumu and not Mumias; in addition, Bell writes in *Bell of Africa* that on his second incursion into East Africa he started out from Kisumu. These facts led us to decide on this version to present for this chapter. For the reader's information, we have included Bell's narrative about arriving in Mumias. Bell picks up his story of departing from Mumias into Karamoja in the next chapter.

In Mumias I found a friend in the government post by the name of Partington, whom I shall call P., who told me what he could about the area north of the Turkwel River, including all about the raidings and doings of the Habash (Abyssinian slavers) then operating in that region.

P. said I must be armed. At his insistence twenty old Sniders (tower muskets) were hauled out of some moldering store. No proper cartridges for these ancient fire tubes could be found, but I tried a Martini round in one of them and it fired. The .450 bullet went rattling up the .577 tube and out in the merriest manner, key-holing all over the place. I at once said they would do.

My finances still did not allow of more than a very modest outfit. Donkeys were beyond my means. But I was not going to be stuck. P. was taking in bullocks as tax payment and I bought a bunch of steers and set about training them to carry loads. What a game we had with those infernal animals. None of them had ever worked in their lives before, but they did now, long and persistently . . . at bucking off our loads.

At last the day arrived when we thought ourselves ready for the road. I had Suliemani, the cook; Swede my head-boy; a headman; and a score of Baganda porters, all devoted to the hunt for elephants. Perhaps they thought their only hope of getting paid lay in the success of their Bwana getting ivory. If so, they were not far out.

With the quitting of Mumias, we would leave all civilized white men with their complicated ways behind us. Any money still left in my pockets was stowed away. From now on it would not buy an ounce of flour. We must feed ourselves.

At last my first safari was ready. After the usual delays of last-minute errands to run, stragglers to be rounded up, and the interminable farewells of wives and sweethearts, we crossed the Turkwel River and headed into the unknown.

although elephant grass is better. It is quite impenetrable to humans except on game paths. It is used by such animals as buffaloes and elephants as a daylight stronghold from which to raid native gardens by night.

I had been warned that buffaloes were quite aggressive when they are in these grassy strongholds, and, as the visibility was a matter of feet rather than yards, the utmost caution was necessary. Everyone was emphatic that nothing less than a double .450 should be used in such cover.

On reaching a native village, by way of canoe and through the Ssese Islands, where I saw numbers of otters in the lake, I found plenty of evidence of buffaloes. They came right into the gardens at night and caused a lot of destruction. The lads of the village complained that nothing they could do would drive them away. In answer to the query where they now were, they pointed to a long swamp filled with elephant grass, which at that time of year was about twelve feet high. It was arranged that on the morrow there should be a hunt.

Two middle-aged natives were ready and very willing to show the white man the buffalo in its lair. They said nothing about the appalling ferocity of these animals. As usual the buffaloes had been in the gardens during the night but had not been subjected to the usual counter-measures the natives would have ordinarily taken against them, such as spear and fire-brand throwing or bombardment from muzzle-loaders charged with bits of anything that came handy. This was at my special request.

The edge of the swamp lay quite near the village, and the three of us simply followed the fresh tracks straight into it. One native led while one followed behind me.

Filled as I was with lively apprehension after all the tales I had heard from white men, I was struck by the light-hearted and even eager way my native companions set about the job. I noted that not only did they carry a number of very paltry-looking spears but that they also did not act afraid. As they entered the fearful grass, the leader handed several of his spears to the one whose role apparently was to follow behind.

I had killed buffaloes before without experiencing anything extraordinary either in the killing of them or in their behaviour. But one or two white men had been killed or mauled by buffaloes in Uganda, and it had been impressed upon me that the Uganda buffaloes were different from all other buffalo in their dislike of white men. It was said that they would show diabolical cunning in waylaying the hunter, charge suddenly out on him, and, in fact, show the utmost resentment and fury should he invade their retreats.

With all these forebodings and gloomy prophecies in mind, I could not help contrasting the cool way my companions were undertaking the actual hunting of these ferocious animals with nothing but a spear in their hands. *Surely,* I thought, *these men, who almost lived with buffaloes, must know their characteristics.* Considerably comforted by these reflections, I set myself the task of making the least noise possible while following my nearly naked companion.

To my surprise, we were still within earshot of the village noises when the leader stopped rock still. He obviously could hear something, for he leant sideways on the wall of stiff grass to let me pass. With rifle at the ready and expecting almost instantly to receive a headlong charge at a two- or three-yard range, we advanced very slowly and silently toward what now could be distinguished as the breathing of some heavy beast.

At this stage the buffalo bull was probably asleep or, if not asleep, quite unsuspicious of his enemies' presence. He was about ten yards distant but, of course, quite invisible through the dense grass. But when we had closed the range to perhaps five yards, there was a sudden end to the heavy breathing. Dead

Thinking it all over by the camp fire, the conclusion was inescapable that the deadly cunning and ferocity of the buffalo was largely a figment of the white man's brain.

silence reigned as I peered about trying to glimpse something. The moment I moved—khaki drill gives off a certain scratching noise when rubbing against strong grass—there was a commotion.

I thought, *Here it comes!* and covered the expected spot with my rifle. Almost instantly I realized that the noise was receding. The poor old buff had had the scare of his life and was hell bent for the far away. The two natives had not moved and were as cool as be-damned.

Well, thought I, *things are not working out the way the story books say.*

We went on and worked that swamp here, there, and everywhere. We got close up on the buffalo several times, but always he heard us and ran away. Only once did I catch a glimpse of a fast-disappearing rump, and into it I instantly put a shot, so fed-up was I with the shyness of the quarry.

Now, I thought, *we'll see some fireworks.* A wounded buff in high grass was supposed to be the very devil, and wounded in such a place, too. *Better look out now,* I told myself.

What was my surprise and delight when, after what appeared about a mile but was actually about one hundred yards, we stumbled right on the kneeling buff . . . and this after the most careful approach. The native was again leading, as the tracking was much fouled and involved when suddenly he launched his spear. Leaning aside, he disclosed the kneeling buff—with the spear still quivering in the animal's stern. I covered the buff with my rifle and was just going to let go when it struck me that the animal must be dead. How we laughed—the natives from joy at the prospect of meat and I from relief.

As always I had used a solid bullet. On inspection I found that it had entered through the large part of one side of the massive hip-bone formation, had raked right forward into the vitals, and, thus, had killed him. Had it been a soft-nose bullet, goodness only knows what might have happened.

On the return to the village, I was leading at one stage when I stopped suddenly in the narrow grass lane, for my eye had just caught something near my tummy. It was the head of a spear pointing toward me. It appeared that the hindmost of the natives had been setting up spears for the buffalo on the chance one of them would transfix itself in the animal.

Thinking it all over by the camp fire, the conclusion was inescapable that the deadly cunning and ferocity of the buffalo was largely a figment of the white man's brain, born of the formidable appearance of the animal combined with the appalling character of its daylight retreats. Certainly those natives, living as they did in proximity with buffaloes from year's end to year's end had no fear of them.

But, at the same time, it should not be forgotten that however docile the animals may be, when scared they may easily run down or stampede over any human being in their path. In the nature of things, a stampede is more likely to harm the human than any deliberate act on the part of a buffalo, but it is poor consolation when your body is badly broken to be told the animal was running away.

Elephants were scarce in southern Uganda, so I was determined to move on to Unyoro.[2] Elephants were known to be numerous and the ivory good. I presently found myself in the very centre of good elephant country.

Again it was rolling country with much cultivation on the ridges and with swamp between. I found the natives extremely friendly toward an elephant hunter, so there was no lack of news of elephants that were raiding plantations.

When one saw the devastation caused by a night's visit of a few of these marauders, one wondered how anyone had the heart to ever plant anything again. Whole groves of bananas would be broken off, plucked up, or trampled underfoot. That plantation would be kaput for that year anyway.

The only reason anyone continued to plant at all was that all the villagers had one or more muzzle-loading, gas-pipe guns. These they would grossly overload and blast into the raiders with great spirit and determination. When I asked to see what sort of bullet they used, they said it did not matter and that anything would do so long as the projectile made a hole in the hide so that the fire from the powder could enter. These people thought it was the fire that killed! This was a widely held view at that time in many parts of Africa.

Queer notion as it may seem, it had this advantage: It took the firer to very close quarters with his game. Inevitably sometime, somewhere, one of these charges would chance to contain something that would penetrate. When these chances happened to combine with further chance of entry in a vital area, the recipient would die and the resultant feast of meat would presumably

---

[2] Unyoro is today known as Bunyoro, western Uganda. (See map at right.) It was one of the most powerful kingdoms in Central and East Africa from the thirteenth to the nineteenth centuries.

Leased to
Wandi
Kabayendi
Baginze
Makraka
King
of the
Belgians
Rimo
Kuterma
Ndirri
Gambiri
Kiri
Luri R.
Bedden
Gomoro R.
Latuka
Tarangolle
Mt Haro
Muggi
Kerefi
Obbo
Labore
Agoro
Dodo
Dongu R.
Vatako
Korobe
Dufile
Tertenia
Fadibek
Ganda
Kibi R.
Akoro
Gale
Sir R.
Lemihn
R. Nile
Fatiko
Bagger R.
Jubbo R.
Liki
Abuda
Wadelai
Vugora
Udat R.
J. Moro
Lobor
Majegba
Mt Emin
Mt Speke
Mt Schweinfurth
Mt Junker
Murchison
Karuma Falls
Asua R.
Mahagi
Magungo
Foweira
L. Kirkpatrick
Panyato
L. Kwania
Mswa
ALBERT NYANZA
2400
Kirota
Kibero
Masindi
WAKEDI
L. Sal
Andjuba
Kavalli
Mruli
3320
CHOGA L.
Manda
Kabarega
Kafu
Katonsa
Kabagambe
Ft Kafu
Ituri R.
Kilanga
Mpologo L.
Kiriama
Kikonda
Lugogo R.
Ugarama
UGANDA
Ripon Fs
Wakoles
Ruwenzori
16600
Kivari
L. Isolt
Kampala
Lubwas
Mengo
Mt Edwin Arnold
Kibibi
Kwaliooma
Ft Edward
Sangwe
Usongoro
Ntara
Napoleon
Ft George
L. Ruisamba
Kikoma
Berkeley
Port Victoria
Kazinga
Naguecha
Ugonsi
Port Alice
3600
Kwa Kaihuru
Antari
Sesse Arch.
Ugowe
Rusinga I.
Igororo
Rwizi R.
Budda
Duma
VICTORIA
Katunda
Nile
Kikondo
3880
Kavirondo B.
Mporora
Kagera R.
NYANZA
Kitangule
Bukoba
Irigwa
Kiantunga
Bukerebe
Mohasi L.
Itolia
Bumbire
Ukara
Karagwe
Mutatre
Nasso
Kadoto
Ukerewe
Speke G.
Emin
Mwanza
Nasa
Eshangi
4850

make up for all the crop destruction. The chief, of course, would look after the ivory. Hence eternal hope kept everyone busy as bees planting and re-planting, right in among a horde of elephants grown used to, and defying, anything the human population could do about them.

These were ideal conditions for the hunter because everyone was eager to report visiting marauders, and the latter were at no great pains to retire in the daytime to any distance from their nightly feeding grounds. In spite of my efforts to reduce their numbers, it soon became necessary for the Government to institute measures directed against elephants to protect the natives against their depredations. That is how the Elephant Control came into existence. This control, from a small beginning, grew into a veritable small army of native hunters, armed with the latest big-bore rifles and with white officers who also took a hand.

The yearly "bag" in course of time grew into the four-figure category and continues to this day. Unfortunately for me, the proceeds—ivory—from these operations were required for the payment of salaries and expenses. I was, thus, obliged to leave a very profitable hunting ground and seek out some less settled country for my operations.

When an elephant hunter behaves in an ordinarily decent fashion toward the natives among whom he is living, he soon comes to enjoy a measure of confidence and intimacy seldom extended to anyone representing Government. Many were the tales told round the camp fire of the so recently dethroned kings of Unyoro and Uganda. Natives are rather proud of the "toughness" of their rulers, in retrospect at any rate.

They thought it great when the king of Uganda made a white missionary swim across the pond in the palace grounds, where he kept a tame crocodile of gigantic proportions fed on human victims, on the understanding that if the missionary reached the opposite shore intact, the king would then believe in the God of Christianity. The missionary accomplished the feat all right with the old croc right on his tail. Whether the croc was not hungry or whether the strange whiteness of the bait was the reason for the missionary's salvation is hard to say.

Personally I inclined toward the latter explanation as I frequently, in subsequent years, swam across the Nile in croc-infested areas where a black man would not have progressed ten yards. An analogy to this might be drawn with that rare occurrence of the appearance on a grouse moor of a white grouse.

When it is seen, everyone wonders what it is and it is out of range before anyone does anything about it.

Whilst still in Unyoro I got a rousing go of dysentery and it was through this that I met Ormsby.[3] This man had been with ex-missionary Stokes on the original Central African trail from Dar-es-Salaam to Ujiji, the great old slavers' route from Zanzibar to the Congo. This was long before white government came to the region. Great were his tales of the doings in those days.

Ormsby was the person who organized and ran Charles Stokes's safaris of so-called "trade goods," consisting largely of gas-pipe guns, percussion caps, and powder. He recounted how a certain bishop, about to visit Uganda, was induced, in all innocence, to allow a couple hundred porters of Stokes's to join his safari, each carrying a load of guns tied up in trade cloth. Apparently Stokes's reputation stank so, especially when it was revealed that he was selling guns to rebels in exchange for ivory, that he was hanged. The whole incident passed over.[4]

Ormsby now undertook to cure me of my dysentery. Treating that disconcerting disease as he would malaria, Ormsby started shoving large doses of quinine down me at frequent intervals, whilst giving me half-hourly doses of Epsom salts. In no time at all, the cure was affected to my great relief. I felt eternally grateful to Ormsby.

About this time the Soudanese troops in Uganda mutinied. When these troops flogged and shot their white officers, all the exceedingly few white men in the country were enrolled to stamp out the mutineers, who were now

---

[3] Sydney William Ormsby was employed by the Uganda Protectorate Service in 1903.

[4] According to several sources, Bell was incorrect: The incident was not "passed over." The Stokes Affair became a diplomatic incident between the Congo Free State and the British government in 1895. Charles Stokes, a British trader and former Christian missionary, was arrested for illegal trading in the Congo and hanged. The Belgian officer responsible for the execution, Captain Lothaire, was convinced that Stokes had been selling guns in exchange for ivory to Kibonge, the assassin of Emin Pasha and the head of the Muslim rebels in the eastern Congo. Since the Belgians were waging war against Kibonge, this act was declared unlawful, and Stokes was hanged without trial on 15 January 1895. The British public accused Lothaire of having failed to provide Stokes with due process of law. Lothaire was charged with murder in Belgium but was acquitted. There was a public outcry throughout the British Empire.

The Stokes Affair mobilized British public opinion against the Congo Free State, already accused of systematic humanitarian abuses in a British report published in May 1895. The campaign would eventually result in the formation of the Congo Reform Association and the annexation of the Free State by Belgium as the Belgian Congo in 1908.

ravaging the country as only primitive savages armed with modern weapons can. The rebels had seized all the rifles, machine guns, and ammunition then in the country, except for one Maxim that belonged to the Uganda Marine. They got hold of the steam launch that mainly constituted the Marine's entire flotilla and managed to hold on to it, even after an abortive night attack with a home-made naval mine.

A Captain Fowler had got away with the machine gun and lost no time in mounting it on a large native canoe. It was he who made the abortive attempt to sink the Government steam launch by swimming out on a small raft in pitch darkness in croc-infested waters. When that didn't work, he determined to sink the launch with the machine gun.

It was said—and was doubtless true—that in order to induce his paddlers to close the range in the ensuing engagement, Captain Fowler pistoled sundry peddlers and bundled them overboard to the waiting crocs. Be that as it may, the range was closed. The captain, plying his .450-bore Maxim with great application to the waterline of the enemy craft, soon had the satisfaction of seeing it founder with all hands, who were drunk as lords. Curiously enough, one did not hear of any enemy survivors from this spirited engagement.

Of course, Ormsby joined the good work, and a tough job they had. He and trader "Jinja" Grant, with the old sailing-ship captain Mayes,[5] were hastily enrolled and given charge of a nondescript bunch of Swahili porters, roustabouts, boys, natives, and riff-raff. Every sort of gun was pressed into service, muzzle-loading trade guns, Sniders, and a few Martinis. Fortunately for them, the mutineers were so drunken on success and native wine and women that their threat as a fighting body was much impaired.

One may ask what caused the mutiny. It was the age-old problem of women. Now Africans have no nonsense about women. They know that women are endowed by Nature with far more stamina than men. They know that women can work harder and longer than men, that they can carry bigger loads far longer distances than men. In their "way of living" the male is a rather delicate fighting—and its corollary—machine, requiring well-prepared food,

---

[5] Walter Mayes was a seaman who volunteered to help British troops in the Sudanese mutiny. He later was given the post at Nandi as Collector for the colonial government in 1902. Found guilty of gross negligence, he was demoted to Assistant Collector in 1905. (See also chapter 25.)

abundant drink of a stimulating nature, and the necessary leisure to enjoy all these good things. This is, of course, to be combined with the minimum of work of any description. The ambition is, therefore, naturally to surround oneself with as many women as possible.

When, then, a high-ranking white man issues an unheard-of order to the effect that no woman must be taken on an imminent expedition, one can imagine the consternation in the ranks. Some of these men had fought all over the Soudan, in Abyssinia, and even for the Turks in Arabia, but always they had carried their women with them. The white man's idea that women were an encumbrance was to them sheer lunacy. When it was explained to them that white men considered women too delicate to stand the rigours of campaigning, they thought these pale-skinned officers were simply mad. They could not believe that these officers were serious.

So when the general made it quite plain that he meant every word of the order, the rebels-to-be quite definitely said, "To hell with the white men and their silly notions. We'll rid ourselves once and for all of them and their nonsense." Which they straightaway did in no uncertain way. Every white officer they were able to catch was immediately caught up, flogged, and shot.

There then ensued a period during which a great time was had by the mutineers. Of course, they took possession of all Government property, including the stocks of arms and munitions. Altogether they had a glorious time, for they commanded everything. They re-introduced the practice of slavery—the abandoning of which at the white man's order had been such a blow to their "African Way of Life." In short, they played merry hell while it lasted.

Now anyone who knew the Soudanese—or any other Africans for that matter—of that time would quite instinctively know what the general treatment of the unarmed natives would be at the hands of these hard, drunken toughs. No one in their senses would expect anything but robbery, murder, and rape, with the sale into slavery of any survivors. So when I read recently that these troops had mutinied "because they refused to have any hand in the oppression of their coloured brethren," I could not help laughing. This extraordinary statement was contained in a travel book and was probably made in all good faith. So is history made.

Ormsby, "Jinja" Grant, and Mayes held the fort until reinforcements arrived from the coast. Now the hunt was on. A very effective gentleman came

Reminiscences of an Elephant Hunter

Bell moved from southern Uganda to Unyoro and then on to Karamoja in search of the great herds of elephant bulls that had been reported as living there. When Bell hunted there, Uganda Protectorate was under British administration.

out with full powers to catch up, dead or alive, all mutineers. His methods were direct and vigorous. After sundry extremely bloody engagements, in which the mutineers' women distinguished themselves with the rifles of their fallen or too-drunken men, the survivors fled into the villages all over the country.

To find the fleeing rebels, this gentleman now applied the simple method of rounding up the stock of any village suspected of harbouring these mutineers. Dead or alive they must be produced. And they mostly were. One or two escaped into Belgian country, but mostly they were run down and captured, tried by martial law, and hanged or shot.

Much of this executing fell to the lot of poor Grant, and he used to recount what a job the women presented. Nubi women are the very devil, as savage as lovers as they are as enemies and as broad as they are long and as thick through as they are broad. When he would ride to the place of execution, he said the women would almost tear him from his horse until he armed himself with a stout *kiboko*. He was a very brave man.

******

All the Arab and Swahili traders who used to do such a thriving trade were by now finding it more and more difficult to carry on business in Unyoro. Government—their deadliest enemy—was spreading out. Prohibitions and regulations were cramping their style. It became essential to find some new country where the cursed white man had not yet established himself. A country where a man could still slit a throat or grab a native girl without being badgered by alien law. Such a country was Karamojo.

By this time I also had heard of Karamojo, but for me the enticement came in the form of tales of great herds of elephant bulls. Given the state of Unyoro, I determined to make my way forthwith to Karamojo.

Kaabong

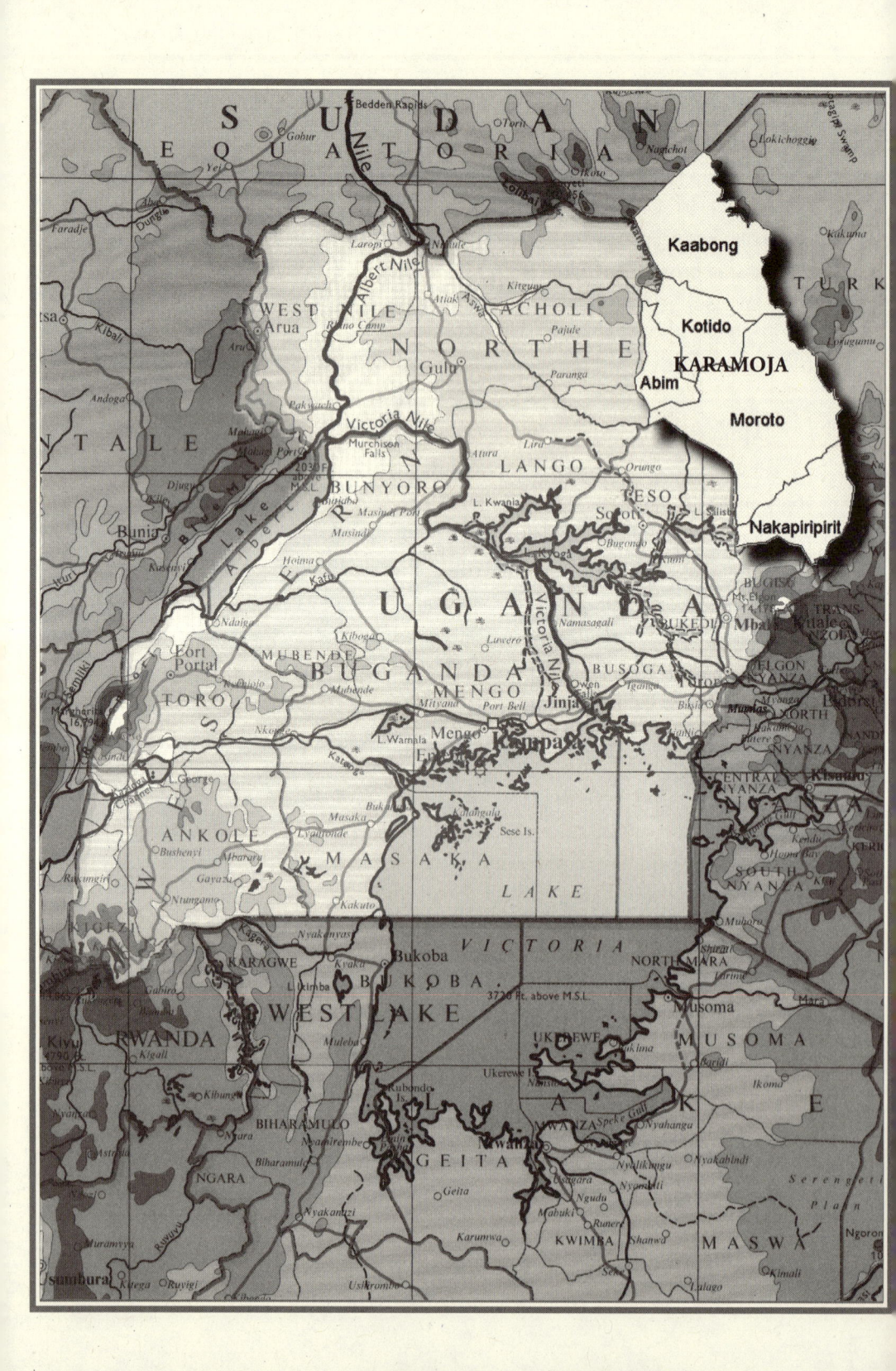

Kotido

KARAMOJA

Abim

Moroto

Nakapiripirit

Karamojo

Chapter 10

Even though some of this chapter is a repeat of events or descriptions found elsewhere, we felt the need to include at least a placeholder of this time so as to provide continuity to Bell's life story for the reader. As Bell said, "A detailed account of these years and my best hunts is given in Karamojo Safari."

In 1902 this unmapped and unopened country of Karamojo was a high, dry, sandy ridge of country, interspersed with rock outcrops and some quite high isolated mountains, running parallel with the Albert Nile, distant some two hundred miles to the west, while Lake Rudolph lay simmering in the heat of its depression about two hundred and fifty miles to the east. While its northern boundary still remained undefined, Abyssinia lay beyond the border to the north. It was very healthy country and mosquitoes were not at all bothersome, but every other variety of pestiferous fly was there in numbers.

The country was thorn bush interspersed with open glades. Toward Lake Rudolph the bush became higher and denser, with fewer open parts. Toward the Nile there were large stretches of plains country covered with high grass that became inundated during the big rains. The rivers on the high ridge where all the Karamojo permanent villages were congregated consisted of seemingly dry sandy river beds that only ran water in the rainy season. The rest of the time humans and wild life alike obtained water by digging in the sand.

Beyond designating the country "British" on the maps, there was as yet no attempt to occupy or administer it. The boundary had not been fixed, so it was a sort of free-for-all scramble in which the British-sponsored native traders from British East Africa were only too willing to join.

All the old slavers in Africa seemed to have found a last stronghold in this land as well. As I said, true Abyssinia lay to the north, and the Abyssinians would come south to raid for slaves and cattle. Swahili and Arab caravans—the old slaving gangs—chased out of the Congo, other parts of Uganda, Tanganyika, and the Rhodesias—still found room there for their so-called "trading" activities. They had little to fear except a large band of Habash [Abyssinians], who were better armed, but both sides were wary of each other and would retire smartly when met.

Added to this sense of lawless chaos, everyone had a firearm except the owners of the land; they had only spears.

This state of affairs was unwittingly assisted by the putting into force of a decree called the "Outlying Districts Ordinance," by which no white man was allowed north of Elgon without a special permit. All this, of course, simply played into the hands of the traders. The last thing they wanted was the presence of a white man in their midst. They proceeded to make the most of their opportunities. The Closed District began to simmer, but a lot of ivory came out and paid heavy dues. Government closed its eyes and raked in the shekels.

Added to this sense of lawless chaos, everyone had a firearm except the owners of the land; they had only spears. The Habash had fairly modern rifles, and the Swahili and Arab traders had a ramshackle assortment of "fire-tubes" from muzzle-loading percussion cap types up to the heavy double-barrel products of all the famous London firms. Ostensibly these arms were allowed for the protection of peaceful traders. Inevitably, they were turned to other uses, for there was not a single authority in the land.

When I drew into Mumias at the foot of the 14,000-foot Mount Elgon, this was the state of affairs in the area. Therefore, I was delighted to find my old friend Partington[1] in charge of the *boma*. A man of great independence of outlook, Partington seized the chance of acquiring, without any cost to the Government, an unofficial agent who could be relied upon to confine his activities to the killing of four-footed game and whose presence in the disturbed area would restrain the activities of those who were more addicted to the pursuit of the two-footed sort. All these considerations played right into my hand.

This Partington was also a man of outstanding, remarkable character. He used to tell me of his idea of a holiday. He would choose the Continent for his hunting grounds. His prey were those couriers and interpreters of every civilized language so thoughtfully provided by States and Railway Companies for the comfort of travelers and, incidentally, the profit of all concerned.

Well, Partington discovered that much fun could be had by pretending he knew no other language but Ki-swahili. Now these gold-braided interpreters rather fancy themselves as lingos. The man was white, wasn't he? Therefore, one of them must know his language. At large centers like Paris he would have gathered round him brass hats who spoke collectively every civilized language in the world. They would get quite excited about it and would work over poor old P. to the imminent danger of his losing his connection. Porters and station functionaries, guards and telegraphy boys would join the throng as they shouted in P.'s ears, thinking he must be deaf, in every known tongue. All in vain. P. would simply reply quite quietly that he did not understand—in Ki-swahili.

Partington set about assisting me in every way possible, and I was soon fitted out for my first journey into Karamojo. Partington knew, of course, that the two-footers would do everything they could to obstruct and hinder his agent, but he judged they would not go to the extreme in the matter. He was right.

---

[1] Hugh Basil Partington was District Commissioner East Africa in the early part of the twentieth century. It was Partington who allowed Bell to hunt in Karamojo, and it was Partington who made sure that no other hunters were allowed in the area where Bell was hunting. Partington died 1 July 1914 in Mombasa of blackwater fever. He was 40 years old. (See also chapter 2 of *Incidents from an Elephant Hunter's Diary*.)

Partington thought that I should have some sort of force for the protection of my safari from the natives, for he knew that they were bound to be hostile. That they could show their hostility effectively was born out by the recently arrived news that a caravan of three hundred and fifty guns had been wiped out, one survivor escaping to tell the news. The leader and organizer of this clever coup was one Pyjalé of Bukora.[2] While P. knew the natives to be hostile, he did not think the traders would resort to any monkey tricks. Nonetheless, as I made my preparations, the devastating results of the recent Soudanese mutiny were still fresh in both our minds.

******

Thus began my sojourn in Karamojo. The natives of the region, once they learned that I meant them no harm, accepted me as a friend, and we lived, hunted, and traded in peace, even though I was the only white man within hundreds of miles. They helped me in my hunts for ivory; I, in turn, provided them with an abundance of meat, that greatest of African luxuries, and defended them from the Arab and Habash raiders. It was a happy partnership, always kept on both sides with the best of faith.

I hunted in this Karamojo-Dabossa country from 1902 to the end of 1907. In that time, I returned five times to Kenya and the railroad to sell my ivory and recoup my safari. The average weight of the tusks from the elephants I shot was fifty-three pounds, including about 10 percent of single or broken tusks.

My life during my stay in Karamojo was filled with abundant adventures. All these jolly doings, detailed accounts of these years, and my best hunts can be found in *Karamojo Safari* and *Wanderings of an Elephant Hunter*.

******

All was now ready for my final *shuka* or retreat from Karamojo to begin. There was no more buried ivory to dig up, and it was not very likely that we would encounter much on the road. The reason for this is that we would be obliged to follow the regular caravan trail because the rains had by this

---

[2] Bell said, "Pyjalé later became my right-hand man and hunting companion. From him, I learned how he had accomplished such a complete and overwhelming victory while using only stabbing spears against firearms." (On maps Bukora is also spelled Bokora.)

time inundated much of our west-of-Dabasian trail, making it impossible for donkey transport.

Before moving, I decided to do a trial of everything that had to be transported. What a sight it was! I had amassed 354 tusks, with an average weight of 53 pounds each from 180 elephants. Now they all had to be transported. The following gives some details for this last hunt:

> Total time of safari: .... 14 months
> Time spent on the actual hunting: .... 6 months
> Average number of elephants per month of hunting: 30
> Bill for wages per month: £150
> Bill for the safari: £2,100
> Bonus to each boy: .... 3 months' wages (£450)
> Cost of stock and trade goods: .... approximately £400.
> Total expenditure: .... approximately £3,000.
> Set value of ivory, all first rate stuff saleable on the spot to
>   the Indian merchants: .... £900 (Rs: 7 per pound, say 10/- per pound)
> Total profit: .... about £8,000

(This was after deducting something for drying-out, shrinkage, and allowing for extras. And we still had a full-power safari.)

There were 31 tusks that required porters to carry them, either because they were too heavy for donkeys or their length and curvature made them awkward when donkey-borne. Of these 31 tusks, 29 belonged to the former class and only two to the latter. These two teeth were more like mammoth tusks than elephants' as they were very long and very much curved. Unlike mammoth tusks, they weighed 70-odd pounds each; all the others were over 100 pounds each.

A line of thirty tusks does not sound much, but actually they constitute a first-class spectacle. When man-borne, each tusk requires at least three yards of the line to itself, and this meant we soon had a caravan a hundred yards long. When each porter is decked up in elaborately worked garments of many coloured beads; the heads bedecked with Karamojan blood-red, white, or black ostrich feathers; and the bodies covered with giraffe manes, lion manes, leopard skins, and baboon manes, the whole thing fills the eye.

It is the genuine stuff all right. What glitter and gaud it has it owes to goodness-to-God sunlight and grease. The film stuff is far too clean. Dirt is just as much a part of life as anything else and should be given its proper place. It always surprises me when I see a Hollywood hero perform the most prodigious deeds and appear quite immaculate after it all.

The Karamojong.

Just as we were in the midst of our preparations, who should come drifting across the plain but Yongellynung[3] with a string of women behind him bearing their pots. He seemed to be pretty well jagged judging by his stouts. Thank goodness I still had some stuff to give his wives—he never seemed to want anything for himself. Dear, old, unselfish beggar, he would have given me anything. Of course he was, for a Karamojan, unbelievably rich.

Alone of all native men in my experience, riches had not accrued to him through superior cunning or aggressive acquisitiveness. It had come to him solely by light of courage in battle. Even in his cups—the final test—he was innately modest. He would not tell of his exploits; only his people would. The fact that his wealth caused no envy in the hearts of his neighbours showed that his character soared triumphant over such moderating influences. He always reminded me of a bull terrier, rushing to meet battle with genuine joy.

There was a tremendous gathering of natives present and a big gathering of bald heads round the beer pots. Speeches were freely spouting. They were all about how friendly they felt toward the "Red Man" (myself) and how he—the "Red Man"—could beat his children—themselves—as much as he liked and how he would give them tobacco and trade goods, cows, and sheep etc., etc., without end . . . as long as the beer held out at any rate.

I warned them not to kill any traders while I was away and not to kill any enemy women. I said that I would soon be back among them and that if I saw anyone freshly tattooed on the left side, I might be unable to resist shooting him. It went on and on, the usual palaver.

---

[3] See chapter 3 in *Incidents from an Elephant Hunter's Diary* for more on this kind old rascal.

The first march was a short one, just to get everything into running order. After that, the safari just rolled along from day to day until the final camp before our entry once more into Mumias and civilization.

As we neared the town, strings of women in the latest product of Manchester cotton mills began to meet us. A great concourse lined the main street to see the safari parade in. It was an important event in the life of a small town like Mumias. Safaris lasted at least a year and sometimes two or three years, and when they returned, there would be thousands of rupees to be sharked from the beer-sodden boys relaxing from the toils of their safari.

The ivory buyers were in great force, too. Only those who had a large sum of hard cash would stand much chance, for I always liked to be paid at once.

After the interminable parade down the main street, camp was made about a mile from the town. A visit would be made with Swede to the shops and some fearfully unwholesome tined stuff, long since condemned, would be bought, together with some liquor such as whisky. Bar the haggling over ivory prices, the clashes of our lit-up porters with the local police, the thieving of our boys to quickly acquire goods, and all the usual money troubles appertaining to a return to civilization, the safari was ended.

The haggling over the ivory, however, had just begun.

******

It turned out to be an amusing auction of my Karamojo ivory. As I said, the safari had been out in the *barra* (wilderness) for fourteen months, so I had amassed a good deal of ivory during that time. There were only two buyers of sufficient financial standing to handle such a quantity. Both had firm orders to outbid his rival no matter what the price might be.

On the one hand was the representative of Alidina Visram[4] with whom I had had a long and pleasurable connection. He was a large, fat man with a henna-coloured beard. His rival was a small, oldish Persian.

---

[4] According to the *Daily Monitor,* Alidina Visram was the grandfather of trade in Uganda. He was born in India in 1851, and when he was twelve years old, he took a dhow to Zanzibar. An astute businessman, he spent many years developing his various enterprises on the eastern coast of Africa, and as they flourished, he moved his ventures into Uganda. This model citizen and honest businessman was known to many for his wide-ranging philanthropy. (See chapter 25 of this book for more on this Ismaili hero.)

The ivory was brought out from the store in the Government *boma* and laid in long rows in the compound. Business was conducted on a shady veranda, all this by permission of the district officer.

At first the large, fat man treated his rival in a jovial, friendly way. One might have almost detected a mood of friendly tolerance in his bearing to what must have appeared the arrival of an upstart. The Persian, on the other hand, was deadly serious and put in the most vicious bids. Soon the fat man dropped his bantering manner and seemed suddenly to realize that he was facing serious opposition. Could he have been misinformed about this little man's financial backing? He, too, became rattled.

The price war had now reached the point where their usual 90 or 100 percent profit began to be threatened. Both referred to their written instructions. Apparently they both drew some comfort from what they read, for from that moment they

It turned out to be an amusing auction of my Karamojo ivory. The ivory was brought out from the store in the Government boma *and laid out in the compound.*

threw caution to the winds. Madly bidding against each other, they soon reached a point far beyond the price for tusks of any known ivory market in the world.

By this time both buyers were in a state of great agitation and anger. I was afraid the fat man would have a fit. At long last it was he who quit, wishing his rival joy of his bargain—with venom in his voice. The little man, too, seemed quite overcome when he realized that he had committed himself so deeply.

They both sank into chairs, completely exhausted.

While tea was served, I said casually to the successful one that I would require about 10,000 rupees in cash for my safari.

"Certainly," said the Persian. "I will have it here in four days' time."

"No," I said. "That won't do. I must have it today."

He didn't have the money, so the fat man won after all.

After a bit of figuring, he turned to me and said, all smiles now, "That passes the £25,000 mark for ivory we have bought from you."

******

My hunting in the vast semi-desert country to the north-west of Lake Rudolph seemed to indicate that the swampy country farther to the north around the eastern tributaries of the White Nile would be very productive for elephants. I also constantly had had reports of great movements of elephants going toward the sources of rivers running into the Nile by way of the Sobat. Consequently, it had been in my mind for some time to push farther north into that area. I now determined to return to London for a new outfit and to approach this country through Abyssinia. My sojourn in Karamojo was over, and I bade farewell to that lovely land.

Although I knew it not at the time, thinking Africa was full of similar delightful countries, I never found another where the ivory was so good. It was a strange kind of country. One could go for a month without seeing elephant and then meet up with scores of them. This was because the long dry ridge of Karamojo attracted the old bulls from the Nile Valley when things got too wet for them there.

So ended my five years solo. I left many friends behind me . . . and some enemies too. My presence had prevented many raids both from the Swahili traders and the Abyssinians. I had nipped two raids and returned the raided stock to their rightful owners. I had entered in unopened country and found a happy people. I was sorry to leave them.

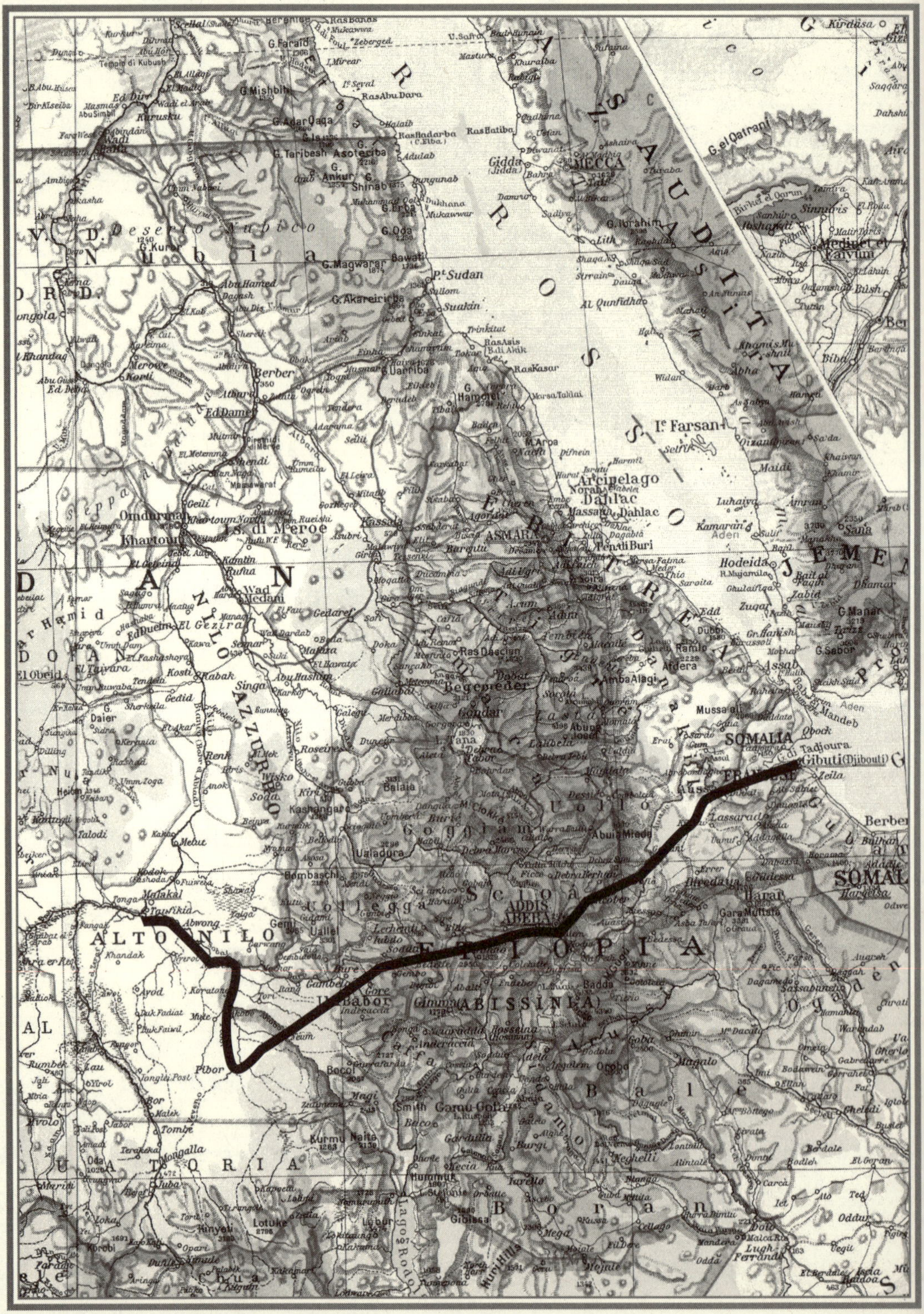

Abyssinia under Menelik

Chapter 11

Sometime later I walked into Thomas Cook & Sons in London and asked the first man I saw to find four of my old boys in Mombasa, East Africa, to clothe them suitably, and to deliver them to Djibouti in French Somaliland against my arrival there. Then Harry Rayne, a friend who was to accompany me on this hunt, and I set about our preparations. We were to travel overland through France and to board a steamer at Marseilles.

When we docked in France, our large consignment of rifles and ammunition were promptly stacked in the Custom House, and all I could visualize was an endless filling out of forms, if not total confiscation. Rayne, however, coolly placed a franc piece between his fingers and leaned on the counter with the palm of his hand showing toward the *douaniera*. In a flash the worthy whipped off the franc and bundled our gear over to us.

"Gosh, Harry," I said, "I wouldn't have had the nerve to do that. And even if I had, I'd not have offered anything less than a gold piece."

And this was Rayne's first visit to Europe! My companion was evidently a man of parts.

When we arrived at Djibouti, we were met by our four stalwarts from Mombasa. Cook's had somehow ferreted them out from their various villages and then transported them to Djibouti. I had asked that they be suitably clothed, and so they were, depending on your meaning of "suitable." Suliemani had on an admiral's swallow-tail coat, without insignia, of course, and very well he looked as to the top half; the tails, unfortunately, reached his heels.

******

In 1908 the country lying around the western and south-western base of the Abyssinian plateau was a true wilderness. As the boundaries had not yet been delimited between Abyssinia and the Soudan on the one hand and Abyssinia and Uganda on the other, I felt there would be more scope for my activities in that region and elsewhere. Our goal was to reach that far-off country where I suspected those great herds of bull elephants were headed when I last saw them trekking north from the Moru Akipi swamps like a train and into the horizon. To reach this country, I was obliged to cross Abyssinia.

The railway in those days stopped at Menelik's frontier. From there on to the capital we had to ride baggage mules and ponies. None of the bridges, where there were any bridges at all, were broader than just enough to pass a single horseman, for Menelik was a wily bird and knew his land-hungry Europeans.

On reaching Addis Ababa, Harry and I found ourselves held up temporarily. We needed to obtain an all-important document that would, we hoped, open the road through western Abyssinia to our hunting grounds. To acquire this important pass one had to approach one's country's minister in due and humble form, for only thus could permission to traverse the hinterland be obtained for nothing. To get it in any other way would have meant the oiling of many palms and considerable delay. Apparently in these diplomatic matters one's financial standing is all important. Luckily, we carried a letter to the local banker.[1]

Our permit to proceed arrived pronto, and we prepared to move. As is the way of all safaris, the first march was a short one. That allows things that have been forgotten to be retrieved, wives to take a last squeeze from husbands, and deserters or run-away mules to be captured.

On our journey through the highlands we were hampered by heavy rains and swollen rivers. But we knew how to deal with natural obstacles. Both of us were experienced travelers and nothing could stop us. Where we had trouble was in dealing with the local chiefs who were far more trouble than were ordinary Africans. These gentry seemed to combine all the objectionable traits of every race.

At first we smiled and produced our pass from the emperor, a prodigious document with seals on it the size of soup plates. To our astonishment they seemed to set very little store by it. We had a rascally interpreter with one ear—the other had been cut off because he had rowed with the Italians at Adowa—who probably got some sort of rake-off. Anyhow, we found ourselves shedding presents at a great rate, but, luckily, we had been warned and had come prepared. Our pass allowed us to move forward on the path but denied us more than one hundred metres penetration on either side.

We came to one quite large river that was in full spate, so we camped on the near side to build a ground-sheet raft to ferry our ammunition, rifles, food,

---

[1] The story of what happened to Bell and Harry Rayne while they were in Addis Ababa is told in chapter 9 of *Incidents from an Elephant Hunter's Diary*.

and stores. To do this expeditiously, we had to get a rope across. As none of the boys would tackle the job, one of us had to do it while the other kept crocs at bay by plastering the surrounding waters with rifle shots. Once a rope is across from bank to bank, the job is soon accomplished.

While we were busy at it, an Englishman came along and camped alongside. Of course, we extended the use of our ferry to a fellow traveler, and when everything was safely over, including the dithering Abyssinians who hate water, much preferring 99.75 percent pure alcohol, we all camped together. In return he told us something that would have made us rich men if we had had the gumption of a barn-yard fowl.

He was a rubber expert straight from the woods and forests of Ceylon and Malay, where he had been planting the Para rubber seedlings that had been propagated from seeds stolen from Brazil. He was now employed by Menelik to report on the wild rubber of Abyssinia, and his pass allowed him free access to any part of the country. He told us that the Ceylon plantations would soon be in full production, that he had put his shirt into shares, and that they would pay fantastic dividends.

He then gave us a written list of plantation names. He told us to invest every penny we could scrape together in the estates he named. We did not do so, of course. Had we only followed his advice, our futures would have been secured. The long forgotten, but to those who experienced it, the ever-memorable rubber boom was in full blast, and anyone with inside knowledge was making a fortune.

Instead, we thought, *Why not plant rubber in East Africa? Land could be got for one and four pence an acre—say thirty cents.* We determined to do it. If we found good elephant country, I would sit down in it and Harry, who was a fine agriculturist, would go on through Uganda down to the coast, buy land, and start it going.

At Gore we found ourselves on the verge of elephant country once more, country untouched by any white hunter. What we also found there was Ras Tsama, who proved quite an obstacle if ever there was one. We knew Ras Tsama was next to the emperor himself in standing and power, and we also knew we would not easily get past him.

It took three weeks of haggling to get permission from the old tough. Between him and our lop-eared interpreter, he became the recipient of one case of fine Cognac, fifty gold sovereigns, one good Westley Richards Mauser, one box of ammunition, fifteen camels, and our mules. The mules did not matter so much as they could not live in the swamp country below the plateau. Elephants were about the only animals that could exist there.

I must admit that once the insatiable robber had bled us white, he did us well. He gave us a guide who led us to the most appalling country. Once the guide had discharged his duties, he left us, and with all our Abyssinian boys he departed for the hills. They simply could not stand the mosquitoes of the low country. We, on our part, were glad to see the last of them.

Now that we were landed once again in good, new country, we had to seek some means of transport. The natives had very narrow dug-out canoes, and these we lashed together as we could not get our backsides into a single one. We now, finally, started hunting.

The big rains were on and the greatest difficulty we had was to find enough land above water for our tents. Everyone had a mosquito net. It would have been impossible to have lived without one. All the native villages were up on the drier ridges below the escarpment.

The grass was terrific, twelve-foot stuff and simply teeming with elephants. Nobody had ever hunted here in the big rains, and no native would go with us, for they hate the wet season. But we had our four Cook's Tourists, as we called my four boys from East Africa. Also we had four Yemen Arabs who hated the thought of crossing Abyssinia by themselves, so when they were offered their return across Abyssinia, they elected to stay with us. They were poor doers and suffered much.[2]

We were so encouraged by the size of the ivory and the quantity of elephants that when we had as much as we could carry on our flotilla, we decided we must get a stern-wheel steamer into this country and simply load it up with ivory whilst living aboard in great luxury. We knew that such steamers plied on the Nile at Khartoum. We knew Cook's had them. We would charter one and make a real job of it. Little did we know what lay ahead of us.

So one steamy day we loaded up all our tusks, only to find that we would have to jettison all sorts of gear to accommodate the ivory. As it was, we were dangerously overladen. The gentlest breeze sent wavelets lopping over the sides. Once we foundered in ten feet of water but managed to make shore

---

[2] In *Bell of Africa*, Bell called them "splendid fellows."

Bull elephants on the Pibor Flats of Soudan, north of Moru Akipi. (Sketch by W. D. M. Bell)

and get everything straightened out again. We made very poor speed in these conditions; more was it a matter of drifting with the current. Finally we reached the Pibor and then the Sobat and so into the Nile at Tawfikia.

Here was a large government post and here we met with a large packet of trouble. The authorities made it clear to us that they were annoyed.

"Why?" we asked in all innocence.

For one thing they were at war with the tribes through which we had peacefully drifted. They asked if we had been molested. We said, "No." This seemed to nettle them.

Reminiscences of an Elephant Hunter

The grass was terrific, twelve-foot-high stuff and simply teeming with elephants.

"Anyhow," they said, "you cannot go back."

"Why?" we asked.

"You just can't," they said. And they took a thumping big royalty on our ivory. Eight years elapsed before I got a refund of £150, representing, in their words, "a slight overcharge on ivory."

What a thundering nuisance these white governments are to perfectly harmless, peaceful travelers. We, the two of us, could have brought those tribes into friendly relations in a very short time. But no, the government must go traipsing around with soldiers armed to the teeth and then wonder why the savages are so unco-operative.

******

Plans had to be altered now. Gone were our visions of steamboats and giant elephant bulls. I now thought I would have a go at the Belgian Congo to see what the elephants were like there while Rayne would start that rubber plantation we had discussed.

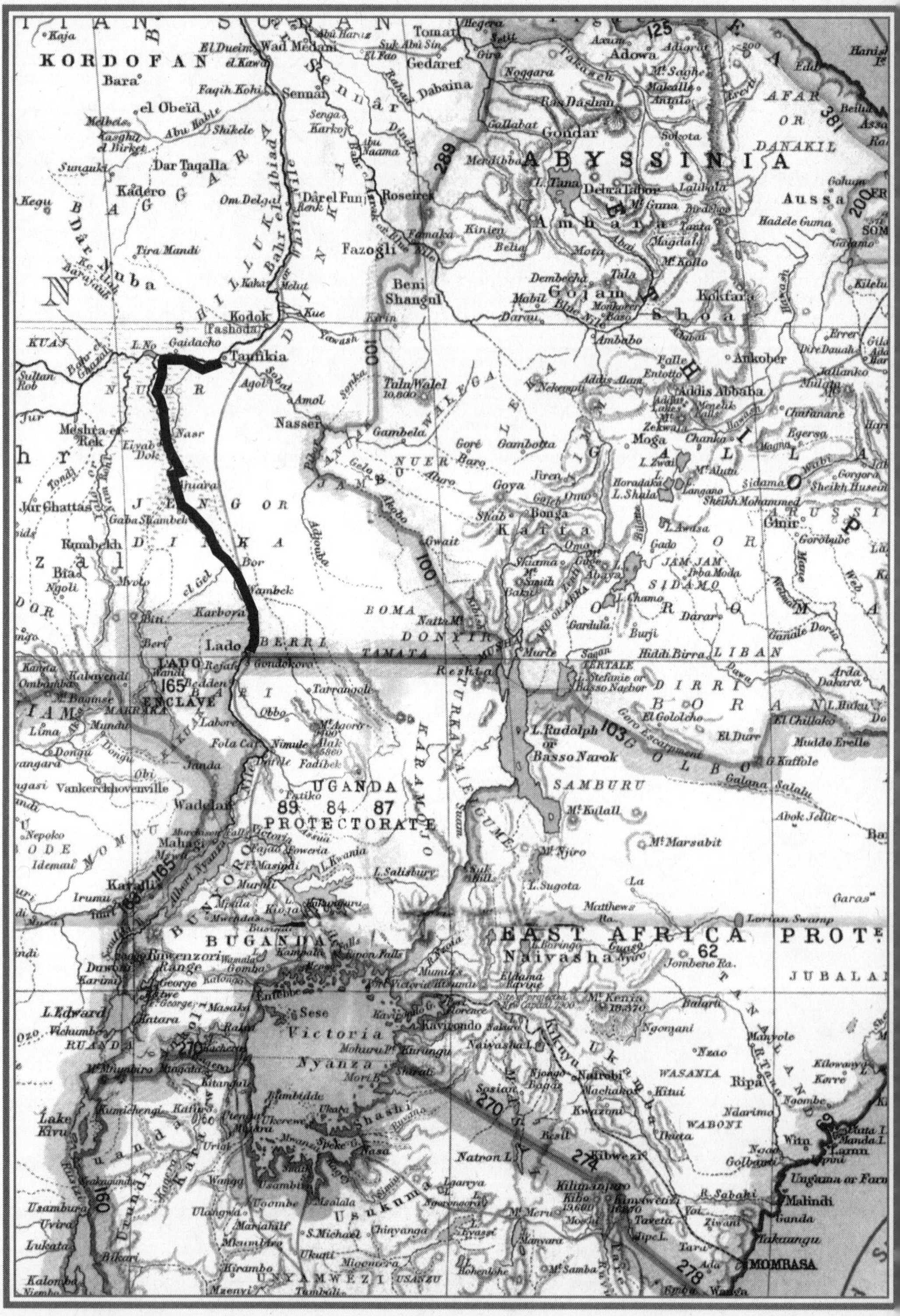

The Lado Enclave

CHAPTER 12

Arriving at Lado, Rayne continued on through Uganda while I applied for a permit to hunt in the Belgian Congo. By the time I got it—it cost only twenty pounds sterling for five months, which was a gift—it was the dry season. All the elephants in creation seemed concentrated in the huge Nile swamps. There was, however, plenty of other game, among them the so-called "white" rhino that were in fair numbers and lent interest to the landscape.

The west bank of the Nile had been leased by the British to King Leopold of the Belgians, but only for his lifetime. The deed or contract stipulated that on the king's death the Belgians should have six months in which to withdraw their installations. About this time (1909), the king died. The Belgians, who had nothing to withdraw, cleared out in a month and the whole of this territory, called the Enclave de Lado, lay unoccupied by white men with the sole exception of myself. I made good use of my fortune, of course, but it did not take long for the news to travel.

Hordes of people came in from every direction. All sorts and kinds of men—masons, builders, farmers, and even engineers—threw down their tools and legged it for the Lado Enclave. Fabulous stories got about of the enormous quantities of ivory. I myself stupidly helped set these rumours going. Having no idea of what was on the way, I landed a large number of tusks at a British post, hired the local natives to carry them from the landing place up to the station, and found that the line of tusk bearers neatly filled the space of about a mile. Had I known that a kind of gold rush was under way and that my mile-long parade of ivory would only fan the fever, I would have buried the stuff.

Most of these new-comers were novices at hunting and novices in the art of living peacefully with savages. Soon there were fearful doings. And nothing could be done about it. The Belgians had gone and the British could not take over until the expiration of the stipulated time. The natives, too, were now on their own. Their old oppressors had departed, and they did not care much for the new ones.

It was an astounding sight to see perfectly ordinary men, many of whom were what we call "family men," suddenly throw off all restraints of civilization to pillage, loot, violate, and, yes, even murder. Perhaps most of us are only decent because the law and the policeman keep us so. We have never developed within ourselves a code of behaviour that would enable us to live together decently—the Bobby does it all for us. Civilization, it would seem, is only skin deep, and below it lurks the savage.

This invasion of white men scared the wits out of the frontier posts of the Belgian Congo. Gold had recently been discovered at Kilo, on their side of the frontier, and they seemed to think this horde of armed men might at any moment start a Jameson Raid[1] on the gold fields. Consequently, they were very nervous and very trigger-happy.

******

When their lease of the Lado Enclave terminated, the Belgians were allowed by the British to retain access to Lake Albert, at the port of Mahagi. It would happen that one of my canoes, against my orders, put into this very spot. The Belgians had a strip only a mile wide, giving them the desired transport facilities. I had told my boys that on no account were they to touch at the Belgian's port but to pass it by. I had preceded them in my steel canoe.

The wind had come on to blow and quite a little sea rose on the lake, so my ruffians, who thought they knew better than I, dismissed my warnings and paddled gaily into the port. They were instantly seized by the Belgian authorities, and they and their—or, rather, my—safari gear were marched off up to the fort.

Meanwhile, I had gone ahead and saw nothing of this. I waited and waited and finally paddled back to see what had happened, visions of the canoe having foundered or been attacked by hippo vaguely coursing through my mind. Never once did it occur to me that they would put into the hornet's nest I had expressly warned them against.

In passing I kept sweeping the shores for any sign of my boys or the canoe. Crossing the mouth of Mahagi Port, my glasses revealed what looked

---

[1] The Jameson Raid (29 December 1895 to 2 January 1896) was a botched raid against the South African Republic (commonly known as the Transvaal) carried out by British colonial statesman Leander Starr Jameson and his company troops ("police" in the employ of Beit and Rhodes's British South Africa Company) and Bechuanaland policemen. Paul Kruger was president of the republic at the time. The raid was intended to trigger an uprising by the primarily British expatriate workers (known as Uitlanders) in the Transvaal but failed to do so. The workers were called the Johannesburg conspirators. They were expected to recruit an army and prepare for an insurrection. The raid was ineffective and no uprising took place, but it was an inciting factor in the Second Boer War and the Second Matabele War. It is easy to understand the Belgians' concern.

THE LADO ENCLAVE

While in the Enclave, I reached a truly wonderful country: high, cool, and with rolling hills. There were running streams of clear, cold water in every hollow, the sole bush a few forest trees lining their banks.

Reminiscences of an Elephant Hunter

In my nine months in the Lado Enclave, I bagged 210 elephants, with an average weight of tusk of twenty-seven pounds.

uncommonly like our big canoe lying deserted on the beach. Going in to investigate, I was met by Belgian native soldiers carrying arms. Not trusting them, I lay off a bit from the shore and parleyed in Ki-swahili, which one or two spoke. They told me to come ashore. I told them to release my safari instantly.

They returned to the fort that commanded a view of the bay from a height of perhaps four hundred feet. Presently they returned, but without any of my boys. Now whether the fort commandant had given them orders to start hostilities—I subsequently heard he was roaring drunk at the time—or whether they did so on their own will never be known.

At any rate, shooting started. When that happened, my boys broke out of the fort and took to the bush, all but one of them arriving back safely. They told me that when the shooting began all the soldiers and the white man seized their rifles and rushed out of the fort, leaving my boys unattended, so they had had no difficulty in escaping.

I suppose the Belgians thought, *This is it, another Jameson Raid!*

******

While in the Enclave, I reached a truly wonderful country: high, cool, and with rolling hills. There were running streams of clear, cold water in every hollow, the sole bush a few forest trees lining their banks. In the wet season the ground was covered with high, strong grass, but it was now burned off and the fresh, young green stuff was just coming along.

In the far distance could be seen from some of the higher places a dark line. This was the edge of "Darkest Africa," the great primeval forest spreading for thousands of square miles. Out of that forest, and elsewhere, had come hundreds upon hundreds of elephants to feed upon the tender green vegetation. They stood about the landscape as if made of wood and as if stuck there. Hunting was too easy. Beyond a few reed buck, there was no other game.

Soon natives flocked to our camps, and at one time there must have been three thousand in all. They were noisy and disturbed game, no doubt, but when it came to moving our ivory, they were indispensable. Without them we could not have budged.

******

In my nine months in the Lado Enclave, I bagged 210 elephants, with an average weight of tusk of twenty-seven pounds. Now, as the time approached for the British to once more take over the country, I knew it was necessary to look for new hunting grounds. I decided this was the time to pay a visit to Witu, in Kenya, where the great little Harry Rayne was planting our rubber.

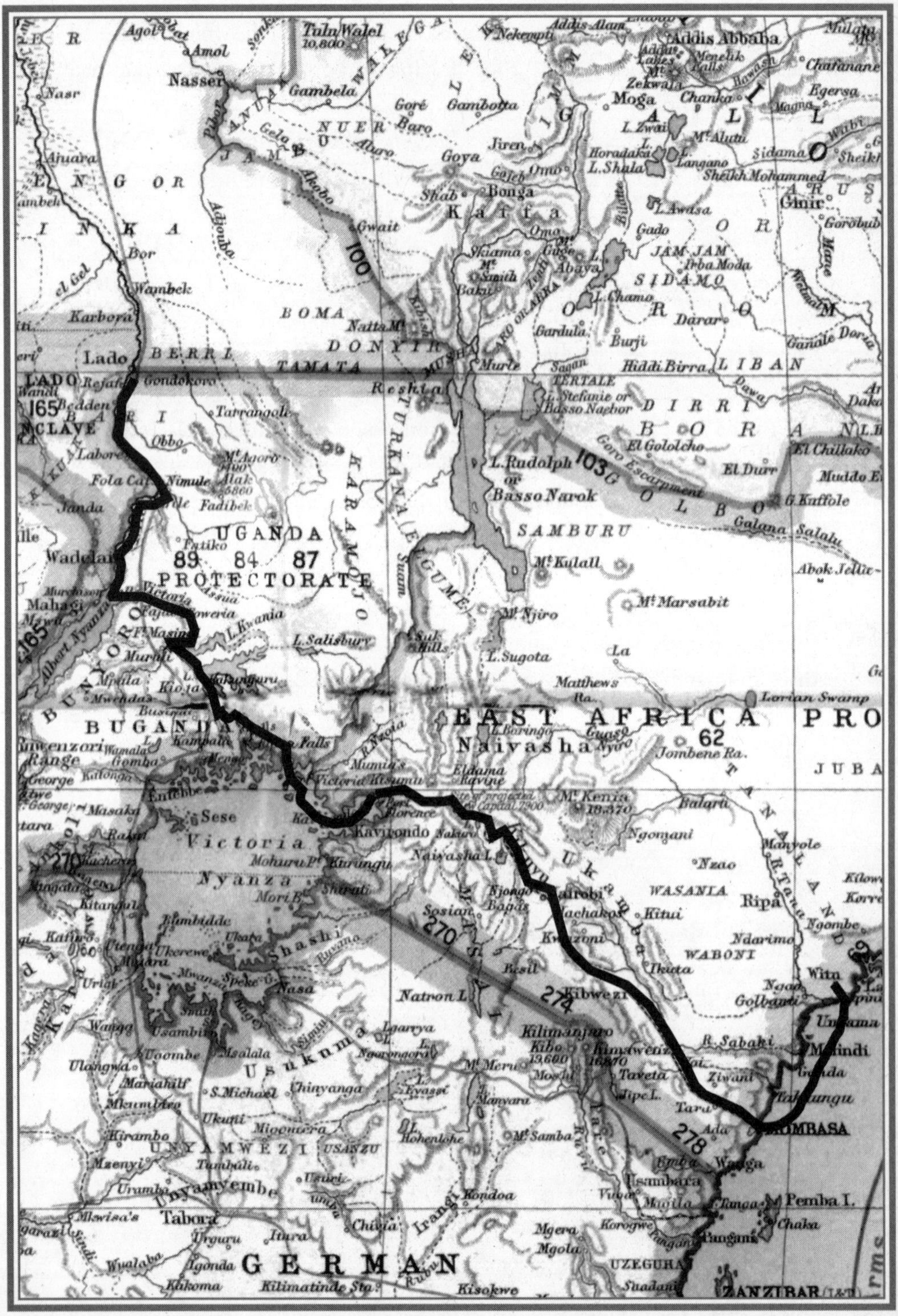

Addis Abbaba
Nasser
Gambela
Goré
Gambotta
Moga
Goya
Bonga
Lado
Gondokoro
LADO
ENCLAVE
Nimule
Wadelai
Mahagi
UGANDA
PROTECTORATE
89
84
87
165
100
103
62
270
274
278
L. Rudolph
or
Basso Narok
SAMBURU
Mt. Kulall
Mt. Marsabit
L. Salisbury
EAST AFRICA PRO
Naivasha
Mt. Kenia
Nairobi
BUGANDA
Victoria
Nyanza
Sese
Entebbe
Kavirondo
Kilimanjaro
Kibo
Natron L.
Witu
Malindi
MOMBASA
Pemba I.
ZANZIBAR
Tanga
Tabora
Unyanyembe
UNYAMWEZI
GERMAN
Lorian Swamp
JUBA
WASANIA
Ripa

Rubber and Whales, an Interlude

CHAPTER 13

In order to reach our newly projected rubber estate at Witu[1] on the East African coast, I had to traverse Uganda on foot. This was a journey of some twelve days. Then Lake Victoria had to be crossed by native canoe, camping each night on one of the deserted islands. All the population had been removed either by sleeping sickness or by government decree should they have survived the scourge. On this journey we were much bedeviled by waterspouts. The native paddlers showed a lively fear of this phenomenon, and, indeed, it looks formidable from the water level of a canoe.

When I arrived at Kisumu, I found the railway regularly operating to Mombasa on the coast. The trains, however, did not yet travel by night as the new track was still subject to displacement from elephants playfully lifting the whole thing with their trunks. At some of the stations, too, the stationmasters were sometimes besieged by lions on the platforms, and their telegraphed S.O.S.'s were often cut off by giraffes walking away with the wires tangled round their long necks.

Witu was then a more or less independent sultanate connected in some vague way with that of Zanzibar. All our dealings in connection with the plantation were conducted through the Sultan of Witu. He was a very good neighbour who often took tea with us, when he would expatiate at length on the virtues of ambergris as an aphrodisiac. As he was about eighty years old, had many wives, and had only recently added another to his harem, he spoke on the subject with some authority. He carried small pieces of the precious stuff in his embroidered waistcoat pocket.

Witu lies about sixty miles north of Mombasa, so to reach it I took passage on an Arab dhow. For a few rupees, the dhow agreed to put into the port of Lamu. The captain sat on a rickety white-man chair by the wheel—also of white-man make—and chewed betel nut the whole time, all the while spraying the surrounding deck with highly coloured saliva.

---

[1] Witu is a small market town in the Lamu county of Kenya, East Africa. Formerly it was the capital of the Witu Sultanate.

REMINISCENCES OF AN ELEPHANT HUNTER

On this journey we were much bedeviled by waterspouts—tornadoes that form over water.

All went well during the night as we discoursed on subjects close to the crew's calling. Inevitably the recent coup of a dhow skipper came up for discussion. This skipper had embarked one hundred labourers for the plantations north of Mombasa, been paid for their passages, and, instead of delivering them to their destination, had boldly put straight out into the Indian Ocean to eventually sell them as slaves in Arabia.

"They would be worth forty gold pounds apiece," the skipper told me.

Rubber and Whales, an Interlude

I asked him if the gunboat that was supposed to look out for this sort of thing bothered them much. He laughed and said the gunboat could not catch a dhow if the latter's bottom was clean. The Arabs smear them with fish oil to give them added speed as well as protection from the teredo, or naval shipworm. The whole affair was considered to be a great joke, slaving in any form being very dear to the Arab heart.

Whales were sighted, and they appeared to me to be sperm whales. The dhow men knew a lot about them and their habits. They said the whales went each year to the shallow waters round the Seychelles Islands to calve and were then very numerous. Seeing them playing around with their blunt tank-like heads well exposed gave me the idea that they might be killed by an accurately placed bullet in the brain.

Because the sperm whale is the only one that floats when dead, none of the usual cumbersome, costly, and elaborate gear for drawing them up to the surface and then inflating the carcass with air would be required. In fact, it seemed to me that all you would need was a fast sea-going launch from which to shoot, a large dhow fitted with try-works, and a gang of dhow men to do the dirty work. Besides oil, ambergris might be harvested, and that was fetching at auction four pounds sterling per ounce for the kind used as an aphrodisiac, down to a few shillings for the inferior grade stuff used by the perfumers.

I determined to look into this whaling project further. Meanwhile dawn was upon us, and half the crew were up the low-raking mast peering at the haze-shrouded shore evidently trying to determine our position. This was a matter of some importance, for should we overshoot the entrance to Lamu harbour, nothing that we could do would prevent our pointed tub from continuing on its northward drift.

After heated argument, a majority finally decided that the land we saw broad on our port bow was indubitably our destination. There was not a moment to lose if we were to make it. Up went the great towering sail with its gimcrack spar made up of mango trees lashed together with coir ropes, and off we headed toward shore. No sooner were we moving smartly through the water than the rudder fell off, disappearing rapidly astern. This would have been regarded as a major disaster on any other kind of ship, but not so here.

Down came the sail with a run while about thirty boys dived straight overboard to retrieve the sportive rudder, a massive timber affair. Soon it was being propelled toward us by the combined efforts of the laughing crew while various bits and pieces of coir rope appeared ready to lash it in place again. The way in which everyone seemed to know exactly what to do made me suspect this was no rare occurrence. Meanwhile, the inexorable current continued to push us past our proper landfall with every moment making it more difficult of attainment.

Soon the lash-up was completed, and the race against time and current was resumed. We just scraped in by the barest margin, but I shall always remember that incident as the finest exhibition of seamanship I have ever seen. I parted from these merry mariners with warm feelings of admiration, and soon after arrived at Witu Rubber Estate, Harry's and my joint venture into the commercial world of rubber production.

It was just like coming home. I had been living for years the nomad life of a hunter, here to-day gone to-morrow, with nothing more permanent than a tent and an antheap oven sometimes. But now I found all the evidences of a permanent living place. Harry had done marvels. He had built a good, solid thatched house of sun-baked brick with a wide, shady veranda all around and with a novel arrangement whereby air circulated through the interior. The thing was eminently suited to the tropics and stood out far ahead of the usual abominations white men erect for themselves in new lands.

Harry had made our abode most homelike by having pet animals all over the place: a goat that unexpectedly butted you in the bottom, a lemur that sprang out of the shade onto your shoulders, or an ostrich that craned its neck from behind you to pick up and swallow the spoon from your coffee cup.

In honour of our re-union, Rayne had opened a box of luxuries, one of which was a Stilton cheese, a very precious item. Unfortunately, the smell from the fruity contents of the jar had persuaded the boys that it had gone bad, so bad, indeed, they thought that not even white men would eat it. After one whiff they had unanimously condemned it and had thrown it out . . . to be devoured by the all-consuming ostrich, who had promptly swallowed it, jar and all.

All around the house enchanting vistas of long, regular lines of growing rubber trees met the eye, while the tall slender coconut palms swayed and rustled in the moist monsoon wind. It was the time of the great rubber boom, and as we walked among our rows of growing trees we thought what a nice thing to have in our old age.

Soon, however, the peace and quietness began to pall on me. I wanted to get back to the *barra* (wilderness) or at least to something more active than the drowsy watching of growing trees amidst the regular siestas of the tropics, to say nothing of the sex-laden nights. With nothing to occupy me, once more that brain shot for sperm whales rose in my mind.

One day a runner from Lamu brought news that a white visitor awaited transport. Who he might be we had no idea. Rayne sent off a riding mule and a few boys to bring in the stranger. On arrival, the stranger turned out to be a young man from London Town. He was interested in rubber and went all over our holding. He then asked, "Are you interested in selling?"

We thought about it a bit and then said, "Certainly . . . for the right price."

His name was Ambrose; it would be. He said his father was on the Stock Exchange, and he was on the look-out for rubber estates. He said that if we agreed, his father had the idea to float Witu Rubber into a company. Although we had never contemplated selling our rubber estate—indeed, we had gone into the business for our retirement—he soon persuaded us to sell with the glib financial talk of his kind. He told us that he would leave straight-away for London, and if things went as anticipated, he would cable us. We were to receive £10,000 in cash and £15,000 in shares.

Off he beetled, and in due course we got a cable to say he had pulled off the deal. We went to London and everything was all right. True, we had some difficulty in getting the cash from the firm. Its address was Old Jewry, London.

Having so successfully pulled that one off, we thought we would buy land at Kismayu on the Juba River, thus repeating the performance. Here again we just missed making our fortunes. The land that we developed was later given by our government to the Italians—compensation number one from the donors and compensation number two from the recipients. Unfortunately, one Gabriel from Manchester bought us out before these pleasant transactions, and it was he who reaped the benefit. Marvelous how they do it!

Meanwhile I went into the sperm-whale-hunting-from-speed-boat project. While I was in London, I studied everything I could find anent the sperm whale, including a large skeleton at a museum there. As far as I could see, there was nothing to prevent a man from killing a sperm whale with a shot into the brain using an ordinary rifle. I also purchased a boat that would keep the sea and would be fast enough. That was my hope, anyway.

Although my idea was to rifle-shoot the leviathan in the brain, I knew so little about the whaling business that I was easily persuaded to mount an orthodox harpoon gun in the bow of the whaler. This gun proved a fearsome

Reminiscences of an Elephant Hunter

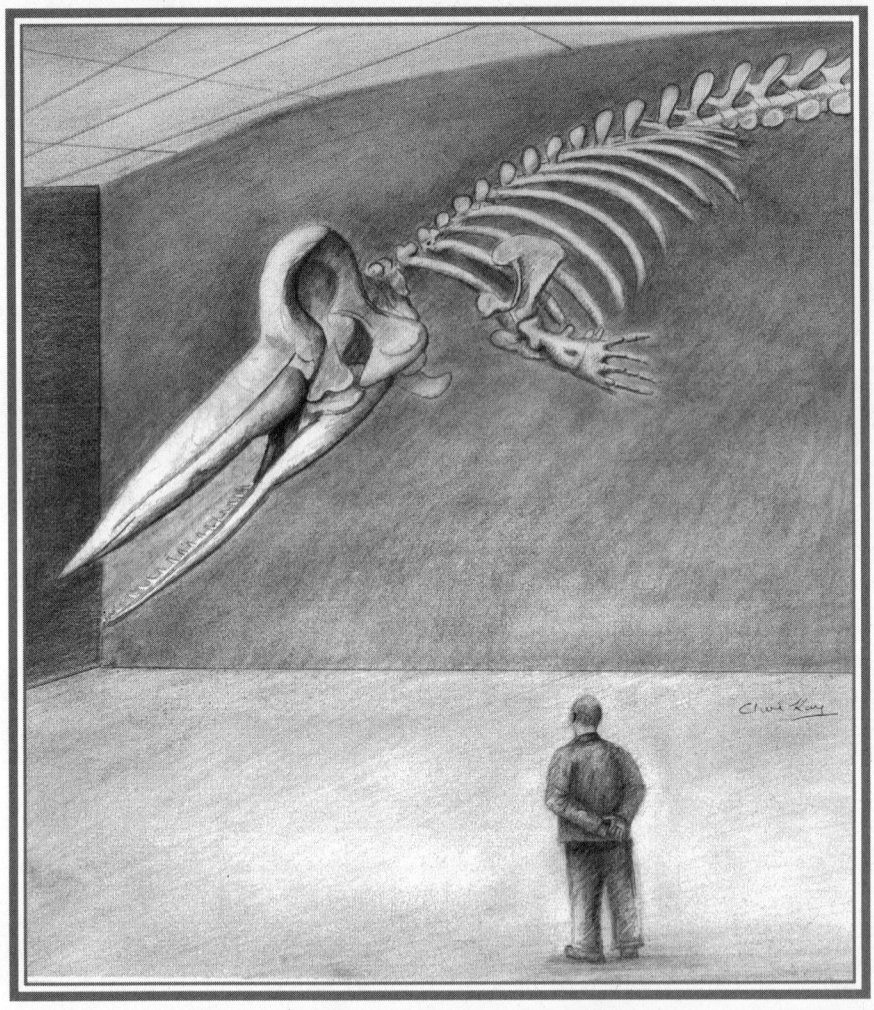

I went to London and studied everything I could find anent the sperm whale, including a large skeleton at a museum there.

affair, and I had many difficulties with it initially. When we had overcome teething troubles, we tried our set-up out on porpoises. We found these nimble creatures rather too nimble, in fact, and we lost several harpoons while practicing on them. So we looked for bigger game and again found them difficult targets. These were dolphins, and although they measure up to ten feet in length and were numerous, we found them also exceedingly hard to hit with the ponderous weapon.

Rubber and Whales, an Interlude

Even on whales of eighty- to one-hundred-foot length, expert whale gunners register many misses and badly placed shots. But I felt consoled by the thought of using the brain shot on those enormous sperm heads, especially as I had had extensive experience with this shot on elephants. I saw no reason why the brain of a whale should not be reached by an ordinary rifle bullet.

To test this out on dolphins was easy, but not knowing the exact whereabouts of the brain, I registered a few misses with but little harm done to the cetaceans. It required fast, accurate shooting on a very fleeting target from such a lively platform as the bow of a small boat. When the shot was successful, the dolphin turned over and sank, the gleam of its whitish belly shewing [archaic for showing] through the water the only indication that the shot had registered.

From these slight experiences I was quite satisfied that sperm whales would prove to be vulnerable to this form of attack, and I was on the point of departure on the long journey out to the Seychelles Islands when I got news that a Norwegian whaling company had acquired the whaling rights there.[2]

They were cunning whalers, these Norwegians. Of course, they undertook this operation in a big way. They started up a shore station and they invested in steam chasers that were able to handle any kind of whale. The investment on their Seychelles establishment paid enormous dividends, and soon they were busy raking in the huge profits I had thought might be mine.

I was about six months too late, so, cutting my losses, I determined to resume once more the search for good elephant grounds. This time it led me to Liberia, the Black Republic of West Africa.

---

[2] For the complete story, see chapter 28 of this book.

SAHARA
DÉSERT
EL DJOUF
AFRIQUE OCC
MAURITANIE
ADRAR
TAGANT
HODH
SAHEL
KAARTA
SOUDAN
FOUTA
BAMBOUK
SÉNÉGAL
GAMBIE
GUINÉE FRANÇAISE
SIERRA LEONE
LIBERIA
CÔTE D'IVOIRE
HAUTE
Port Étienne
C. Blanc
B. d'Arguin
Atar
Tidjikdja
Oualata
Tombouctou
Nioro
Kayes
Kita
Bamako
Ségou
San
Sikasso
Bobo Dioulasso
Labé
Boké
Kankan
Kong
Conakry
Freetown
Monrovia
Bingerville
Kumasi
Harper
C. des Palmes
Côte des Graines
Côte de l'Ivoire

Liberia, Where the Black Man Rules

Chapter 14

Bell told the story of his excursion into Liberia in both Wanderings of an Elephant Hunter *and* Bell of Africa. *While the events are largely the same in this chapter as they are in these two books, there are elements in this version not found elsewhere. Inclusion was also necessary to provide continuity to Bell's life story for the reader.*

In 1911 the search for new hunting grounds led me to Liberia, the independent black republic founded in 1822 by American philanthropists for the settlement of freed slaves. I landed at Sinoe Town, south of Monrovia, the capital, and immediately saw that things were different here. Nowhere in the Africa of that day was the white man the underdog except in Liberia and in Menelik's Abyssinia.

The moment I stepped ashore I witnessed the way in which any attempt to evade or disregard black rule was quickly and forcibly resented. I saw a white being held powerless by a crowd of natives. The man's face seemed familiar, so I took a closer look and was astonished to recognise one of the officers of the tramp steamer from which I had just disembarked. He cursed incoherently when I asked him what was the trouble.

Just then a very polite native official in blue uniform and badge cap informed me that the officer had struck a native and that he would have to go before the magistrate. The officer was then dragged before the beak, who promptly fined him twenty-five dollars and the ship's captain fifty dollars, although the latter had not left his ship!

This made me wonder what I had let myself in for. I found, however, that the man in uniform was the local Customs official, and he was extremely courteous and anxious to pass my gear without delay. He seemed to have absolute power and let me off very lightly indeed, even suggesting I might be a scientific mission for all he knew to the contrary. I always treated the Liberians politely and as a result was always treated politely by them.

Cleared through Customs, I looked out for a lodging of some sort. There were no hotels, of course, but I found an Englishman who represented a rubber company. He very kindly put me up. The white community was comprised of my host and one German. My host, whom I will call B.,[1] was much interested in my proposed expedition into the interior. He told me frankly that I would have a devil of a time, for he said the jurisdiction of the Liberians extended inland for only ten miles; beyond that the original natives held sway. They had guns and a few rifles, were constantly at war with each other, and sold their captives on the coast.

B. advised me to call on the governor, and he strongly suggested that I take him a suitable present. He recommended a case of beer and a case of kola wine, the governor being partial to a weird mixture of these beverages. He also told me that if I pressed a golden sovereign into the governor's hand, I should get a permit to hunt elephants.

In order to present the governor with his gift, I first had to engage a boy or two. B. said I could either hire them or buy them, explaining that slavery was rampant. He said alcoholism was so prevalent and widespread that scarcely any children were born to the Liberians, so they simply bought bush children from the warring tribes of the hinterland and adopted them.

B. was going to a dance that night and asked if I would go with him. I agreed but later on was surprised to see B. in full evening dress. He explained that everyone dressed for these dances. That was awkward for I had not brought my evening clothes, but B. said it would be all right. As we were changing, a fine buxom black girl burst into our house, marched right upstairs, and threw B.'s door open, revealing B. in his shirt only.

I closed my door but could hear her engaging B. for some dances. Then my door was thrown open. I was far from dressed myself, and something about my appearance seemed to tickle the lady immensely, for she went into peals of the jolliest laughter. She spoke English with a strong American accent, as nearly all the Liberians do. Turning the place upside-down, she left us after promising to dance that night with me. I hastened to ask B. what they danced. He told me they liked waltzing best.

After dinner we sauntered off to a large barn where a musical din denoted the dance. Here was a fine lay-out. Lavish refreshments consisting of cakes, cold pork, gin, and beer were provided free for all. Everyone was in tremendous

---

[1] In *Bell of Africa*, this man is referred to as "R." In Bell's two versions of his autobiography and in *Wanderings of an Elephant Hunter*, this man is referred to as "B."

spirits. The girls were nearly all in white or pink dresses, but not very décolleté. A tall, coal-black gentleman in full evening dress was master of ceremonies, but introductions seemed unnecessary.

Round the refreshments gathered the old men, some in frock coats of a very ancient cut, others in more modern garments. I was hospitably pressed to drink. The musicians drank without any pressing. Everybody drank, women and all. What added to the hilarity of the gathering was the fact that the fines imposed on the steamer captain and his officer had paid for the feast. German export beer and Hamburg potato spirit cost only a few pence per bottle then, and the dance became a debauch, seasoned drinkers though they were.

The din and heat became terrific. Starched linen soon turned to limp rags. The fun became fast and furious, with no thought of the inevitable head-sufferings on the morrow. I shall always remember the hurricane wildness of that night and the incongruity of shining black faces atop bizarre white-man clothing as something that could only have happened in Liberia, the borderland of the savage and civilized worlds.

Next day I set off to visit the governor with my cases of beer and kola wine. Bush with clearings planted with coffee describes the country between the town and the residency, which was situated in a large coffee plantation. The house was of lumber construction and two stories high, well-built and the largest I had yet seen.

I marched up to the front door, followed by B.'s two boys carrying the present, and was met immediately by a splendid-looking old black. He was very tall and dressed in a long black frock coat, high starched collar, and black cravat. With snow-white hair and an Uncle Sam beard with accent to match, he received me in a really kind and hearty manner.

I must confess I was a bit embarrassed as I stood there fingering a few hot sovereigns in my pocket with my two cases of cheap liquor in the background. However, the bluff old fellow soon put me at my ease. Seeing the stuff out there on the boys' heads, he beckoned them in, helped them to lower their loads, shouted to someone to come and open the boxes, sent the boys in to get a drink, and ushered me into his sitting room, all in the jolliest manner possible. Here we talked a bit, and I told him what I wanted.

A permit to hunt elephant! He roared with laughter. The idea seemed to tickle him immensely. Of course, I should have a permit. He wrote it there and then. That it was quite inoperative ten miles inland was, perhaps, what really tickled the old gentleman. But he did not try to sting me.

"You'll stop for dinner?"

I said I would be delighted. Then we had beer and kola mixed drinks until lunch was announced. Now the old boy threw off his coat and cravat, inviting me to do likewise. In the dining room there was a long trestle table laid for about twenty people with a white tablecloth, cutlery, and all the accoutrements of good dining. As we seated ourselves, in trooped some enchanting little black girls all dressed neatly in clean print dresses, with arms, necks, and legs bare. Then Mrs. Governor appeared with some larger girls. After shaking hands, we all sat down to a very substantial meal.

It was all perfectly charming. Everyone was at ease. The old man was an excellent host and the old lady just as good a hostess. Conversation never flagged. The host was full of his brother's doings. It appeared that his brother was a lazy, good-for-nothing fellow who would let his cows stray onto his neighbours' plantations.

My host had repeatedly remonstrated, but without effect. So that morning on seeing some marauding cows, he had got his shot-gun and rendered at least one incapable of further depredations. This act had stirred his brother profoundly, but in an unusual way, for he could be heard for miles bawling religious songs from his bedroom window. Whenever there was a lull during lunch, we could hear the monotonous chant. This appeared to amuse my host immensely.

All the girls were called their children, but the old couple were quite childless and these were adopted bush children from the interior. My host told me that he had been a slave in the Southern States and could well remember being flogged.

He said elephants were numerous in the interior, as also were "bush cows," the small reddish-brown buffaloes. He said the natives were a rough lot and had plenty of guns; he also told me that Liberia was almost constantly at war with them. The tribesmen had recently raided a neighbouring town, looted the stores, got roaring drunk, seized the governor, stripped and tarred and feathered him, and enjoyed themselves generally.

When the Liberians set up Customs to levy duty on imports, they very soon found that a thriving smuggling racket sprang up. Steamers would stand off-shore and sell overboard to clouds of canoes for spot cash or gold dust whole cargoes of gin, gunpowder, percussion caps, and articles of general trade.

Liberia, Where the Black Man Rules

All the girls were called their children, but the old couple was quite childless and these were adopted bush children from the interior.

To stop this, the republic bought an old steam yacht that had once belonged to Leopold of the Belgians. They installed a gun on her, engaged a white as captain, and told him to stop the smuggling and pay himself while doing so. He succeeded in doing both.

Having got the permit and some boys together, I was soon on the road. Now I would get a glimpse of Africans on their own. The Liberians were civilized, but now I was to see Africans without any such background, armed with firearms and quite without any sort of government.

On the whole conditions were not as bad as one might have expected. There was no great fighting or killing going on. True, there were exchanges of shots. But the easy-going African can do a lot of that without doing much harm. He is a lazy man when on his own. The chief activity of these Africans seemed to be directed toward snaffling children to sell on the coast. At the very first camp I was offered a slave, a very nice one, too. Also gold dust, but it was largely mixed with brass filings.

As usual, when they grasped the fact that I was only after elephant, I was welcomed everywhere. At first they thought my rifle was too small to kill an elephant, but when I sent a bullet through a tree, they thought it might be worthwhile to try me out. Once I had killed an elephant, the trouble was over; the whole country then wanted me to come and hunt for them. In fact, my success made it difficult to get out of the country. Once I realized the ivory ran too small, however, I determined to once more resume the search for new country.

The village from which I had done so much hunting had acquired great riches with the meat I had given them. In spite of this, or, perhaps, because of this, they showed strong opposition to my going. At first I paid no attention to their protests, continuing calmly with my preparations for departure, weighing and marking my ivory. When my loads were ready, I announced my intention of leaving on the morrow. This was a mistake. What I should have done was to have kept my intention entirely to myself, then suddenly to have fallen in the boys, shouldered the loads, and marched off. All would then have been well.

As it was, when the morrow came, the boys did not. They could not be found . . . and I could not move without them. I found the village headman, accused him of playing this mean trick, and demanded the boys. He then tried all the persuasions he could think of to induce me to stay. He offered me any woman I fancied. This is always the first inducement in the African mind. Slaves, food, anything I wanted if I would only stay.

I got angry and cursed him and threatened to shoot up the town. He said quietly that the king was coming, and I could talk to him. Meanwhile I had to wait. I was furious.

I became suspicious, and the belief that they were after my ivory began to poison my mind. I argued with myself that they knew the value of ivory, that they knew what a lot of gin and trade goods they would get if they sold my tusks on the coast. And a white man, a hunter of elephants, "done in," what would it matter? People would say, "Serves him right," probably. Then my suspicion turned to my rifle. I convinced myself they wanted it. They had seen it kill elephants with one shot. It had wonderful "medicine."

Curious how near I came to wanting to shoot someone. But that would not have helped matters. Then sense and experience came to the fore and . . . I laughed. As soon as I laughed, they laughed. I felt master of the situation.

"Where was the king?" I asked.

"Drinking beer," I was told.

"Let me talk to him," I stated.

I sat down in front of my hut. In a short time the king arrived with an escort of some forty guns. He seated himself in front of a hut directly across the street from me. I would have shaken hands with him, but I did not wish to take my rifle with me, nor did I wish to leave it behind me, as it was to play a part in the plan I had determined to try.

No one could reach me from the back as I leant against the wall of the hut. I assumed a belligerent attitude from the first, demanding to know why all my boys had been taken. The old king was, luckily, still sober—it being early in the day—and very calm and dignified. After I had stated my demand for their instant return, the king replied. He said that his people had shown me elephant; that without them I could not have found them. He said his people had treated me well. They had offered me wives of my own choosing. Food I had never lacked. Elephants were still numerous in the bush. Why should I wish to desert them in this manner?

I admitted that all he had said was true, but I begged to point out that I was not a black man. I could not live there always among them. White men died when they remained too long in the tropics and so on. Then I pointed to the fact that I had never sold the meat of the elephant I had killed, although I might have done so and bought slaves and guns with it. I had given it all freely to him among others, and now when I wanted to go, he had seized my porters.

Then he tried another tack. He said I could go freely if I gave him my rifle. He said I could easily get another in my country. I turned this suggestion down so emphatically that he switched to another approach.

He said that when black men went to the coast they had to pay customs duty on everything they took to or brought away from it. This was entirely a white man's custom and yet they enforced it upon black men, putting them in prison if they did not pay. He, therefore, would be obliged to make me pay a duty on my ivory. He thought that if he and I divided it equally, it would be a fair thing. At this I could not help laughing. The king smiled and everyone smiled. I suppose they thought I was going to pay.

"But," I said, "there is a difference between your country and white man's country. When a traveler arrives at the gates of the white man's country, the very first thing he sees is a long building and on it the magic sign 'Customs.' Now on seeing this sign, the traveler knows what lies before him. If he objects to paying customs, or if he has not the money with which to pay, he departs without entering that country.

"But when the traveler reaches the gates of the king's country, he looks in vain for a 'Customs sign.' Therefore, he says to himself, *what a very wise and good king rules this happy country. I will enter, for there is no 'Customs.'* But if, having entered the country on this understanding, the king levies 'Customs' without having a 'Customs House,' that traveler will recall what he said about the king and will depart, cursing that king and spreading his ill-fame so that no more travelers or elephant hunters will come near him.

"Therefore," I ended, "the whole matter resolves itself into this: Have you a Customs House or have you not?"

Here I peered diligently about as if searching among the huts. The whole lot—king, court, escort, and mob—roared with laughter.

They were not done yet, though. The palaver ran its usual interminable length. The king accused me of disposing of the pygmy hippo meat in an illegal manner. Pygmy hippo were royal game and every bit of it should have been sent to him. I had him again with the same gag as the Customs one, i.e., that when he made a law he should write it down for everyone to read, or if he could not write, he should employ some boy who could. And so on and on it went.

Wearied to exhaustion, I determined to see what a little bluff would do. I had hoped that I would not have to use it, but it was now or never. If it came off, and the porters were forthcoming, we could just make the next village, hostile to this king, before dark.

Suddenly seizing my rifle I covered the king. No one moved. The king took it very well, I must say. I said I was going to fight for my porters and begin on the king.

He said that to fight was a silly game. However well I shot, I could not kill more than ten of them before someone got me. I replied that that was so, but that no one knew if he would be among the ten or not.

That did the trick. They gave up. I kept the old king covered and told him not to move until the porters arrived. He sent off runners at once. They came on the run, picked up the loads, and began to march. I stopped a moment to shake hands with the king, and the insatiable old rascal begged for at least some tobacco. I felt so relieved and pleased at seeing my loads on the road at last that I promised him some when we caught up with the safari.

******

B. told me on my arrival back at the coast that during my absence in the interior the inspector of his company had come on a visit straight from London. He had started from the coast with head carriers to visit another of their trading posts. He had been promptly arrested, carried before the magistrate, and fined twenty-five dollars for traveling on the Sabbath.

The fine had been paid and someone sent off to purchase gin. The magistrate knocked the neck off a bottle, took a pull at it, and then offered it to the prisoner. B. explained that the inspector had been very haughty with the Liberians, and they were out to get their own back.

It must not be thought that they are unfriendly toward whites. If treated politely, they are very nice people; indeed, they will do anything to help. But they must be treated just as if they were ordinary white foreigners. I liked them immensely; they were great fun. I regretted having to leave their country, and I only did so because the ivory ran so small.

El-Goléa
El-Erg
Ghadamès
Plateau de Tademaït
Touat
In-Salah
Tidikelt
Timassinin
Tassili des Azdjer
Mourzouk
Rhat
FEZZAN
Gatroun
Plateau de Mouydir
Atakor n-Ahaggar
Adzjer
Mts de Tummo
Ouallen
Bîr el-Gharama
Tummo
TOUAREG
Tassili des Ahaggar
Bîr Assiou
Os Djébado
GRAND DÉSERT
Os de Yat
Tao
TIBES
Aouelimmiden
Tin-Telloust
Oasis de Kaouar
Adrar el-Ghebli
AÏR
Os de Bilma
Os d'Agadem
Agadès
Gogo
Songhaï
Bourré
DAMERGHOU
LAC TCHAD
Tessaoua
Zinder
Barroua
Mao
Abechr
Kabbabich
Kobeh
EGYPTIEN
Fodja
KORDOFAN
GOURMA
Saï
Vournou
Sokoto
Katséna
Kouka
Bari
OUADAÏ
Kolkol
El-Facher
Ouaghadougou
GANDO
Kebbi
Kano
Ngornou
Yaoua
Midogo
L. Fitri
Tourah
Martafal
Darra
Taouaïcha
Fada-Ngourma
Gomba
HAOUSSA
BORNOU
Dikoa
Karnak-Logone
Massenya
BAGHIRMI
DARFOUR
Chekka
Sansanné-Mango
Yaouri
SOKOTO
DAR-ROUNA
Dongo
Taïmo
Boussa
Kouandé
Rapides
BORGOU
Yakoba
Yola
Marroua
L. Iro
Hofrah en-Nahas
Pays des Rivières
Rabba
Bida
Keffi
Mouri
Mt Alantika
Laï
El-Kouti
DAR-FERTIT
Mechra er-Rek
NOUPÉ
Ilorin
YOROUBA
Loko
Bénoué
Korero
Goundi
DAHOMEY
Ibadan
Abeokouta
Lokodja
Youkari
Katsena
ADAMAOUA
Mpoko
Dem Ziber
Roumbek
TOGO
Lagos
Ado
BÉNIN
KOROFA
Ngaoundéré
Yagoussou
Ganda
Onitcha
Tibati
Kounde
HAUT OUBANGHI
DAR-BANDA
Ombanga
Côte des Esclaves
Delta du Niger
CAMEROUN
Creek Town
Kémo
Bangasson
Zemio
Mt Cameroun
Banghi
Ouadda
Ndorouma
Akassa
Calabar
Cameroun
Zongo
Abiras
Djabbir
Nyam
I. Fernando-Po (E)
Sta Isabel
Bama
Ouellé
Makoua
Bé de Biafra
Batanga
Nyong
Oupoto
Roubi
Tangasi
GOLFE DE GUINÉE
R. Campo
Mt Goumendjoko
Mobéka
Congo
Ngoko
Ouesso
I. du Prince (P)
San Benito
C. St Jean
Mts de Cristal
Mfang
Hokou
Basongo
Arouhouimi
Yambouya
Itouri
I. et Bé de Corisco (E)
Libreville
CONGO
Bangala
Loulongo
ÉTAT
Falls Station
Chûtes de Stanley
Sangha
I. St Thomé (P)
Gabon
Ogooué
Njolé
Madiville ou Lastoursville
Equateurville
Tchouapa
Lac Albert Edouard
C. Lopez
Lambaréné
Lirranga
L. Mantoumba
Lomami
I. Annobom (E)
Opika
INDÉPENDANT
Francevilla
Lékéti
Loukoléla
L. Léopold II
L. Kivou
Olenda
FRANÇAIS
L. Rougourou
Riba-Riba
Mayoumba
Makabana
Makaka
Bena Kamba
DU CONGO
Tchilounga
Brazzaville
Stanley-Pool
Loukenyé
Kassaï
Sankourou
Nyangoué
Kasongo
Loango
Léopoldville
Ibanchu
Lousambo
Landana
Cabinda
Boma
Manyanga
Louebo
Kapouka
Moussomba
Kabambarre
Banana
Matadi
C. Padrao
CONGO
ROYME DU MOUATA-YAMVO KASONGO
Kikassa
Loulouabourg
Loupoungou
Loukouga
Ankoro
Mpala
Ambrizette
Kilouata
Makiyombo
Bembé
Ambriz
Encoje
LOANDA
Rme DE CHINGA
ROYME DU MOUATA YAMVO (LOUNDA)
Kisiméné
KASONGO
Kilemba
L. Kassali
St Paul de Loanda
Ambaca
Kadinga
Mona Kissenghé
L. Moero
Punta das Palmeirinhas
ROYME DU MSIRI
ANGOLA
ATLANTIQUE
TANGANIKA
FRANÇAISE SOMALI
MER ROUGE
Cheikh Saïd
I. Périm
Dét. de Bab-el-Mandeb
GOLFE D'ADEN
Obock
Ras Bir
Tadjoura
Is Moucha
Ras Djibouti
Zeila
SOMALIE ANGLAISE
ATLANTIC
SOUTH
Ascension
St Helena
Tristan da Cunha
Nigeria
French Congo
Congo State
ABYSSINIA
Sudan
Algeria
Tripoli
PERSIA
Madagascar
Cape Town
Port Elizabeth
East London

French Equatorial Africa

CHAPTER 15

There is no doubt about it, the French are the greatest lovers of individual freedom, and the best practicers of it, in the whole world. And not only for themselves. They wish to extend the hand of freedom to everyone—well, almost everyone. The French government makes laws as plentifully as the next government, but each separate Frenchman judges whether he shall obey that law or not.

When I landed at Brazzaville on the Congo in French Equatorial Africa in 1912 and said I wanted to hunt elephants, I was metaphorically clapped on the shoulder and told, "Bravo! Why not?" instead of being met with suspicion and reserve. Great lads, the French. I like them immensely.

I was told to make for Bangui, on the River Ubangi. I went up the Congo River into its tributary, the Ubangi, on a small stern-wheel river steamer captained by a Dane named Larsen. Of course, we burned wood and stopped frequently to replenish our fuel stock. I made a friend for life of Larsen by killing some hippo for him. He told me the islands were full of elephants at certain seasons. I asked him to lend me a boat so that I could have a look.

I landed on a sandy spit at one end of a near-by island and literally had not gone ten paces into the heavy forest when I came face-to-face with a large bull elephant. I could hardly believe my eyes. I killed him instantly and then returned to the boat and hailed the steamer. Larsen sent a gang to cut up the so-precious meat. Because the people of that part exist on a staple diet of cassava root, meat is simply priceless.

In fact, cassava is so deficient in protein that its consumption leads to a fearful craving for meat. If it is not forthcoming, cannibalism is practised. While the gang was at work, I made an examination of the bush; there were signs of heavy elephant traffic. They were all bulls, too. The ivory was forest stuff but quite promising.

I stored this incident away in my memory. There were heaps of islands but one would require to have water-borne transport to work them properly. I amused myself with plans for such a lay [vessel], and subsequently there emerged an order to my agent in Scotland to get me a small steamer, built in sections weighing not more than one hundred and twenty pounds each, that would steam on green wood, and to hurry it up and ship it out to me at Bangui. I knew it would be about a year before I got it. Meanwhile, I had an immense country to explore.

During my hunts for elephants in the French Congo [Ubangi-Shari], I had many varied and interesting experiences. Some of these incidents included my introduction to a species of game new to me—the man-eating leopard. I found myself next to villages that were notorious for the disappearance of people under mysterious circumstances, and I saw with my own eyes the consequences of protein deprivation—cannibalism. It was but a short stretch from there to realize that there were human man-eaters at work in the region. My understanding of the suggestive power of witch doctors grew accordingly. I hunted elephants on islands, and I led fire-driven hunts for elephants, which has to be among the most exciting hunts ever. I realized my dream of hunting with the Pygmies, and I found a land devoid of humans because of the fear of evil spirts roaming there.[1]

******

From the forest regions I now broke new country up on the watershed between the Shari River system running into Lake Chad and the Congo system. The pursuit of elephants landed me in a predicament. Without knowing it, I had entered a concession area. These concessions are private trusts that were arranged in Paris with the aid of very incomplete maps, and it was frequently difficult to know when you had entered a closed region.

I had collected some ivory when there arrived in my camp a representative of a French concessionaire. He demanded that I sell to him all ivory from elephants killed in the concession, and although I was quite willing to get rid of my stuff, indeed anxious to do so, he named such a ridiculously low price that I refused.

He finally left camp, but six or so weeks later I received a summons to appear with my ivory at the court in Bangui, about three weeks' journey from where I then was. The concessionaire had decided to make a test case of this affair. When I arrived in Bangui, his directors tried to frighten me by saying they would carry the case as far as Paris if necessary. They had no idea of what was about to happen.

---

[1] All these stories can be found in *Incidents from an Elephant Hunter's Diary*.

The native judge before whom the case was to be tried was of pure African stock and had been graduated from the University of Paris with honours. The day before the trial he looked into the concession deeds and found nothing that gave the concessionaire any right to buy from a white man. The directors only had the right to buy from the natives of the concession. Knowing that I was a stranger with only a smattering of the French language and that I had no legal representative available, he sent for me and told me in perfect English that I need say nothing and do nothing. This act of pure kindness is one that I shall always treasure.

After the directors had stated their case at the trial, the judge bluntly informed them that they had no case, and the court was dismissed.

Immediately after this setback, the directors again asked me to sell my ivory. I explained that I had lost a lot of time coming to Bangui and that I should have to add that to the price.

"Name it! Name it!" they said.

I reckoned up what my losses came to, added that to the current price of ivory at Bangui, trebled it, and named the sum, thinking that would give them pause. Not a bit of it. They whipped out a cheque book and hastily scribbled the sum named. How I wished I had multiplied it by ten!

******

On my way out of the concession area toward the Shari watershed, I made a point of calling on my friend, M. Tourte, a trader established some way up river from Bangui. My friend was a Frenchman known far and wide as a *quel type* [what a guy!] or often as *quel phénomène* [he's phenomenal!]. He was a trader now but he had been an actor in France.

M. Tourte and Madame Tourte were, indeed, a find in the wilds of Africa. With a genius for imposing the "French way of life" on their surroundings, however grim they might be, they had established themselves in a clearing of the forest on the bank of a river and made it a small piece of France. Wine flowed freely and Madame's cooking was of the very best.

Tourte was a most engaging fellow and could re-enact his tallest tales and bring them to the life. One of these lingers specially in my memory. He used to describe how he attended his own wedding in disguise. He showed how he assisted in the hunt for the missing bridegroom, joined in the abuse of that unmentionable individual, and enjoyed the scene immensely. Only when the bride was on the point of departing in a flood of tears and in a four-wheeled cab did he tear off his false beard.

Both he and his wife were the most hospitable people, and they urged me to pitch my tent in their compound and stay the night. Of course, I was invited to dinner. French cooking has always been a standing wonder to me, but an even greater wonder is the way the French manage to carry their whole way of life with them even to the nethermost wilds of Africa. How anyone could take all that trouble about food always astonished as well as pleased me.

At this time I had a mongoose as a constant traveling companion. Those who know these animals will not be surprised to hear that I took the precaution of shutting my pet in a iron cage—as he'd have eaten his way through a wooden one—before going to dinner. Just as Tourte was merrily relating his missing bridegroom story, Madame Tourte said, "Listen! What's that noise?"

Needless to say, it was my mongoose loudly announcing that he wanted to be let out. Madame was terribly sorry for the little dear and insisted that I release the prisoner immediately. I explained that if I did so he would wreck the place. She would hear none of it; the mongoose must be freed!

For a time all was quiet. I am certain the little devil was merely debating which particular piece of mischief he should first attempt. Then from the adjoining room where the parrot lived there issued some of the most piercing screams interspersed with muddled scuffling. We rushed in to find my mongoose engrossed in the task of pulling the feathers of Madame's talking parrot one by one through the bars of its cage. There was nothing to do but shut the beggar up again in his cage.

Madame was desolated at the defeathering of her parrot, of course. She loved her parrot. Tourte seemed not so desolated; in fact, I heard him mutter something suspiciously like *sal bête* [the beast]!

The mongoose always slept in my bed under the mosquito net. When I was restless and happened to disturb him, he would nip one of my toes. That night when I turned in, I let him out and he came to bed with me as usual. Suddenly in the small hours there was a terrible outcry from Tourte's house. I could distinguish amidst Tourte's blasphemous roars the sound of dishes crashing. At once I missed the mongoose.

Just then Tourte shouted out, "Come fetch your ---- mongoose. He's tearing down the house!

"Shoot the blasted thing!" I yelled in exasperation.

Quick! Shoot the blasted troublemaker! (The Royal Magazine, *Volume 21*, London, C. A. Pearson, 1908)

Before I could get across to the house, I heard a loud report. I arrived to see Tourte in a long nightgown with a shot gun in his hand, gazing open-mouthed at a gaping hole in his corrugated iron roof. He had completely missed the mongoose.

On all sides destruction met the eye. Madame Tourte was very house proud and had placed her china dishes on shelves along the walls. My mongoose had amused himself by walking along these shelves and sweeping each piece of Madame Tourte's precious china to the ground, where they lay in pieces.

As Madame Tourte and I looked at each other and the mayhem spread before us, we were overcome by convulsions of laughter at the comic scene. The Tourtes were really good sports, and, seeing the humour of the night's adventure, took it as a joke, fortunately. We opened another bottle to drink damnation to all mongeese.

Reminiscences of an Elephant Hunter

I drew into a handy island, put the mongoose ashore, and steamed off. The mongoose started hunting quite unconcernedly, obviously taking his marooning with the utmost calm. (The Royal Magazine, Volume 21, London, C. A. Pearson, 1908)

One often sees these animals in zoological gardens and not unseldom is there a plaque with words on it like:

Donated by the Wardroom of Such-and-Such Ship

Evidently, the Tourtes are not the only sufferers at the hands of these mischievous rodents—if rodents they be.

Now the fate of this particular mongoose played out thus: One day as the flotilla was labouring up an island-studded stretch of river, I heard a *plop! plop!* behind me. I turned around to see what the noise was about and . . . to my horror

I saw Mr. Mongoose throwing cartridges overboard and deriving no small amount of satanic amusement from the deed. How the little devil succeeded in getting the cartridges out of the their box, no one knew but himself.

In exasperation, I drew into a handy island, put the mongoose ashore, and steamed off. The mongoose started hunting quite unconcernedly, obviously taking his marooning with the utmost calm. About an hour afterward, we were all back at the island begging and howling for the mongoose to come back. Yes, the weird little creature had so strangely fashioned and wound a web around the affections of both white and black man that we felt compelled to go back and rescue him.

******

I now began to penetrate what I came to call the "fly river" country because of the extraordinary number of tsetse flies. These flies were such a pestilence near the rivers flowing into the Shari that even the thick-skinned elephant came to drink and bathe only by night, leaving again before the sun came up and the flies got busy.

We, the hunters, had to track them a long way back. As we started when the flies were active, they followed us in clouds, stayed with us all day, and bit us the whole time. Apparently, they would face any dry country. Luckily for us there was no native source of sleeping sickness about.

Honey was abundant in this country and the honey birds that guide you to a beehive were very numerous. By twittering and diving and swooping, these small birds attract the natives' attention and lead them to the wild hives when the honey is full. For their reward, they receive a portion of the honey that is left on the ground near the tree. So numerous were they in these parts that their constant twittering alarmed the elephants. At one stage they became such a nuisance that I decided my only recourse was to visit a medicine man.

"You have come about the honey birds," he said before we had an opportunity to explain our visit.

That was easy because all my boys had been complaining about them. Time after time they had frightened off the elephants.

I said, "Yes, we want you to make 'medicine.'"

"All right," he said, "but I'll need a fowl."

He got it, read its guts, and announced that I would kill on the morrow. And I did. What the canny old fellow had done was to send the lads to the likely

Reminiscences of an Elephant Hunter

Bell and his pet mongoose.

places in the bush in such numbers that the honey birds had been distracted or satisfied. When I came along, there wasn't one to be heard or seen. To the African that is real "medicine."

******

One day I returned to camp to find that a small native boy attached to my safari had been wounded by a leopard and required attention.[2] After dressing the wounds with strong permanganate solution, I sent for the head-man of the nearest village with a view to organizing a leopard hunt. The forest was such that only with the help of the villagers and their dogs would there be any chance of coming up with the leopard. Now I knew in a general sort of way that man-killing leopards infested the whole of this particular country, but I did not know that they had acquired such an ascendancy. On questioning the head-man closely, a terrible tale of cannibalism was unfolded.

So now a two-legged variety of man-eater was at large. I decided to investigate this more closely, and I moved camp to a site near a native village that was notorious for the disappearance of numbers of people under mysterious circumstances. It was here I had the strange experience of catching in the open and destroying a whole of a small herd of buffaloes. This set me up with the villagers and made possible my further queries.

The whole country had once been heavily forested, but through centuries of felling and burning and planting, large areas had been cleared of high forest and had, after two or three years of cultivation, reverted to a frightful growth of elephant grass—a form of vegetation the most damnable for the elephant hunter. Twelve feet high and with sharp-edged leaves and myriad detachable spines, it made the attaining of a good bag of anything practically impossible, for it prevented both movement and visibility.

As usual the village was craving meat. The medicine man who dominated this region said that he would arrange for me to kill something. I told him to go ahead, and we agreed to go out on the morrow. At this particular time of the year, the elephant grass was only about three feet high, so I thought we were most likely to find only bush-buck in the open.

---

[2] The complete story can be found in chapter 31 of *Incidents from an Elephant Hunter's Diary*.

I had just received a .22 Hi-Power Savage rifle with ammunition, all of the soft-nose-bullet variety. I chose to carry this weapon, thinking it would do for anything we would likely meet. I knew that the elephants at that time were off on one of their mysterious migrations probably connected with the seasonable rise of sap in bamboo, or for some reason known only to themselves.

Bright and early the medicine man and I left the village on one of the many paths that converged from it. He led the way and I had time to examine him and the numerous charms that hung around him. My first thought was that he could not have washed in years. Then I took note of the many curious things that hung from every point of his anatomy. These were quite unknown to me. They were permanently fixed, too. Among them were human teeth—those small white, even dentures one sees and admires so often among Africans. As the old boy kept closing diverging paths so as to show the meat party the correct trail to follow, I thought to myself, *What a tale those teeth would tell.*

We had gone perhaps three miles when my guide stopped, and with a wand hung with charms he pointed dramatically at a small disturbance away over the grass-covered slopes. The glasses showed this to be a tight little bunch of rapidly traveling buffaloes coming directly toward us. They were on our right hand and the horizon on our left was the tall, abrupt edge of an untouched wall of forest. They had been caught out far from cover and were hell-bent for shade and safety. We had nothing to do but wait.

I felt a bit uneasy about those soft-nose bullets. I knew they would be no good for end-on shots into these heavy bone animals. I would have to wait until the buffaloes afforded a chance at their broadsides. I decided the best chance would be a lung shot, thinking in terms of getting one or possibly two animals before they disappeared in a cloud of dust. While I waited until I got a shot at a large cow, I tried to count how many animals were in the advancing herd, but it was impossible to do so.

When a cow presented an opportunity, I took the shot. Immediately she swung from her previous course, galloping and bellowing across the front of the herd. In doing so, she turned them broadside to my rifle, which continued to slam into them. The result was that in what seemed an incredibly short time, there was nothing living to be seen. Even the dead ones were almost hidden from sight by the grass. All was now deathly stillness.

I wondered if I was dreaming and looked at the old witch doctor behind me. He had not moved, but he now wore a smug look that said, "I told you so" and "Alone I did it!"

Suddenly we were both seized with excitement and rushed across to where the herd had been stampeding along so bravely and so lively only a few seconds before. There, in a patch about the size of a tennis lawn lay twenty-three buffaloes, stone dead. That seventy-grain bullet had robbed them of life almost instantaneously.

The ensuing scene defies description. I sent off a runner to the nearest *poste* with a chit for the *chef de poste,* who happened to be a friend of mine. He, in turn, sent out a posse of native police to take over a carcass.[3] For years thereafter he loved to recount how M. Bell had sent him a whole buffalo for his dinner. Thousands of meat-hungry natives met in a clash over the slain, but the witch-doctor managed in a masterly way to guard his own three carcasses from the milling throng.

******

It was in this country that I first began to hear of the mysterious Bahr Aouk River. This large and unexplored body of water lying far north was said to be the haunt of great herds of elephants, but I had never met anyone who had been near it. A blank space marked it on the maps of those days, and from the natives all I could learn was that it was a tabooed region, not to be entered. I made a mental note that someday the Bahr Aouk would need looking into.

Word came that the launch I had ordered from Scotland while I was hunting in the French Congo had finally arrived at Brazzaville. By the time I got the news, I knew that it most likely would already be at Bangui, so I hastily wound up my safari, dug up the ivory, and headed down country with great excitement.

There it was, complete to the last nut and bolt, but lying on the pier in sections as I had designed it. Two French engineers volunteered to help assemble it, and the whole town turned out to superintend the job. When completed, the boat was thirty-five feet long with six-foot beams; it had a water-tube boiler with a working pressure of two hundred and fifty

---

[3] See chapter 28 in *Incidents from an Elephant Hunter's Diary.*

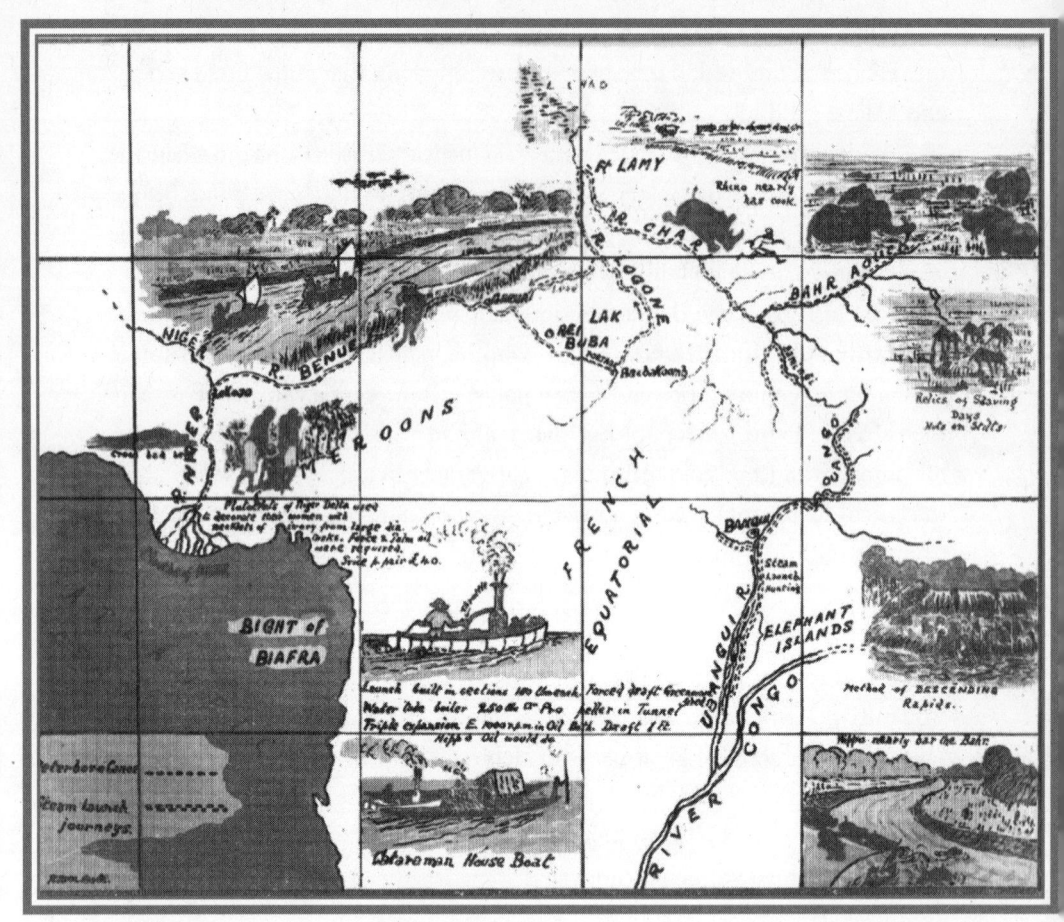

Bell's hand-drawn map of French Equatorial Africa, the Benue, Congo, and Ubangi Rivers, and drawings of his steamboat. (Sketch by W. D. M. Bell)

pounds per square inch, forced draft, a propeller running in a tunnel, and a triple expansion engine immersed in an oil bath running at one thousand revolutions per minute. Most important of all, it operated on green wood. Altogether a dandy little outfit.

The engineers were crazy about it, so I decided to repay their generosity in helping me by taking them on a hunt up one of the Congo's tributaries. Bangui had been built at the river's highest navigable point. There were quite formidable rapids just above the town. To everyone's surprise our little boat walked right up them.

French Equatorial Africa

Now I had to devise some sort of a floating home, for with a boiler and engine on a boat thirty-five feet long there was not much room for anything but wood fuel, a stoker, an oil drum, and a steersman. I took two forty-foot dugout canoes and built an elevated platform across them. Then on the platform, under which there was ample "garage space" for the launch, I built a small grass-roofed house.[4]

For some months this was my home. I pushed it wherever I liked, tied it to a sand bank, and withdrew the launch to go off hunting. It proved an ideal and most comfortable arrangement. No longer did I need a safari of hundreds of natives, all to be fed and cared for with great diligence. Whenever I killed an elephant, the local natives were only too glad to chop out the ivory and load it on the boat for the meat alone.

This novel form of hunting was also inexpensive. Fuel was to be had for the cutting. True, green wood was required to get a forced draft, and the sparks from the funnel would often set fire to the sun-awning, my clothes, or my hat, but to a young elephant hunter such things were quite expendable.

******

One day I met a white man who was drifting downstream in a large native dug-out. The canoe was a grass-covered shelter, and a native woman was occupied with a fire in the bottom of the canoe. There were three paddlers, and one of them was steering. Quite naturally, the craft drew alongside and here, to my astonishment, was one Phelizot, a youngster I had met in Kampala in Uganda years earlier.

At the time of this meeting in Uganda, P. was working for a commercial house, but was very anxious to take up elephant hunting and had asked me how to set about it. This was several years before the present meeting and Kampala was a far cry from the Ubangi River. As soon as we recognized each other, we agreed to land at the nearest suitable camping place and exchange news.

Now this P. was a curious mixture. He had a French mother, an Irish father, and was a U.S.A. citizen. His profession in America had been that of an erector of high smoke stacks. He was a man of delicate constitution and,

---

[4] A more complete description can be found in chapter 8 of *Incidents from an Elephant Hunter's Diary*.

189

in order to counteract his lack of physique, he had taken up and constantly practiced those Sandow[5] exercises most calculated to develop his naturally meagre defensive equipment. Thus had he attained a formidable muscular development, although he continued to be nothing much to look at. He confided to me that his punch was quite devastating and had often stood him in good stead with men twice his weight who were inclined to strong-arm methods in the settling of a difference of opinion.

By the camp fire the news rolled out. I had advised P. to buy himself a double .450 and a .318 Mauser and to try them out before deciding—after practical experience—which rifle he preferred. P. had asked me how I actually set about making a bag of elephants, and I had told him what my methods were. Specifically, I had said that it is essential to keep cool, to place one's shots correctly, and to understand that the diameter of the bullet did not matter so much as where it was placed.

Well, it appears that P. had tried these methods. Time after time he had applied the lessons, but in each case no kill had resulted. So, in desperation one day he had thrown all advice to the wind and had charged in close up to the elephant, given him both barrels anywhere in the body, and rushed after the fleeing animal while pumping in lead as fast as he could. Result? A kill!

From that he had continued to develop this highly individualistic technique until now, he said, it practically never failed. He had added a second .450 to his battery but confessed that he thought it was the .318 that really killed on most occasions.

Evidently my cool, calm method was not suited to his particular make-up, and he had branched out on his own. I was greatly interested in this and longed to see it in action, so we arranged to make a joint hunt, P. stipulating that there should be only a single elephant. He explained that he never hunted anything but solitary bulls.

Then he showed me a stick that he had cut to the diameter of a large forefoot. He would give this stick to a village and explain that if an elephant track corresponding to those dimensions could be found that he would follow it and they should have the meat. I thought that he would not get very many that way, and P. agreed.

---

[5] Eugen Sandow was born on 2 April 1867; he died 14 October 1925. Sandow was a pioneering German bodybuilder, now known as the "father of modern bodybuilding."

"Look at what I do get!" he said, uncovering some enormous tusks in the bottom of the canoe.

He undoubtedly had some beauties.

"About one a week, on average," he said in reply to my query.

As for price, he could ask almost anything for such ivory. Some of the ivory would go to Niger where the wealthy chiefs decorated their favourite wives with ivory necklets that slipped over the head. A pair of such necklets commanded a price of forty pounds sterling. Of course, these necklets had to be cut from a tusk of outstanding diameter, as, apparently, no method of squeezing the human head through a smaller necklet had yet been devised, although the search for it no doubt continued.

He explained that when he amassed about £3,000 worth of ivory, he sold out. He would send £500 to his gunmaker to hold against new equipment and a return ticket, and he then repaired himself straight to Paris. He would contract himself a temporary wife, hand her what was left of his money, and enjoy life to the utmost while it lasted.

And last well it did, he explained—much longer in the hands of an expert Parisienne than if he had the spending of it himself. They knew where to eat well and cheaply, what ought to be paid for wines, and so on. These women were extremely honest and quite loyal to their temporary husbands, he said. Often he would take them into a jeweler's shop and tell them to choose something for themselves. After pricing a few trinkets, they would whisper they knew where the same thing could be got for half the price. Once his money was finished, he went back to the bush.

P. was in Paris when the 1914 War broke out. He and hundreds of other Americans joined the French Foreign Legion. The next I heard of my friend, he was dead of tetanus, contracted through a head wound sustained in a scuffle with a fellow legionnaire.

******

After leaving P., my thoughts returned to the Bahr Aouk country. I thought I could get my steam kettle a long way up one of the tributaries of the Ubangi during the big rains, break it down into small sections, and then make quite a short portage over the watershed.

I decided to hunt my way toward the headwaters. Continuing upstream, I reached a tributary running in from the north that I thought would shorten my land travel across to the Shari river system. I knew that I would not get very far up before the heavy rains set in, but I could profitably employ the wait by hunting in the watershed country.

I landed at a French military post that had been set down along the river to prevent British encroachment from the Bahr el Ghazal region. I felt the presence of the French was somehow connected to the expansionist policy of the thrusting British, whose far-reaching tentacles were already making their influence felt. At least that is the only reason I can give for the fort's presence that far from the Soudan, for there were very few natives in these parts.

The commandant promptly informed me that the river was low and that I would not be able to continue farther up until the rains came. There wasn't another option, so I left the launch there and once again took to the bush.

I now entered an amazing country. Nowhere had I seen nature in a wilder mood since I had hunted the *nabwa*[6] of Dodosi in Karamojo. Everything was on a stupendous scale. The trees were twisted by fire into the weirdest shapes, contorted into the most fantastic convolutions. Many lightning-struck trunks of trees stood starkly about like the bones of extinct prehistoric life. Ravines cut deeply here and there told of great deluges. Where any grass was still unburnt, it stood eight to twelve feet high, whitened and bleached. This was the time of year when the natives laid in a stock of meat for the rainy season, for no self-respecting African will venture out once the weather has turned.

I had been there for a while when I received a letter from the commandant. It said that he was liquidating the post and that I had better send someone to look after the launch. Then in a postscript he casually added: "It might be of interest to you to know that war has broken out. France and Great Britain are at war with Germany. We are nearly all called up and I am departing forthwith."

When I received this letter, I was hunting in the farthest-out parts of the Ubangi-Shari river system in the French Congo. I returned poste haste to the French outpost where my flotilla lay at the head of navigation. There I found great preparations afoot. As every possible man had been called up, the Government had decided to close down this station for the duration. Steel whalers were loading the stores and paraphernalia belonging to the troops.

---

[6] *Nabwa* is uninhabited, wild country. See *Karamojo Safari*.

The commandant seemed to take it for granted that I would be staying on. It seemed incredible to him that anyone should go to war without receiving his call-up papers. He was astonished and gratified when I said that I, too, was going to war. He doubted if a passage could be secured as all French ships would have automatically come under mobilization orders, but he thought perhaps the commander-in-chief might make an exception in my case. Therefore, I determined to go down to Bangui and try.

I invited my friend to go along with me on my steam flotilla, but I took the precaution of letting him know just what poor catering he might expect. He was, after all, French. The jovial Frenchman soon put that right, assuring me that he had enough "necessities of life" for all hands. This meant such an abundance of white flour, sugar, coffee, fresh vegetables, and wine as almost to sink the flotilla.

Meanwhile departure was delayed only for as long as it took his cook to bake enough loaves of bread for the journey. War or no war, one must eat white bread! Amongst all this provender, to which I was quite unused, was a bidon [can] of about ten gallons of strong red wine and most excellent French army-ration wine. This wine circulates to the most isolated outposts and is subjected to violent changes of temperature. In order to preserve it, quite a lot of alcohol is added to the natural wine. It then becomes a very fine drink, indeed.

On the down-stream journey we employed except on two occasions the usual but very dangerous method of rushing the rapids. At these two places where there were numerous rocks breaking the white water, I demonstrated my usual method of negotiating such places, much to the admiration of my passenger.

This consists of turning the bow up-stream and throttling down on the steam until the current is just neutralized by the propulsive effort of the engine. Thus, the boat stands still and a touch of the rudder sends it straight across the stream to either side, when, by closing down still further on the steam, the craft goes slowly astern. In this way can quite formidable rapids be passed in comparative safety. The speed of the current plus the speed of the craft means disaster if you hit a rock, however.

When we arrived in Bangui, all was bustle and activity. Almost everyone had had his call-up papers. I had to see about my passage home, and my friend said that he would see if he could do something about it. While I was selling my ivory, I was wondering what to do with my launch. Then M. Tourte arrived and offered to buy it. He had not been called up. He got the launch and what a farewell party was on! On the day of departure, I said au revoir to my dream of ascending the Bahr Aouk, good-bye to my launch, and good-bye to elephant hunting—for the time being. I now began the long journey home.

******

The ship was crowded to its utmost limit with French and Belgians. But room was found somehow for a few women. What a time we had! Everyone was animated with the idea of "Eat, drink, and be merry, for to-morrow we may die." Food was abundant and good wine plentiful. At my table there were four Frenchmen and a Belgian and his wife. Such sparkle, wit, and freedom from inhibition could never have been found among a similar gathering of Anglo-Saxons.

Every meal was an orgy of the spiciest conversation, often led by the lady herself. At the early morning gathering in the saloon for "soupe a l'onion"—on which they seemed to set great store—everyone, male and female, appeared in their night attire. It was at and after luncheon that they brightened up, and at dinner, they really got going.

Among the passengers was a mother with a marriageable daughter, a pretty enough girl in her own right but possessing that priceless thing known as youth. Probably in an ordinary crowd she would have attracted hardly more than a glance, but in this crowd, she really appeared to be a "pearl among swine."

With that characteristic appreciation of the passing chance, the mother proposed to auction the girl. Everyone was mad about her. She, in her turn, was enjoying the opportunity to the utmost. Guarded by her able and worldly wise mother, there was little chance of her precious lamb being devoured by the ravenous wolves. The crowded state of the ship no doubt helped.

One of my cabin mates—there were three—was simply potty about this girl. He spent all his time out of the cabin ogling the beauty and licking his lips. All the time he was in his cabin he spent audibly dreaming of her charms. In spite of his considerable age, he fired up at once when one of the cabin inmates cynically remarked he would bet she wasn't a virgin.

"Guaranteed! Guaranteed!" he would shout. "And I am willing to bet one thousand francs that I am right."

******

As the ship approached La Belle France, news came in over the radio of reverses and bloody battles. This was before the war had assumed its static character that later drained away the very life blood of France. More and more resort was had to the bottle, and gayer and gayer did everyone become.

FRENCH EQUATORIAL AFRICA

On sighting land I suggested in my innocence, "But you'll get some leave once we dock."

"Leave!" they roared and burst into bitter laughter.

They told me that their trains would be standing with steam up and ready to take them straight to their units wherever they might happen to be, including the front-line trenches.

On arrival at Bordeaux, one of my cabin mates found he had an hour or two to spare before being swallowed up by the war machine. He proposed to show me the town. We immediately set out on a round of the hotels to view their registers. This apparently afforded great fun to my companion, for it revealed who was bedding with whom. Then on we went to a round of the good restaurants.

"See that man over there? He's so-and-so. Owns such-and-such a vineyard. Let's see what he's drinking!"

Having seen, or ascertained from the waiter, the name of that particular wine and its vintage, a bottle of it would instantly be ordered. Then another celebrity of the wine world would be seen and the same performance would be repeated, all the while dozen after dozen of those small oysters would be consumed. I wondered at the capacity of the French. Drunk or not, orders were orders, and I saw my friend to his train for the front.

******

When I first set out on my elephant-hunting career, I set my goal to take one thousand bull elephants, and to that end I hunted in Karamojo, the Lado Enclave, the Belgian and French Congos, Ivory Coast, Liberia, Uganda, Abyssinia, and the East African coast. When I returned to England, I took with me some huge tusks as almost my sole personal baggage.

Instead of suitcases, the railway porters had nine- or ten-foot-long slippery tusks to handle. They slid off the barrows and when they did stay put, they raked the mob of baggage-seekers just about knee high, to their indignation. Nobody seemed to know what they were. Then when they were hove into the guard's van, they took charge and barged into piles of normal luggage. Altogether quite a scene was created.

The tusks were duly presented to my sisters, who promptly sold them and invested in diamonds.

LONDON
Colchester
Clacton on Sea
Chelmsford
Brentwood
Basildon
SOUTHEND ON SEA
Grays
Thurrock
Gravesend
Sheerness
Rochester
Gillingham
Chatham
Margate
Broadstairs
Ramsgate
Herne Bay
Whitstable
Faversham
Canterbury
Deal
Dover
Folkestone
Hythe
Ashford
Maidstone
Tunbridge Wells
Tonbridge
Sevenoaks
Caterham
Reigate
Guildford
Crawley
East Grinstead
Horsham
Cuckfield
Burgess Hill
Lewes
BRIGHTON
Worthing
Seaford
Eastbourne
Bexhill
Hastings
St Albans
Welwyn Garden City
Harlow
Hoddesdon
Hemel Hempstead
Walton
Leatherhead
Dorking
Crowborough
New Romney
Winchelsea
Dungeness
Thames
KENT
SUSSEX
Strait of Dover
Pas de Calais
CHANNEL
Oslo 650, København 683, Szczecin 834
Hamburg 412, Kiel 441, Szczecin 662, Gdańsk 798, Leningrad 1212
Rotterdam 160, Amsterdam 185
Dunkerque 95
Southampton-London 184, Rotterdam 244
Shanghai 10381, Rio de Janeiro 5855, New York 4038, Gibraltar 1359, Gdańsk
Le Havre-Dunkerque 163, Londres 186
Oostende (Ostende)
Blankenberge
Dunkerque (Dunkirk)
Calais
Rosendaël
Saint-Omer
Hazebrouck
Armentières
Boulogne-sur-Mer
Desvres
Étaples
Le Touquet Paris-Plage
Montreuil
Berck
Bruay-en-Artois
Bully-les-Mines
Liévin
Lens
Arras
Auchel
Béthune
Saint-Pol
PAS-DE-CALAIS
Baie de Somme
Saint Valery-sur-Somme
Cayeux-sur-Mer
Abbeville
Le Tréport
Eu
Dieppe
AMIENS
SOMME
Doullens
Beauvais
OISE
Creil
Clermont
Fécamp
Étretat
Bolbec
Yvetot
SEINE-MARITIME
PAYS DE CAUX
LE HAVRE
Harfleur
Honfleur
Trouville
ROUEN
Elbeuf
Louviers
Évreux
EURE
Les Andelys
Vernon
Gisors
Pontoise
Mantes-Gassicourt
Dreux
Caen
Lisieux
Bernay
Pont-Audemer
PARIS
VERSAILLES
Seine

I JOIN THE ROYAL FLYING CORPS (R.F.C.)

CHAPTER 16

On my arrival in London, I met a friend in the regular forces who said, on hearing that I wished to join the Royal Flying Corps, that he could help me at the War Office. I never discovered what my friend said about me, but I was presently summoned to be interviewed by a certain eminent person whose job it was to conduct these interviews so as to form some idea as to the applicant's suitability for the role of aviator. Very little was known then about this subject and even less, apparently, by the interviewer because I was asked, after some hesitation, if I could ride a bicycle and all that. After I reassured him on this point, he said he would put my name down and that in due course I would be appointed to a flying school.

Hearing nothing further about the matter, I thought I might as well see what lessons I could pick up at a private flying school at Hendon. It was run by an enterprising gentleman who advertised a complete course in flying for the sum of £70. This seemed reasonable enough until one perused the formidable document that all aspiring aviators were required to sign. It consisted of a long list of items ranging from whole wings to undercarriage wheels and against each item was neatly displayed exactly what the pupil would have to pay should he damage it. If the whole machine was a write-off, it would cost the student a small fortune.

Now I had had a little previous experience, if not of flying at least of handling an aircraft on the ground. For no sooner had the news of Blériot's cross-Channel flight[1] reached me on the coast of East Africa than I came hurriedly home with the sole object of learning to fly and to apply this somewhat precarious mode of getting about to my elephant hunting.

With this in mind, I joined the Blériot School, also at Hendon. There was one other pupil and one machine, with a few French mechanics and an

---

[1] Louis Charles Joseph Blériot (1 July 1872—1 August 1936) was a French aviator, inventor, and engineer. He developed the first practical headlamp for trucks and established a profitable business manufacturing them, using much of the money he made to finance his attempts to build a successful aircraft. In 1909 he became world famous for making the first flight across the English Channel in a heavier than air aircraft, winning the prize of £1,000 offered by the *Daily Mail*. Blériot was also the first to make a working, powered, piloted monoplane, and he was the founder of a successful aircraft manufacturing company.

Blériot parasol.

instructor. Whenever the air was tranquil—and tranquil it had to be—the crate would be wheeled out and the instructor would fly a circuit or two, and then the precious affair would be wheeled back into its shed. Then everyone would go off, saying, *"À demain! À demain!"* [tomorrow, tomorrow], leaving the two students cursing on the empty field.

One day the instructor, rendered bold from some hidden source, or maybe ashamed by the wistful look in his pupils' eyes, beckoned the two of us over and began in French to instruct us on the art of taxying these tricky monoplanes on the ground. He emphasized that on no account should the throttle be opened, for, should that happen, the machine would leave the ground! This, to his mind, was sufficiently terrible an affair to daunt anyone in their senses from touching the little lever. He was quite oblivious to the fact that his two miserable pupils had been standing around for two or three weeks in the hope of accomplishing just that exact, identical thing.

I Join the Royal Flying Corps (R.F.C.)

The whole contraption was of the utmost simplicity. This particular one had a three-cylinder Anzani motor of a reputed twenty-five h.p., a contact switch, and a throttle. There were no ailerons; a lateral movement of the joystick caused a warping of the wings, thereby serving the same purpose. The rudder was a straight-forward bar. Both of us pupils felt confident that if we could only get aboard the affair, the rest would be easy.

At last one of us was allowed to do so. It was, of course, a single seater. The engine was started up, the air was tranquil, the machine was pointed to the wide-open spaces, and off I trundled slowly along while the blanched faces of the instructor and the mechanics showed with what apprehension they viewed the gyrations of their precious machine.

Now, with the tail on the ground and the drag of the tail skid, taxying these craft at very low speed was the devil. It was impossible to keep a straight course. But if you opened the throttle a bit and got the tail up off the ground, all was easy. This I discovered as soon as I was far enough away from the anxious crowd.

To their consternation, their precious airplane began to race away with the tail up and the steering set for a dead straight course. Throttling down as the boundary was reached, the *sacré* pupil—me—effected a turn so that now the plane was pointed directly at the hangar. Giving her the gun, the parasol got her tail up and came racing toward the crowd.

They were all terribly shaken, but that was nothing, for now I gave her full throttle, eased back on the joystick, and left the ground . . . still aimed at the center of the hanger. The strong men on the ground first hid their eyes and then fled the scene. At that point, I closed the throttle and eased her to the ground in time to bring her to a perfect stop in front of the hanger. This experience was enough for me to realize that when aircraft were cheap and procurable, I would cable for one myself.

In the meantime, I found a new flying school. This time I had an Irish instructor who used a Wright two-seater, box-kite biplane instead of the single-seater Blériot monoplane. Like most of his race, Kelly was an optimist. When later he was called to give evidence in a case where a pupil had been fired as hopeless and had tried to recover the fee he had paid, the judge asked him if he, too, shared that view. "No," he said, "but then, I'm Irish."

Instead of two pupils to one bus, as at Blériot's, there were now thirty pupils to two buses. Again, the air had to be tranquil. Owing to the

World War I–era biplane.

unfortunate habit of the instructor taking his best girl for a flip in the early morning after a hectic night before, neither of the two machines was ever in a robust enough state for pupils to handle.

I was now fed up with trying to learn to fly at private flying schools, but my appointment for R.F.C. flying school still had not come through. I decided, therefore, to write the R.F.C. authorities and state the facts about my experiences with these private flying schools. The result was that I got a

I JOIN THE ROYAL FLYING CORPS (R.F.C.)

summons to go to the R.F.C.'s own flying school at Brooklands, where a very different state of affairs prevailed.

For one thing, the instructors had returned from France with actual war-flying experience. Moreover, to begin with one flew with the instructor in a two-seater contraption called a Long Horn, so the student got actual instruction while in the air. Of course, there were far too many pupils for the number of machines.

My chance came one day, however, when my instructor took me up. There were no dual controls; the pupil sat behind and watched over the instructor's shoulder what he did with the controls. The pupil also kept his eye on the rev. counter and the air speed instrument. As it happened, it was a lovely day, and the instructor said, "Let's go and lunch at Richmond."

We landed in the park and went for lunch. The machine was in view from our table, so we could see when a lot of fallow deer began collecting round the machine.

"Better chivvy them off, they're no better than b-----[2] goats," said the instructor.

The deer had done no damage; even fallow deer could not stomach the castor oil with which the whole machine was drenched. It had the famous, or infamous rather, rotary engine Gnome, and castor oil was simply laid on by turning a handle and pouring it through the engine in a constant stream until the supply was exhausted or when you came down and landed voluntarily and turned off the handle.

On the way home, the instructor suggested to me that I now knew all about flying a biplane. I, who thought that nothing could be simpler, said that I felt good about it although I did not feel too sure of the landing.

"Well, watch carefully," said B., the instructor, as we took to the air.

On the ground once more, B. asked, "How d'you feel about it?"

I replied, "All right."

"Well," said B., "why don't you go for your ticket?"

He then explained what had to be done. You had to take off solo, make so many figure-of-eight turns of the aerodrome, climb to two thousand feet,

---

[2] It's interesting to note that the word *bloody* in Bell's time was sufficiently vulgar that he doesn't spell it out.

cut off the engine, and land within a hundred yards of a flag. A tallish order considering that I had had at that point one and a half hours in the air—and even that was stretched out to its limits.

"You needn't worry about the flag," said B. "I'll make sure to hand it off to the flag man who will then run like hell to where you are going to land. If you don't break anything, you'll get your ticket. Right?"

"Right, sir," I replied, and off B. went.

The taking off was easy, so was the control in the air. But the landing—Oh, Lord! Hitting the ground at much too steep an angle, the thing bounced twenty feet and hovered, then hit the ground again, and bounced considerably less. Three such bounds and it came to rest at last. B. and the flag man raced up to see if anything was broken. Not a wire was even strained.

B. laughed with relief and said, "Off you go, and don't fly into the ground this time."

The next landing was considerably better—the flag man was getting his second wind. The third time was quite passable, and I got my ticket.

I was now passed over to a more advanced course in which I handled single-seater Avros. I was given to understand that if I conducted myself well, I would fly in company with my instructor to Netheravon, which was then the central flying school.

Before setting off on this cross-country flight, which I was given to understand that if successfully accomplished would go far to gain me my coveted "Wings," I was invited by a new instructor to go for a flip. We took off in a two-seater Blériot parasol all right, but the engine cut out, and we landed in the middle of a sewage farm. Not that this was an unusual ending to a flight, but what interested us was the swarms of snipe we disturbed. We reckoned we would have to get mud-boards so as to get at them.

It is interesting to note that sewage farms have now become almost the last sanctuaries of these birds, and it is quite likely to remain so as it is a messy business getting them out of it. As well as snipe, there were partridge at Brooklands. They would squat right in front of a landing machine, yet never was one hit. They seemed to know exactly where the machine would touch ground, which was a good deal more than the pupils knew!

The test for "Wings" consisted in taking up a strange machine and landing it in a small field three times. This was done without engine, flying over a

I Join the Royal Flying Corps (R.F.C.)

high line of trees or a cottage and then landing as close to a mark as could be contrived. The Wing Commander stood by the mark and after each attempt passed caustic remarks on the aspirant's attempts.

I gave the obstruction a good, safe clearance but got into the field all right. The Wing Commander waxed facetious about Brooklands as a training centre. He said the fields in France were the size of tennis lawns.

"Try again," he said. "Shave it this time."

I determined to do so and cleared it by a few feet, only to overshoot the mark again by twenty yards. The Wing Commander again passed pointed remarks. The third time I came down below the level of the cottage roof with plenty of flying speed. I was lost to sight of the Wing Commander, who, scenting a crash, started toward the cottage. Just then I came floating over the roof top with just enough flying speed to clear it, and I landed nearly on top of the Wing Commander who was in full flight to one side. This time I was twenty yards short of the mark, and the Wing Commander said he wouldn't have believed it.

I got my wings all right, although the Morse examiner said I had scored fewer marks than anyone he had ever had through his hands. I was now handed three so-called scout machines of types that had proved to be unmanageable and was told to do what I liked with them. The sooner they were written off, the better the C.O. would be pleased.

I mounted wooden dummy guns on these and used them to make mock attacks on other machines, much to everyone's annoyance. One of the more advanced pupils complained of my activities to the C.O. This man subsequently got the V.C. in action against Zeppelins.

The Great War in East Africa

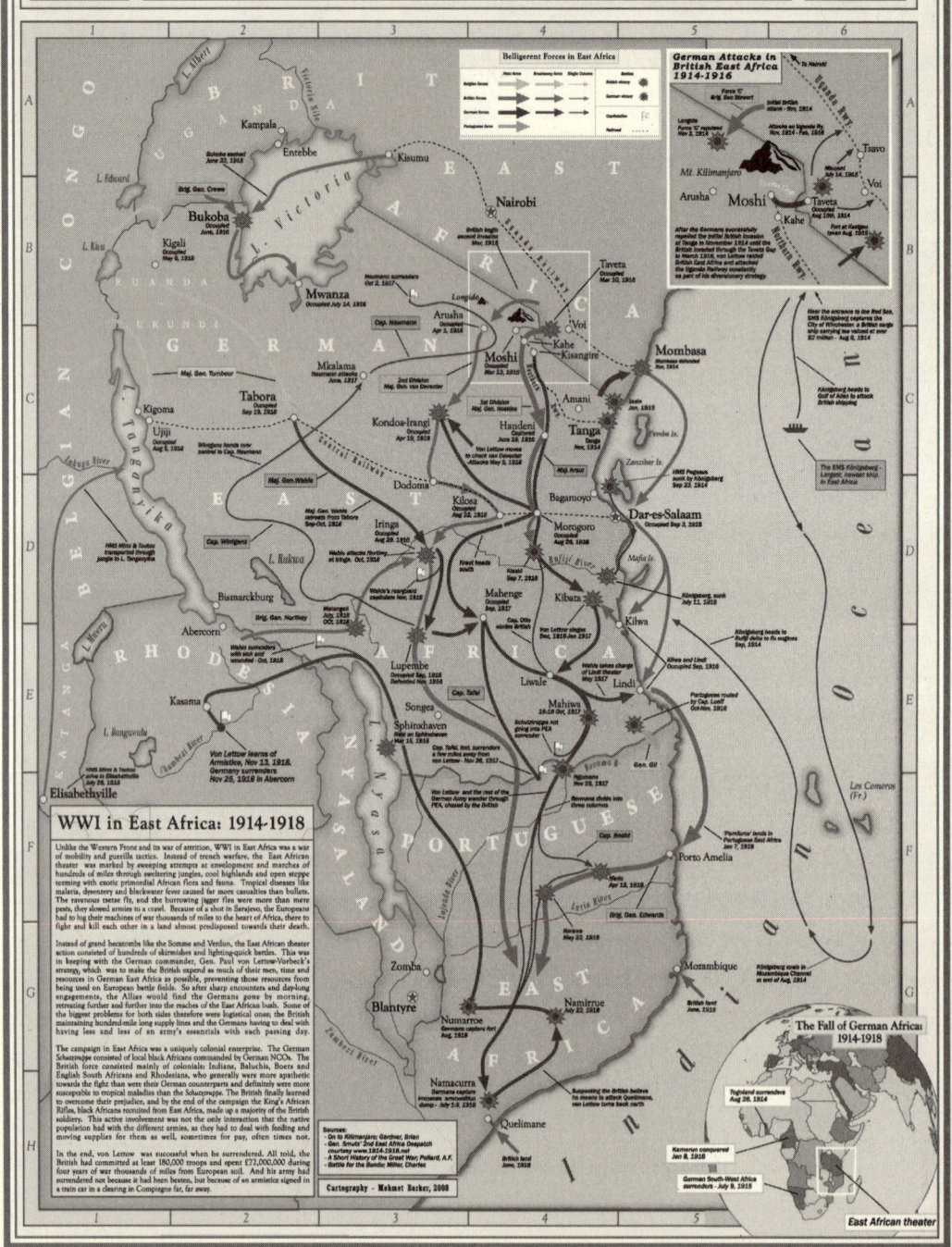

WWI in East Africa: 1914-1918

Unlike the Western Front and its war of attrition, WWI in East Africa was a war of mobility and guerilla tactics. Instead of trench warfare, the East African theater was marked by sweeping attempts at envelopment and marches of hundreds of miles through sweltering jungles, cool highlands and open steppe teeming with exotic primordial African flora and fauna. Tropical diseases like malaria, dysentery and blackwater fever caused far more casualties than bullets. The ravenous tsetse fly, and the burrowing jigger flea were more than mere pests, they slowed armies to a crawl. Because of a shot in Sarajevo, the Europeans had to lug their machines of war thousands of miles to the heart of Africa, there to fight and kill each other in a land almost predisposed towards their death.

Instead of grand bloodbaths like the Somme and Verdun, the East African theater action consisted of hundreds of skirmishes and lightning-quick battles. This was in keeping with the German commander, Gen. Paul von Lettow-Vorbeck's strategy, which was to make the British expend as much of their men, time and resources in German East Africa as possible, preventing those resources from being used on European battle fields. So after sharp encounters and day-long engagements, the Allies would find the Germans gone by morning, retreating farther and farther into the reaches of the East African bush. Some of the biggest problems for both sides therefore were logistical ones; the British maintaining hundred-mile long supply lines and the Germans having to deal with having less and less of an army's essentials with each passing day.

The campaign in East Africa was a uniquely colonial enterprise. The German Schutztruppe consisted of local black Africans commanded by German NCOs. The British force consisted mainly of colonials; Indians, Baluchis, Boers and English South Africans and Rhodesians, who generally were more apathetic towards the fight than were their German counterparts and definitely were more susceptible to tropical maladies than the Schutztruppe. The British finally learned to overcome their prejudice, and by the end of the campaign the King's African Rifles, black Africans recruited from East Africa, made up a majority of the British soldiers. This active involvement was not the only interaction that the native population had with the different armies, as they had to deal with feeding and moving supplies for them as well, sometimes for pay, often times not.

In the end, von Lettow was successful when he surrendered. All told, the British had committed at least 180,000 troops and spent £72,000,000 during four years of war thousands of miles from European soil. And his army had surrendered not because it had been beaten, but because of an armistice signed in a train car in a clearing in Compiègne far, far away.

Sources:
- Go to Kilimanjaro; Gardner, Brian
- Gen. Smuts' 2nd East Africa Despatch courtesy www.1914-1918.net
- A Short History of the Great War; Pollard, A.F.
- Battle for the Bundu; Miller, Charles

Cartography - Mehmet Barker, 2008

The War Years

Chapter 17

Sometime toward the end of my courses on learning how to fly the rickety crates of those days, I had been warned for France; instead, I suddenly received orders to join a South African Squadron forming at an aerodrome for service in East Africa under General Smuts. In due course we all embarked and sailed on our own without escort.

What course we steered no one knew, but we must have traversed some of the most unfrequented areas of the oceans. Not only did we sight no land, but we never saw a ship of any sort. As with all long sea passages, it started with everyone on the best of terms and ended with everyone loathing the sight of each other. I was fortunate in that the skipper took a fancy to me, so I spent long hours on the bridge with the old man. He was a relic of sailing ship days, loved sailing, and employed the endless days sewing himself a suit of sails for his small boat that was hanging in davits.

At last the ship arrived in Kilindini harbour. It was like coming home again for me, and I found things had altered almost beyond recognition since my former days there. The Uganda Railway now operated, and where I used to pitch my tent under a mangrove tree, there were now rows of bungalows and store houses.

It was here I heard for the first time that C., who, seeing the way of things to come, had with great astuteness bought up all the native-held plantations on the foreshore. He had then waited with his title deeds all in order. When the Government required land, they had to go to him. It was here he slipped up. Instead of being satisfied with a decent profit of two hundred percent or so, he demanded so outrageous a figure that the Government got a special bill passed for compulsory purchase, and poor old C. got only half. Even at that he must have done extremely well and retired a rich man.

The squadron got itself ashore and installed itself at a natural aerodrome on the game plains under Kilimanjaro, whose snows looked down on what must have been a strange scene to that hoary-headed mountain. It was a magnificent mark for finding your way about in the otherwise rather featureless bush.

The machines we brought with us were B.E.2.C's, and there was much speculation among the fliers whether they would get off the ground in view of the four-thousand-foot altitude of the flying ground. We need not have worried. These planes took the air if not with the spring of a partridge at any rate like that of a meat-gorged vulture, with which, by the way, they often just missed colliding.

As well as B.E.2.C's, there were some Henri Farmans. These latter were most interesting craft in view of later developments. They were pushers—that is, the engine was behind the occupants. The engine was a museum-piece—a water-cooled radial with nine cylinders. The frame of the wings was constructed of steel tubing, and it withstood the vagaries of the tropical conditions admirably. The whole was fabric covered, of course, as were all machines in those days. The pilot sat out in a sort of gondola in front of the wings and had a splendid view all around. He could and often did fall asleep at the controls.

It was very interesting to fly over many of my old hunting grounds, but I was surprised to find the visibility from an airplane poor. The amount of game you could see from the air was disappointing; animals just did not show up well. Even on photographs, they did not show up well unless there was a backdrop of water or a swamp.

I had not realized how much we earthlings depend on silhouette to give us perspective. For instance, giraffes viewed from the air looked like donkeys with jockeys on their backs. Elephants in bush were difficult to find unless they kicked up a small dust storm. Hippos, of course, were easy when they showed at all. The main trouble to seeing things on the ground was the unpredictable performance of the engines. With the possibility of a forced-landing site being so scarce in the all-pervading thorn bush, no one liked to fly low.

For some unknown reason there raged among the pilots a heated controversy about aerobatics in the tropics. Some held the view that if you got into a spin or looped-the-loop, you would not come out of it because of the rarified air. Others thought this was all bunk, holding that the air at five thousand feet on the equator could not be very different from the air at say six or seven thousand feet in the temperate zones. Aided by the hot sun and abundant liquor, the arguments became a perfect pest, and eventually I was deputed to put the matter to test.

I was assigned the first plane assembled and told to put it through the usual tests. Unfortunately for me, the C.O. adhered to the rarified air gang and was against settling the matter by test. I, however, felt that in the role of test pilot, I was well within my rights if I chose to put a machine through any of the recognized test maneuvers.

I thought that if the machines were going to develop any strange tricks, they might as well do it over the aerodrome instead of out in the blue. Not that I thought they would do so; on the contrary, I felt sure the whole thing was a scare-up. When I put it through the usual tests, it was just as I thought. I found all was well in the air.

But not so on the ground. The commanding officer was so furious at the enthusiasm with which I performed my acrobatics that he grounded me for two weeks. The document detailing my grounding must have been unique. Delivered to me by the adjutant, it stated that I was confined to the ground.

As I was on my native heath, so to speak, I applied for a job with ground intelligence. Before doing this, however, I had the pleasure of drawing attention to the serious loss of petrol resulting from the method of stowing it in two-gallon cans. In spite of the knowledge of the recent calamity that befell Scott in the Antarctic,[1] here was the same thing happening at our aerodrome, just on a larger scale.

As on Scott's voyage, here we were using for stowage the same sort of can and in the same upright position that had resulted in the drying out of the leather washer in the cap of the can and the consequent evaporation of the contents. Hundreds of thousands of cans were sucking in air past the shrunken washers as the tins expanded in the heat of the day, only to pump it out, laden with gas, when the cool of the night contracted them. Passing to leeward of the dump one day, the stink of petrol was enough to gas anyone.

Bet you, they've stowed those cans bung up, I remarked to my companion. "Let's see."

They had. The man in charge was astonished at the news. He'd heard of Scott all right, but not of the petrol leakage that was so largely, if indirectly, the cause of the tragedy that overtook the polar party. At once an examination was

---

[1] Capt. Robert Falcon Scott, CVO, RN (6 June 1868–29 March 1912) was a British Royal Navy officer and explorer who led two expeditions to the Antarctic regions: the Discovery Expedition, 1901–1904, and the ill-fated Terra Nova Expedition, 1910–1913. On the first expedition, he set a new southern record by marching to latitude 82°S and discovered the Polar Plateau, on which the South Pole is located. During the second venture, Scott led a party of five that reached the South Pole on 17 January 1912, four weeks after Roald Amundsen's Norwegian expedition. On their return journey, Scott's party discovered plant fossils, proving Antarctica was once forested and joined to other continents. A planned meeting with supporting dog teams from the base camp failed, despite Scott's written instructions, and at a distance of 150 miles from their base camp and 11 miles from the next depot, Scott and his companions perished.

made and most of the tins were found some half and others two-thirds empty, What a scare! When laid on their sides, the washers remained wet and tight.

Another problem was the bombs. They did not explode. Only the primer went off, but the main charge remained. On examination it was discovered that the T.N.T. had liquefied and soaked into the primers so that the latter failed to explode the main charge. Thereafter, primers were stowed apart and only inserted just previous to loading them on the machines; this resulted in satisfactory explosions. Having made myself thoroughly unpopular with my C.O., I got my appointment to ground intelligence and bade my squadron au revoir.

I was given the job of prowling about the bush to learn what I could. I quite enjoyed this new job. There was no boss, and I could do as I pleased. Now that I was back to foot-slogging among Africans in the bush, I had a very good time. One day I met P. J. Pretorius,[2] who was on the same job. We all worked from an advanced camp in the bush. One evening Pretorius and his mate, another Dutchman, came back from a bush-prowl in a fearful state, clothes torn, arms scratched, and black and blue with bruises.

"What the hell has the Hun been doing to you?" I asked, full of interest.

"Hun nothing," they said disgustedly, "It was a bloody rhino!"

I reported the presence of native troops in brand new khaki uniforms on a river. They were in small numbers and I was in a position to see them quite plainly. For the life of me, however, I could not be certain whether or not they were the King's African Rifles because the headgear was not the usual one worn by that body of native troops. I could easily have shot one from where I lay and might have stampeded the others and so might have got a new uniform to show to Intelligence.

It was a priceless opportunity to try out my .303 Farquharson semi-automatic that I had acquired with such difficulty from the inventor, Colonel Farquharson. The colonel had but three fitters and one work bench at his shop in Birmingham and was laboriously building up two or three rifles for War Office trials. Farquharson had amused me by firing his rifles into a heap of ashes in the backyard, right in among buildings.

---

[2] Maj. Philip Jacobus Pretorius was a South African elephant hunter of repute, adventurer, and the scout responsible for finding and sinking the German battleship SMS *Konigsberg* in East Africa during World War I. His famous autobiography, *Jungle Man*, is a classic in big-game hunting literature.

THE WAR YEARS

Maj. Philip Jacobus Pretorius was a famous South African elephant hunter.

Well, here was a chance for it. The trouble was that I was not certain enough if this was the enemy. There might have been a new issue of uniform to our troops that I was unaware of. The particular item that attracted and held my attention was a khaki neck-protector dangling down from the cap behind and partly to the sides. It looked like the things the explorers of Stanley's era wore, at least in their pictures anyway.

I hastened back to headquarters to report what he had seen. As far as Intelligence knew, no British troops, coloured or white, fitted the description. My report, however, electrified headquarters. It was either the first indication of the Germans having got a ship through the blockade or it confirmed some rumour to that effect. Whatever it was, it certainly caused some upheaval. The army had apparently gone into winter quarters, quite in the old tradition. The Flying Corps had declared it impossible to function in the rainy season. Extensive leave had been given, and half the pilots were away shooting or otherwise disporting themselves.

My new chief consulted me as to what to do now. I had seen a flat-open strip in the bush that only required a few ant-heaps to be leveled off and a few trees cut to make quite a decent little aerodrome. I demanded that a machine be given me, together with a tender and four mechanics. I said that with this outfit I could operate over the enemy lines. Orders came through to prepare the landing ground.

The moment the landing strip was ready, a machine from the squadron arrived and landed safely. The pilot, a Flight Commander, said, "Your name is mud. The C.O. is furious." He told me that everyone had been recalled from leave, and he gave further prognostications of the awful things that would happen to Second-Lieutenant Bell.

Presently the tender with all the things I had asked for arrived. The Flight Commander returned whence he came, and there I was, set up with my own plane, aerodrome, and personnel. I was detached from my squadron and attached to Intelligence. Of course, I now had the time of my life. Such a situation must be unique. Only a commander-in-chief like Smuts could have brought it about.

From this bush aerodrome I operated all over the place. Once I was asked if I thought I could take a ground officer as passenger-observer over the lines. Without much thought, I said I could. Down from headquarters arrived a stout individual with general's insignia and his staff officer, a much slimmer man.

In looking at the general, I asked him his weight. When I heard it, I had some doubts as to my machine's ability to clear the tallish trees surrounding my little bush aerodrome. When the general wanted to bring along a rifle, I had to turn his request down. I explained the difficulties and suggested there would be a better chance if I took the staff officer. But the general would not hear of that. So I then explained what might happen should we hit the trees. The general hastily discarded a hefty pack of provisions he had previously intended to take along with him, keeping only an enormous water bottle filled with brandy.

I waited for the breeze to harden and took the longest run possible, and even so, the machine, with its double load—for I was no feather weight myself—just managed to clear. Even then the wheels grazed the tree tops. The general was able to see the lay of the land and seemed satisfied.

Shortly after this, the whole campaign was set in motion once more, rain or no rain. The squadron came pouring through the bush and air to my aerodrome, very much to my annoyance, be it said. The C.-in-C. himself paid a visit. The only thing he said to me was, "For God's sake, cover your head. Don't you know the danger of sun?"

I was wearing my R.F.C. cap, a ridiculous headgear little calculated to afford any protection from anything whatsoever.

Rather to my surprise, my C.O. had nothing to say to me except, "Good work, Bell, the C.-in-C. has given you an M.C."

So is it always the unexpected.

The whole army now rolled on. As it progressed, bush strips were cut for the planes. We bombed columns of the enemy winding through the eternal bush in single file, carrying their white officers in hammocks. We had no bomb sights and simply let go when we thought the right moment had come.

We also had no armour plating on the machines, and the enemy machine gunners were mighty good at hitting flying planes. Our all-out speed was only about sixty or seventy miles per hour. Since we had a healthy aversion to low flying, we consequently did not do much damage, especially as the bombs we had simply blew up a lot of dust into the air with no lateral effect whatsoever.

Then there came a time when news arrived from the base that a Farman had broken in the air at three thousand feet, killing the test pilot. This incident, coming on top of a forced landing in the bush of another Farman, forced the pilots furiously to think. For some reason or other, the Farmans were not popular. Now the pilots said they were not fit machines for bush work and proposed to tell the C.O. something to that effect. When I was asked to join in the protest, I said I liked the Farman.

This machine, with its nose wheel and independent brakes on the main wheels was the forerunner of the present tricycle undercarriage. The engine, too, was quite fairly reliable if left alone. Of course, when the engineer thought fit to transfer the water-circulating pump drive from its proper place to that of the magneto in order to get livelier cooling, any engine was entitled to jib at such treatment. This little effort had actually been responsible for the forced landing. It was a French engine, and by way of mastering its peculiarities, the English engineer without a word of French had been sent to France to "learn" the engine in a week.

Unfortunately for me, my championing of the Farman was seized upon by the C.O., and I was asked to go back to base to find out what was wrong with the Farmans. When I arrived there, I was provided with a newly assembled one to test. I naturally looked it over carefully but could find nothing wrong. So I prepared to take it up.

Just as I was about to leave, a mechanic asked if he might come, too. *Can't be much wrong if he is willing to risk his neck,* I thought. Parachutes being unknown in those days, we set off. We circled and circled, gaining confidence all the time. Nothing happened, so I thought I would take the machine over a neighbouring lake where I knew from former experience the air was very bumpy. Sure enough it was.

Suddenly my companion and I saw a balloon forming on the wing. To our horror, it grew bigger and bigger. Throttling down hastily and flying as gingerly as possible, we headed for home, all the time watching that fearful bulge on the wing covering. We both knew that if it burst, we were for it. However, it held and we landed safely.

We found the linen fabric was rotten. I had the time of my life poking my finger through it all over the machine and bawling out the people, majors and captains and all, for not detecting the faulty covering before. The corps had ample stocks of good, sound Irish linen, and when the machines had been covered with this, they functioned right along.

As there was no opposition in the air, the enemy having no airplanes, of course there was no fighting. This and the apparent reluctance of the staff to use aeroplanes for anything but reconnaissance and photography induced me to apply for a transfer to some more active front. In due course I went to Egypt, and from Egypt to the Balkan front.[3]

---

[3] The Macedonian Front of World War I, also known as the Salonika Front, was formed as a result of an attempt by the Allied Powers to aid Serbia in the fall of 1915 against the combined attack of Germany, Austria-Hungary, and Bulgaria.

THE WAR YEARS

Artist's rendition of a Farman on reconnaissance over British East Africa during World War I.

Reminiscences of an Elephant Hunter

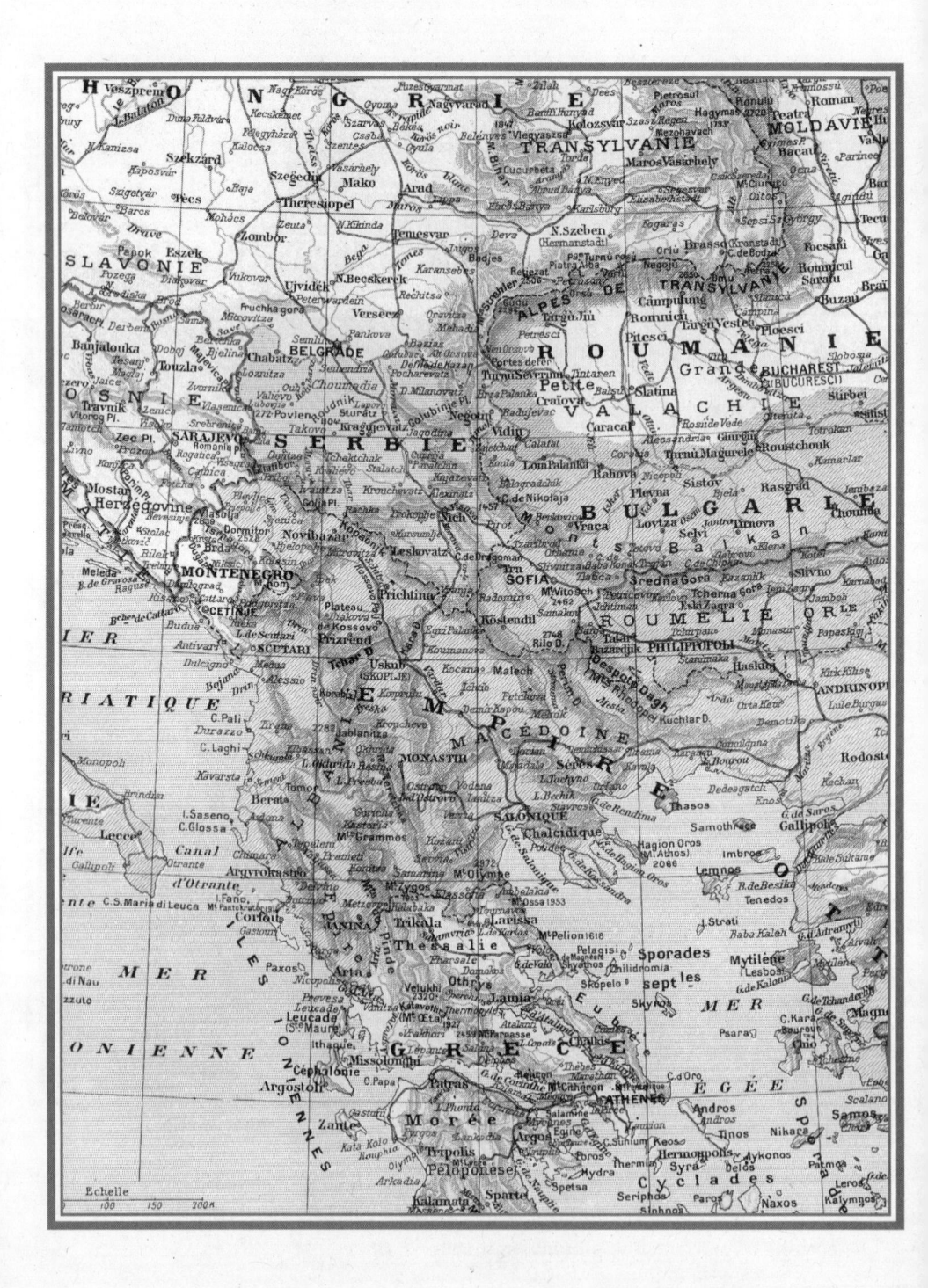

The War Years

Soldiers from various Allied countries at the Macedonian Front of World War I.

At Salonika I found a curious assortment of all kinds of rejected machines from France. Among them was a vicious-looking bird cage with a pusher screw, a water-cooled engine, and a long beak in front in which sat the pilot with a Lewis gun. This gun was very close to and fired straight past the head of the observer who also had a Lewis gun.

It was quite a formidable machine except for the fact that it had a very poor performance rating. But it would dive like a streak out of hell. None of the Huns would take a go at it even though it was totally blind from behind and even though the Germans had quite smart Fokker monoplanes. I had great fun with this machine.

Owing to its apparent immunity from attack, it was sent daily over the Hun aerodrome. The occupants would laugh to see the Hun fighters being kicked off their aerodrome by their C.O. One dive from the bird cage with both Lewis guns roaring would send them scattering. What they said when they returned to their aerodrome I always wondered.

It was not possible to make a long dive in this crate because the plugs oiled up and you would find yourself without an engine. Otherwise, there was nothing to prevent close-ground strafing.

My first air fight was somewhat unexpected. I had just received a new machine, and, wanting to try it, I thought I might as well combine business with pleasure. So I had the machine-gun filled up—it was a belt-fed Vickers firing through the prop—and I took along two, twenty-five-pound bombs in the cockpit just to chuck overboard if the A.A. [anti-aircraft] guns annoyed me.

I climbed to ten thousand feet—that took quite a while in those days—and crossed the lines. Enemy A.A. started to plaster the sky, and, as usual, nowhere near the machine. I threw my bombs overboard, hoping they might hit something. The A.A. fire stopped abruptly. I was thinking I must have tickled them up by some extraordinary fluke when there flashed past me a vividly coloured Albatross covered with the Hun black crosses. It was not firing.

In a matter of seconds I had him covered, sighting the machine by lining the row of tappets on the engine, the only sight I had. As I drew near, I could see the enemy quite distinctly crouched behind his gun and firing over his tail like billy-oh from the after cockpit. I started my Vickers—*pop! pop!* blank, *pop! pop!*—about as fast as it takes to write this; obviously, the interrupter gear was working smoothly. All the while brown tracer streaked from the Albatross.

After about twenty rounds (actually twenty-one), to my astonishment and delight the Albatross went out of control, turned over on her back, and out fell the two occupants. I was thrilled to realize I had shot down my first E.A. [enemy aircraft], and I hoped it would fall within my own lines. I did not know my exact whereabouts, but just then A.A. fire opened up and left me in no doubt on that score.

Thinking I might as well celebrate a bit and lose height at the same time, as the batteries seemed to have my range, I started a few stunts and then returned to my aerodrome. I was still doubtful if my combat had been seen, but these were soon allayed, for, on entering the mess, I was greeted with shouts of, "What did you do to that Hun?"

"Why, I filled the Boche with lead," I told them, midst shouts of laughter.

Two men who had been spotting for our heavies at three thousand feet said they had had the shock of their lives and needed a drink badly. They then related how their shoot had been going on nicely and all was peace and quietness when out of the blue quite suddenly two human bodies had shot past them quite close. They had seen no aeroplanes about. No. Just two bodies plunging earthward. Shoot or no shoot, they were seeing things and needed refreshment. Hence the meeting in mess.

THE WAR YEARS

Air fight over the Balkans, World War I.

The whole incident had been seen from the frontline trenches, so it was known that the Albatross had been downed and the bodies had fallen in no-man's land. So that night both sides met out there in the dark, and it was our fellows who prevailed after quite a scrap. The pilot and the observer were both shot through the head.

One might have thought that this fight showed good shooting. Many people did so. But I was much puzzled in my mind about it. I was conscious that while I was firing, my impromptu sights were off the target. The Albatross was not going straight away but in a curve, probably involuntarily caused by the pilot looking over his shoulder in his desire to see his officer shoot down the enemy. I was conscious, too, of having to hold off so as to get him across the arc of flight, but he was constantly over-ruddering. By some miraculous combination of flukes, two of those twenty-one bullets had found billets from that gyrating platform. With these thoughts in my mind, I was not greatly surprised when I test-fired my gun to find my shots were nowhere near the point of aim.

About this time an Irish friend of mine got the tail of his machine cut off neatly behind the pilot's seat while coming up from below to attack another aircraft. It was the enemy's propeller that got him. My friend was at eleven thousand feet when the E.A. came up behind him, cut the back of his plane clean off, and what was left of his machine turned on its back and went spinning slowly down. His cockpit machine-gun fell off, but luckily Pat's belt held. By the time a rescue party reached the spot, Pat had disentangled himself and was sitting smoking a cigarette quite unhurt.

But he was an appalling sight. Blood had invaded and completely suffused the whites of his eyes. The iris being of a pale blue, the effect was quite startling, and Pat enjoyed it enormously. The medics ordered him a fortnight's leave to Egypt. As it happened, I was due for a spot of leave, too. I had done two-and-a-half years of continuous flying. So it was arranged we should sail together.

It is often said misfortunes never come singly. Off one of the Aegean islands our ship—a ten thousand tonner—got a torpedo amidships, in the engine-room, in fact. Now the captain had allotted boat stations and had announced that all should assemble at their proper places and wait for the "abandon ship" signal. This was to be a continuous blast on the ship's foghorn. Unfortunately, the explosion had made it impossible to do this.

It was about five minutes after the explosion, and some one thousand, two hundred troops had by that time all fallen in at boat stations when the ship

THE WAR YEARS

R.M.S.P. Ocean Cruising Steamer "Arcadian" (Twin-Screw-12,050 Tons Gross).

Off one of the Aegean islands our ship—a ten thousand tonner—got a torpedo amidships, in the engine-room, in fact. The Arcadian, Bell's ship, was torpedoed 15 April 1917. (Courtesy of Terry Castle)

219

simply sank on a level keel. As it happened I was on the boat deck at the time and had a good view of the bridge. I saw the first mate with the loose end of the foghorn cord in his hand saying something to the skipper. I spotted at once that the game was up and it was best to get into the sea. The stern suggested itself as being the best place.

Meeting Pat, I told him to get into the water at once. I got a rope and lowered myself gingerly into the sea so as not to wet my cigarettes and matches in the upper pockets of my tunic. Pat, fully alive to what was going on, followed suit but, unfortunately, chose to go overside just where the crew was throwing over the Carley life floats, which are great, huge box-like affairs.

As they swung the floats overboard without glancing overside, they shouted, "Stand from under!" in the most unhurried and everyday manner as if discharging cargo. Well, poor Pat got one of these floats smack on his head. It stunned him, but someone got a hold of him and pulled him aboard a raft.

The scene that met my eye was this: The ship had disappeared, and in the calm, warm sea the evening light shone on innumerable black dots, obviously human heads. There were larger dots where rafts and one or two boats had got clear, and in the offing round and round the scene tore the escort ship occasionally firing at something they thought might be a periscope.

While this was going on, I made my way toward a deeply laden boat and got aboard. There were seventy men in the boat that was marked for forty-five. As it happened, I was the only officer on board, so I took charge. It seemed to me that the escort should pick us up, so we waited. We had a grandstand view, and presently the escort drew near, slowed down to ten knots or so, and lowered a boat. Then she tore off again, firing away at wreckage and whatnot.

In the meanwhile the escort boat had filled up rapidly with floating men, and again the escort drew near to pick a life boat up. Just as the boat was made fast, the gunner in the bows of the escort let fly at something or other, having, one supposes, orders to shoot on sight. Forgetting the deeply laden boat alongside, the officer on the bridge ordered full-steam ahead and that was that. As the escort jumped away, the life boat capsized, and all were in the drink again.

On seeing the way things were going, I determined to get my boat moving and to go to the nearest island, only about four miles distant. Seeing some men in naval uniform, I naturally turned to them to get the oars out, only to discover to my amazement that they had no experience whatever of small-boat handling.

The boat was fearfully over-loaded and had that sickening wallow of all boats in that condition. The oars were covered with men and whenever we tried to move the oars, the boat would give a sickening roll and scare everyone stiff. However, the oars had to be got out and were. The island was duly made . . . only to discover another trouble. This time it was boots, or rather the lack of them.

The islanders were extremely hospitable, especially so as they were paid so much for each rescued mariner. But the island was very rocky and a lot of the lads had thrown away their boots—why is not clear as the life belts were easily capable of floating a good deal more than boots. The village lay up some very stony paths, and the naked soft feet of the troops could not face them. However, as the reward depended on good treatment of shipwrecked mariners, donkeys were soon forthcoming to carry the unshod. All assembled in the town hall where a spread was laid out.

I felt quite ashamed when one of my men sampled a wine flask, spat out the mouthful on the clean town hall floor and said, "Oh, Christ!" in front of the villagers.

When all the survivors of the ship had been collected together at the naval base, I was overjoyed to see Pat again, quite recovered. I had lost my rifle when the ship sank, and besides the loss of my precious semi-automatic, all our kit was lost as well. Talking it all over without heat, we came to the conclusion that it had been a poor show, indeed. We were furious with the navy for losing our kit, and we declared, quite openly, that we would hire a sail boat and sail her back when our leave terminated. "Safer that way," we said.

At this assembly camp there was a white-haired padre strolling around talking earnestly to a group who had been torpedoed. I felt there something familiar about the appearance of the reverent gentleman, albeit his khaki uniform was black with ingrained soot. Pat and I stopped to listen. He was recounting how he and his brother padre had been sucked down when the ship sank, how his brother padre had shaken his hand at some unknown depth, and that then a sudden gush of air had shot him up the funnel.

Pat whispered to me, "He's gone nuts."

To the padre, Pat said, "Why didn't you come up the main stairway?"

******

When one thinks back on the faux pas perpetrated by reputable firms in those days, it makes one shudder to think of similar ones to come. Only with this difference: They now have much more incalculable forces to play the ass with.

As an example of those days, take the interrupter gear fitted to those war machines. It consisted of a steel rod some ten feet in length connected to the mechanism of the gun at one end and making intermittent contact with knobs on the hub of the propeller at the other. The rod was fitted with a micrometer adjustment whereby you got the gun to shoot between the blades.

This you did on the ground when maybe the sun was out and the rod expanded to ground temperature. When you got to ten or twelve thousand feet, it might well be freezing. As any schoolboy could have foretold, that ten-foot rod would contract and almost every shot would hit a blade. However, most times the gun packed up before you lost a blade. Anyhow, it was extraordinary how many shots those wooden props could withstand before breaking.

I had another unusual dogfight when a Halberstadt single-seater engaged me, this time over the French front. You can't imagine a more ridiculous affair. Both machines flew all-out straight at each other, and we passed by a hair's breadth. Not a shot from either side. As we passed, we both tried to get on the other's tail. Still not a shot from either. We both were frantically trying to clear our guns, and so it went on while the French front-liners cheered and afterward testified that they heard the machine-guns roaring at each other.

I was the first to get my gun to fire, and I sailed in to give the Halber a burst. Result: one shot and the gun again jammed. What was my astonishment when I saw the Hun start diving the Halber down but not to the German pilot's own lines, which he could easily have reached, but hell bent for a comfortable berth in the middle of no-man's-land between the lines. I watched as I followed the other plane down, and I saw him flatten out, land OK, get out, and then run like hell for his own lines. Almost simultaneously the French batteries started to pound the abandoned machine, soon scattering it to atoms.

Well, I thought, *that's a queer go. Can't make a fight of that.*

So I merely stated in my combat report that I had engaged an S.A. but that my gun had jammed after one shot and that the E.A. too had broken off the fight. That was not the end of it, however, for presently the C.O. came in with a telegram in his hand from the French congratulating him on the result of the combat.

On receipt of this, he had telephoned the French battery concerned, and they said, "Yes, yes, we saw the whole affair and heard the machine-guns roaring!"

A Halberstadt.

After that they confirmed that they had demolished the E.A. on the ground with the superb *tir* [shooting] of their seventy-fives.

"Well, what do you say to that?" asked the C.O.

Again I explained exactly what had happened: that both guns had jammed and that anyhow the Hun was just as fed-up with the German's dud machines as we were with ours, and that he saw this merely as an opportunity for a write-off. The C.O., an otherwise quite sane person, was furious and said that he was not going to lose a claim and that I would be credited with shooting down the machine whether I liked it or not.

"What," I asked, "with one shot, Sir?"

"Yes, and be damned to you!" and off he stomped.

Such is squadron history in the making and such was air fighting in those days. How very different now, with multiple cannon, armour plating, parachutes, and fantastic rates of speed and climb, to say nothing of radar. I collected a bar in this campaign to add to my M.C.

Every day the enemy sent out a very high-flying reconnaissance machine to photograph the shipping in Salonika harbour. It was known as the "Iron Cross flight," and it was said that any Hun making three successful recces was awarded that decoration. Consequently, everyone tried to intercept this machine.

The French had got out from France one very smart little scout called a Spad, which was quite the latest thing and the apple of their eye. On it they

A recruiting poster for the R.F.C. (Courtesy of Terry Castle)

mounted two additional Lewis guns secured to the outer struts and fired by Bowden wire from the cockpit, thus giving, together with the normal gun firing through the prop, an unheard-of rate of fire—in those days at any rate. They chose their best pilot, and one fine, clear day they launched their attempt at the "Iron Cross" machine.

As it happened Wynne-Eyton,[4] a man in my squadron whom I liked very much, and I were also up and bent on the same lay. We, however, were somewhat handicapped by the ceiling of our machines standing at fifteen thousand feet or so, whereas the Hun used to come over at twenty thousand feet. As we were floundering around in that floppy way of machines at their ceiling, suddenly there was a burst of fire behind me and a small machine flashed by me in a dive.

Without a thought I put my nose down and started my Vickers pop-popping. As luck would have it, the Vickers, which nearly always gave up after a few rounds, continued to fire at its best rate. Wynne, seeing me engaging a machine, joined in. His gun, too, operated. It would!

Presently we saw a piece of the enemy machine detach itself. Still we followed the German down, down. We thought, *"We've got him!"*

We also knew what would happen to him if he came down inside our lines, for we had seen Hun machines stripped bare by hungry souvenir hunters in incredibly short time. So taking no chances, we followed our victim right down until he crash-landed, the plane collapsing flat.

We then landed close by and rushed over to the plane. Suddenly, coming from one of the wing guns, there was a burst of fire. Behind it was a fierce-looking little man evidently in a state of great excitement. We invited him to come forth and explain himself. He did so . . . in French.

"It's a ruddy Frenchman! Hell," we said, "Let's clear out quick!"

We did so, pretending we knew nothing about the episode. That plane was the marvelous, the magnificent, the formidable Spad! My only souvenir? A neat group of bullet-holes in my machine.

---

[4] Robert Mainwaring Wynne-Eyton would be Bell's best man at his wedding in January 1919. Both Bell and Wynne-Eyton were captains in the Royal Air Force in World War I and both received a Military Cross for "exemplary gallantry during active operations."

Islande (D.)
Reykjavik
Trondhjem
Is Færœr
Bergen
Is Shetland
Kristiania
Kristiansand
Stockholm
Is Hébrides
Inverness
Riga
ILES
Edimbourg
Glasgow
Copenhague
DANEMARK
Londonderry
BRITANNIQUES
Liverpool
Berlin
Varsovie
Valentia
Londres
ALLEMAGNE
Le Havre
Prague
Kiev
Kharkov
Paris
Vienne
St Nazaire
FRANCE
AUTRICHE
Odessa
Bordeaux
Lyon
Trieste
Marseille
Belgrade
M. NOIRE
la Corogne
Vigo
Porto
ESPAGNE
Rome
PORTUGAL
Madrid
Naples
Lisbonne
Valence
Palerme
EMPIRE OTTOMAN
Gibraltar
Cadix
Alger
Tunis
Malte (A)
Crète
Oran
Fez
Algérie
Benghasi
Madère
Mogador
Ghadamès
Tripoli
Alexandrie
Ténériffe
MAROC
Is Canaries
Tripolitaine
le Caire
In Çalah
Mourzouk
EGYPTE
Rio de Oro
S A H A R A
Taoudéni
Ouadi Halfa
Nubie
Tombouctou
Touareg
St Louis
Agadem
Sénégal
Khartoum
Omdurman
Kayes
Niger
Sokoto
Kouka
L. Tchad
El Facher
Bamako
S o u d a n
Fachoda
Kong
Salaga
Boussa
Chari
Freetown
Lagos
Mourovia
A F R I Q U E
Cameroun
Batanga
Congo
Français
ÉTAT DU
CONGO
I. Annobon
Brazzaville
Léopoldville
Loango
Cabinda
Banana
Ascension (A)
Ambriz
Loanda
Pernambouc
Benguela
Angola

Another Go at Africa

CHAPTER 18

At the conclusion of the war, I returned to England and married the best girl in the world. (I should know as I have vast experience on the subject!) Katie, who was from Devon, was the daughter of Sir Ernest and Lady Soares, and I had met her while on leave. We settled in London for a while, but we had great schemes for settling down to a quiet life in the Scottish Highlands. Eventually we settled in "Corriemoillie," our highland estate at Garve in Ross-shire, Scotland.[1]

But first there was one last bit of wandering to be gotten out of my system. My health, however, was suffering from a double infestation of malaria of the Balkan variety plus my old African bugs, and initially after the war, this curbed my activities quite a lot.[2]

My friend and fellow squadron member Wynne-Eyton and I had often talked about what we would do after the war, and, upon telling him of my proposal to ascend the Bahr Aouk, he instantly declared that he would join me. We agreed to have a go at it as soon as we were discharged.

Having received our families' blessings, we prepared to push right off after the war, but our womenfolk pressed us to get our medals. We pointed out that there was not going to be an investiture for some time, and we stated that we could not wait until then, and that anyhow the army would post them.

"No! No!" they declared. "You must go through the ceremony!"

---

[1] Bell is vague about who bought Corriemoillie, but it was most likely Katie Bell's family. Valuation rolls from the 1930s list Kate Rose Mary Bell as the proprietrix of Corriemoillie. Had Walter and Katie Bell bought the property together, the valuation rolls would most likely have listed W. D. M as the owner, especially given the patriarchal culture of the 1930s. (See chapter 34.)

[2] Malaria was a scourge in World War I. About 40 percent of the French and British troops in the Balkans—about 120,000 men—contracted malaria and became unfit for active service.

Bell leaves a bit out in this account. While it is true that he was suffering from various forms of malaria, Bell was repatriated to England, according to his military records, because he was suffering from "Neurasthenia," the precursor to what is now known as PTSD. He returned home on the hospital ship *Formosa*, which sailed from Salonika for Malta on 4 December 1917. This also means that he didn't return "at the end of the war" but about eight months earlier. Bell flew for two-and-a-half years without a break, and when he finally was able to get leave, the ship he was on was torpedoed. It's hardly surprising that he finally caved under the pressure and strain.

Bell was awarded Great Britain's Military Cross with bar. (Courtesy of Terry Castle)

Through the ceremony we went.

As it happened Wynne's sister was working at the War Office, and she said that she would see if anything could be done about it. Finally, a general was persuaded to present the medals. Having entered into civilian life, it never occurred to us to don our uniforms; instead, we went in overcoats and bowler hats, as if to a funeral. To top it off, we both were suffering from colds, so our appearance was lugubrious at best! We caused quite a sensation at the War Office.

When the general came into the room where we were waiting, he was so overcome by the sombre clothes and unhealthy pallor of the war heroes that he burst into fits of laughter.

"Never, no never," he roared, "have I ever invested anyone wearing bowler hats!"

******

Before the war broke out in 1914, I was making preparations to explore the Bahr Aouk and its mythical lake. Now was my chance to resume where I had left off years earlier. Once in Cairo I had seen a map made by Kumm, one of those methodically plodding German explorers who lived with the native tribes, learnt their languages, and wrote everything down.

These Germans spent years on the job, and their books were still treated in the 1920s as the standard works on many of the less well-known parts of Africa. Kumm had heard native rumours of the lake and had tentatively dotted in on his map what he called "a reported lake" and an outflow that would approximate the Bahr Aouk. Only he guessed that it flowed east into the Bahr el Ghazal. In question marks he had labeled it "?Inundations?" That the lake was caused by flood water in the rains and only existed at that season was unknown then.

As was my wont whenever I wanted anything from any part of the world, I ordered a small fleet of Peterborough canoes from Canada through the Army and Navy Stores in London. They were to be shipped direct to West Africa where we, the would-be explorers, would pick them up. Everything went according to plan.

Before leaving this subject of ordering things that you wanted from anywhere, it should be remembered that there were no restrictions on currency as at present. The good old British pound note was still welcome everywhere. The notable London firms could get you anything, anywhere. Thomas Cook and Sons afforded another example of outstanding service.

Once I had occasion to require four of my East African boys to meet me at Djibouti, French Somaliland. I walked into Cook's place in Ludgate Circus, London, and wrote down the details, merely giving the names. Cook's arranged everything perfectly. Another instance of the marvelous service of this firm took place in the Belgian Congo. At one stage of the hunt I found myself becoming embarrassed by the number and weight of my ivory. Usually on reaching such a stage of plethora, I buried the stuff. But on this occasion I met a Greek trader moving down country with a lot of empty porters.

I asked the Greek if he would take the ivory down with him to Khartoum and once there collect his expenses from Cook's. He agreed readily, and I gave him a letter to the Cook's agent along with a list of the ivory that detailed their weights. Of course, the tusks were all stamped with my mark, but it is easy to remove any mark by simply filing it off. The ivory went off with the Greek, and I continued to hunt.

About a year later I got the proceeds from the London auctioneers. Cook's had paid all expenses and recovered them from the sale price of the tusks. The expenses listed were very reasonable, indeed. In spite of this, however, the price netted was hardly up to that given by the Indian traders, who would come out anywhere in the bush to buy.

Although the weights and numbers of the ivory that went via the Greek to Cook's tallied with my list, there seemed to be an extraordinarily large number of defective tusks. I read in the auctioneer's report such things as "rotten centres" and "shot bodies," phrases that figured frequently in the descriptions but that were not at all applicable to the tusks I had sent off. It is natural to suppose that a little juggling with the tusks took place somewhere, probably before they were handed over to Cook's.

******

We found the Niger Delta country reeking of palm oil, sex, and money. It was surprising to see such affluence because at the end of the war-that-was-to-end-all-wars nothing in the shape of provisions could be got in Britain. In fact,

REMINISCENCES OF AN ELEPHANT HUNTER

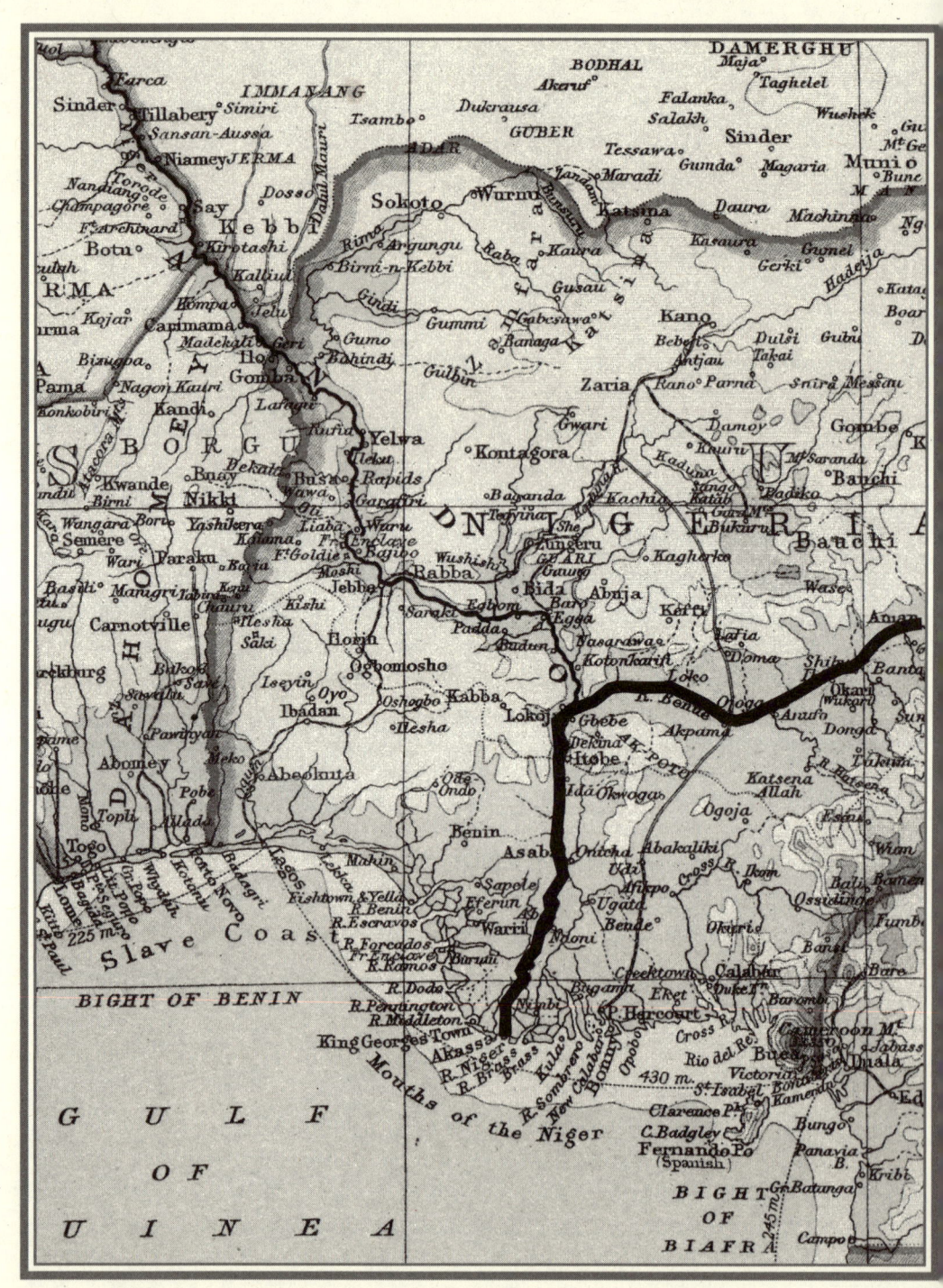

Bell first went up the Niger River in canoes before he then turned east onto the Benue River.

nothing could be had at all except rifles and ammunition. We were prepared, therefore, to live off our rifles, a shot-gun, and the country.

The expedition up the Bahr Aouk has been described for the most part in *Wanderings of an Elephant Hunter*, so it will suffice to say here that we ascended[3] the Niger in canoes, went four hundred miles up the Benue, made a portage of one hundred miles to the Logone, descended toward Lake Chad, went upstream on the Shari, which is a main feeder of Lake Chad, to Fort Archambault (Sarh). From there we went into and up the Bahr Aouk.

We did some fair hunting, but the ivory was small and the elephants much harassed by bands of wandering Arabs. Wynne and I did have a couple of interesting adventures that I now remember are not in *Wanderings of an Elephant Hunter*, so I will touch on those.

It was on our portage to the Logone that we ran across Buba Gida,[4] the last of the great African potentates left at that time (1919) outside of Abyssinia. His empire lay in the German Cameroons, but with the war just over it had come under French administration. No one, not even the Germans, had attempted to interfere with the wily Buba. I suspect they found it convenient to have such a man as Buba who could, and did, furnish at a moment's notice a colossal labour force. At the time we arrived in his country, this absolute dictator of the Logone-Benue watershed was carrying on just as he had begun.

Buba was a frightening example of what can be done by courage, energy, force of character, and extreme cunning allied to ferocious cruelty. For this owner, body and soul, of literally tens of thousands of slaves was no scion of a kingly race. Mothered by a Lakka slave and fathered by a scrub Fulani of sorts, everything he had and was he owed entirely to his own abilities. He had amassed power that was almost beyond imagination, and he exerted complete control over all his dominions. For a while, that included us, too.

Buba Gida had an intelligence force that would rival a modern-day state's in its information-gathering abilities. He set upon us a villainous following

---

[3] In *Bell of Africa*, Bell wrote that he first went to Ivory Coast to hunt elephants before meeting up with Wynne-Eyton. Bell makes no mention of that in the diaries on which this autobiography is based.

[4] The story of Buba Gida is told in detail in *Wanderings of an Elephant Hunter*. A synopsis of Bell's encounter with Buba Gida is mentioned here only to place him chronologically in this autobiography.

REMINISCENCES OF AN ELEPHANT HUNTER

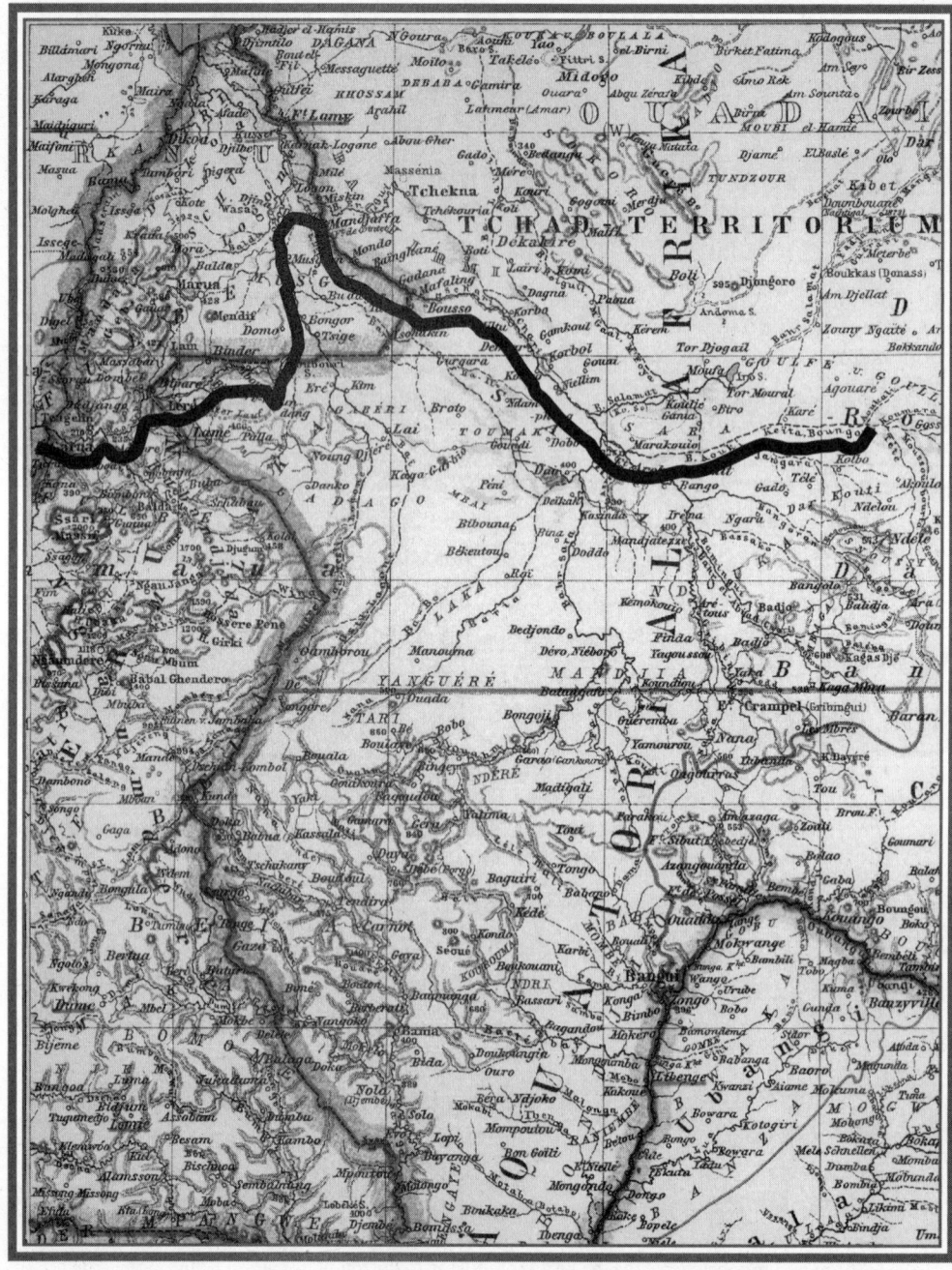

Bell was somewhere near the end of the Benue River when he went overland to the Logone River, took it toward Lake Chad, went upstream on the Shari River to Fort Archambault (now Sarh), and then went up to the Bahr Aouk River. He probably also went up the Aoukale River or one of the side branches of the Bahr Aouk.

that was hard to shake, but shake it we finally did. Once we were rid of his spies and his slavers, we soon became friends with the natives. After that, we enjoyed quite fair hunting in the Lakka country.

When we had reached the Shari-Chad-Logone watershed, it was time once more to embark in our canoes as we needed to avoid the rains. There were still many miles to cover before we would reach the waters of the unexplored Bahr Aouk. Thus far we had paddled five hundred miles up the Niger and Benue Rivers and portaged one hundred miles overland. Now we had a descent of two hundred miles down the Logone to its junction with the Shari, near Lake Chad. From there it would be a steady plug against the current of the Shari for three hundred and fifty miles to where the Aouk joined it. From now on we would be independent of all, beholden to none. It was a relief.

Before the advent of motor cars, canoes proved to be by far the most economical means of transport. Not least of their advantages being that their use enabled the personal boys to do their share in the transport of the safari equipment. Where otherwise the cook, headman, gunbearers, and servants would be idly strolling along, carrying nothing, they could all paddle or pole.

It seemed never to strike them that they might claim, with some justice, extra pay for this addition to their day's task. The fact of the matter is that these lovely craft were so easily propelled that it was preferable to paddle than to sit idle all day under a broiling sun. Our average speed carrying about two tons of stuff was little short of twenty miles per day against the current, while with it naturally it was much greater.

This whole country was theoretically occupied by the French, and the commandant, who should have known something about it, told us that in his opinion nothing short of a well-equipped military expedition could penetrate this region as it was the refuge and last stronghold of the Khalifa's[5] die-hards. This subsequently proved to be wrong. But that painstaking German explorer had been right. He need not have queried the "?Inundations?" Only the direction of the river was in error.

The day arrived at last when we reached the mouth of the Aouk. As we paddled into it, we were all very merry, the boys because they did not know where they were, such is the happy disposition of the African, and we because

---

[5] Khalifa was the successor to the Mahdi.

Reminiscences of an Elephant Hunter

As we paddled into the Bahr Aouk, we were all very merry, the boys because they did not know where they were, and we because we did.

we did. Visions of a new land teeming with elephants rose before my eyes. We had with us the wherewithal to sit down in it and hunt to our hearts' content, which is exactly what we did.

The plan was that if we found good elephant country, we would make a base camp and bury all the ivory. None of it would we take out, for I had found from bitter experience in the past that if you did so, others immediately came in and spoiled your hunting. The Lado Enclave was a good example. A deluge of hunters and would-be hunters descended upon me there, spoiling not only the game but also the natives. So on this expedition, not a word had been said about our destination. Should things fall our way, one of us would return home for a spell and then relieve the other.

We entered the Bahr Aouk in the dry season. Much of the grass had been burned off, and one could circulate freely to watch the game. It was a lovely country at that time of year, but in the heavy rains it must be an almost continuous sheet of water with perhaps only the dry ridges showing above it. Now there were only the swampy hollows holding high reeds and water, a perfect paradise for elephants. Antelopes were numerous enough, but nothing as plentiful as they are in East Africa.

It seemed to me we had struck it lucky at last. Here was a truly virgin country abounding in game. There were practically no natives living in the country owing to severe slave raiding. Certainly we missed the assistance only meat-hungry natives can give in chopping out ivory, carrying it to base, building huts, getting firewood, and doing the innumerable chores of a permanent camp. On the other hand, we were not burdened with all the cares the safari leader shoulders.

Rhinos were also numerous and very aggressive; they would sometimes follow you for miles. Once I saw a cow and bull rhino in the morning and made a little detour to avoid them. Well on in the afternoon I turned at a shout from a boy to find the same two rhinos hunting him like terriers after a rat. I had to flatten them, and when the boy subsequently went to get their horns, he found the carcasses in possession of lions. He shouted to chase them off, and they growled and threatened him. Only after we gave him a gun did he obtain those precious horns that, when ground to a powder, one held in high esteem as an aphrodisiac.

It was a grand sight to see game so indifferent to, and even contemptuous of, the presence of man. This had its drawbacks, however.

Lions were very numerous and they were bold. Once we camped near but downwind from some elephant carcasses. Being so short-handed, we had to leave our downed elephants to rot so that on the fourth day we could draw out the tusks without any ax work. I have seldom heard such a racket. There must have been a score of lions eating away at the putrid carcasses. They were large lions of a distinctive dark-olive tinge with small manes lighter in colour than the body.

At first Wynne carefully skinned and preserved those lions he shot. But presently, what with stumbling over lions or having them constantly dispute our passage, he began to get tired of them. They were bulky and a nuisance in the canoes. So one day I was amused to see Wynne throwing overboard what had hitherto been his treasured trophies. They were a lazy lot, those lions, and much preferred us killing their meat for them to hunting prey down for themselves.

Living on what could be shot, the twelve-bore was about the most valuable gun on the safari. Cartridges were heavy and limited in number, so they had to be used with discretion. As regards elephants, the best day's bag was ten. They were in a deep swamp and thought they were safe, as they would have been from anything but a modern rifle.

Reminiscences of an Elephant Hunter

Portaging canoes overland.

The river brimmed with hippos. In the dry season the Bahr Aouk is not much more than thirty to forty yards wide, and at every bend there would be a deep pool at the outer edge and a sand bank at the inner side. As we came silently paddling along, a mass of hippos would rise from the sand bank and enter the deep water. One wondered why they did not dam up the whole stream. We would dodge along the sand bank side as close as we could get. Even so, Wynne's canoe once ran slap onto an enormous rising back and was lifted out of the water. Wynne's immediate reaction was to dig his paddle into the beast's neck. I don't know who was the more surprised.

We tried night shooting only once. We made some grass torches and sprinkled them with kerosene. By their blaze we could see well enough to shoot fairly accurately, but it resulted in the elephants ceasing to visit that spot, so we gave it up.

As the dry season wore on, we began to wonder what would happen when the rains came. There was no sign of any mound that might afford a dry spot when the big floods arrived, which would result in what Kumm had called Lake Mamoun. Then one day we discovered the very old remnants of huts built on quite high piles. Who built them or why we never discovered. Yet their presence was a pretty broad hint as to the state of the country in the rainy season. We, too, could build raised huts, but we knew it would be unlikely that the game would continue to haunt what must become a veritable sea.

Away to the south lay the high ground of the Zande country. I thought that just as the Karamojo elephants left the Nile swamps and came up to the drier ridges in the heavy rains, so would these of the Bahr Aouk climb to the watershed country lying to the south of us. And so it proved.

We journeyed down to the Zande country to see what it was like. A wild and forbidding land of mountainous grass, hurricane winds, and the most devastating thunderstorms! Iron-stone outcrops seemed to attract the lightning, for it flashed and fizzled all over the place. Blinding bright sunlight one moment and then a purple black cloud would come swooping along—a fantastic and beautiful sight.

Once I saw this happening and I took a photograph of it. Then we raced for some grass huts a short way off. We just made it when we heard: *bang! flash! sizzle!* Our hut had ignited! Hastily we got our gear into another hut. No sooner were we safely in there than sparks from the burning hut caught on this one, too. I knew what the boys were thinking: *You would go photographing thunder clouds, would you, and of all places in this land of medicine?*

With the coming of the rains I knew the time had finally arrived to put my wanderings behind me and embark on the greatest adventure of all, the adventure of life in a home. Wynne decided not to stay on by himself, so we closed camp, packed our gear, and began the trip that would carry us back to our families.

This was, with the exception of a quick tour of North Africa from Kano to Khartoum[6] with the Forbes brothers' motorized expedition, my last visit to an Africa that had been so kind to me and that was disappearing so rapidly in the mystery we call progress. Africans all dressed up in pants, shirts, collars, and specs—the sight horrified me. I fled from it to the country from which nearly all had fled, the Highlands of Scotland, where on a day when rain covers the moors and there are moments for reflection, I can think back over a life that was good because it was free.

---

[6] This story can be found in chapter 15 of *Incidents from an Elephant Hunter's Diary*.

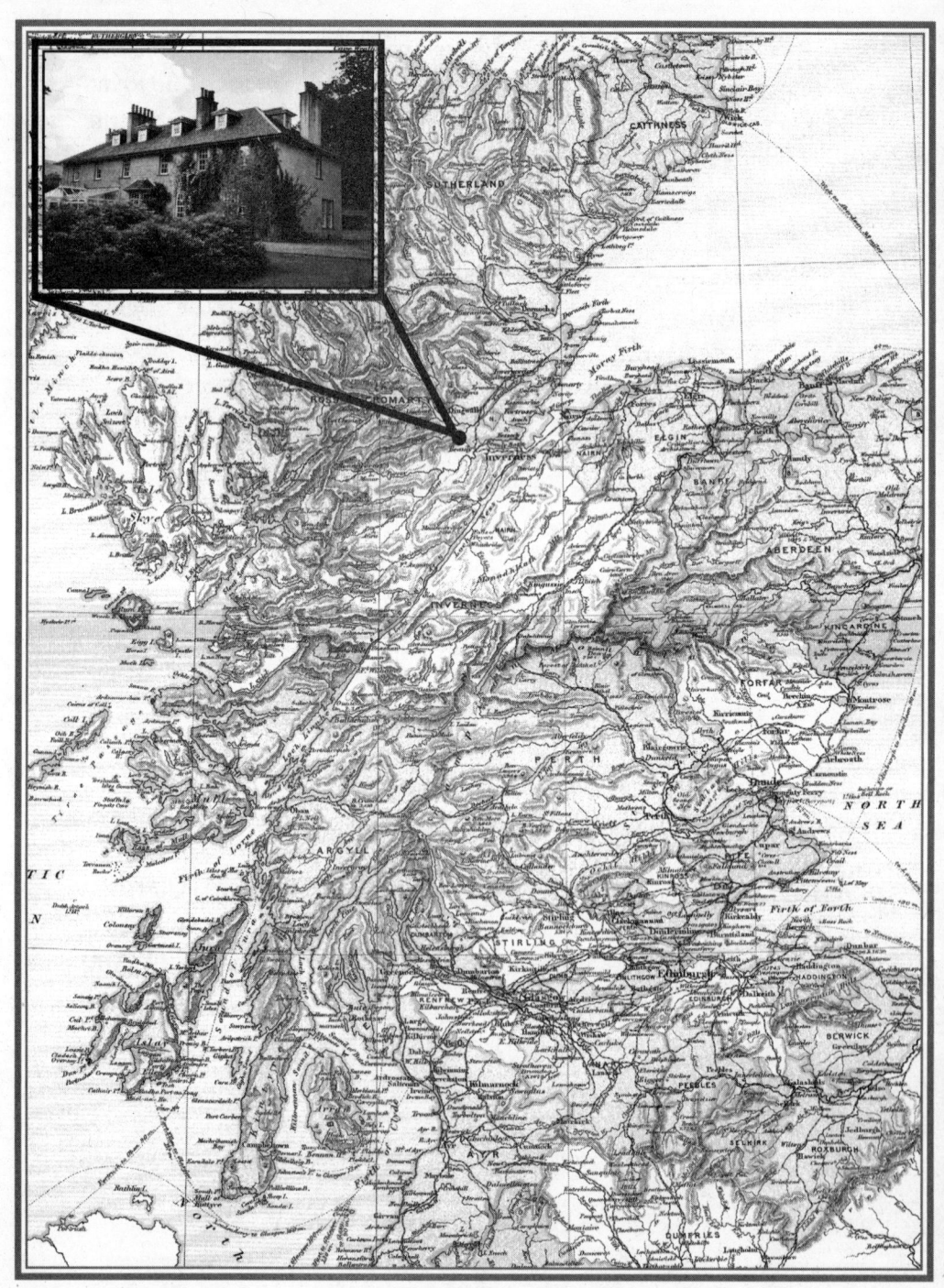

Corriemoillie, Bell's estate, is shown in the inset above. (Safari Press archives)

Home in the Highlands

CHAPTER 19

After my safari with Wynne-Eyton, I did not re-visit Africa for a considerable time. As I said in the last chapter, it was with American friends and motor cars.[1] All motorized, we simply rushed through the bush and arrived at the other side of Africa with little time for hunting. The urge each day seemed to be to see how far one could get. It was found that the motor car and lorry could circulate without roads practically anywhere in the dry season. Sometimes one could crash along through light bush at thirty and even forty miles an hour. As for serious hunting as I was used to, it was out of the question.

All along the edge of the Sahara it was a desolating sight to see the sand trickling relentlessly south. Trees with their bases barely covered stood, still alive, in the foreground, while farther away just their tops stood out of the steadily advancing ocean of sand, the branches white and dead and resembling the bleached bones of perished animals. Nothing apparently could be done to stop the relentless advance. At any rate, nothing was being done then. One imagines that in time the whole of Central Africa will be swallowed up, the climate changed, and all will become waterless desert.

At the Sudan frontier we met an enterprising gentleman who wanted desperately to buy our motor transport. He did not say so directly. Rather he tried to show that it would be impossible to traverse a certain range of hills that lay ahead. He said even camels had to be off-loaded and their loads portaged by hand past the bad place. He recounted how a Rolls Royce armoured car had got through, but only by sheer manpower. A battalion of Egyptian troops had lifted it bodily up and got it through on its side.

I could not but admire my young American friend's attitude to this situation. Malcolm Forbes had but left Harvard University yet he saw clean through all this sales talk, and when the commandant kindly offered to buy the motors and to supply camels in their place, as if he were actuated by kindness only, Malcolm turned down the offer without hesitation. The passage of the

---

[1] The complete story can be found in chapter 15 of *Incidents from an Elephant's Hunter Diary.*.

Artist's rendition of Corriemoillie, Bell's home in the Scottish Highlands.

narrow defile was successfully negotiated by building up stone ramps on either side and going over the top.

After this expedition and while preparing to settle in the Highlands of Scotland, I started to write. I sent my first article to *Country Life*. When hearing nothing further about it, I thought it had simply gone into the wastepaper basket. What was my astonishment when I not only got an acceptance but a very polite letter from the editor to say that he was keeping my article for the Christmas edition. I produced a series of articles for this journal, and *Country Life* later produced *Wanderings of an Elephant Hunter* from them.

As I had never been a photographer, I got into the habit of illustrating my stuff with drawings. Although these efforts of mine raised some ribaldry, still they went off all right, the commonly held assumption seeming to be that they were on a par with the efforts of cave-men and were not to be judged by ordinary standards. That, aided maybe by the unfamiliar subject matter of these drawings, actually induced a committee of the Royal Academy to give a painting of mine hanging room on the walls of that august body.

I had sent in three oil paintings, and the rejection slips had duly arrived as expected. One day Katie, my wife, discovered that there were only two rejection numbers on the slip. I received this news without any heat, thinking the third one had got lost or something. However, the whole matter was settled when an admission card to varnishing day arrived, and we suddenly realized that one of the pictures was actually going to be displayed.

Prices for the pictures had already been discussed. The family thought I would be lucky to get five guineas, but I thought fifty guineas would be nearer the mark. So argue-bargue [bandying words about], we compromised on thirty-five guineas. It sold instantly much to our subsequent regret, be it said, for never could I get another picture accepted, and often I wished I had not sold it. After all, it was a distinction for me to have painted a picture acceptable to artists without my having had a single lesson or course of study.

My first book, too, brought out an interesting batch of criticisms ranging from the highest praise to that of a critic at the *Manchester Guardian,* who said the author should have lived thirty thousand years ago. I loved that and took it as a great compliment. The *Manchester Guardian* said that the drawings were archaic in the extreme but full of life. The paper also said that the book could be read at a sitting, meaning, of course, that it was very short. I, on the other hand, loved to think that it was so interesting one could not put it down.

My wife and I long had had an idea to build or acquire a sizeable sailing craft. We wanted one that would offer a fair amount of comfort. The idea now crystallized. As it happened, there came along a competition for just such a boat, open to the designers of the world. The affair attracted a lot of interesting designs from all over the place. After the prizes had been allotted, the promoters of the scheme published a book containing not only the prize-winning designs but also some of those that had not, in the opinion of the judges, qualified for a prize. We bought the book, and my wife and I pored over the entrancing pages. A condition of the competition called for proper working drawings, and the aim of it was to evolve a deep-sea racing boat that would at the same time fulfill the role of comfortable cruiser.

Knowing nothing whatever about the intricacies of the subject, we boldly chose what to our minds seemed to be the best boat in the book. As it happened, it was by a young American designer, Olin Stephens by name, afterward to win such a prominent place by designing so many outstanding racing yachts, including the successful defender of the America's Cup *Ranger* and the unbeaten *Baruna*. I knew nothing of this at the time.

Having made up our minds that we had found our ship, we proceeded to name her. Katie came across an account of King Richard Coeur de Lion's red galley that he used in the Crusades. This vessel was always the leader of any fleet,

Reminiscences of an Elephant Hunter

Five Tuskers, *original painting by "Karamojo" Bell.*

Home in the Highlands

whether by virtue of superior design or whether it was in nobody's best interest to pass her, is not known. The name of King Richard's boat was the *Trenchemer*.

Looking up names in Lloyd's Register, we found no Trenchemer. So far so good. Now for the Board of Trade. "No," the reply came back to us. The Board had no objection to the name. So that was that. Now to build the ship.

After making out a list of the dimensions as detailed in the book, we sent a copy round to the leading yacht yards asking for estimates of the cost of building such a ship. This was in 1932 when timber was abundant. The answers were daunting in the extreme, the lowest being £9,000.

As would-be mariners, this gave us somewhat of a shock. We ruminated over our project in our Highland home, and came up with an idea: What about the local yards? Had not a friend of ours got himself a boat built locally? Not only had it been well and truly built, but the finished boat had come out some two feet longer than the specification called for.

Alas, these yards would not, or maybe could not, work to anything but their own ideas as to form. They simply built boats and cut them off to the desired length and then sharpened the ends. It was decided that such rough-and-ready methods would not do for such a craft as the *Trenchemer*.

Next we considered the modern shipyards at Aberdeen. A company there had built many fine sailing ships in the past, and although it mostly dealt in much bigger craft than the *Trenchemer*, we thought it possible it might tackle the job. Our letter of enquiry brought an immediate reply; the company was open to building such a boat.

Straightaway I cut out the pages of the book of designs containing the very sketchy drawings of our choice and rushed off to Aberdeen with it. Here was a very different lay-out from our local boat makers. Nothing rough and ready here. If you ordered a boat seventy feet long, it would be seventy feet long. This was the home of scientific ship-building. It was presided over by a mathematical genius, Colin Maclay, and owned by a descendant of the original firm.

At the interview, I produced the pages of my book and said I wanted an estimate for the building of that ship, inwardly trembling that such a firm would even contemplate the building of such a tiny vessel. The whole place was decorated with the loveliest models—some almost as big as the *Trenchemer*—of ships built in the past by the famous firm.

To my joy and relief, after looking at the drawings, the designers said they could build her but only in steel. This was rather a poser, for Olin Stephens's design called for wood construction. The hull was a series of the most beautiful and delicate curves, and I could not believe that they could be reproduced in steel. The keel, for instance, was one continuous but ever-altering curved profile, and I asked how they could possibly do that in steel.

"Well," they said, "we treat steel as you would paper."

I then asked how they would manage that curved keel-profile, and they explained they would simply take a long sheet of steel and double it up. But even when done with paper, it was quite difficult to bend. However, they said with conviction, they could do it. All they wanted to know was should she be built to Lloyd's scantlings (shipbuilding standards).

Here I made a mistake. However good Lloyd's may be in the case of large vessels, when it comes to small racing craft, it is undoubtedly a mistake to apply its rules—that is, if you want the utmost sailing ability from your boat. Of course, from the aspect of durability and long life of the vessel, it is undoubtedly advantageous to build under Lloyd's supervision—as well as always being a good selling point. All these considerations were then quite unknown to us budding deep-sea racers, and when the estimate came in at less than a quarter of the cost of those of the yacht yards, we whole-heartedly accepted it and the building began.

There are few greater pleasures in life than watching the building of a ship that is to be one's very own. First of all to see the thing drawn out full size in chalk on the loft floor is thrilling in the extreme. Then comes the unfolding of the lovely form in the model maker's shop. Next arrive the plates that go into the pickle to remove their scale. All is entrancing: the innumerable quarter-inch-to-the-foot scale drawings, the fairing of the lines, the accommodation plan mocked-up actual size in the carpenter's shop, the planning.

This seemed especially so in Hall Russell's yard where everyone seemed so interested in the sailing boat. Steam and motor vessels were their daily bread and, consequently, had a certain monotony in their construction. But a sailing ship was different—at least in their kindness the staff allowed us—the prospective sailors—to think so. What a pest we must have been in reality. We took a house in Aberdeen so as to be near the yard. We were always there watching the growing of our dream ship, asking endless questions, pottering about, and getting in everyone's way. Never were we shown anything but the most boundless patience, toleration, politeness, and kindness.

As anticipated, the bending of the steel keel plate was a job. Because it was of .3-inch thickness, it required a heavy mold to be built and much manipulating of

Reminiscences of an Elephant Hunter

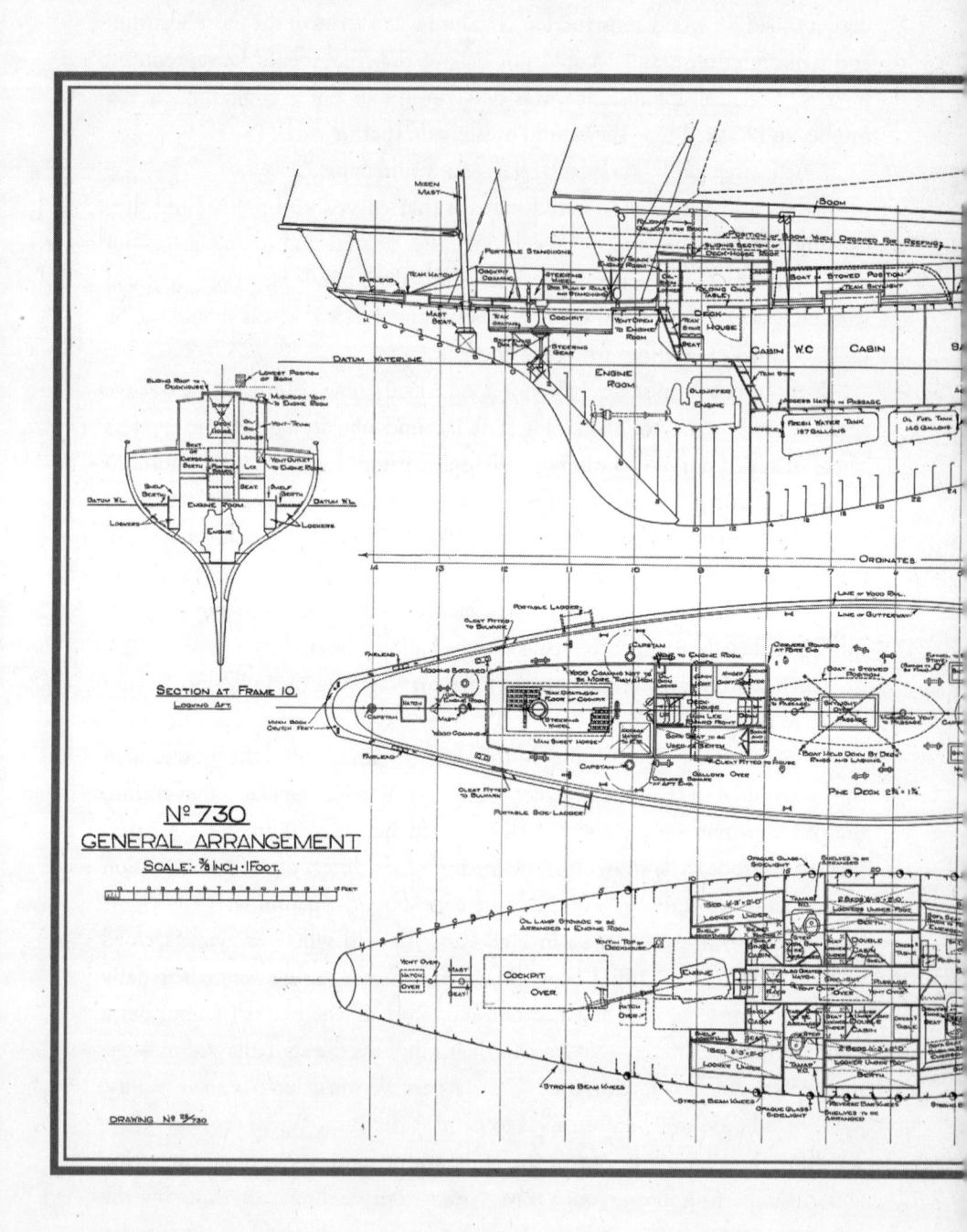

HOME IN THE HIGHLANDS

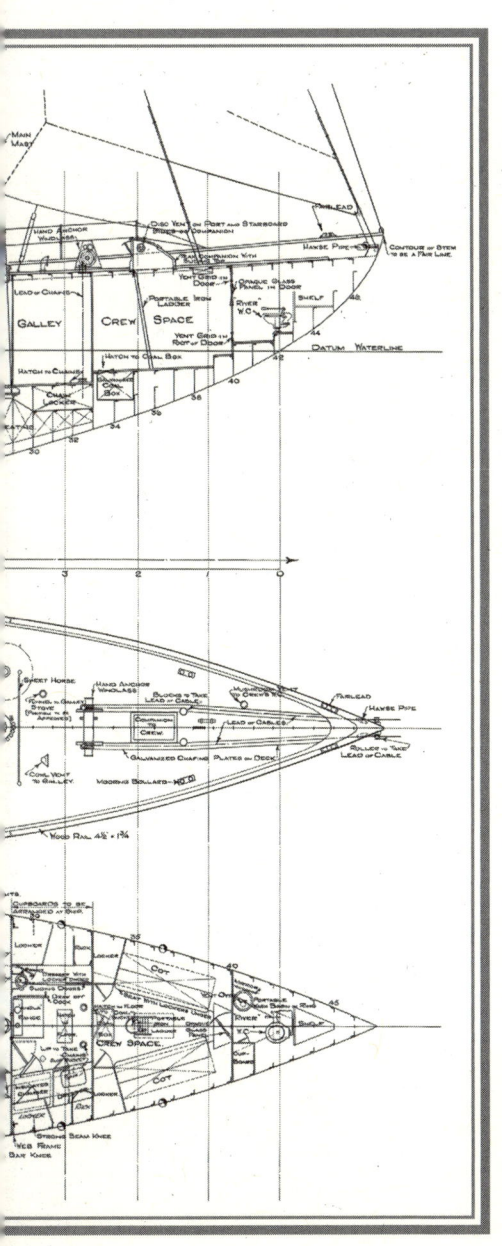

This is what Allen Tony of the website WreckSite has to say about the history of Bell's yacht: "SV Trenchemer *(1934–1965) was built for ocean racing and is believed to have been the first built in Britain for that purpose under the 55-rating class of the Royal Ocean Racing Club. Rigged as a Bermudian yawl with a 36-HP Gleniffer high-speed diesel and designed by Olin J. Stephens, this was the first steel yacht built in Britain. Built for Walter Dalrymple Maitland (W. D. M.) "Karamojo" Bell (1880–1954), a member of the Bell's Whisky family* [not confirmed and probably not true] *and a famous ivory hunter, who reputedly killed more than a thousand elephants and made a fortune* [questionable—a very comfortable sum, but probably not a fortune] *from ivory. Author of* Wanderings of an Elephant Hunter *published in 1923 and* Karamojo Safari, *published in 1949, Bell was also a pilot in the First World War in Africa and the Balkans. The last owner listed in Lloyd's Register of Yachts 1963 is recorded as Robert Somerset, Aberdeen, the heir presumptive of the Duke of Beaufort. He and two lady friends were drowned when the* Trenchemer *ran aground on rocks at Rhodes on 27 February 1965."*

This is from The Times *(London) 2 March 1965: "Two Bodies Found off Rhodes, from our correspondent in Athens.*

The bodies of Mr. Robert Somerset, the 66-year-old heir presumptive of the Duke of Beaufort, and of Miss Caroline Gibbs who were killed last Saturday when the yacht Trenchemer *was wrecked off Rhodes were recovered by divers today. The body of Miss Gibbs was found wedged between two rocks under the water. Mr. Somerset lay under the wreckage of his ship, his arms clasped to his chest as if he had been holding his dog Jessie. The search for the missing body of Miss Fiona Rutherford will be resumed tomorrow if weather permits."*

247

the hot plate to bring it to Stephens's beautiful curve. Then the molten lead had to be poured into its proper position, all of which had to be minutely calculated by the drawing office. Finally, the completed hull was launched. What a joy it was to see it floating correctly to its light load line. What a lovely thing she looked set off by the squat, powerful figure of the attendant tug.

Next came the arrival of the mast. A hollow spruce stick of just under a hundred feet in length, it rode on two railway trucks separated by two trucks in between. The only crane high enough was the enormous sheerleg[2] used for lifting boilers and other heavy machinery onto steamers. It belonged to the port authorities and a scale of charges for its use had been made out on the assumption that only heavy lifts would be its lot. The minimum lift contemplated was five tons, for which a charge of thirty-five shillings was made. So for that trifling sum the slender mast, weighing about 1,400 pounds, was hoisted up and lowered down into its tulip-red hull.

Standing eighty-five feet from the deck, it certainly looked a devil of a height. The sail-boat element of Aberdeen was quite anxious about it. One old salt tackled Hall Russell's people about it, saying, "You can't send that boat to sea with that mast. She'll capsize!" Only they called it "cowp." Of course, they knew nothing of the Bermudian rig or of the minute calculations made by the drawing office staff, or of the lead down in the keel.

The sailing trials were the greatest fun. Luckily the harbour master had been a master of a sailing ship in days gone by. Sail was in his blood. Confronted hourly by nothing but steam or motor vessels, he fell in love with the *Trenchemer* instantly. He allotted her a buoy in a quiet spot in the harbour where she could sail up and lie quietly out of the constant to and fro'ing of the trawlers. Not that these busy craft crowded her in any way. On the contrary, they all seemed to welcome a sailing boat, would stand out of her way, and show her every courtesy. The harbour master said there had not been a sailing ship in the harbour for many years. The last one to come was a Scotia schooner. She had tried to beat up the Channel but had run aground.

One day Katie was on the very popular and populous beach as "T" was out at sea sail drilling when she heard the owner of a large telescope—more usually employed in watching the bathing belles—sing out: "See the tallest mast in the world: penny a peep!"

---

[2] A sheerleg is a floating vessel with a crane.

HOME IN THE HIGHLANDS

This is an actual photo of the Trenchemer. *Hall, Russell & Co. Ltd., Aberdeen, Engineers and Iron Shipbuilders, founded in 1864, built the* Trenchemer *for the Bells. The firm was a partnership between James and William Hall, sons of Alexander; Thomas Russell, a Glasgow engineer; and John Cardno Couper of Sussex. From 1864–1992, the company built iron and steel ships of every kind ranging from cargo vessels to warships.*

Bell (lower left) and his crew aboard the Trenchemer, *which finished second in the Fastnet Race. (Safari Press Archives)*

As soon as the *Trenchemer* was in good working shape, all thoughts turned to her first race, the six-hundred-mile "Fastnet." Swing McGruer was responsible for the rigging, and one day he asked me to "take a swig" on a rope. I did so—a good hefty one—and promptly went overside in a particularly filthy part of the harbour, too, to the great merriment of the usual crowd of watchers. The worst of it was some local journalist saw it, and I found myself in the evening paper. His "Yachtsman falls overboard but gallantly swims for shore!" sounded as if without the gallantry I'd have stayed where I was among the dead cats and rubbish.

The time finally arrived for a shaking-down cruise to get the amateur crew accustomed to the boat. A fog had to come down, of course. Trawlers take no notice of anything when the price of fish is good and the holds are full. Round you, over you, or through you, they must get on. I hove-to well out in the North Sea, but apparently I had positioned myself directly in the road of every trawler in the area trying to get his fish to port.

Two of the crew were detailed to stand watch, to keep the bell ringing, and to shine an electric torch on mast and sail as a warning to the jostling foghorns blaring in every direction. In the small hours, on hearing a shattering blast very close aboard, I rushed on deck and on stepping into the cockpit felt something soft. It was the bodies of the watch. They were sound asleep on deck . . . while just free of the ship was a blaspheming trawler going full astern.

In the morning the fog persisted, and I asked the accomplished navigator where we were and what course to steer for harbour. I was given a course that would have landed us, if I had persisted, very far away, indeed.

Now it was time to get away down south for the first race. In due course we made it to Falmouth. No sooner was the anchor down and sails stowed when up comes the Scottish crew—two fishermen—who were actually the only real sailors aboard. Certainly they were the only people who knew where anything was, as they had had the job of stowing all the multifarious gear that seems essential to a racing boat.

Well, what was it? I asked.

"We want to go ashore," they said.

"What's the hurry?" I questioned.

"We want the first train to Scotland!"

I tried to find out what the matter was. "Oh, it was too late in the season for racing," they said.

It was obvious they had made up their minds to leave. Nothing would induce them to stay. They made it quite plain that they had no confidence in either the skipper or the amateur crew. These West Coast sea-farers are very superstitious and an unfortunate incident during the voyage down had done nothing to help.

The incident occurred when a very gallant member of the amateur crew had had the misfortune to lose his glass eye. That in itself was nothing as everyone knew he had a glass eye, but the infernal thing bounced about the deck, pursued by its owner. That was all right. Nothing to that. But when he put it back in wrong side out, that finished it! The effect was appalling. He didn't even know what had happened until someone whispered him, "For heaven's sake, put your eye right side out!"

Whether it was that, combined with the reckless sailing so often displayed by the ignorant, or a combination of the two, the two Scotsmen had had enough. They were off. There was poor *Trenchemer* close to the starting date and no crew who knew where anything was. Luckily, friend Luard had promised to navigate, and I was soon in touch with Bill Buley, a grand Brixham sailing trawler skipper. Although he had never sailed in anything like "T," by the time the passage to Cowes had been accomplished, he knew exactly where everything was and always knew what to do.

A born seaman, Bill Buley had that innate sea sense that only a life-time at sea can give. He was somewhat impatient of the less gifted members of the crew. He used to curse them in the most salt-junk-and-hard-tack style, and I had to ask him to moderate it a bit. He took it in grand style but flew to the opposite extreme. Instead of cursing, he became painfully polite. He would address some suffering amateur, perhaps clinging determinably to a rope that Bill wanted to make fast, in these words:

"Mister Smith, Sir, will you please LET GO OF THE BLOODY ROPE!"

Delivered thus in a slow and commanding voice, it proved devastatingly effective because it drew everyone's attention to the episode and the culprit.

Bill, with a life-time of sea behind him, would often remark: "You do this for fun, don't you? Well, if I had the money, I wouldn't spend it on this."

Really, sometimes I had to agree. Especially when the boat was awash below with the corpses of the off-watch slithering about the saloon floor, I often had to remind my amateur crew that it was for pleasure we were doing this.

Through superlative navigation on the part of Luard and the good steering of several of the experienced racing amateurs, the *Trenchemer* came in second in her first Fastnet, beaten out of first place by her small sister *Stormy Weather* on time allowance. This was not so bad for the "fishing boat," as the Cowes people had been inclined to call her.

We continued to race and cruise the *Trenchemer* right along until the war broke out in 1939. She then lay in the fresh-water basin at Inverness, which meant she was too far away to help with the Dunkirk evacuation. One day I got a telephone message to appear alongside her at eleven A.M. the next morning.

I did so, and I found a ship surveyor, a gang of men, and a lorry standing on the bank. A document was presented to me to the effect that the "T" had been requisitioned by the Admiralty for war service. Firstly, the surveyor wanted to see the engine and to see it running. It was a Gray diesel. To the surveyor's astonishment, it started instantly the button was pressed.

"That's not a diesel," he said, looking accusingly at me.

"All right! If you think that, then smell or taste that if you like," I replied as I handed him some of the diesel fuel oil.

Satisfied on this point he said, "If you want any of these tools, you better take them now as you'll never see them again." He said this as he seized an oil can of the pressure-pump type and squirted streams of lubricating all over the place. "Gosh, that's a good oil-can! I could do with that for my car." Then, turning to the foreman of the gang, he said, "Get busy."

With crowbars they smashed and levered up the deck over the engine room so as to get the engine out. Picking up a splinter of the deck, the surveyor declared it to be that priceless yellow pine. Actually, it was spruce. I asked him what they were going to do with the hull—it was only too evident what they were going to do with the engine.

"Oh, we don't want the hull; it's the engine we want."

"Why not leave the hull and just buy the engine?" I asked.

"As to that, you had better write the Minister of War Transport. I can't do anything."

This was done, and for once commonsense prevailed and the boat remained in my possession. Unfortunately, that was not before the curious phenomenon of pilfering of government property by perfectly honest men had been fully demonstrated. These are the same type of men who would not have thought of touching a thing of privately owned stuff, yet the moment it was known that the poor *Trenchemer* had been requisitioned, she was stripped of practically all small, portable items of gear. Even the naptha balls in the sail bags went.

In looking back to the early days of the *Trenchemer*'s sailing, I cannot help wondering at how lightly we undertook the hardihood mid-winter passages. When most other yachts would be safely laid up under cover or at moorings, my wife and I would be out and about. Sometimes the salt spray froze solid and closed every cleat on the deck. Always we thought we were not sailing unless a foot or two of the leeward deck was solidly awash. We thought nothing of taking a passage through Pentland Firth when an equally quick one could have been made through the Caledonian Canal.

This toughness was partly due to ignorance and partly to confidence in the immense strength of everything on board. The *Trenchemer* has several times hit objects at sea but never had she sprung a leak or broken anything but the most minor items of gear. Once at night she came in most violent contact with something, gave a leap bodily into the air, and proceeded on her way. Any ordinary ship would have almost certainly have shed an outside keel or sprung a leak.

As it happened, I had just relieved the man at the wheel and he was still standing by and lighting his pipe. As a precaution, I told him to tell those below to put on their life-belts. This hand, a dour West-coaster, walked slowly to the hatchway, and just as slowly bawled out: "Pit on yer life-belts. We're goin' doon!" while puffing away at his pipe.

Walter D. M. "Karamojo" Bell

Postscript

Chapter 20

Looking back on my life it seems to me that the happiest people I met were invariably those the furthest removed from our civilization. Somehow, often despite the greatest personal catastrophes, the African was always brimming with laughter and good spirits, enjoying, as we of more complicated ways have long forgotten, every day for the pure delight of living.

True, as the social worker will be quick to point out, not until the advent of the white man did the native have a chance for education and development. True, in his native state his life was surrounded by ignorance, filth, disease, and cruelty. But what have we placed in their stead? Confusion, suppression, resentment, and often a flaming hate. We have built schools, and the native has learned to fear us; we have taught justice, and the native has felt our lash; we have preached a religion of brotherhood, and the native is not allowed to shake hands. Gifts such as these are better not given.

But the African will endure. I do not speak of the endurance that comes from physical or moral strength, or of the statistical endurance of abounding reproduction. I speak of the endurance that comes with the ability to laugh in the face of the severest blows that men of other races and of an ever-vigilant nature are all too ready to hand out.

I like to remember the true episode of the German scientist who commanded the natives to carry a whole elephant from the bush to his camp. The unbelievable task was accomplished, not by tractors and bulldozers, but by the unaided efforts of the multitude stirred, as we stir our race horses, with whips. That strangers could go traipsing around your country doing that sort of thing with impunity, and that you had no answer to it, would be enough to get anyone down.

But not the African. That simple little story never failed to produce real belly laughs; it was but one of many similar stock jokes among the natives. If life has anything to teach, it is that those who can laugh at such a carry-on will eventually outlast those who could perpetrate it. After all my years in Africa, and especially given my experiences in the Lado Enclave, I have learned that civilization is but skin deep, and without restraints a white man can be as lawless and as savage as the native African.

Another of the stock jokes was this following episode. You are a free-born native African and you visit a town. On a street you happen to meet a white man walking with his white wife. You in all politeness say, "Good evening, Mister." Thereupon the white man commands you to lie down in the open street. You do so, whereupon the white man gives you a severe beating.

Then he calls you to attention. You spring up and salute. "Now," the white man says, "Do you understand why you were beaten?"

You in your ignorance say, "No, Mister."

"Well," he explains, "when you meet a white woman, you always address her in your salutation." Then the white man marches off, well satisfied with himself.

You go about your business, but your luck just isn't in, for the very next day you encounter the same white man with the same white woman. This time you think you have learned your lesson, and you say in all politeness, "Good evening, Mistress."

To your bewilderment you are again commanded to lie down in the open street. It is dirty; you have on your one and only garment. No matter, you obey. You are again beaten, more severely than the last time. Again the question, and again you do not know.

"You should say 'Good evening, Mistress. Good evening, Mister," he tells you.

That simple little story never failed to produce roars of real belly laughter. If life has anything to teach, it is "He who laughs endures."

******

I don't suppose anyone will deny that all men are born hunters. Some want wealth, some power, fame, women, men, children, fun, or what you will. That goes for book reviews, too. They are all hunting something.

Having so neatly forestalled any hostile or too critical review of my book, I can now announce that my particular form of hunting was the pursuit of the African elephant. It is of no use to blame me; I was born with the craze. And after all, I was only doing what the different elephant controls now do on such a vast scale in the effort to give the African farmer some assurance that he will not wake up to find his banana plantation laid flat or his corn crop ruined.

Mine was a great life because it was a free one. I once computed that for every elephant bagged, I traveled on my flat feet no fewer than seventy miles.

Naturally, I sought out the largest and oldest bulls as they carried the heaviest ivory. So long as my hunting afforded me the means to continue in my way of life, I cared not two cents for the financial result. Although it may sound like boosting, I claim to have struck down a greater number of bulls with the instantaneous and painless brain shot than any organized control measures could ever attain. This result was arrived at only through the most rigorous physical and mental control allied to close concentration and study of the location of the elephant's brain.

Mostly I hunted in country where money as we know it was not yet in use. What a joy that can be. It would be hard if not impossible to find such conditions anywhere in the world to-day. More's the pity.

THE END

Endnote:

Bell's last chapter of his autobiography ends here, but in a massive outline in one of his diaries, we found references to two future stories, which he obviously intended to include but never did. These are: "Home Guard in World War II" and "Meet Bill Powers."

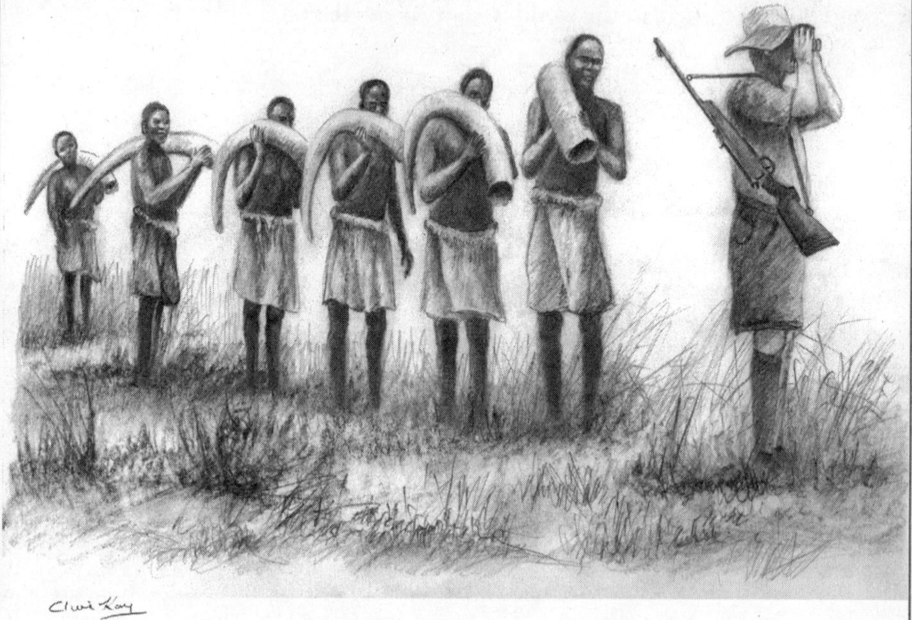
Clive Kay

The Obituary of Capt. W. D. M. "Karamojo" Bell

CHAPTER 21

BY
Maj. B. G. Kinloch*

The advent of modern transport, leading to the extensive use of the hunting car in place of the foot safari, the pacification of warlike tribes, and the opening up of most of the previously wild and largely unknown country in Africa have greatly reduced the elements of danger and physical endeavor involved in the pursuit of large game, elements that are an essential part of any sport worthy of the name.

As a result, the sport of big-game hunting has, in many quarters, fallen into disrepute. There is one animal at least the successful hunting of which with a rifle, if the element of luck is ignored, still involves, as in the past, considerable expenditure of physical effort, and frequently no little danger. This is the African elephant, the largest, the strongest, and the most majestic of land mammals, and to many people, the real King of Beasts.

The elephant has been hunted since time immemorial for its tusks, for its meat, and for sport. There has always been a demand for its ivory from the Far East to the Americas, and in the early part of the present century, when the Dark Continent was still largely unknown, there grew up in Africa a select body of men calling themselves professional elephant hunters. From many walks of life and of varying characters, they had a least three things in common: a love of the wild, a sense of adventure, and a passion for hunting. Added to this they were almost without exception held in thrall by the peculiar fascination that the elephant appears to exert on nearly all those fortunate enough to come in contact with it.

Among this almost legendary band of adventurous spirits are many famous names, but without a doubt one of the greatest is that of Capt. W. D.

---

*Maj. Bruce Kinloch, a former game warden in Tanganyika and Uganda, wrote *The Shamba Raiders: Memories of a Game Warden*, an enduring classic, about his experiences as the director of Uganda Game and Fisheries Department during the establishment of that country's first national parks. Major Kinloch was also a former member of the British Indian Army. Kinloch's obituary of Bell was published in *The Uganda Journal,* Volume 19, Number 1, March 1955.

M. Bell, better known as Karamojo Bell. The very name Karamojo Bell has a romantic lilt about it, and it has stirred the imagination of many a budding hunter; indeed, Bell's career was both romantic and adventurous. Hunting and sailing were his ruling passions in life, and he became a master of each of these crafts. Bell himself wrote that his earliest recollection of his boyhood was of his sole and insatiable ambition to hunt. First he wanted to be a bison hunter in America, but after reading Roualeyn Gordon-Cumming's books on Africa, he determined to become an elephant hunter, and in due course an elephant hunter he became, one of the greatest of them all.

In his early teens he voyaged around the world as an apprentice on a windjammer and lived briefly in New Zealand doing odd jobs after working his passage there. In 1897, aged seventeen, he landed in Mombasa and was employed as a hunter by the Kenya-Uganda Railway, which was under construction at the time. He then left Africa to take part in the gold rush on the Yukon, finding little gold but making a living by shooting game to supply Dawson City with meat.

This was followed by the South African War (the Boer War), in which he served with the Canadian Mounted Rifles, was taken prisoner, but managed to escape. Finally, in 1902 he returned to British East Africa to become a professional elephant hunter for close to twenty-five years. His hunting career was interrupted only by the First World War, during which time he served with the Royal Flying Corps. He was awarded the Military Cross and a bar, and was five times mentioned in dispatches.

Bell hunted elephants in various parts of Africa, but the area in which he achieved his greatest successes was Karamoja and its environs in Uganda. His amazing exploits in the Karamoja region finally earned him the world-famous nickname of Karamojo Bell. Even now Karamoja is one of the wilder areas of Africa, sparsely inhabited and that by still primitive but proud people who scorn to hide their fine physiques under Western garments. In Bell's day, it was a savage land—unexplored, uncontrolled, and unadministered—torn by inter-tribal strife, armed raids, and blood-shed, but abounding with elephants carrying magnificent ivory.

His almost incredible adventures are recorded in two books, *The Wanderings of an Elephant Hunter* (1923) and *Karamojo Safari* (1949), both of these being classics that should be on the shelves of all students of the chase. He was the first white man to be seen by many of the Karamojong and other tribes in whose

The Obituary of Capt. W. D. M. "Karamojo" Bell

country he hunted alone for a number of years, and to whom, as a result of his exploits he became an almost legendary character.

Bell was an exponent of the use of the small-bore, high-velocity rifle for killing elephants. He was a brilliant marksman, an artist with a rifle, and he knew the anatomy of his quarry so thoroughly that he could instinctively place a killing shot from any angle. His favourite was the brain shot because it caused an instantaneous and painless death. At various times he used a .256 Mannlicher, a .303, and a .318, but he killed the majority of his elephants with a .275 (7mm) Mauser. Although elephants were undoubtedly far less sophisticated in his day, his success with the small-bore was certainly due to the fact that he carried his rifle everywhere until it became almost a part of him; his success was also due to his intimate knowledge of his quarry, its habits, and its characteristics.

His total bag of elephants is uncertain, but his prowess as a hunter is shown by the results of one of his most successful safaris in the Karamoja region. In six months he obtained 354 tusks, these having the high-average weight of 53 pounds each. This is a result of shooting 180 elephants, for an average of 30 a month. Anyone who has hunted elephants for heavy ivory will appreciate what this means, particularly the physical endeavor that would be involved even at the best of times.

To many this must appear to be merely a tale of slaughter, but it must be remembered that conditions were very different in those days and the region in which Bell hunted was teeming with elephants. There is no doubt that like all truly great hunters, he genuinely loved and was fascinated by his quarry, an apparent paradox not generally understood by the average person. He was that not too frequent combination, described by Negley Farson in the preface to *Karamojo Safari,* of professional killer and artist adventurer. He adds: "A man must have something of the poet in him to become a great hunter."

At the end of his professional hunting career, Bell retired to his home near Garve in Ross-shire in the Highlands of Scotland. His hunting was then confined to stalking red deer, although he was not above keeping his eye in with a .22 rifle on rabbits with which the area abounded. Rifles, particularly high-velocity small-bores, fascinated him, and he made a close study of them, becoming a ballistics expert consulted by several British gun firms, and exchanging information with his opposite numbers in the United States. He used to write to me from time to time in recent years, asking for my help in

REMINISCENCES OF AN ELEPHANT HUNTER

Bell's drawing of Corriemoillie, his home in the Highlands of Scotland.

providing a piece of elephant skull or the heavy bones of a game animal on which to test some newly designed and specially constructed bullet.

His hard-earned leisure now enabled him also to indulge in his second passion, sailing, and in this, too, he achieved success. His ocean-racing yacht, the *Trenchemer,* which he kept on the Clyde,* won several notable races and he came in second in her for the Fastnet Race in 1934. [*Bell kept his boat at Inverness.]

I had the privilege of meeting Bell and his charming wife when I visited Scotland in 1951. The night before I called on him at his home I stayed at a hotel in Garve where I noticed on the wall a glass case of harness trappings beautifully carved from ivory. In reply to my inquiry, the proprietress told me that they had been carved by her grandfather from an elephant tusk given to him by the same Roualeyn Gordon-Cumming whose books had inspired Bell to become an elephant hunter and whose coachman her grandfather had been.

The next day my wife and I visited Bell's home Corriemoillie. We were welcomed by an elderly, white-haired man of soldierly bearing, great charm of manner, and remarkably blue eyes. It was not long before the ice was broken and we were poring over maps and re-living Bell's travels in Uganda. Our brief call ended with an invitation to stay for several days, which we gladly accepted, and the time passed all too quickly.

Reticent as he was about his accomplishments, he was intensely interesting when persuaded to talk about his travels and his hobbies. I recollect him saying, "You know, when you first called, I wondered what sort of person you expected Karamojo Bell to be—probably a tough, swashbuckling old ivory poacher, and I felt that you would be surprised to be met by someone who looked like a retired country parson." He was not far from the truth!

Apart from his other accomplishments, Bell had great artistic ability. I well remember his pictures hung round his house, in particular a magnificent one, painted by himself, of a pride of lions and a lone old bull elephant drinking on opposite sides of a water-hole in the moonlight.

His gunroom contained a variety of weapons, and he showed me a take-down model .318 in a special light case. He said rather wistfully that he had planned to visit Uganda by air in 1939 for a last elephant hunt, but that the war had intervened and that he now felt he was too old for such a trip. At that time he was nearly seventy-two but was still stalking red deer.

I said good-bye to him with regret, and sad to say for the last time, for he died at his home at the end of June 1954. The death of Karamojo Bell marks the ending of an era of professional elephant hunting in Africa that will never again be known, and brings to a close the colourful career of a very great hunter, sailor, and gentleman. Surely no more fitting lines could be found as an epitaph to his memory than those in Robert Louis Stevenson's "Requiem":

> Under the wide and starry sky,
> Dig the grave and let me lie:
> Glad did I live and gladly die,
> And I laid me down with a will.
> This be the verse you grave for me:
> Here he lies where he long'd to be;
> Home is the sailor, home from the sea,
> And the hunter home from the hill.

ORIGINAL STORIES BY W. D. M. BELL

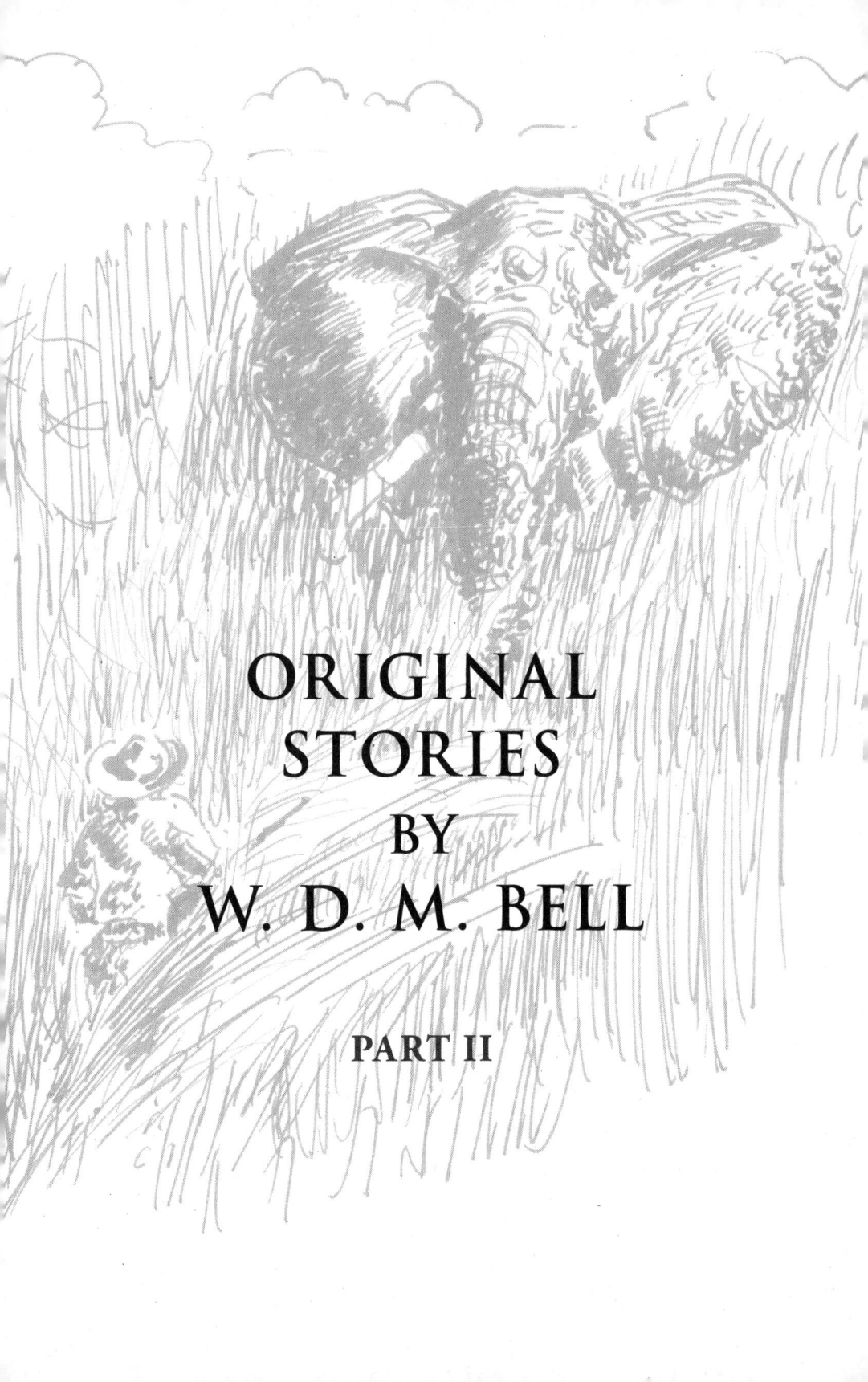

PART II

Bell's drawings of his British Lee-Enfield .303. sporting rifles.

WALTER BELL'S HANDBOOK ON AFRICAN BIG GAME

CHAPTER 22

Walter Bell's diaries filled four huge three-ring binders when transcribed. We estimate that there are about 1,800 handwritten and typed pages in this collection. Many, many times, he repeated the same story but wrote it from different perspectives. Each variation in the story told something different and gave new information, and each iteration offered new insight into Bell the man and Bell the hunter. The title above and the categories below are Bell's. We found only Part I in his notes, and the fact that he wrote on each of these five topics in great length elsewhere led us to believe that he never got back to this particular essay.

BEING A GUIDE TO THE HUMANE KILLING OF WILD ANIMALS

Part	I.	The Tools for the Job	
	II.	Personal Proficiency	
	III.	Elephant	
	IV.	Buck	Rhino
	V.	Crocs & Hippo	Hippo
	VI		

Introduction

This little handbook is an attempt to convey on paper enough of the experience gained in a life time of rifle shooting to enable a beginner to accomplish the clean and most merciful death of his quarry with the least pain to the animal and the least danger, fuss, and bother to the hunter. That this medium has its faults will be apparent from the following story.

One day a man burst into my den in the Scottish Highlands in a high state of excitement. Looking accusingly at me he said, "You are the man I've wanted to meet for twenty years. You wrote *Wanderings of an Elephant Hunter* didn't you?

I admitted it.

"Well," he stormed indignantly, "I studied that book inside out, got a chance at an elephant, sat down ten yards from him cool as be damned, and even bent my back against a tree, and gave him one right on the knob. This was all according to your instructions, and all he did was turn his back side to me and crash away. Never even shook his head."

"And where was this?" I asked.

"In India, of course."

"But my book dealt with the African elephant," I ventured.

"I know," he roared. "I should have known there was a difference."

Part I

The Tools for the Job

Any rifle shooting a jacketed bullet at a decent velocity can kill any animal provided it is properly directed. It should not be assumed, however, that all rifles are equally good killers. There is much more in the directing of it than in the rifle itself. And that is the vital point of the whole business.

So many people think that it is only a matter of acquiring the proper rifle, pointing it in the appropriate direction, and the rifle will do the rest. It will not. At least no sporting arm so far invented would of its own power lay out an elephant when directed casually into the gray. A bazooka might. I don't know. The direction of the rifle at the instant of firing is what determines the issue. It is not the weight of the bullet, or its velocity, or its striking energy, or its cost, reputation, maker's name, or anything else.

Man being what he is—a case-hardened know-all of extremely fragile construction—it is almost impossible to get two of them to agree on what is the best rifle to use. Ever since man started to decimate game herds with fire tubes, he has shown most agreement perhaps in pursuit of that will-of-the-wisp "shock." Hence, we got the Boers with their "roers" [powerful elephant guns], Samuel Baker with his 8-, 4-, and even 2-bores, and Roualeyn Gordon-Cumming with his double 4-bore weighing 34 pounds.

Think of what Gordon-Cumming's pony, probably a small Basuto, had to carry as that huge man sallied forth to what was a veritable battle, lasting sometimes the better part of a day with some pachyderms rendered furious by repeated injections of hardened lead bullets fired—one must suppose—into the gray. Or Sam Baker lying up for a week after firing his famous "Baby" (the 2-bore) or lending it to an Arab hunter who in an unfortunate moment of bravado fired it and came out of the encounter with nothing more severe than a broken shoulder.

Think also about the effect on the recipients of those colossal bullets. Frequently old Sammy was charged viciously by elephants goaded to desperation by repeated doses from his 4- or 8-bores. So was Roualeyn. Time after time he was chased right off. Pony after pony would be exhausted and a change would be required as in a game of polo.

We don't hear of the hunters themselves succumbing to fatigue. For hunters, it was more a matter of shoving down a few more handfuls of powder. I have often wondered if it was the visible presence of the ponies that caused these apparently authentic charges. With their ponies, they could ride very close to their game before discharging a broadside, and the pony would quite readily catch an elephant's eye, especially when in motion. On the other hand, I have myself shot elephants from horseback at a few yards range with a 7mm, and they showed no inclination to offer hostilities. In the case of Sam and Roualeyn, it must have been the maddening effect of their outrageous weapons plus the sight of something to vent their rage upon that caused such repeated charges.

Here is just one more example of the ridiculous lengths to which this "shock" school led. Stanley was commissioned by the newspapers to find and rescue Emin Pasha.[1] With unlimited funds at his disposal, we find a huge safari fitted out to cross the great primeval Congo forest, the veritable home and H.Q of elephants. What was the result? Fifteen hundred men die of starvation, and Stanley recounts how he and his British army officers are reduced to "a handful of native beans." Yet he carries to this stamping ground of elephant herds what he calls "the latest product of Bond Street" in the way of a heavy double rifle.

Even as the belly bands of the soldiers were drawn in to the last notch, Stanley determined to see what the Bond Street product could do to relieve the situation. I can only imagine the search for this double rifle in its case among the thousands, and I can also imagine too the eagerness of the starving boys as they unpack the marvellous *bunduki* [Swahili for gun]

---

[1] Mehmed Emin Pasha was born Isaak Eduard Schnitzer (28 March 1840 – 23 October 1892). He was an Ottoman German-Jewish physician, naturalist, and governor of the Egyptian province of Equatoria on the Upper Nile. The Ottoman Empire conferred the title "Pasha" on him in 1886, and thereafter he was referred to as "Emin Pasha." The Emin Pasha Relief Expedition of 1886 to 1889 was one of the last major European expeditions into the interior of Africa in the nineteenth century. Because Gen. Charles Gordon had been killed by the Mahdist forces the year before, Henry Morton Stanley led an expedition to relieve the besieged governor of Equatoria who was also being threatened by Mahdist forces. The expedition came to be both celebrated for its ambition in crossing "Darkest Africa" and notorious for the deaths of so many of its members as well as for disease unwittingly left in its wake.

Reminiscences of an Elephant Hunter

I did not decide on my choice of rifles lightly. As I said, my war experience had taught me that the British .303 was quite a useful weapon, and I thought that coupled with a 215-grain, solid-jacketed bullet, the combination should serve me well for elephant hunting.

that is going to provide meat for all hands. Bula Matadi[2] himself is going to operate the miraculous weapon—I'll hazard a guess he had never fired the thing before.

An elephant is soon located on the river bank. A close approach is made and both barrels are whanged into him by the great man himself. The result is a cloud of smoke and a vacant landscape and yet further starvation. Bula Matadi condemns the weapon as being useless and finally "gives it to a chief." He continues to live on a handful of native beans, I suppose.

Faiths die a hard death, apparently, for to this day, 1950, one may still hear of such monstrous and clumsy weapons as the .600 and .577 bores being used, so wedded is man to the idea that what punishes him must necessarily punish the other fellow more.

---

[2] Stanley's African name was Bula Matadi; it means the Breaker of Rocks.

Endnote:

Bell wrote about twenty more pages on small bores versus big bores, how to become an expert rifleman, and the advantage of the neck shot. Because these topics can all be found in various chapters of Incidents from an Elephant Hunter's Diary, *we chose to discard the rest of this section rather than inflict on our readers undue redundancies. For those who wish to read about these subjects, see chapters 32, 36, and 37 in* Incidents from an Elephant Hunter's Diary.

AFRICA.

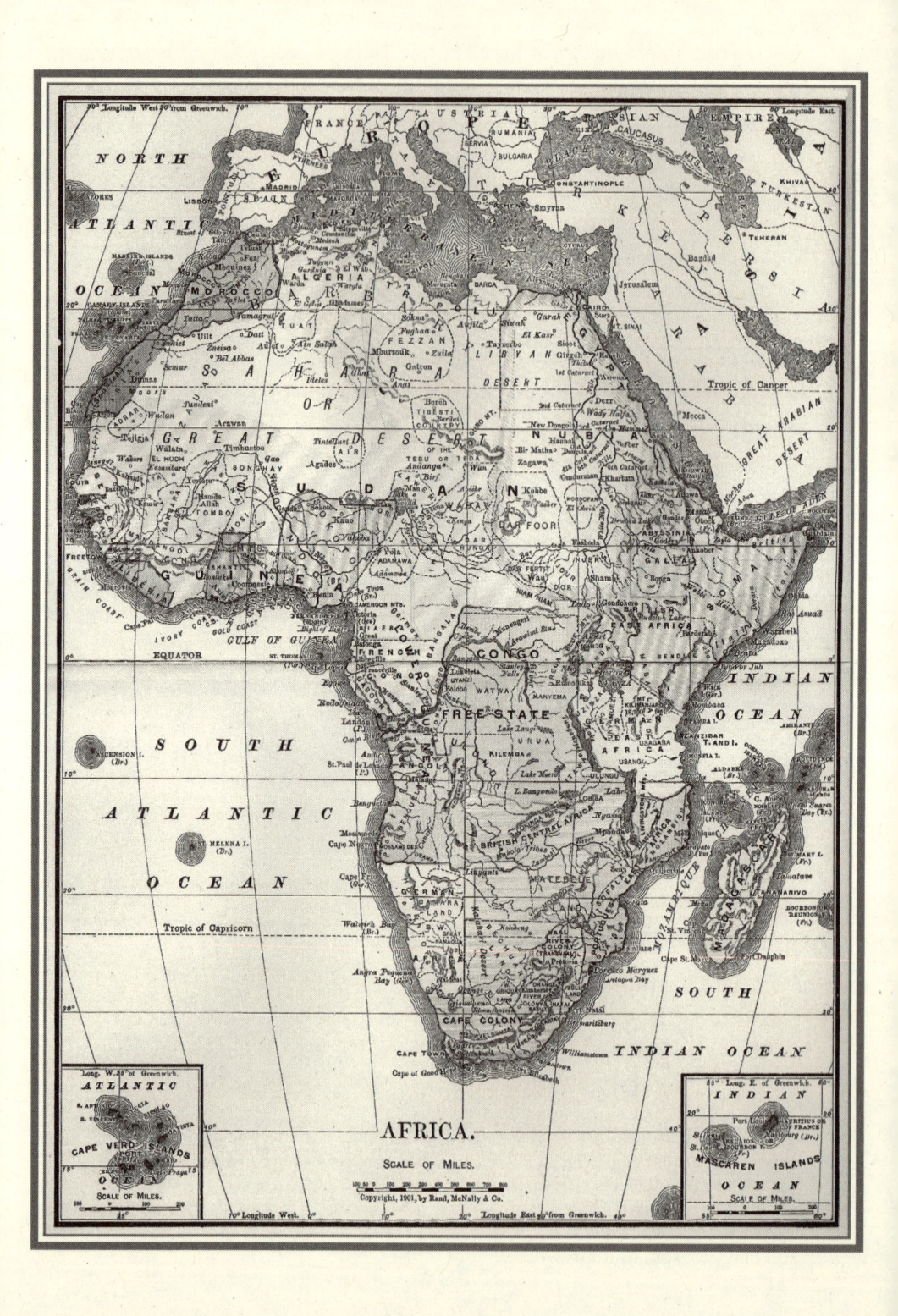

SCALE OF MILES.

Copyright, 1901, by Rand, McNally & Co.

The Repulsive Saurian

Chapter 23

When one thinks of Africa in comparison with other continents, one is struck by the enormous richness of its wild life. The mammalia in all its diverse forms include the elephant weighing four to five tons and its tiny cousin the shrew mouse weighing as many ounces. Contrast the giraffe, standing eighteen feet fast with the tiny dik-dik antelope standing perhaps ten inches. Then there are the beautiful crested crane and the hideous ground hornbill.

Among the reptiles too, one finds just as great a contrast: The python is twenty-two feet in length and capable of swallowing a bush buck whole while the wisp-like green mamba is no thicker than a pencil and stands on its tail and sways about like a stem of grass. The black mamba flashes past you erect at thirty miles per hour while the bloated puff adder is so lethargic you can and do tread on it.

Among the insects, too, you find such an infinity of form as to make one pause and wonder at the magnitude of the output and the ingenuity and imagination of what we call Nature. We can but liken it to some gigantic drawing office filled with the most ingenious and industrious draughtsmen.

Who, I wonder, was responsible for inventing the dung beetle? Let us imagine the decorative department of the drawing office has launched its schemes to fill the landscape with all the beautiful antelopes, zebras, giraffes, etc. It passes to the Control of Animal Increase. They in turn get busy designing lions, leopards, and various other carnivora. Then it passes to the Scavenge Department. They design the hyena, the jackal, the vulture, and, not least, the dung beetle.

Here apparently a slight miscalculation cropped up. The beetle was a perfectly good beetle. It could stand offensive smells; indeed, it liked them. It sought out dung in preference to any other material. It knew how to roll it into a perfectly round ball and how to roll it away. One problem arose: It just had not enough power in its front legs for the rolling operation. "Turn it upside down," said the designer responsible. So to this day the dung beetle rolls its evil-smelling balls by standing on its front legs with its hind legs up on the ball, thus progressing backward with nothing but hindsight to control direction. You can see them at it anywhere.

As with the mammals, so with the fishes. Some marvelous forms of fish exist in the sweet and salt waters of Africa. Food being so abundant that a check on fish life had to be thought out. Hence we have the crocodile, quite the most evil, hateful creature ever invented but a thoroughly efficient destroyer of fish. As a sort of counter-check on the crocodile population, the large fish were given a taste for the young crocodiles. And so it goes, everything eating everything else.

Let us stroll along the sandy shores of one of the great inland lakes. Here we see the whole scheme working at its most hectic rate. As we pass through the sparse grass covering the hot sandy banks, we are surrounded by a moving mass of baby crocodiles. The whole place rustles with them. This is a crocodile breeding farm. They lay their eggs in the sand where the heat of the sun hatches them without any further bother to the parents.

When enemy man appears on the scene, these young crocodiles do not seek refuge in the waters of the adjacent lake, as might be expected. Oh no, that is the last place they wish to go. Lift one with your foot and heave it into the water. Instantly there is a boil and your baby crocodile has disappeared down the capacious maw of a waiting barbel perhaps weighing one hundred or even two hundred and fifty pounds. As you watch, maybe there is a bigger commotion. A large crocodile has in turn seized the barbel!

Perhaps at your first essay, you did not reach deep water with your baby crocodile missile. He scuttles back to dry land with the utmost haste and alarm and will land at your very foot rather than delay a second longer in the dangerous water. Time and time again this may be repeated with the same result.

Meanwhile out on the sand banks of the lake, hundreds upon hundreds of large crocodiles may be seen lying sunning themselves and looking like rows of logs that had escaped from some gigantic lumber camp. The difference being that the crocodiles arrange themselves side by side in parallel rows.

The submarine and the crocodile employ very similar tactics against their surface victims. Both have periscopes and both expose them so as to see their prey. But where the submarine fires a torpedo and blows you up, the crocodile submerges, sneaks up under you, and pulls you down. His eyes are not extensible—that refinement was left to man to evolve—but they occupy the highest point on his head.

He will lie for hours with only these evil eyes exposed, motionless in the reflections of a bank while waiting for some innocent buck or a human to come to the water's edge. Once a large crocodile seizes its prey, no matter how powerful the latter may be, there is no escape. The sheer weight of the saurian aided by the slope of the land make it certain the crocodile will prevail. Quite large rhinos have been seen to be drawn into deeper water and drowned.

I have seen crocodiles emerge from the river dragging with them large antelopes like hartebeests out onto the bank—there to enjoy their meal in the warmth of the sun. After killing a crocodile, I invariably found that its latest meal, whatever animal it might happen to be, had been kept until it had reached a semi-putrid state. Apparently they like their meat well hung.

Native man's attitude to the crocodile varies enormously in those parts of Africa where I used to roam. Passing along through the tribes inhabiting the shores of the upper White Nile one observes quite distinct behaviour toward crocs. One may camp near a village one day and hear nothing but evil of the crocodile coupled with warnings on no account to bathe and to draw water only at protected places.

There will be found elaborate defenses erected to guard against crocodiles from seizing women who are drawing water. Every watering place will be stockaded off. Complaints will be numerous of stock and humans having been taken. No one goes near the river if it can possibly be avoided. In such dread is the crocodile held that no one will assist any attempt to deal with the marauders. Here the crocodile is on top of man.

Then one passes on perhaps only twenty or thirty miles and what a difference can be seen. Here man is on top of crocodile. Maybe you see a lot of black dots in the sky-reflecting river. You get your binoculars to bear on them. They are human heads. Mindful of the warnings of the tribe you so recently left, you ask what on earth these people are doing standing motionless in the crocodile-infested water. They are waiting for crocodiles, you are told. They are crocodile hunters. Somehow the tables have been turned, the roles reversed. Here man is on top of the crocodile, and it is the latter who is terrified.

When I first met with this extraordinary difference in outlook, I took some pains to investigate more closely the conditions of such a curious form of hunting. It seemed to me that man was but poorly equipped to tackle Mr. Croc in his own element.

For one thing how could he see the crocodile? The Nile is far from being a clear-water river running over silvery sand. On the contrary, its waters are so charged with minute organisms as to be quite opaque. Combined with a dark muddy bottom, it is quite impenetrable, to northern eyes at any rate. How then can these hunters see their quarry?

This puzzled me for some time. By close observation it appeared that they did not actually see through the water. What they saw was a line of bubbles released by pressure from the gas-laden mud on the bottom, some bubbles from the crocodile itself possibly, but above all they perceived the pressure-wave caused by a large body moving through comparatively shallow water. One sees a very pronounced bulge on the surface of the water when a hippo is moving along the bottom of a pool, so here, too, a crocodile moving anywhere near those waiting figures is immediately spotted and dealt with by the paltry-looking spears of these crocodile hunters.

"Are they never attacked by the crocodiles?" I asked.

"Oh no," they said, rather shocked by the ignorance implied in the question. "The crocs are afraid."

Possibly, too, they feel on their naked bodies the pressure that bulges the surface. Anyone who has used hand grenades for the purpose of stunning fish while partly immersed in water will understand how these pressures may be felt, and especially on the more tender parts of the body. This is so even when the grenade is thrown a considerable distance.

I was much emboldened by the general bearing of these natives toward the terrible crocodile. Everyone swam about and bathed freely in the river. No precautions were taken to safeguard the women and children at the watering places.

The opposite bank from where we were encamped was quite free from native settlement. Asked why this was so, the natives said that the land was impossible to cultivate owing to the depredation of elephants. This might have been so at that particular time, but the reason for all the population of the riverine area being confined to one bank probably lay in slave-raiding days.

I always used a steel canoe built in sections for easy portage when crossing the river. One day, however, after a neat and successful hunt I made my way down to the river bank, leaving my boy to guide the natives to the kill. Being hot and sweaty I plunged into the river and started to swim across. I had done it before and thought nothing of it because of where I was—this place man was on top of crocodile. Naturally, I would not have done it for any money where the reverse was the case.

The Repulsive Saurian

Native man's attitude to the crocodile varies enormously in those parts of Africa where I used to roam.

On reaching the bank by our village, the old chief said he had watched a large crocodile following me across. This was curious. If I had been a black man, the crocodile would have been scared stiff, but because I was white, he followed me. Whether this was out of curiosity I do not know.

So here we have two diametrically opposed instances of crocodile behaviour. The first instance occurred where King Mwanga's tame crocodile refused a white missionary,[1] although fed regularly on living blacks, and now here my crocodile almost accepted a white man but refused all blacks. This all goes to show that you never, never know.

During my African career, crocodiles caused us serious trouble only twice. Once when three of the boys took a native dug-out to ferry some ivory over the Upper Nile. The canoe was just a casual flat bed and, as so often happens, was in a bad state of repair. In this case the whole of one end was only held in place by clay. Now anyone of the least imagination would have rejected such a conveyance for the two-mile crossing in an area where the saurian was very definitely on top of man.

At the very least they would have taken the precaution to wet the clay and trample and puddle it into some sort of adhesion to its surroundings should it have been necessary at all cost to make the traverse. Not so with my bright lads. Off they went with my precious ivory. About midway the end fell out. One of the boys could swim; the others could not. The swimmer struck out for shore and was drawn under, never to be seen again, while the non-swimmers stuck to the rolling canoe and were saved.

The second incident occurred when a boy was seized in deep water from behind as he sat on the low stern of his heavily laden canoe. Seeing his companion disappearing in a commotion in the water, the other boy in the canoe fired his gun. We, who were following in canoes some way behind, hearing the shot, paddled as hard as we could toward it.

Once there, we found the boy safe. The crocodile on hearing the shot had released the boy, who had swum back to the canoe and clambered aboard. He seemed quite unconcerned although his back was in a frightful mess.

He lay down while we tried to dress his wounds. There was air coming from one of the tooth punctures, so it was almost certain a lung was involved. The kidneys were uncovered and the whole back and buttocks terribly lacerated.

---

[1] See chapter 9 of this book for this story.

The Repulsive Saurian

But he wasn't scared or faint, his pulse was strong and regular, and he didn't seem to be in pain. I have always recognized and admired primitive man's toughness, but here was a supreme example.

We were fortunately at the end of our journey, having come down through perhaps the most heavily crocodile-infested water in Africa, and were near a mission station. The missionaries had a doctor among them, and they took our boy into their hospital. He was given every attention but died three days later.

******

However piercing your young eyesight may be, it pays not to be too proud to carry and use a good binocular. Not nearly enough use is made of these invaluable instruments. Use them to find things and to distinguish what the naked eye has already found.

One evening we were camped by a native village near the confluence of the Niger and Benue Rivers. These waters have an evil reputation for man-eating crocodiles. Searching the reflections for those tiny twin periscopes with my 6X40 Zeiss glasses, I soon found one lurking opposite the village. It was a longish shot, and you must have your rifle really well sighted-in for these kinds of shots.

This you must do yourself. No matter what price you have paid for your rifle, the test-firer will have been only concerned to group his shots. To do this he will have blackened the front sight bead and have taken into the notch of the backsight only the merest fraction of the blackened bead front sight. He will have got his group all right, but when you come to fire it with the full white bead, perhaps out in Africa, you will be inches high of an object—like a crocodile's eyes. I don't suppose these eyes protrude more than one-and-a-half inches from the surface of the water.

Well, on this occasion "the shot" came off all right.

Now when a crocodile wants to lie motionless just under the surface, he can adjust his buoyancy to such exactitude that he can remain for hours in one position without having to alter trim and so cause ripples on the surrounding placidity. If he wishes to sink and lie motionless on the bottom, he takes in water to the desired amount. He expels it to rise and, in fact, is so much more highly developed in these maneuvers that one would expect submarine designers to have large crocodile-equipped tanks for the sole purpose of studying their masters' technique.

I have seen crocodiles emerge from the river dragging with them large antelopes like hartebeests out onto the bank—there to enjoy their meal in the warmth of the sun. (Sketch by W. D. M. Bell)

On this occasion the crocodile remained awash until we reached him. He was a large crocodile but no larger or in any way different from hundreds of other crocodiles. But when we cut him open, the incredible met our eyes.

I don't suppose there is any more widely told tale than that of a woman's bangles being found in the stomach of a crocodile. Hoary with age, it had long since been dumped on the junk pile of travelers' tales and fishing stories. So you can imagine our surprise when a bangle was produced from that crocodile's stomach, and not only that, the bangle was instantly claimed by the sister of the victim. We found nothing else in its stomach. Sometimes, it doesn't do to know too much.

The Repulsive Saurian

Perhaps some day someone will devise and develop some means of catching the crocodile by means of some lure. I imagine it to be a gigantic tackle that would take a fish of fifteen or twenty pounds. If this were towed behind an able boat, it might show results, although Mr. Croc is a wily customer and extremely wary. How he would be handled after hooking him opens up a vista of pleasant speculation, never forgetting that he would only weigh in water a tenth part of his dry-land weight.

One thing seems probable: He will put up a veritable battle. He can be drowned, however; that is certain. He is not a fish. When brought to the surface, it would be certainly necessary to blow his brains out with a rifle or shot gun. Perhaps when Americans become really interested in Africa, as they are certain to do, some such move will be set afoot. They have the ingenuity, originality, and leisure that others seem to lack.

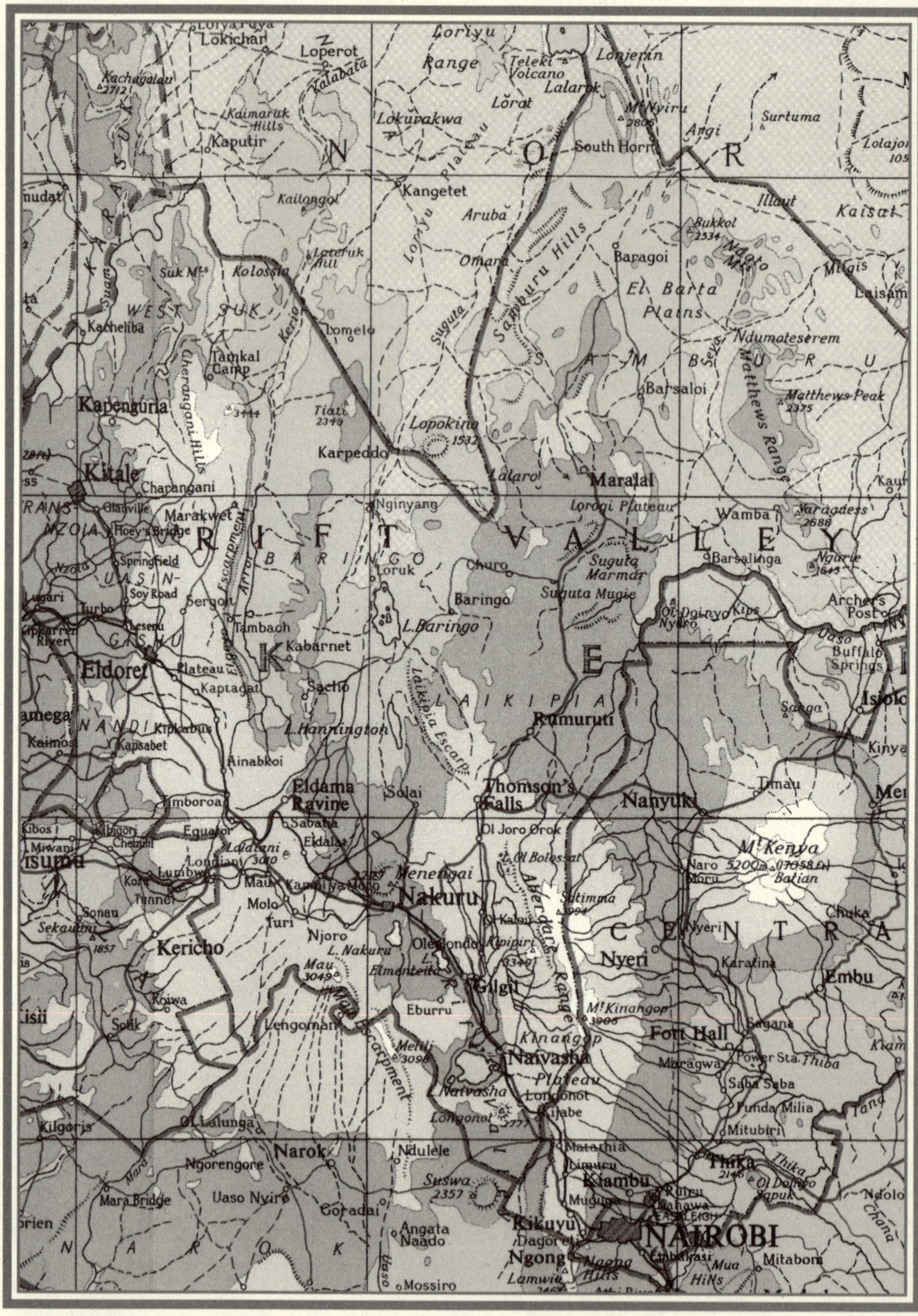

A Nandi Epic

Chapter 24

The first time I met Partington was when he had the job of controlling a then wild and truculent tribe of mountain dwellers called the Lumbwa.[1] These charming but undisciplined warriors had recently shown in no uncertain fashion their strong objection to the behavior of the Indian coolie gangs toward the Lumbwa goats. To the pure-minded Africans, such goings-on were quite inexplicable. Too soon their abhorrence of such an un-natural vice carried them to a pass where they felt that nothing short of spearing a gang or two of Indian coolies would relieve their passion.

At the same time the Lumbwa, it must be admitted, found the little steel wedges used for locking the rails of the newly laid railway track to the wooden anti-termite sleepers just the very thing for fashioning spear heads. The copper wire of the newly constructed telephone line was also found most acceptable for ornamental and trading purposes. Whole miles of these commodities would mysteriously disappear in the night in spite of armed patrols all along the line. To P. fell the job of putting a stop to these depredations.

As to my presence in this turbulent country, it was partly due to my hunting activities and partly due to the fact that I had assembled a herd of native cows to await the arrival of a short-horned bull, together with a heifer in calf, I had imported from Scotland. I hoped thereby to establish a cross breed of animals that would be a bigger and better beast than the pure native cattle. It must be confessed, too, that I hoped that such agricultural activities would act as a set-off against my purely hunting ones.

Unfortunately, the importation of these two animals had no result. Although only a yearling, the bull was much too heavy for the native cows. Even when supported by a gang of boys, it was seldom that the poor but willing bull could accomplish the feat of propagating the stock. The boys, who regarded the bull as some formidable monster, always let go at the critical moment and down would fall the miserable cow flat on the ground.

---

[1] The Nandi traditionally lived in the highland areas of the Nandi Hills in the former Rift Valley province of Kenya. The map to the left shows the Uasin Gishu Plateau to Turkwell and Sotik, the areas where Bell hunted during his time with the Nandis.

Soon my imported bull and heifer succumbed to heat, unfamiliar food and, in the case of the bull, perhaps disappointment.

I will never forget my first meeting with P. Here was an unusual type, in these surroundings at any rate. In fact, he looked the most unlikely person to control a formidable gang of spearmen-cum-bowmen. He was a slight, pale-complexioned man with a soft smile, pleasant manner, and a sandy beard, which was eternally garnished with a much-burned pipe filled with native tobacco. He dressed in khaki slacks, open shirt, and khaki drill coat, and as headgear he wore a slouchy felt hat. He always carried the butt end of a native spear as a stick. He might have been mistaken for some humble trader.

Actually, he had been in a London bank until some complication caused him to foreswear his career and to enter colonial service, and here he was. As the saying goes, we "took" to each other. I cannot say what he saw in me. But in him I sensed a most unusual personality.

Under the conditions of his surroundings it was easy to do so, but I could not help wondering how his bosses in the administration had come to recognize his peculiar abilities. Someone, somewhere, must be a man of unusual perspicacity, for P. was given unique powers. He was C. in C., magistrate, judge with life-and-death powers, and everything else. Beyond a Goanese clerk he had no assistant.

The Lumbwa had long been a thorn in the side of the administration. They had held up and sometimes massacred safaris that considered themselves strong enough to resist the Lumbwa demands for *hongo* (tribute) in the old caravan days. That was before the advent of the Uganda railway. Now they continued to raid and steal the very vitals of the railway itself, pilfering any part that was transportable by manpower back into their densely wooded mountainous fastnesses.

Repeated attempts had been made by the military to bring to book the elusive Lumbwa but with such conspicuous failure that it was finally abandoned. Indeed, in the last engagement, the Lumbwa had attacked at dawn a strong column of regular troops reinforced with numbers of Masai auxiliaries. As usual, the column was in a chosen position, with good field of fire, and surrounded with the customary man-proof thorn zareba. In the rush from close quarters that constituted the attack, the Lumbwa spearmen with astonishing valour placed their shields on top of the thorn hedge, leapt upon them, and hurled themselves into the dense and now firing throng within the zareba.

At least one of the machine guns had been brought to bear on the milling throng by some trigger-happy gunner, and down went friend and foe alike—chiefly friendly auxiliaries who were in their native war paint and hard to distinguish from the enemy. Then the cattle that had been so laboriously scraped together at considerable cost in casualties from native poisoned arrows, of course, stampeded in all directions, flattening the thorn zareba as if it were non-existent. Altogether a clear triumph for the Lumbwas.

In desperation the Government had turned to P., this funny-looking, odd, retiring, and least martial of men. He was quite willing to try his hand so long as it was a lone hand. He demanded that he should be given an absolutely free rein to run the show in his own way. His wish was acceded to.

All the military must be withdrawn was his first demand. It was done. Then this queer figure, totally unarmed—P. never carried or used or even had a gun or pistol of any kind—wandered placidly through the hostile country. Glowered upon from every dense clump of forest by bowmen itching to loose their deadly, freshly poisoned arrows, he quietly led his dithering safari through ambush after ambush, smoking his pipe, glancing neither to right nor left, greeting the nervous expostulations of his boys with his funny little smile and a gentle, "On! GO on!"

His boys and small force of civil police were as much mystified as were the native spearmen by these tactics. Hitherto the procedure of a government safari through the country was quite a different affair. The vanguard would be composed of a dozen or so of those tough old fighters, Nubi or Soudanese. With them would be a score of porters carrying open boxes of ammunition. Each of the vanguard would start off with two hundred rounds each. In those days it was Martini-Henry stuff and heavy. As they went along, they poured a stream of lead into any cover that might harbour enemy spear- or bowmen, replenishing from the open boxes as they went along.

Of course, if the way were long, it became very costly in ammunition. On one such safari I saw a bugler hurriedly brought up to the front and given orders to sound the cease-fire as soon as the terrain and the flights of arrows would allow, such was the drain on the ammo.

Behind the advance guard would generally be found the white soldier in command and the political officer. Sometimes these valuable and precious people would seize the large buffalo-hide shields carried by the auxiliaries and hold them on each side while the little poisoned arrows pattered like rain upon them, all the while volley after volley of shot would pour into the bush in every direction. All were quite oblivious of the cease-fire. Creating a good imitation of the modern smoke screen, the black powder from the Martinis poured into the still air on the narrow forest track. The din and stink of sulphur can only be imagined.

Every now and again one of the number would be arrow-stricken. If the poison was fresh, the victim would be dead in two or three minutes even though when only scratched superficially. Should it happen to be a Muslim who died and should the arrow have sunk in over the barbs, what a palaver there would be. Firstly, the iron had to be got out but without cutting. No true believer could be buried with any iron in his precious anatomy, and none must be disfigured by cutting.

How we used to curse at the deliberation of the performers as the *zip! zip!* of the arrows continued all around us. Many were fired at extreme range from high trees and arrived from the most unexpected directions.

Instead of instilling fear in the native breast, all this noise and fuss had the contrary effect. While an occasional bullet found a billet on a native body by the law of chance, the most obvious effect was to demonstrate the funk of the advancing column and the futility of firearms in dense cover. So the natives were quite happy when dealing with such tactics.

When a lone, unarmed white man came strolling along, however, peacefully smoking his pipe at the head of his safari—a position more usually associated with a stream of fire, bullets, and noise—the local inhabitants were filled with wonder. It smacked strongly of "medicine." Here was a man obviously unconcerned and unafraid. Even the boldest and toughest hesitated to deliver the so easy spear thrust or to loose the arrow at such a "sitter." On went P. until he reached such a place as was suitable for his purposes. Not a shot from either side had been fired.

In course of time contact was gradually established with the natives. Never did P. show impatience or anger with anyone. Never did he raise his voice. His Kiswahili was atrocious, yet he somehow commanded instant obedience. Everyone was scared stiff of this still man. By that queer and undefinable quality we so conveniently call "character" or "personality," he completely overcame the Lumbwa without killings or violence. Where machine guns had failed, this quiet London banker prevailed.

While this unostentatious yet so momentous revolution in the contact between savage and white man went on its allotted course, it might be enquired what I, an unattached white man, was doing in the country. I was raising cattle and lowering elephants.

In my role as hunter I was welcome everywhere. The immunity from molestation by the natives extended to my cattle and belongings. Even when I accompanied one or two expeditions against the natives, they did not appear to take umbrage. They never knowingly shot at me. Once when they killed a boy of mine, they came to apologize. On my part I never shot at them, and they knew this. It all seems very odd, but so it was. Without any arranging, it just happened so. They seemed not to resent my taking part in the fighting and marching against my hosts. The whole thing was a huge joke anyhow and an affair to be laughed at.

P. seemed to like my company, and after a few weeks in the bush I would spend a few days with him. It used to fascinate me to watch him apparently doing nothing yet getting things done. Already he had a body of young Lumbwa warriors drilling and preparing to enter his police force. He used to say that in due course he hoped to be able to induce the Lumbwa to make roads, in spite of the fact that it was considered demeaning for any warrior to do any work whatsoever.

P. was a very good friend to me and considered that my residence among the natives was a good thing for everybody concerned.[2] He turned a blind eye on my hunting activities, for, of course, game laws were now supposed to be in force. This arrangement suited all the parties concerned, and whenever I had a pit full of buried ivory, I would ask P. to get me permission to dig it up and sell it.

It amused him intensely the first time I said I wanted to open a pit. "The governor can't possibly refuse," he said. "There is no alternative. To leave it rotting in the ground would be stupid."

And off he wrote straightaway demanding permission. The authorities could not deny P. anything. For once they knew when they had a good man. Their precious railway was now secure from the embarrassing attentions of the native raiders. The coolie gangs were no longer molested and could circulate freely once more. All this at very little cost to the government.

---

[2] See chapter 9 of this book for the complete story.

Permission to sell my ivory would arrive and out of the pit it would come. An agent of Alidina Visram[3] would attend at the pit head out in the bush, my own spring balance would be used to weigh the ivory, and the resultant total would be accepted by the quite poor-looking Indian agent. Then I would be handed a scrap of paper, generally a page torn from a small notebook, covered with Gujarati characters that meant nothing to me. The Indian would take the ivory and go on his way while I would send the dirty little note to my bank in Mombasa where, in due time, it would be honoured.

I once asked my banker if it was all right to accept these chits. "Yes," was the reply, "the Gujaratis will always honour their paper. In the case of very large sums, you might have to wait until the stuff reaches railhead, but no longer."

Alidina Visram was a marvelous firm, and his system of disposing of what would otherwise have been an embarrassing amount of stuff worked very much in my favour. The company would send a ragged-arsed agent out to the wildest country. So long as it was known that he was coming to my camp, no one would molest him. And the price they paid was astonishingly high when one considers the outlay they had to face. Everyone had a cut at ivory. It was deemed capable of bearing outrageous taxation. The government had first whack at it with a thumping great royalty tax. Then the freight charges on the new railway to the coast were on such a scale as to almost pay for the whole ramshackle affair in one consignment. And the forms that had to be filled out!

---

[3] In 1863, at the age of twelve, Alidina Visram traveled on a dhow from India to Zanzibar; at Bagamoyo he worked as an assistant to Sewa Haji Paroo. Soon he branched out on his own and started organizing his own caravans into the interior of Tanganyika. He opened branches of his firm at Dar-es-Salaam, Sadani, Tabora, Ujiji, and Alima and Tindo in the Belgian Congo. With the ongoing construction of the Uganda Railway, he opened stores along the railway line and became the supplier of food to the Indian workers. He got the contract of paying the railway workers their salaries as well as providing funds to the railway authority. He was practically a bank: cheques given to him on the coast could be cashed in the interior for a commission of 3–5 percent. By 1904, he began to branch into agriculture and within a few years owned seven large plantations for sugar cane and rubber, with experimental plots of grains, fruits, flowers, tea, and cotton, employing over 3,000 workers on his projects.

Alidina Visram was well known for his kindness and generosity. By 1905 he began encouraging immigration from Kathiawar, India, first as his employees and then as his agents. He also sponsored and employed as many non-Ismailis as came his way. Those he mentored spread out to Homa Bay, Mumias, Sio Port, Kenya, and then into Uganda. It is said that 90 percent of the Khoja Ismailis who attained prosperity in Kenya and Uganda owe their advance to him. See chapter 10 of this book for more on Alidina Visram.

No. It certainly paid to unburden oneself of the stuff quietly and discreetly out in the bush and to let the other man do all the dirty work.

It also concealed the extent of my hunting activities, for, of course, no Indian trader would divulge to another where he got such a number of lovely tusks. As regards the effect of burying them in damp forest soil, they all gained in weight from two to five pounds. One tusk once scaled seven pounds more when it came up than when it went down.

******

In course of time my hunting activities extended to the opposite side of the extensive valley through which the railway approached Lake Victoria. Here was situated an even more wild and unruly tribe called the Nandi. While P. continued from strength to strength in his uncanny sway over the Lumbwa, no-one seemed able to do anything with the Nandi.

Their depredations finally reached such a pitch—for they were accompanied by quite serious killings—that the home authorities at long last gave orders for an expedition against the Nandi on an unprecedented scale. This happened, however, only after minor-scale operations had failed lamentably to make any impression on this sporting and lively little tribe. It was considered by the pundits that only by capturing and forcibly removing their stocks and herds could their subjugation be secured.

The country itself was difficult. It was quite small but consisted of wild mountainous country that was densely clothed with forest. As were the Lumbwa, the Nandi were armed with stabbing spears and bows and arrows. So far the honours of the conflict leant to the side of the natives, in spite of one success on the part of the authorities.

That was when a lot of Nandi natives—men, women, children, and cattle—retreated to some large natural caves in the face of an assault. It was a fatal mistake on their part. The pursuing columns failed to take the place by frontal assault, so their recourse was to dynamite the cave. The results can be imagined. Never again did the Nandi try to hold a defensive position. As for being subdued by this catastrophe, it only seemed to imbue them with redoubled daring and resolution to fight their foes to the death.

Among these unruly but sporting natives I lived and circulated freely. They never molested me or my boys or even my stock. The latter must often have been a sore temptation. The young bloods would often accompany my hunting safaris across the Uasin Gishu Plateau to Turkwell and Sotik. They often taunted me with the fact that they could kill me any time they liked, and then I, on my part, would demonstrate how futile their shields and tree cover were against bullets that would penetrate either with ease.

At this time I had a riding pony and a mule. Often when I visited the armed camp that was the government *boma,* I would laugh to find them practically beleaguered in their fortress. To send a letter down-country, as many as thirty soldiers would be required as escort.

The man in charge of the political side was an old sailing ship captain.[4] A trader up to the time the Soudanese troops had mutinied, he and all other white men had been drawn into the conflict. He had been given the choice between a large monetary reward or a post in the administration. He had chosen the latter, and as he had proven to be a tough and stout-hearted old warrior, he had been posted to Nandi. Here he had built himself a regular little fortress with a deep moat, drawbridges, and machine-gun emplacements all in true frontier style.

If you were invited to stay with him, you were, indeed, lucky. As a general rule no male guest was allowed to sleep within the fort. The officers, who occupied an entrenched camp on an adjacent hill, were never allowed to do so. Why? The captain was a jealous old devil. The cause of this jealousy? He ran his whole establishment with women.

He dressed the choicest and prettiest of young native girls in short khaki drill skirts. Their legs and feet were bare, and their firm, pointed breasts pricked out the cloth of their neat little khaki blouses in the most ravishing way. Their well-developed posteriors caused their skirts to bulge and swing to the complete undoing of any beholder. So used were we to seeing all the divine female form in complete nudity that we never realized what exquisite proportions it contained until we saw it partially veiled by suitable garments. Hence, of course, was Bluebeard's jealous guard on his harem.

I don't know how many of these entrancing imps he had—they were always changing as is the nature of things—but they were all over the place. They took the place of boys, so they cooked, washed, and served at table; in fact, they did everything. I tell you guests could hardly take their eyes off them

---

[4] This was probably M. Walter Mayes. See chapter 9 of this book.

as those tantalizingly sharp breasts almost perforated your ear as they handed you a dish. With a background of many womanless years at sea in sailing ships, the host was a pretty potent man and the turn-around in personnel was correspondingly rapid.

I used to roar with laughter to see the skipper begin prizing off his guests long before midnight after one of his dinners. He would first tell one of the girls to call out across the moat—the drawbridge was up, of course—to the lantern boys and escorts that their bwanas were ready to depart. This pretty broad hint would be stoutly rejected by the soldiers—there were no other whites in that land except myself and these men—who were by this time feeling quite mellow on the skipper's whisky.

Finding this made no impression, he would yawn and stretch and say he had a heavy day ahead of him; he wasn't a bone-idle soldier, nor was he a herring-gutted one. Then he would order one of the girls to remove all drink from the table, but this would not be accomplished before his guests had seized the bottles and replenished their glasses, all the while pinching the girls' bottoms and otherwise distracting them. The skipper meanwhile glowered with venom on these jolly proceedings. Little wonder he was reluctant to have male guests sleep in his fort. It is a moot point just how much the defensive lay-out of his fortress was directed against the natives or against his white friends and protectors.

The truth of the matter was he could not afford to quarrel with the soldiers, nor they with him. By mutual agreement sundry credits accrued to all concerned not unconnected with the sale of cattle. These were beasts taken from the natives as reprisal for some treacherous spearing of mail runners or what-not, there being no dearth of excuses.

Once I had ridden in and had no safari with me, so perforce I had to be accommodated in the fort. I was given a camp bed in the dining room. To my astonishment no sooner had I gone to bed than sundry dusky maids silently laid their sleeping mats on the floor and forthwith fell asleep. About five o'clock in the morning the skipper appeared, kicked various posteriors in his passage to the whisky and soda on the sideboard and announced that all these sluts were in the family way anyhow.

This man could do nothing with the natives. They laughed at him and—had they been Americans—would have called him a "cheap skate." This native attitude toward one who appeared to me quite a stout-hearted man often puzzled me. That he was pretty easy-going and not too scrupulous, judged by white men's standards, could not be denied. But those traits of character were also to be found among the men they did admire.

Why should they stand in palpable awe of a man like P. and laugh and scoff at one like the skipper? The one a man of honourable dealing but without show or pretense, of poor personal presence, guileless and quiet. The other brimful of energy, bounce, force, and guile as any of their own leaders. Yet there it was. The skipper could not go more than a mile into the forest without a gang of police and soldiers and then it was a case of continuous fire from one side against a continuous flight of arrows from the other. It was ambush after ambush every mile of the way. Then there was P. who could circulate anywhere without a shot being fired. I think it was a matter of personal courage. I cannot think of any other reason for it.

Anyway, things went from bad to worse. All the time Nandi were nightly raiding the precious new railway, lifting miles of telephone wire, spearing their way through any opposition. Armoured trains were tried only to become de-railed. Finally, London became seriously worked up about it. Orders issued that at all cost these pestiferous Nandi must be wound up. Affairs passed into the hands of the soldiers. No longer was it an affair of civil administration and its terror of having to meet the cost of operations from their meagre resources.

As is usual, the army set about the job in a big way. There would surely be medals if the campaign were important enough. Great numbers of troops were gathered together from all parts of Africa. In due course the attack was launched from different points. Columns converged so as to trap and capture, they hoped, so much of the native herds that starvation would succeed where all else had failed. The skipper was withdrawn and P. was appointed political officer to represent the interests of the administration, a lamb among wolves if ever there was one. Or so they thought as they gazed curiously at the queer, still little man in his slouchy get-up.

Well, they marched and counter-marched up and down the length and breadth of the quite small land, blasting their way through the forest by fire-power, over-running ambushes, building formidable camps with machine-gun platforms, commanding suitable fields of fire and the camp-encircling thorn zarebas. The expenditure in ammunition was prodigious. And always that funny man with the beard went along unconcernedly smoking his filthy pipe, saying nothing yet seeing all.

As the army collected cattle, they were sent down to the main camp. These convoys had to be escorted by such numbers of troops that all other operations were halted in their fortified positions. Even then it was a continuous battle as the plucky natives gave them no rest night or day. One particularly decisive action resulted in the complete annihilation of thirty picked troops who were escorting a letter from the C. in C. to base camp. They stopped for a drink at one of those clear, cold streams that intersect the country in all directions. Not a shot was to be fired, so complete and sudden was the surprise.

P. told me of another brilliant coup—this time effected by Nandi boys. One of them crept up right under the eyes of the sentries and scraped a hole big enough to crawl through on one side of an enormously strong camp, while another youth made a similar hole through the zareba on the opposite side. It was in the dead of night, of course.

Then the band collected together, crept silently through the first hole, ran down the rows of closely packed sleepers stabbing the sleeping forms on one side with the head of a spear and puncturing those on the other side with the pointed iron-shod end. They killed or wounded quite a number before they reached the prepared exit holes. The resultant machine-gun and rifle fire accounted for many more, but not among the Nandi. This and similar exploits tended to bear out the native saying that man is at his bravest as a boy, best at actual fighting as a youth, and only a woman at middle-age, no good for anything but breeding.

In course of time some eighteen hundred head of cattle had been captured and were sent down to base. It was thought that if these were withheld from their owners, starvation would compel submission. So the columns withdrew to base, pursued by their active opponents to the last, there to await events.

Nothing happened. Time passed. No emissaries came from the enemy. Expenses of the army in the field mounted ever higher. Then a young officer had an idea. If he could arrange a meeting with the laibon of Nandi, he felt convinced he could persuade him to submit. What these means of persuasion were was known only to himself.

Now the laibon occupied a position among the Nandi that might be likened to that of king or czar but that included powers of magic or "medicine" quite unknown to our rulers. His word was law even to these unruly devils. So that should he give the word, there is little doubt the Nandi resistance would have collapsed. P. in his role of political officer was requested to arrange a meeting if it were possible.

He soon found a native who would undertake the task of carrying a message to the laibon. The message arrived and was pondered by the old man. With great courage he agreed to meet the army representative at a stated time and place, unarmed and with only one armed orderly, in his case a spearman, and stipulating that his opposite number should also come unarmed attended by one armed orderly. P., of course, had no part in this palaver beyond that of providing a messenger to contact the laibon. All the rest was in army hands.

The meeting took place. The laibon was a frail old gentleman of some hundred and ten pounds, the officer of some hundred and eighty pounds. Both had one armed orderly. What actually happened at the meeting is any man's guess. There survived from it only one person—the officer.

Now whether treachery had from the very beginning been intended by both sides in this interesting drama or whether it was merely a case of mutual distrust will never be known. What is known is that behind and hidden in the bush the laibon had two or three hundred spearman while the army had a similarly hidden body of riflemen.

When, therefore, a series of shots was heard to shatter the silence, there was a mutual rush from the opposing escorts and a most frightful clash over the dead bodies of the laibon, his orderly, and that of the army representative's orderly. Alone of the actual palaver party the officer remained alive, the convenience of which coincidence by no means escaped the prosecution at the ensuing court martial insisted upon by those inconsiderate people of the administration.[5]

P. was filled with fury about this affair. As was his way, the only sign of this was to go a shade or two paler than usual and quieter and stiller.

---

[5] Bell never mentions Richard Meinertzhagen in his notes by name, but it is Meinertzhagen he refers to when he says, "a young officer." Many believe Meinertzhagen, with aforethought, lured Laibon Koitalel Arap Samoei of the Nandi to his death. Even though many British officers felt shamed over Meinertzhagen's actions, he was recommended for a Victoria Cross for this escapade. The outcry over this, however, was so great that two courts of enquiry were held concerning the massacre and Meinertzhagen's part in it; both times Meinertzhagen was exonerated. British Colonial Commissioner Sir James Hayes-Sadler was so unhappy with these verdicts that he protested to the Colonial Office in an effort to have Meinertzhagen's verdicts overturned. Meinertzhagen said in his memoirs, "[I was told that] my actions resulted in the reputation of the British Government for fair dealing and honesty being called into question, and the Colonial Office consider it undesirable that I should continue to serve in East Africa." Instead of being awarded the Victoria Cross, Meinertzhagen left under the cloud of an official reprimand. Today many believe Richard Meinertzhagen's legend to be one of colossal fraud.

Although the army was mostly rather ashamed of this affair, still there were those who thought much good might come of it even if it were as evil as the political people made out. Unfortunately, instead of bringing submission, the killing of the laibon seemed rather to act as a powerful stimulant. Infuriated Nandi parties raided and killed to the very confines of the base itself. Half the army now guarded the captured herds by day while the other half did so by night.

P. now threw in his hand by refusing to have any more to do with the show. Stalemate, complete and absolute, became the status quo. Something had to be done.

Finally P. was asked to resolve the situation. He was very firm and said he would only tackle the problem if his conditions were agreed to. He was asked to name them. He did so. Firstly, all military were to be withdrawn from the country. He was to have a free hand. He wanted twenty-four policemen and some spare rifles and uniforms. No other white men except one white non-commissioned officer as instructor.

They agreed with many misgivings, for, really, there was nothing else they could do. P. departed on his new mission as soon as the last of the army had withdrawn.

Very much the same procedure was gone through as in the case of the Lumbwa and with equal success. Not a shot was fired and not a bow-string twanged as that bearded figure walked at the head of the column right in among the heights on either side covered with the silent throng of spear- and bowmen.

When he arrived at the site of the old government *boma*, P. set about re-establishing it. But where his predecessors had gone to lengths strengthening its defenses, P. started gardening operations, sowing lettuce and radish seeds. So far there was little or no contact with the still suspicious natives, who contented themselves with keeping careful watch on the doings at the *boma* from the safety of the surrounding heights.

Nothing appeals so much to the savage, both male and female, as drilling with firearms. P. knew this well, so he had his men out marching and parading every day. At first these military preparations were viewed from afar with great suspicion, for there were memories of machine-gun fire tearing into any gathering in the old days. With the new regime, however, never was a shot fired. Gradually the watchers became more numerous and bolder.

Then Nandi emissaries began to circulate among the natives. These emissaries told the natives that the white man wanted to enroll Nandi warriors as policemen. They were to have uniform, pay, food, and housing. This was a new idea entirely. At first only one or two joined up, for they were still suspicious of such a revolutionary idea. Gradually, numbers increased, and now a lot of people gathered to watch their own people all dressed up being put through drills by the instructors. How they laughed when one of their own lot stepped off with the wrong foot or otherwise distinguished himself on the parade ground. All the while P. plodded around peacefully bent on his gardening operations, seemingly paying no attention to anyone.

Gradually the natives came to regard the *boma* and its doings as we might treat a free cinema show. They lost their fear to the extent of mingling with the camp followers; finally, they began to bring in stuff to exchange against trade goods, salt, etc. Quite a little market sprang up . . . and still nothing violent happened.

As soon as P's native recruits were firmly gripped by the sense of power the wearing of uniform seems to arouse in the primitive breast, P. began to use them more and more on missions to the native chiefs. There were cases where they outstripped their instructions, of course. That is unavoidable with primitive material.

Once or twice small chiefs who had proved un-cooperative had been tied up and brought in forcibly. There had been no killings, however, and here I think P. had been fortunate. On the whole things went very well, mainly because P. was so patient. Finally, he won over nearly all the influential chiefs.

He had now most of the best of the young bloods—just the lads to start a row—in his police force or working for him in his native palavers. With this, the Nandi were done for as a tribe of independent raiders and robbers that had been their chief occupation for who knows how long. Gradually their cattle were restored to their original owners for service performed, and the land settled down to peaceful ways.

While all these merry goings-on had been afoot, I had been away north on the Turkwell River, everlastingly on the trail of elephants. Returning to my cattle ranch, a few hours' pony ride from the *boma*, I found my two old pensioners still in possession and everything as before. I had a lot of stuff with me that was immediately buried where it would be safe and where it would gain weight by contact with its damp surroundings.

Somewhat weary with the chase—about seventy miles travel was entailed for every head killed in this country—my boys and I lay off for a few days and listened to the news of all these interesting happenings. When we had left Nandi, the skipper had been in charge, the army had come and gone, and the laibon had been killed. Now P., my great friend, had come, and all was peace once more.

As soon as I arrived, P. told me the news of all the doings in his quiet, modest way. Only I with my intimate knowledge of P. and of the natives could fill in the blanks of his chronicle. What a man!

Then he told me his plans. He was going to make roads.

"Not with Nandi labour?" I said.

"Oh, yes, they'll work all right," he replied.

The lordly raiders at pick and shovel! That was a facer! They came to it in the end, however. Gone were the days when they strutted around in their war paint, their only occupation to see that others worked for them.

"And I'm going to put down parent-murder," P. said, as if he were announcing he was going for a stroll in the garden. "I've got a lad who took his old father into the bush and knocked him on the head with his knobkerrie because his father wouldn't cough up some cows to buy a wife for him. I'm determined to make an example of him, but I'm a bit worried about the thing.

"You see, King's Regulations lay it down that the firing party must be twenty-five paces distant, but Sergeant XX tells me his lads cannot hit a man at that range. I told him I would sew a piece of white cotton round the man's chest and paint a large black bull on it, but he says he can't guarantee a hit even then. He insists on a five-yard range."

The peace-loving man was in a new, cold-blooded role, indeed. In the end, however, he stopped the time-honoured custom of patricide.

My friend Partington, who was of a delicate constitution, died of blackwater fever a few years later.

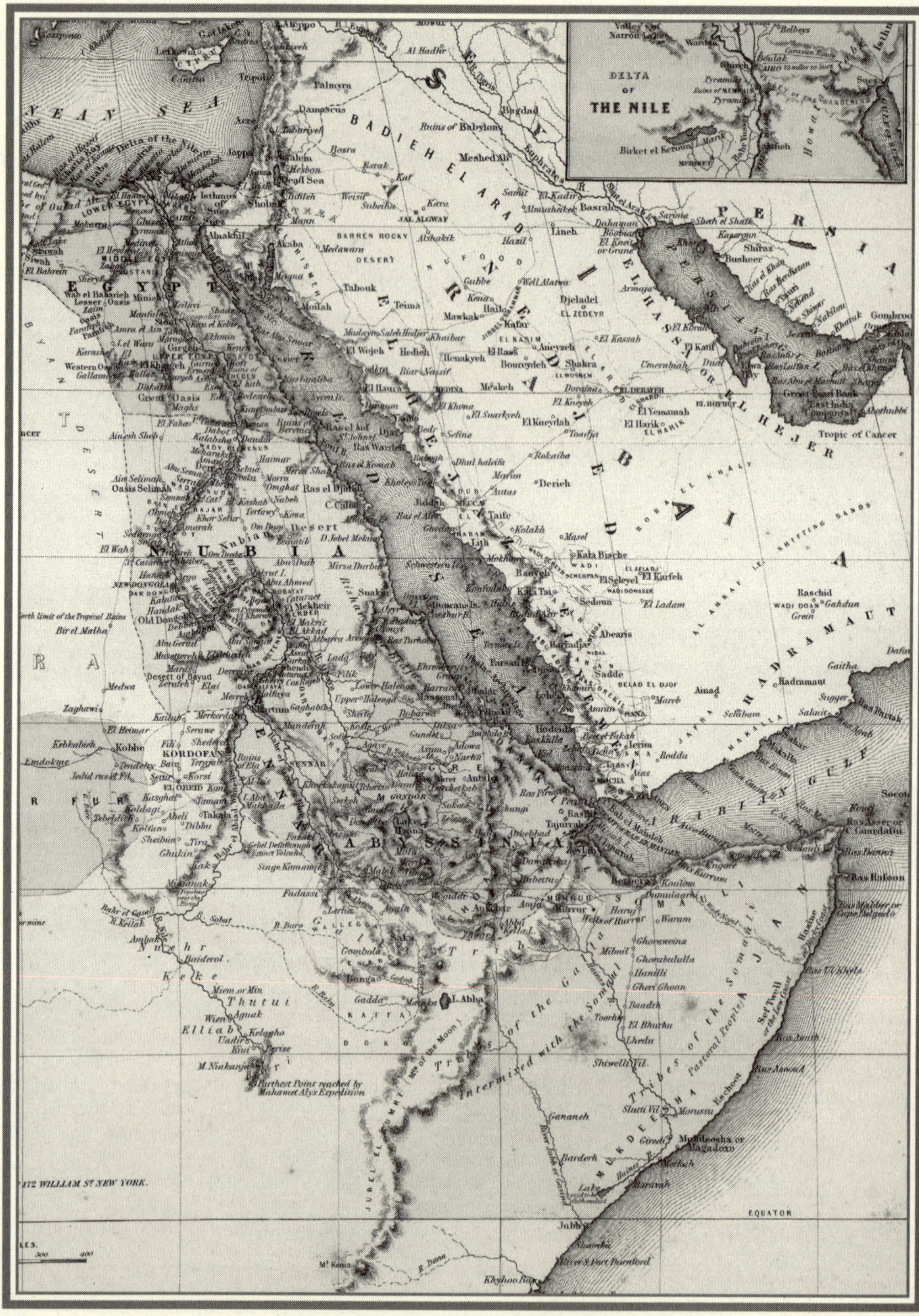

The Somali Virgin

Chapter 25

Alima was her name. She was now about sixteen years of age. Her life so far had been normal enough: milking cows and camels, attending to all the chores of a nomadic people, and constantly moving from place to place in search of grass and water for the numerous herds of cows, camels, goats, and sheep. She was a beauty. Even among Somalis, a people of outstanding beauty of form and feature, she stood out a mile.

The Somalis are a people of mysterious origin. Although you will find among all other races who have come to Africa from outside signs of intermixing with the indigenous Negro peoples, you will hardly see any examples among the Somalis of any such intermarrying. They retain their long black hair, delicate features, fine bones, small heads, light but muscular bodies, and their undefinable air of breeding. Possibly this is due to centuries of interbreeding. Or it may be due to their pastoral habits and to their diet of milk and meat.

Naturally of a fierce and pugnacious character, they are, by our standards, a cruel people. Even the women are always fighting among themselves. When on their own, they are eternally raiding stock and killing each other. In many respects they resemble the Scottish clans in the old days when every clan was fighting every other, the victor massacring the vanquished even to the women and children.

They have very highly developed one trait, and it amounts to selective breeding. They will not tolerate imperfection of body, whether it be bandy legs, knock knees, or even an outsize stature. Any departure from normal is so ridiculed that the poor victim is practically forced out of the tribe through no fault of his or hers. Where clothing is of the scantiest, no physical blemish escapes notice. These prohibitions apply more particularly to the females. There is but one thing left for them to do. They must become prostitutes, where they can conceal their defects with clothes.

Now Alima, as I have said, was a beauty. Straight legs, hard pointed breasts, beautiful body, lovely hair, smooth skin, and fine teeth. She was neither tall nor short. But she had one little defect. She was still a virgin after repeated attempts to undo her. Not that she had resisted these attempts. On the contrary, she had acquiesced in them. Her greatest desire was to prove herself quite normal in that respect, but it simply could not be done. No doubt our doctors have a name for this affliction and quite a minor operation would have put things to rights.

Her people, however, knew nothing of this, so out she had to go. She was taken by her brothers to the nearest town to be sold for as much as could be got. She fell to the lot of a stranger who became deeply enamoured of her beauty. There is no telling what he paid for her. She accepted her fate with smiling fortitude and tried to make herself as agreeable as possible. Actually, she was glad of her new position, covered herself with the silks her doting owner provided so lavishly, and quite enjoyed herself.

There is a custom among these women to immerse their bodies in incense, thereby, they feel, rendering themselves extraordinarily seductive. They tie a long, loose robe without sleeves—a long sack, in fact—tightly around their necks. A brazier of earthenware is loaded with live embers. On the embers is placed a handful of incense. As it smokes, the girl stands over it, letting the robe down to the ground on all sides. There the naked body is smoked all over by the sweet-smelling smoke. They come out of it with a bloom like that on black grapes. They are then ready for their lords

Alima was a beauty. Even among Somalis, a people of outstanding beauty of form and feature, she stood out a mile.

and masters. It is much more effective than powdering yet producing a similar effect. The smoking is done after a bath, of course.

Now Alima's new owner—I suppose one should call him husband—was a man of some age besides being of somewhat dissolute habits. There was, indeed, no lack of those envious persons who saw in the alliance the proverbial pearl cast to the swine. The latter, however, was greatly pleased with his acquisition and boasted that his wife was still a virgin. Malicious tongues suggested she was likely to remain so, as far as he was concerned, anyway.

Then one night when, as usual, she was all bloomed-up and ready, he came home himself pretty well oiled up. Try as he might, he could accomplish nothing, although she withheld nothing from him and assisted in every way. Of course, it was a physical impossibility; he was not likely to succeed where much better men than he had failed. In drunken exasperation he told the poor girl to get the hell out of his house and tantalize him no longer.

Poor Alima was in a fix. To whom could she turn in her dilemma? She sent for her brother. When he arrived, he listened in silence to her tale of woe. *Hell,* he thought, *the man will be wanting his money back. Can't have that.* As he wondered what he should do, it was Alima herself who suggested a solution of the difficulty.

"Get someone to help you," she said. He soon found a friend to assist him. The girl led the two men to a remote part of the bush. Selecting a large diameter tree she lay on her back with a leg on each side of the tree trunk. "Tie my legs," she directed.

They did so. "Now open me with this cowhorn," the dauntless creature said, handing it to her brother.

"Now hold my arms firmly," she told the other man, stretching her arms out beyond her head where he sat upon them.

What excruciating torture she suffered perhaps only a surgeon could guess at, for not a whimper came from that courageous creature. Thus and thus only did Alima lose her virginity.

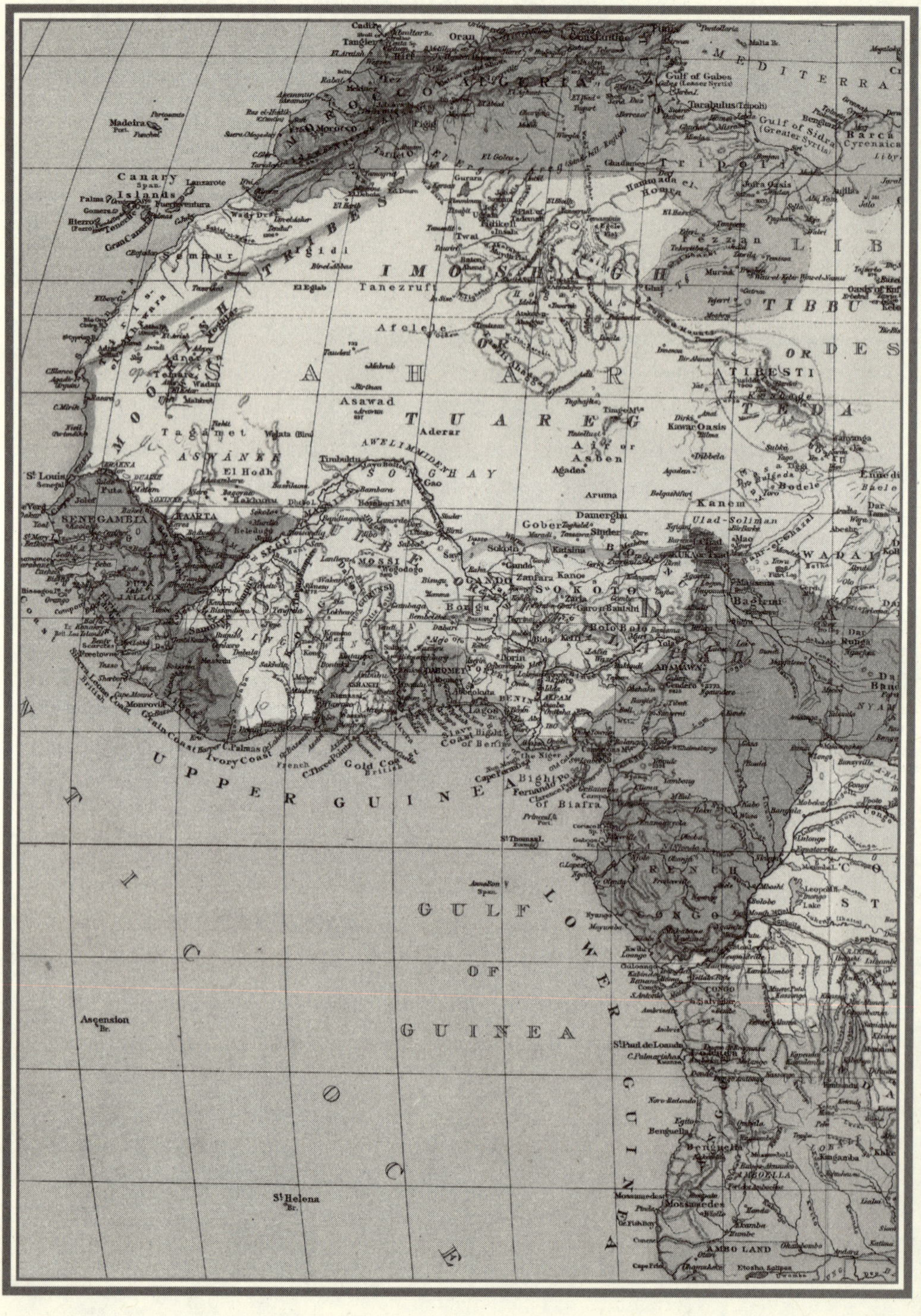

MOROCCO
ALGERIA
MEDITERRA
Gulf of Gabes
Gulf of Sidra
Tripoli
Fezzan
LIB
TIBBU
OR DES
TIBESTI
TEDA
IMOSHAGH
Tanezruft
Afelele
SAHARA
TUAREG
Asawad
Aderar
Air or Asben
Agades
Kawar Oasis
Kanem
Bodele
WADAI
Bagirmi
Madeira
Canary Islands
Lanzarote
Fuerteventura
Palma
Gomera
Hierro
MOORISH TRIBES
Tagânet
El Hodh
St. Louis
SENEGAMBIA
KAARTA
Timbuktu
SONGHAY
Gao
Bambara
MOSSI
Gober
Damerghu
Sokoto
Kano
Zanfara
SOKOTO
Bornu
ADAMAWA
DAHOMEY
ASHANTI
Lagos
Monrovia
Freetown
C. Palmas
Ivory Coast
Gold Coast
Slave Coast
Bight of Benin
Bight of Biafra
Fernando Po
C. Three Points
UPPER GUINEA
St. Thomas I.
Annobon
GULF OF GUINEA
LOWER GUINEA
FRENCH CONGO
CONGO
St. Paul de Loanda
Benguella
Mossamedes
AMBO LAND
Ascension
St. Helena
ATLANTIC OCEAN

A Sojourn among Practicing Christians

CHAPTER 26

I had been hunting in the dense coastal forests that cover much of the West African seaboard. The ivory was small, but elephants were numerous enough. In years gone by great quantities of ivory had issued from this coast, hence its name, Ivory Coast. In the comparatively easy country of the interior with its mixture of bush and savanna, the herds had been much reduced. As so often happens, however, the strip of really thick forest bordering on the sea had been totally neglected owing to the natural difficulties of circulating in the country, the hostile attitude of the tribes, and the impossibility of surprising a village. For it must be understood that the name Ivory Coast referred to black as well as white ivory. Indeed, it was largely from this coast that the Western hemisphere drew its supply of slaves.

When Britain decided that she, at any rate, must stop countenancing this traffic in human stock, it must have been a tremendous blow to the firms engaged in this trade. The supply of the white variety of the precious stuff depends solely on what could be killed by the natives with their primitive spears, arrows, or pits, what was picked up in the bush, and what few could be killed with flint-lock or percussion guns of the muzzle-loading type. So when the close-down on slaving was signaled, trade and revenue dropped with a bump, and, very kindly, the country was handed over to the French.

Many of the old, well-established firms continued in business under the new regime, adapting their lines of goods to the altered circumstances. In the capital there was quite a considerable white community comprised of French officials and French and British traders. There was a club and one hotel-restaurant.

It was here I had a room. In those days steamers were few and far between, and as I wanted to move on to the Cameroons, then under German occupation, I had a considerable time to wait for one that would take me there. Someone suggested that instead of paying rather extortionate prices at the hotel, the thing to do was to take a house in the town. They were reasonable in rent, and if one had native retainers, as I had, the scheme offered obvious advantages. We went to look over one or two such places, met the owners, all English-speaking natives, and finally closed with one oldish man who had a house to let in a very favourable situation in the town.

The house itself, for some reason or other, overlooked all the other houses in the neighbourhood. It towered above its surroundings and, consequently, enjoyed a view; besides this, it was quite airy. There was an outside stairway by which one climbed to a complete little suite comprising an all-around veranda, a bed-cum-sitting room, bath and W.C., shower, and kitchen.

The owner showed me over his house with some pride. He was dressed in a faded frock coat and trousers and without collar or tie. His terms were quite moderate, and we soon agreed. I asked him where he lived and stepping on to the veranda he pointed out his home.

"Married?"

"Oh, yes!"

"Children?"

"Oh, yes, sir. I am a preacher. That is our church," pointing to a building of some size with a bell attached, which had a little grass-roofed shelter of its own. I asked if there were any white ministers living in the town.

"No," he said, "but we have a visiting minister."

"And are you a strong community?" I asked. "I mean are you numerous?"

"Oh, yes!" he said, "all this part is Christian," sweeping most of the town with his arm. "The Mohammedan part is over there."

After some little conversation I said I would now go and settle up at the hotel and bring my things along.

"Very bad place that hotel," he remarked.

When I thought of some of the goings-on there, I could but agree. Then he suggested he could provide a hand-cart to bring my gear along. This was most convenient. Then he suggested I might require a housekeeper who knew the local conditions, the market, its prices, someone in fact who would see I was not done brown [deceived] and also someone who would cook for me. I agreed that it would be most convenient to have such a person, thinking all the time of some town-boy who would at least see that no-one else robbed me.

"Well," he said, "I have a daughter who is an excellent cook and who will look after you."

"And what should I have to pay this lady?" I asked.

"Oh, just give her a small present when you leave," he said.

A Sojourn Among Practicing Christians

And so it was arranged.

It seems almost too good to be true, I thought.

On returning to my new abode with my baggage piled on the preacher's hand-cart, I found an attractive-looking girl of possibly eighteen years of age bustling about the house, sweeping, dusting, and opening the windows; she already had a fire going in the kitchen. She certainly was not the blowsy fat lady of mature age and experience I had anticipated. This creature of seductive and youthful curves greeted me with a smile and in the most matter-of-fact way imaginable.

"Are you the housekeeper?" I asked, expecting to hear that it was her mother who was to fill that exacting post and that this pleasant-looking girl was her daughter only here temporarily to help mama.

"Yes, I'm housekeeper," she said.

Good heavens, I thought, *I'll have to mind my step with such a delectable thing around . . . and with such a father, too.* I had never contacted the Christian element among Africans, and I had visions of serious complications arising vaguely in my mind should I indeed neglect to mind my step. I need not have worried.

I shall never forget my first meal in my new abode. It happened by chance to coincide with the cooking of that magnificent dish called a palm oil chop, which was being prepared chez the Reverend XX's house. My housekeeper, Mary, having asked if I would eat at home, suggested she should bring over from her home some of this ravishing dish and so save on cooking. I agreed to this instantly. This dish when prepared by native male cooks is good, extremely good, but when made by competent native women, it is superlative. For those poor mortals unacquainted with it, here follows a sketchy outline of some of the ingredients.

The whole base upon which the marvelous edifice is erected is the superfine oil of the flesh of the fruit of the oil palm. It will not keep, cannot be exported, and must be freshly prepared. It is as like the commercial palm oil taken from the kernel of the fruit as the purest alcohol is to crude petroleum.

Into a bath of this lovely oil anything may be introduced: herrings, fresh West African chicken, hard-boiled eggs, prawns, in fact, almost anything. The gravy may be thickened with the meal from freshly ground peanuts; to this is added the young, tender flesh scraped from a green coconut; and then the whole rich mass is seasoned with green and red peppers and other condiments.

I used to like it best with boiled, mashed green bananas, but it may equally well be eaten with rice, fou-fou,[1] or native grain. As when approaching a Persian pilau, you want to come hungry to the feast; assuredly, you will not want to eat again for some considerable time. Beer, yes, our own hop beer, is the best drink with this fiery dish—and iced if possible.

People get coast-wide reputations for their palm oil chops. Each individual cook has scope to introduce some subtle little difference that may make or mar her reputation. Should a cook be lucky and hit off a successful combination, nothing on earth would drag the secret from her.

The effect of eating such food in the tropics—and you cannot but eat a lot of it—is alarming, as might be imagined. The most jaded and weary perk up in the most extraordinary fashion—that is, after a heavy sleep that allows digestive processes to turn that seething mass of vitamins into energy. Whether this oil is entirely responsible for the extraordinary sexual accomplishments of the lucky owners of the soil, no-one who has experienced a good, proper palm-oil chop can truthfully deny its attraction.

Mary's mother's chop more than met the foregoing description. Wicked thoughts seethed through my mind as Mary bustled about clearing up and I lay stretched on the large bed.

I wonder, I wonder! They are pious, aren't they?

Waking from a heavy sleep, there was Mary with iced beer!

What a girl! I thought to myself. *Just how pious are they?* arose unbidden in my brain.

In the late afternoon there was a great commotion in the street below. I went to see what was doing. There was quite a procession led by a magnificent-looking young woman walking alone and dressed in the most wonderful manner with solid gold anklets, solid gold armlets, and a necklace of huge native gold nuggets, all of the most gigantic proportions. On either hand walked men all dressed in spotless garments.

"Here, Mary," I called, "what's this?"

She explained it was a Fanti custom to parade marriageable girls with their dowry displayed on their persons. The girl was ready to marry any

---

[1] Fou-fou, also fufu, is usually made from cassava and yams; it is sometimes combined with cocoyam [taro], plantains, or cornmeal.

A Sojourn among Practicing Christians

People get coast-wide reputations for their palm oil chops. Should a cook be lucky and hit off a successful combination, nothing on earth would drag the secret from her.

suitable suitor. According to Mary, these girls were highly trained in all the domestic arts.

There were schools where all these arts were taught. They were run by chosen young men of handsome appearance. Not only were the students guaranteed to be good cooks, but they were deeply instructed in the making of clothes and in their proper maintenance. Where the male instructor came in was in the province of bed-worthiness. They put their pupils through the whole thing. You would not get a virgin, but when you paid your money, you acquired a competent mistress of your house, one thoroughly instructed in money matters as well as in all those arts that make for a comfortable home.

"But," I said, "are there not a lot of complications such as the advent of inconvenient babies?"

"Oh, no!" said Mary vehemently. She was quite shocked at the idea of a schoolmaster so forgetting good manners as to allow his feelings to run away with him.

"It's unbelievable," I said.

I doubt if white men could so contain themselves and said so. Mary seemed to take a dim view of this idea.

I remarked there must be several hundred pounds (sterling) worth of gold on the hopeful bride-to-be. Mary cooked an appraising eye on the free-moving lissome figure.

"About six hundred pounds," she announced.

"And had they any choice in the matter of bridegrooms?" I asked.

"Of course not," she replied indignantly. "Wasn't a man a man?" she remarked.

It seemed to me this system had its points. There is quite a lot in the old saying, "The older the fiddle, the better the tune."

Mary was a mine of information on the doings of the town. She had some scathing remarks to make on the immoral doings of the white community. She told me of how her father and his friends had taken in some shipwrecked sailors once from a ship that had come to grief on the coast. They housed and fed and even clothed them, but they had got very drunk and had misbehaved themselves in a scandalous fashion not unconnected with the young ladies of the community.

Looking at Mary, I thought, *How easy it would be to misbehave.*

This reminded me of the judge who was trying a case where a man was claiming damages from another who had laid siege to his wife. The judge asked to see the lady, who came into court all muffled up. The judge asked that she be unveiled. On seeing the lady without her wrappings, the judge exclaimed, "I'd have done the same. Case dismissed."

For real, solid comfort, my sojourn among these Christian Africans could not be beaten. I gave Mary so much money out of which she provided everything, telling her to ask for more when it was finished. Well, it hardly ever was finished. It went unbelievably far in her experienced hands. And mind you, we lived well.

There was always beer and ice, whisky and soda, and a wide variety of fish, flesh, and fowl to say nothing of the fruit. As for the cooking! After years of suffering at the hands of so-called safari male cooks, Mary's cooking was heavenly.

She never tried to force her religion on me, either. Neither did her father. I shall never forget that airy little house so spotlessly clean, my immaculately laundered clothes, Mary's bright, cheerful presence, my beautifully prepared meals, and the welcome I got even when returning in the small hours from that hard-drinking gang at the Cercle.

I wonder if perchance these lines should come before her eyes will she remember the hunter whom she mothered so long ago, and whether she would recognize herself as the Mary—that was not her name, of course—of this true tale? If it should so happen and her memories of that brief period are half as sweet as mine are, I would, indeed, be happy.

E T H I O P I A
LAKE RUDOLF
Lake Stefanie
N O R T H E R N
RIFT VALLEY
C E N T R A L
S O U T H E R N
NAIROBI
Mombasa
Moyale
Marsabit
Wajir
Lodwar
Moroto
Mbale
Tororo
Kitale
Eldoret
Kisumu
Kericho
Nakuru
Nyeri
Fort Hall
Thika
Machakos
Magadi
Kajiado
Narok
Embu
Meru
Isiolo
Garissa
Kitui
Bura
Malindi
Kilifi
Voi
Taveta
Arusha
Moshi

Among Friends

CHAPTER 27

It was during my stay in Karamojo that I began to meet the native friends who contributed so much to my success. Outstanding among these was a native of Bukora, Pyjalé. He was a grand fellow. I don't think I have ever felt quite the same for any other man, white or black. I liked Bill in the Yukon and admired him. I cannot believe he let me down; I believe something must have happened to him. I have met plenty of men whom I liked, respected, and admired, but Pyjalé brought to our joint hunts courage, sagacity, tireless energy, plus the devotion one gets only from a loving woman.

It is an arresting thought that a completely nude savage who had never had any contact with a white men could have the qualities Pyjalé possessed. He had but recently taken a leading part in the massacre of a trading caravan, when three hundred guns and eight hundred people had been completely scuppered.

When I said, "You need not have speared the women."

He replied, "They stank so."

"How do you mean, they stank?" I asked.

"They were clothed," he answered.

My boys were, of course, both clothed and clothes conscious. Anyone strolling about as nature made them were simply written off as pagan or bush savages. "Bush bastards," Suliemani called them. Although my boys were at the most only one generation removed from a similar state themselves, they professed the utmost scorn for nude people, a scorn as firmly held by the so-called pagans for those people who clothed themselves.

When contrasting the magnificently oiled and burnished bodies of the natives, their elaborately decorated headdress, their polished iron neck bands, their giraffe-tail elbow ornaments, their shining spears, their perfectly fitting sandals, and their dull glowing shields with the filthy rags of cheap trade cotton worn by my following, I could not help thinking that clothing and other white ways bring nothing but grief to the African.

The undressed savage has just as good a way of living as we have. In fact, if happiness is any criterion, it is a much better way. There can be no doubt about their unbounded capacity for happiness. Only when fortune smiles on them—a successful raid on neighbours, a bountiful harvest, a meat feast without limit—are they just a little happier. We cannot show them anything to replace their innate happiness. Unless or until we can, it seems wrong to tamper.

This evidence of happiness is so general that one takes it as just a pleasant part of the scheme of things. It is only when one returns to our way of living, with its evidence of strain on all but the very young, that it is borne in on one that something is lacking, something left behind in those happy pagan lands.

One day, there burst into my camp a great celebrity. He was a huge coal-black Negro clothed in a spotless robe of white. This was Shundi.[1] A man of great dignity and commanding character, Shundi was convoyed by a numerous following of dingy, mean-looking traders like a pack of hyaenas and jackals following a lion. He had very good manners and asked if he might speak with some of my porters. In doing so I could not help overhearing the conversation.

Shundi was threatening that if they did not hand over their pay packets at the end of the safari, he would shoot them and replace them with others. They were his slaves. It was one of his slaves who had killed the monster elephant whose tusks still hold the record for weight. He killed it with a muzzle-loader on the slopes of Kilimanjaro.

Shundi told me all about it and something about himself, too. He started life as a naked pagan Kavirondo. Sold as a slave to a dealer, he soon acquired the right to freedom by embracing Islam. From that point on nothing could stop him. Soon he became slave owner and a *tagir* [rich man], the leader of a large trading caravan, and the owner of great numbers of women. I saw some of them; they were from every tribe indigenous to East Africa.

How these traders must have loathed my presence here in their happy hunting grounds. They were not hunting elephants, and they dared not hunt slaves, so they were raiding cattle with which to buy ivory from the native Karamojans. There was quite a lot of killing in these raids, and inevitably some girls would find their way into the harems.

---

[1] In *Bell of Africa*, Bell states that he met Shundi at Mani-Mani before then moving on into Bukora where he met Pyjalé. The sequencing changed somewhat here.

AMONG FRIENDS

It was during my stay in Karamojo that I began to meet the native friends who contributed so much to my success.

My elephant-hunting activities brought me into very close association with the natives. Although they were rich in cattle, sheep, and goats, they would never kill any of their numerous beasts. Meat for nothing was, therefore, a tremendous blessing in their lives. Had it not been for this, I could not have entered this land at all. The native was still complete master of his country. In my capacity of meat provider, I was suffered to do as I liked, go anywhere, and was welcomed everywhere.

One day a very great man in the Bukora world brought me a bullock as a gift. I noticed that Pyjalé paid him marked respect. Evidently he was a V.I.P. of some sort. He was an oldish man, distinguished among these tall tribesmen for his small stature, but what he lacked in height he made up for in breadth and depth of chest—a chest, too, that was smothered with the tattooings that denoted the killing of human victims, right side for men, left for women. As if to accentuate that barrel-like trunk, it was supported by two inadequate-looking knock-kneed shanks. Pyjalé told me he was the richest man in their world and the best fighter.

"What should I give him in return for his handsome present?" I asked.

"He doesn't want anything; he wants to be your blood brother," answered Pyjalé.

"All right," I said, "what do we do?"

"You kill a sheep and roast the meat. Then he makes a cut on his body, takes a piece of the meat, smears it with his blood, hands it to you and you eat it. You do likewise and he eats it."

I told Pyjalé I knew a far better way. So I shook hands with the fine old man, a very strange gesture to him, and there we were blood brothers. He immediately adopted my name, Yongellynung (Red Man), and I was supposed to adopt his, but it was so unpronounceable that I never mastered it.

The safari boys enjoyed life to the full, too. Well fed on elephant meat and fat, they attained an amazing condition. When the day's work of carrying a tusk of a hundred and twenty pounds or so for ten to fifteen miles, building a donkey *boma* (fence), pitching tents, gathering firewood for the large fire in front of my tent would be done, they would play football.

The playground would almost certainly be littered with ant-heaps, boulders, thorn-bush, and sharp grass. But that mattered not at all. We evolved a game of our own with no boundaries, no umpire, and no limit to the numbers engaged. There were just two marked goals. Everyone joined in, including myself. It need not be thought that they showed any hesitation in tackling the boss. Far from it.

Whenever I had possession of the ball, a perfect deluge of husky lads would fall upon me. They were fast and tricky, tough and enduring. What did tire was the ball itself. They would wear one away every month. Friends have told me that this distinctive style of football has been adopted as the morning exercise of the King's African Rifles and is called Karamoja.

Primitive man is an astounding athlete. I have seen Pyjalé run down and spear an eland when the black soil was wet and clinging, apparently the naked human foot affording less adhesion to the mud than the antelope hoof. Then there was the lad who covered three hundred miles non-stop in one hundred hours to bring in some donkeys. And then the fifty runners who covered the regular Olympic marathon distance, all coming in together in the white record time, not stopping but continuing to circle the Kampala show ground, whooping and yelling.

In short, I have very warm memories of those people, and I cannot help wondering if we have anything to give them. Why introduce money among people who have got along very well without it? Often I have argued on these lines with missionaries only to be told, "Wait five hundred years; then there will be a difference."

GULF
C. Guardafui
(Ras Asir)
Ras Hafun
Ras Mabber
Nogal
i.e. Stony Country
Haud i.e.
Stoneless Country
Ras el-Khyle
Obbia
(Obiat)
Ras Aswad
Shoa
Ankober
Balok
BORAN
GALLA
SOMALI
Lugh
Berdera
Geldi
(El Rode)
Warsheikh
Mukdishu (Magadoxo)
Marka (Meurka)
Barava
Kismaju
Webbi
Lorian L.
UGANDA
Victoria Nyanza
Kenia
Kilima Njaro
Teita
Mombasa
Pemba I.
ZANZIBAR
Dar-es-Salaam
Mafia I.
Kilwa Kisiwani
Lindi
Mikindani
Cape Delgado
ZANZIBAR
Seychelles Is
Br.
Mahe I.
Amirante Is
Br.
Providence I.
Aldabra Is
Cosmoledo Is
Farquhar I.
Galega Is
Glorioso Is
C. Amber
Comoro I.
French
Comoro Is
Johanna I.
Mayotta
Nossi Be
Antalaha
Andranovelona
Mozambique
Mozambique Channel
Angoche Is
Quilimane
Zambesi
Sofala
Bassas da India
Europa I.
Bazaruto I.
C.S. Sebastian
Inhambane
Delagoa Bay
Lorenzo Marques
LORENZO MARQUES
GAZA
COUNTRY
MADAGASCAR
Ambongo
Imerina
Antananarivo
Tullear
Androy
C. St. Mary
Tulangara
I. Ste Marie Fr.
Tromelin I.
Mascarenhas Is
Mauritius Br.
(Isle de France)
Port Louis
I. de la Réunion
(Bourbon)
Fr.
INDIAN
Nazareth

A Whaling Project

CHAPTER 28

I boarded the Arab dhow late in the afternoon. We were to sail that night. It was Mombasa in the good old spacious days when one could go anywhere in the world free from papers, formalities, Customs, and all the bugbears that make modern travel such a pestiferous affair. My hoped-for destination was the ancient Arab and Persian city of Lamu, some hundred-odd miles up north on the East African coast. For a few rupees the dhow skipper had agreed to land me there.

It was the season of the south-west monsoon when we left, so there was a prevailing reverse wind. Dhows only travel with the wind; they cannot beat to windward because they have no keels. But off the wind these primeval tubs are fast. With their fine bows and high sterns, they run before a strong wind and a heavy sea with impunity.

The south-west monsoon is a constant and regular wind current that follows the north-east monsoon after a few weeks pause between them. All sailing dhows depend on these winds: firstly on the north-east monsoon to bring them from the Arabian coast or Persian Gulf ports to the African coast, and secondly on the south-west monsoon to return them whence they came. Such is a dhow's speed under these conditions that they could pass steamers of ten or eleven knots with ease, while the ancient gunboat—those ships that patrolled the waters to make sure dhows did not make off with a cargo of passengers to sell as slaves in Arabia—was often left astern and helpless.

I had now leisure to observe the conduct of the ship as I lay on my camp bed on the high poop deck. Getting under weigh[1] was quite a business. I watched the performance from the high poop. Everyone of the thirty-odd crew shouted directions to everyone else. There was some fine chanting as the anchor rope made of coir [natural coconut fiber] was brought aboard.

---

[1] Bell used the term "under weigh" instead of the correct "underway." The term "under way" first came into being around 1740 specifically as a maritime term, and some seafaring individuals immediately linked it to "weigh anchor," thus erroneously creating the term "under weigh." Some of the best English authors have used this alternative form including Melville, Dickens, Lord Byron, Thackeray, Washington Irving, and others. Bell was in good company.

This particular dhow had a white-man-type anchor they had picked up from some scrap heap somewhere, and with such a strong crew they simply walked it aboard. Soon the huge yard with its sail stopped to it began to climb the mast. When all was set about, a dozen of the crew gave a mighty shout. With a giant heave on the single-part sheet, away burst the stops, the sail filled, and off we went steering for the entrance where we could see evidence of a powerful breeze blowing and a considerable sea running outside.

Soon we were into the south-west monsoon. As this wind blows steadily from the same direction for some four or five months, it sets up quite a strong ocean current. I was not surprised, therefore, to see the sailors lower the sail when we had gained a good offing. Now we ran under bare poles and yet had good steerage way. The strong wind and a three-knot current would carry us north-east for the hundred miles to Lamu, and we ought to be at our destination by sunrise. If we overshot our objective, it would be good-bye to Lamu because these craft cannot sail to windward but must always run before it, which means we would land at some other port farther north.

It was interesting to examine the sailing gear on the vessel. First there is a very short but stout mast, leaning forward at quite an angle. Then there is an enormously long yard, which at the moment is lying on the deck and with the sail attached to it. You never saw such a junk heap. It was made up of all sorts of bits and pieces, some quite short, and it made me wonder how such a thing could stand at all. The pieces were simply overlapped and lashings of coir rope held them more or less in position. The lashings were quite loose when dry. There would be a rough scarf and a short splint over the joint, then the lashings. I imagine it was the sail that prevented the whole thing from disintegrating.

The first activity that drew the eye was a constant stream of four-gallon kerosene tins passed up from the hold and dumped overboard. The crew was baling ship. It never stopped during the whole journey. I asked the Arab who had taken my fare and who I supposed was the captain, if the ship always leaked so badly.

"Yes," he responded as if it were of no importance.

Just below us on the main deck by the break of the poop, there stood four open-top kerosene tins full of water with foliage spread on the top to prevent spillage. A dipper lay handy. From time to time some of the crew came to drink

A Whaling Project

Dhows only travel with the wind, but off the wind these primeval tubs are fast.

and even to pour water over their half-naked bodies. It was hot and humid as only the south-west monsoon weather can be.

I asked the skipper how much water he carried. Pointing to the four tins, he said that was it—say fifteen gallons. Anyone could drink his fill and waste as much as he liked, there being no check on it. There was a happy-go-lucky attitude to the sea of these care-free mariners. Anyone of those cheerful mariners would lay down on deck for a snooze whenever he thought fit. There seemed to be no discipline of any sort.

The dhow I was on had wheel steering and the tiller lines were of coir rope simply wound round the shaft that carried the wheel. There was a very rickety white-man type chair by the wheel and anyone, apparently, could sit down and do a trick at the wheel. You could leave it and join any group of diners sitting round the platters of rice. In other words, it seemed the ship looked after itself.

It was touch and go landing at Lamu, but Luck, who must love these carefree mariners, enabled us just to manage it.

******

We had seen a whale or two out at sea, and I had ample time to talk about them. An old, one-eyed mariner told me that cachalot or sperm whale were quite numerous at certain times. He said that they bred round the Seychelles islands some twelve hundred miles off in the Indian Ocean. This was interesting news, indeed, and I took pains to corroborate it from other sources. It appeared that great numbers of these whales repaired at calving time to the warm and comparatively shallow waters of this group of islands to have their babies.

Now the sperm is the only whale that floats when dead. That is why it had been the object of the old type of hand-harpoon-and-small-rowing-boat-kind of whaling. If the sailors could once get a harpoon into the leviathan and then kill it with lances or shoulder guns, it floated and the parent ship would then draw up to it. The sperm was also one of the largest and most valuable of the whales then. It yielded sperm oil of great value besides spermaceti and occasionally ambergris from its interior.

All this part of the East African coast receives flotsam and jetsam from the Indian and even the Pacific Oceans, whose currents set in there. Great long, wavy, parallel lines of stuff—boxes, crates, fruit, bottles, and whatnot—may be seen creeping slowly inshore to be finally washed up on the beaches. Among this debris are found lumps of ambergris [2] varying from half an ounce to as much as twenty-eight pounds. The latter was a record for the coast then.

During the season when the stuff is coming ashore, the whole of the suitable parts of the fore-shore is divided into claims and is constantly patrolled by natives on the look-out for ambergris. Any thus found is declared "treasure-trove" under the white man's law and has to be surrendered to Customs. There it is stored and graded.

When the season is over, buyers come from all parts to the auctions that are then held. Prices used to vary from a few shillings to three or four pounds sterling per ounce depending on the quality, and those pieces considered to be the most efficacious as an aphrodisiac fetch the highest price. The offensive stinking stuff used to go to the perfume makers, strangely enough; it had the property of "fixing" a scent.

When the stuff was sold, the proceeds would be divided between government and finder, the latter getting just enough to keep him industriously looking for more.

Well, all this bore out the dhow men's statements about the sperm being in great numbers somewhere off the coast, and I formed the idea of hunting them in a small, fast motor-boat. My idea was to shoot them in the brain, and, of course, they would remain floating on the surface. I would have a two-hundred-ton dhow fitted with tanks and try-works, and with a goodly crew of dhow men following on behind ready to handle the carcass and do all the dirty work, I would be free to scour the seas for further victims for my rifle. Yes, it was to be just an ordinary small-bore rifle, the kind I used on elephant, in fact.

Besides going after sperm whales, I thought that a few small motor-boats might profitably be set to patrolling those distinct lines of jetsam. My aim was to nobble the ambergris before it reached the shore and before it reached the

---

[2] Ambergris is a solid, waxy, flammable substance of a dull gray or blackish color produced in the digestive system of sperm whales. Squid is the main diet of sperm whales, but since the beaks cannot be digested, they need to be passed out without hurting the whale. A compound known as ambrein coats the beaks, thus preventing damage to the whale. (Only sperm whales make ambrein.) Intestinal slurry from the whale is ejected into the ocean where it hardens as it floats on the surface. This slurry is ambergris, and it has been used throughout the ages as a perfume fixative that allows the scent to last longer. A rare from of ambergris is also used as an aphrodisiac in some cultures, and it is quite costly. Some refer to it as "floating gold."

three-mile limit and, thence, the coffers of the greedy government. What a howl there would have been if it had come off!

The project obviously called for some capital. I would also have to study the location of the brain in that enormous head. As far as I could tell, the sperm whale traveled much upon the surface, when making a passage at any rate, and the brain would, thus, normally be vulnerable to a bullet. From what I could gather, the speed of the animal was considerable, so a sea-going, comfortable launch would have to have a good turn of speed.

Fired with these ideas, I came home to lay before my friends and relations how easy it would be to make all our fortunes. The idea was to form a small company, build a special boat, and then automatically the dividends would roll in. To my astonishment they did not seem at all keen on the idea; in fact, they thought it a pretty crazy idea. So instead of taking shares in the venture, they were prone to laugh at it. Unable to make any headway with this stupid lot, I determined to set about it on my own.

I went to a London yacht designer. He was an oldish man rather addicted to the bottle. I explained the type of vessel I required. He had a good deal of sea experience—which is more than some of them have—and drew out a very nice-looking craft. She was to be built of galvanized steel and lined with an inch of cork cement. What between visits to the museum to study a stuffed sperm whale they had there in an underground kind of cellar, and the designer's drawing office, where we had continual noggins from a cupboard on the wall, I had an interesting time. From the studies of the former I could see nothing to prevent the brain shot from being operable, and perhaps even easy.

The designer thought I ought to have a harpoon gun, a small one. He said the Norwegians were bringing out all sorts of new ideas in whaling gear to handle the bottle-nose, the blue, and other whales that sank when killed. I did not know anything about these whales or even whether they existed where I proposed to hunt.

Anyhow, my ship would be much too small to handle anything but the sperm. The others required all sorts of tackle to play them, and they even had to be drawn up to the surface to be then inflated with air to make them float. I was persuaded to purchase what was considered to be a light gun that could be attached to the rails of two- or three-hundred-ton chasers.

The ship took shape at a Thames yard and was christened *Cachalot*. How to power it caused much concern. Lightweight diesels were not then on the market. I doubt even whether Dr. Diesel was then known at all widely. He might well have been still in swaddling clothes or shaking a rattle for all I know. So it came down to petrol engines. These were already quite highly developed and of a suitable weight and consumption rate. Petrol was then five pence per gallon, incredible as it may now seem. There were to be two, six-cylinder engines of sixty horsepower, with each running at one thousand r.p.m.

One of the requirements was a range at cruising speed of three thousand miles on her tanks alone. Much more could be carried on deck for any especially long passage. After trials were run in the North Sea and found to be completely satisfactory, I then took the ship over.

My first task was to retrieve the Norwegian whaling gear that had arrived in Antwerp. Because the harpoons had explosive heads, which screwed on to the iron harpoon itself, no ship would bring them over to England. We had to fetch them.

As crew there was myself, the ship's carpenter from the yard who had not quite completed his job aboard, and two engineers who had installed the engines. None of these men had been to sea before, but when I suggested they should accompany me to Antwerp, they were keen as mustard. Off we set then and soon found ourselves at Flushing.

Pilotage being compulsory, we had to engage a pilot for the river passage. We soon found a hearty-looking man to take us along. The first question he asked was if we had anything to eat on board. He seemed to attach great importance to this; especially was he anxious to know if we had fresh meat and vegetables on board. He showed plenty of good sense, that Dutchman, for I don't think we were very well provided in that line. Anyway, I gave him money and he soon returned on board with an enormous quantity of fresh green stuff and some enormous steaks. *What ho!* we thought; *we're to have steak and onions.*

That Dutchman took us from the wharf where we had tied up, put us into the well-buoyed channel, gave up the wheel, told us we couldn't miss the way, and retired to the galley. Here he threw off his coat and got down to cooking. Steak nothing—it was to be a stew, and in the largest cooking pot we had on board. Presently a delicious odour wafted on the wind from the galley as we steadily plugged up the perfectly straight-forward channel buoyed for deep-draughted ocean-going ships of ten thousand tons or so and drawing, maybe, thirty feet. We drew four feet, six inches.

When the stew was ready, the Dutchman, all red with cooking, laid the table in the saloon helped by one of the engineers. It was cold and we were all pretty keen set to eat when the mountainous stew arrived. All hands set to with a will. It was excellent . . . until someone suggested the meat was funny.

"Fony!" shouted the Dutchman with his mouth full, "Not fony! Good! Best beefstek!"

First the carpenter then an engineer began to fiddle with the pieces of meat on their plates.

"I think it's a horse," said one.

"I'm damn sure it is," said the other.

And no more would those choosy Englishman eat. Seeing the way things were going, the Dutchman roared with laughter, no longer denied the insinuation but applied himself with the utmost fervour to the task of finishing the stew.

When we arrived at Antwerp, the Dutchman laid us alongside a wharf and departed on his mission of finding the address I gave him. Luckily, it was close at hand, and we soon had on board a quite formidable-looking gun, a quantity of the loveliest-looking Italian hemp-rope, and the harpoons. These latter were terrific affairs, weighing one hundred pounds each. I wondered how little *Cachalot* was going to fire these. The recoil was bound to be tremendous even with quite a small charge.

The strangest thing of all, however, was that no one came near the ship. No one bothered at all about us. It may have been that they mistook our gray-painted boat for a naval craft of some sort, especially as we were flying the Blue Ensign as our club membership entitled us to, or perhaps they thought us so small as to be of no account. Anyhow, we didn't worry if they weren't. Soon as we were ready, we set off back to Flushing with our pilot during the passage sleeping off his overplus of stew.

When we arrived at Flushing, we got rid of our passenger and set course for Dover, where we were met by an aggressive launch full of Customs men. They asked where we were from.

"Antwerp."

"Why haven't you your ensign upside down or with a knot in it?" they asked as they clambered aboard.

Now the gun lay on the cabin floor as we had been unable to stow it anywhere else. Whether they did not notice it as they stood on it or whether they saw it all right and did not know what to do about it is not known, but they knew what to do with a bottle of schnapps we produced.

For gun trials we slipped along the coast to the Isle of Wight where there were miles of sand uncovered by the tide and where we would have a chance to fire our harpoons without damaging them. The designer's idea of a mounting was a six-inch steel pipe fastened to the keel and protruding to a convenient height through the deck. The head of the pipe was braced by stout wire ropes with tension screws to take up the recoil. It looked all right and I had no hesitation in firing it. How I wish I hadn't.

When I pulled the trigger, I got a severe punch that knocked me overboard. Luckily, we were anchored close in to the edge of the sand. I fell in quite shallow water and so did the gun, but on the other side of the ship. I clambered aboard and looked for the gun. The fellows who had taken cover when I got knocked overboard now showed me where it had fallen, and we soon had it aboard again. I asked what had happened to the harpoon.

It had been free; that is, it had no rope attached to it as it would have under working conditions. I expected it to have gone some distance over the sand banks as I had given the gun about a 30-degree elevation. The boys pointed in the direction it had taken. They told me that they had been able to see it sizzling like some gigantic arrow through the air. No one could see it even with glasses, so we set off over the flats to find it. It had traveled a tremendous way. When we found it, quite undamaged, I paced the distance and found it had flown eight hundred yards.

On returning to the ship we examined the mounting. To our surprise we could find nothing wrong with it. There was obviously too much whip in the affair, although it was apparently strong enough. I looked once more at the instructions for mounting that had come with the gun. It showed a simple metal socket sunk into an enormously heavy bulwark. They called it a stanchion gun and seemed to treat it as a kind of pea-shooter.

I got hold of an engineer who had been in the Armstrong Vickers works and who said he knew just what was required. The ship had to go into dock, of course. Then the deck was lifted forward and a steel sheet fitted all over the front part where the gun stood. Of course the designer's pipe was thrown the hell out with this new design. Then a light but rigid steel cone was fabricated and the flanged base bolted through the deck to the steel plate below.

Reminiscences of an Elephant Hunter

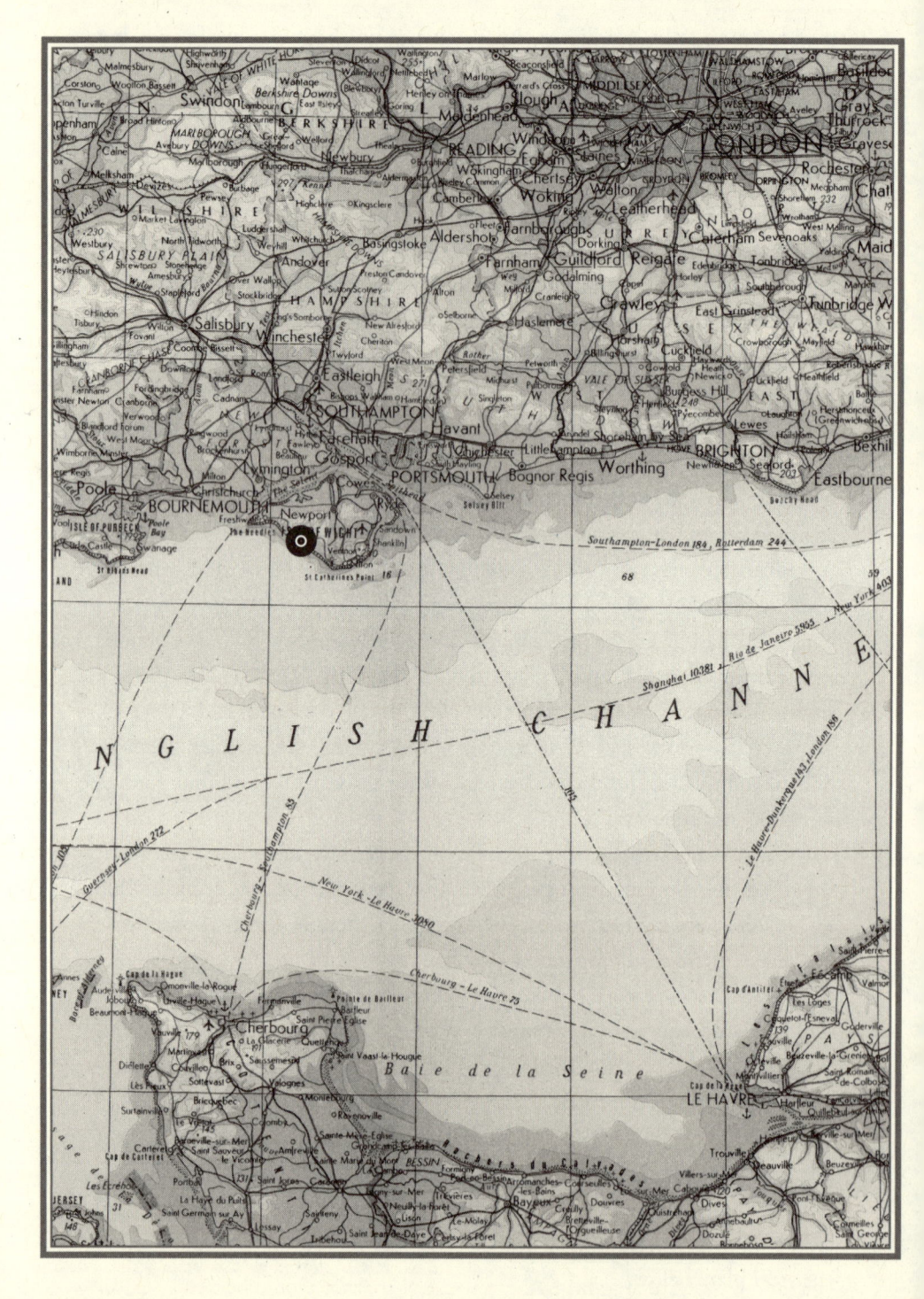

A Whaling Project

This time she held, and as it was quite cheap to fire, the charge consisting of a small bag of blasting powder fired by a revolver cartridge, we had some good artillery practice. Now to try it out at sea with the rope attached.

With a free harpoon one could make quite fair shooting with the thing—that is, if you could hit an orange box at fifty yards with fair frequency. I found it was altogether another affair to hit a similar object with a rope attached to the harpoon at even twenty yards. The boat was small and lively for one thing, and the rope had a very unsteadying effect on the flight of the missile as it tore along behind in great coils sizzling through the air. We lost two or three harpoons because of the rope getting snarled up on stanchions and whatnot. After this practice, we now felt ready to tackle some living target, so we set off to sea to look for porpoises.

We found them all right, but we could not hit them. It was much easier when we used a hand harpoon. The difficulty then was to stop the ship before we pulled the harpoon out. Although all controls led to the wheel and the helmsman could, theoretically, go instantly into reverse, it never worked quickly enough. It would have been better to have had the engine controls on the upper flying bridge and under separate control.

However, we thought we were now fit to try a shot at a "blackfish" as the small species of whale that frequents the Channel is called. These whales run up to quite a length and, anyhow, should be easier to hit than porps. Porps are mighty fleeting targets and do not clear the water for more than a second or two.

At last we fell in with what we sought. There were several "fish" evidently traveling, for they kept coming up in a series of "blows" that made a more or less straight course. The French coast was visible away on our port bow. Everyone was tremendously excited as the fish looked almost as big as the ship herself. I had a sharp knife ready in case the rope got foul of anything and had to be cut away. It seemed to me that should something like that happen, the rope was quite strong enough to capsize the boat. I also laid my loaded rifle in a handy place in case a chance of a finishing shot should present itself.

The fish seemed to be traveling along quite slowly, yet it took us a considerable time to make up on them. As soon as we had a "blow" near us, we slowed down a bit. Now it became apparent that their course was not at all in a straight line as it had appeared to be when they were still distant. In fact, they came up in the most disconcerting way on all sides and even behind us, and before we could turn to bring them ahead of us, they would be down again.

What had appeared to be a slow, leisurely roll was actually of only a few seconds duration and not nearly long enough for us to turn the ship. Of course, the gun could be fired through a considerable arc, but for the first shot anyhow, I wanted one coming up close under our forefoot and straight ahead. It seemed extraordinarily difficult to get just such a chance.

We maneuvered for hours about those wretched fish. Sometimes they stayed down and we lost them for a time, and then someone would see a blow a mile or two away, and off we would hare in pursuit. Then I took a chance at one a bit off on the starboard or right-hand bow, but missed it clean.

We had an explosive head on the harpoon, along with a safety pin and lanyard. You simply tied the end of the lanyard to any part of the gun, and, when you fired, the lanyard pulled out the pin, and this set a fuse going that exploded the charge in the head of the harpoon about a second after the discharge. On this occasion we missed the whale, so the explosion took place some distance under water, but we thought we heard it. The rope had run out nicely, so we had no difficulty in recovering the harpoon. It was quite evidently easy to miss these animals altogether, let alone hit them in the right place.

After the shot, the fish took fright and we lost them for a long time. Toward evening, however, we saw either the same lot or a perfectly new group. In any case, they seemed considerably more leisurely than at first, and we were helped by the wind dropping to a light breeze, although there was still a considerable swell. It would not do to have another miss, and I determined to wait for a sitter.

Helped by the light and the unruffled sea, I saw him coming up from beneath our forefoot. He broke surface perhaps fifteen yards straight ahead of us, and when I saw his full length displayed, I fired. Apparently, the sights on the gun were calculated to counteract a great drop of the heavy harpoon at just such a distance because I could see the harpoon bury itself about the middle of its body.

Full astern both, I signaled. We were not going more than five or six knots, but even so the line led right back under the ship, and I was terrified it would get foul of the propellers. However, all was well as the fish had gone deep on getting the iron. The ship stopped her forward way, and now the line, still running out, began to point forward. As we gathered stern way [backward movement], we soon had the line straightened and now we began to check it on the bollards.

A Whaling Project

We had an explosive head on the harpoon, along with a safety pin and lanyard. You simply tied the end of the lanyard to any part of the gun, and, when you fired, the lanyard pulled out the pin, and this set a fuse going that exploded the charge in the head of the harpoon about a second after the discharge.

We had no idea how much we dared check it, but, gathering confidence as we went along, we soon had a fair strain on it. It now became apparent we had not much line left and would have to check it hard to avoid it all going out. On feeling the line, we thought it seemed to have a mighty strain on it, and looking over the side, it was apparent we were going ahead although both engines were still going astern.

Must be a mighty big one, we thought. He had not looked very big when I fired at him.

"Stop," I signaled to the man at the wheel.

Now we tried to get in some of the rope. There was still a dead weight on it.

"Come ahead slow," I signaled.

Now we could get in some line. We were all much too excited to coil it down properly, and had the fish not been at its last gasp, we might have lost the line, the fish, the harpoon, and all, as the rope almost certainly would have fouled something.

Suddenly the rope we were hauling in went slack. At first we thought, *Damn! The harpoon has come away.* Then it struck me the fish might be coming up.

"Haul away," I told the fellows while I grabbed my rifle.

I then signaled to the helmsman to see how the rope led and to come ahead slowly. In came the rope and lay in a perfect tangle all over the place. *Hope it doesn't rush out again,* I thought, *or someone will get snarled up in it.*

Still the rope came in leading well ahead. At last the dead or dying fish broke surface some way off and still the rope led down, showing there must be a huge bight in it. As soon as the body of the fish showed, I poured in a few shots from the rifle toward what I thought might be the brain. The thing gave one last convulsive sigh and began to sink again. It was evidently at its last gasp.

Now we had a strain on the rope again, quite a heavy one at that, but steady. Almost certainly the fish was dead, but it was sinking. We took the rope to the anchor windlass and hove away. Still the same steady strain. With the engines stopped, the boat now followed the rope until it led straight up and down. Presently we could see the fish, and it was dead all right. We soon had it up and alongside.

By placing a bowline over its tail and by going ahead on the engines, we had it in a position to examine our prize and to recover our harpoon. This latter had buried itself almost centrally in the body about a third of its length from the head; it must have exploded right in among its vitals. The fish was only about half our length, but it was some contract getting that harpoon out. We had none of the proper implements for doing so and relied on an ax and knives. We laid course for home and went below for a drink and something to eat. We had been hours at it and were all hungry as hell with excitement and the sea air.

Now we began to wonder what to do with the thing we had got. We were a long way from a sheltered beach where we could handle our prize; anyway, we did not know quite what to do with it even should we get it there. This is the point where the whalers hand the corpse over to the trying-out gang, who cut it up and boil it down. We, of course, had nothing of that sort.

It now dawned on us that it was one thing to kill a fish but quite another to boil it down to oil. We were making poor progress with our tow, and, finally, we cast it adrift.

It seemed to me my original idea of shooting the sperm whale in the brain was the simplest method. I felt it to be the only one possible without the elaborate and expensive lay-out necessary to deal with the whales when killed. All this harpoon business was all very well for a fully equipped company but not for a one-man show. I still backed the rifle.

Just about then I received a prospectus from my relations that showed a whaling company about to start a shore station on my own precious islands, the Seychelles. There were to be five catches of the latest type, and the shore station, it was estimated, would cost ten thousand pounds sterling. Of course, it was a Norwegian company.

It was over-subscribed as it started, paid 340 percent the first year, 400 percent the second, 300 percent, 200 percent, and so on until the ground was exhausted.

I sold my boat and returned to Africa.

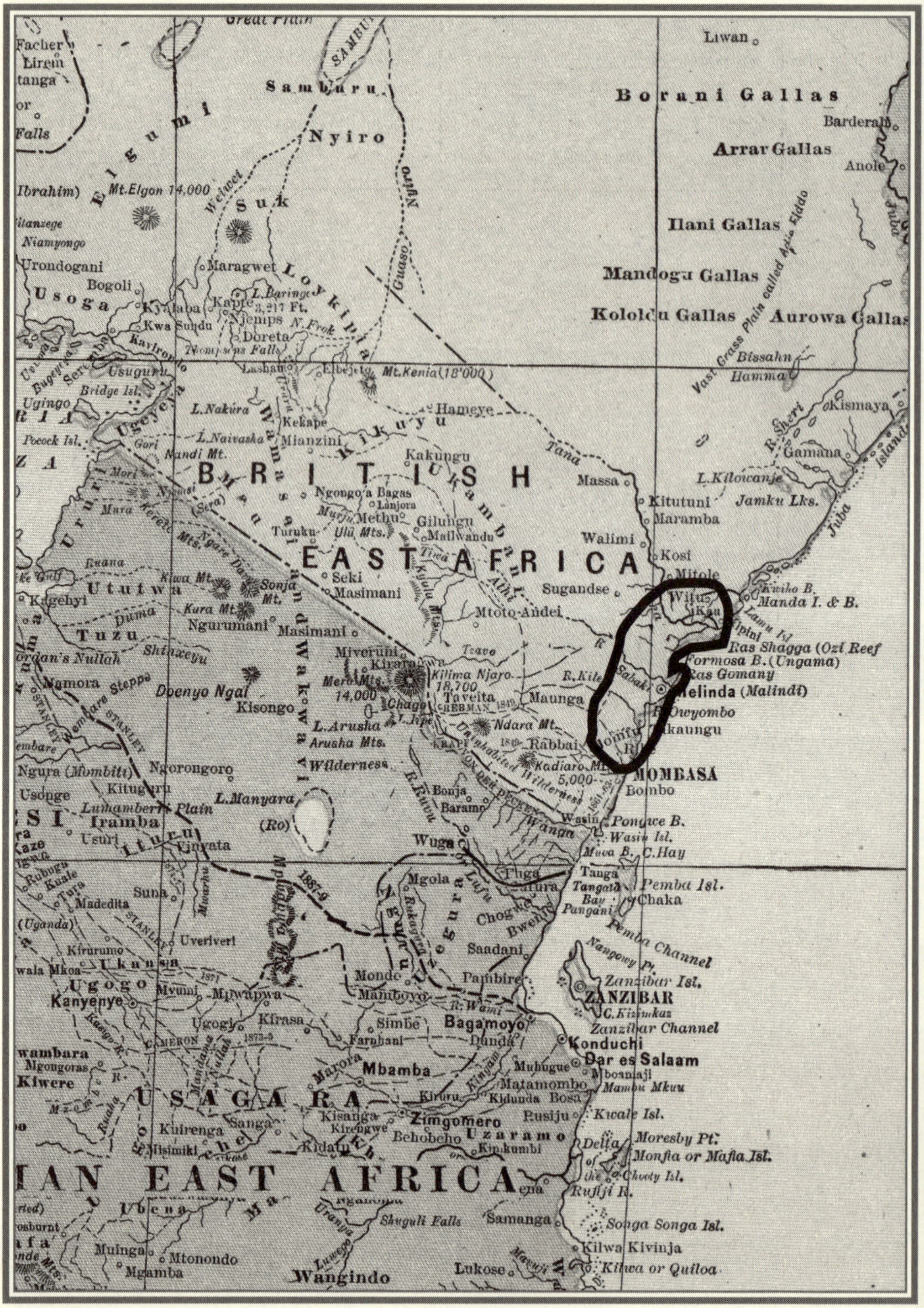
BRITISH EAST AFRICA
IAN EAST AFRICA
Borani Gallas
Arrar Gallas
Ilani Gallas
Mandogu Gallas
Kololdu Gallas
Aurowa Gallas
Vast Grass Plain called Adio Eldo
Liwan
Barderah
Anole
Juba
Samburu
Nyiro
Suk
Elgumi
Mt.Elgon 14,000
Loykipia
Mt.Kenia (18'000)
Kikuyu
Kisumu
Tana
Usoga
Usuguru
Bridge Isl.
Ugingo
Pocock Isl.
L.Nakura
L.Naivasha
Mandi Mt.
Nyiro
Guaso
Maragwet
L.Baringo
N.Frok
Njemps
Doreta
Lashau
Elbejet
Hameye
Kekape
Mianzini
Kakungu
Massa
Kitutuni
Maramba
Walimi
Kosi
Mitole
Witu
Kau
Lamu Isl.
Kiwiho B.
Manda I. & B.
Ras Shagga (Ozi Reef
Formosa B. (Ungama)
Ras Gomany
Melinda (Malindi)
Owyombo
Kaungu
MOMBASA
Bombo
Sabaki
Ngongo a Bagas
Lanjora
Methu
Ulu Mts.
Gilungu
Mallwandu
Turuku
Seki
Masimani
Sugandse
Mtoto-Andei
Athi
Tsavo
Kilima Njaro 18,700
Meru Mts. 14,000
Taveita
Chaga
Maunga
Ndara Mt.
Rabbai
Kadiaro Mt. 5,000
Uninhabited Wilderness
Ukambani
L.Kilowanje
Jamku Lks.
Kismaya
Gamana
Bissahn
Hamma
R.Shari
Ututwa
Kagehyi
Kiwa Mt.
Sonjo Mt.
Kura Mt.
Ngurumani
Masimani
Tuzu
Shinzeyu
Duma
Jordan's Nullah
Namora
Wembare Steppe
Doenyo Ngai
Kisongo
L.Arusha
Arusha Mts.
Wilderness
Ngura (Mombiti)
Ngorongoro
Usonge
Kitugaru
Luhamberri Plain
L.Manyara
Iramba
Usuri
Iturua
Vinyata
Bonja
Baramo
Wasin
Pongwe B.
Wasin Isl.
Muoa B.
C.Hay
Wanga
Umba
Wuga
Mgola
Tanga
Tangata Bay
Pangani
Chaka
Pemba Isl.
Pemba Channel
Nangowy Pt.
Zanzibar Isl.
ZANZIBAR
C.Kizimkazi
Zanzibar Channel
Suna
Madedita
Uveriveri
Kirurumo
Ukansa
Ugogo
Kanyenye
Mvumi
Mpwapwa
Ugogi
Kirasa
Mondo
Mamboyo
Pambire
Saadani
Chogwe
Bwene
Simbe
Bagamoyo
Dunda
Konduchi
Dar es Salaam
Mboamaji
Mambu Mkuu
Kwale Isl.
Farahani
Mbamba
Marora
Muhugue
Matamombo
Kidunda Bosa
Rusiju
Kiruru
Zimgomero
Kisanga
Kirengwe
Behobeho
Uzaramo
Kimkumbi
Kidatu
USAGARA
Kwimba
Mgongoras
Kiwere
Kuirenga
Sanga
Misimiki
Ubena
Delta of the Rufiji R.
Moresby Pt.
Monfia or Mafia Isl.
Choody Isl.
Songa Songa Isl.
Kilwa Kivinja
Kilwa or Quiloa
Samanga
Shuguli Falls
Lukose
Wangindo
Muinga
Mtonondo
Mgamba
Ulanga
Luwego
Mpwapwa Mts.
1887-9
1871
1873-5
CAMERON
STANLEY
Rubuga
Kuale
Tura
Falls
Ibrahim
Urondogani
Bogoli
Kwa Sundu
Kavirondo
Ugeyeya
Uganda

Hunting With
The Waboni

Chapter 29

It was during a traverse by mule, camel, and pony in Emperor Menelik's Abyssinia that my partner and I met with a white man from the Woods and Forests Department of the Ceylon Administration. Whereas we were restricted to a strip one hundred meters wide on either side of the road, he had a permit that allowed him free access to any part of the bush. We wondered about this and asked him.[1]

It appeared that he had been engaged by Menelik to discover and report on any sources of rubber he might be able to find in the extensive forests of the high plateau that comprises the Abyssinian-inhabited part of that country. That night after dinner and by a huge campfire a tale unfolded that made us prick our ears. It was a year or two before the great rubber boom, and here away out in the wilds of Africa we were being given gratis a tip that if followed could not have resulted in anything but our becoming rich men.

This all came as news to us. H. told us he had sold his shirt and had put every penny he possessed in rubber shares. He gave us the names of plantations that he knew personally and made us write them down. He said their shares could be acquired at a moderate price as the trees were not yet in full production.

We wrote everything down all right, but instead of doing what he told us to, we, poor saps, thought we knew better. Why not buy land down on the East African coast, where it was cheap, and plant rubber ourselves? In pursuit of this idea, we bought land at a ridiculously low figure at what we considered a suitable place. We knew nothing of rubber at all . . . and we planted the wrong kind of trees. But it was all very interesting and certainly we had our fun.

This is where the Waboni[2] came into the picture. The plantation was situated in that belt of dense forest that runs parallel to the seaboard and extends right down to the sands of the shore except where mangrove swamp

---

[1] Elements of this story appear in chapter 9 of *Incidents from an Elephant Hunter's Diary* and in chapter 11 of this book.

[2] The Waboni people [also known as the Aweer] are an ethnic group inhabiting the coastal area of southeast Kenya.

intervenes. This forest belt was, and still is, much frequented by big game. Elephants, buffaloes, and the bush-loving antelope were common.

The Waboni found that here they could enjoy the freedom that they considered made life worth living, and, at the same time make use of a ready market where they could exchange any surplus from their hunting activities for palm toddy. This was practically the only commodity they envied their cultivating neighbours. They themselves had no use for planting things, nor did they care for permanent houses, fine clothes, or money—except in so far as money would procure them toddy.

Even ownership of stock such as cattle, sheep, or goats, they considered only led to trouble. Other people stole them or took them by force. Property of any kind was unanimously held to be a mistake. If robbers did not get it, then the Government would in the shape of taxes. So, there you had side by side two opposing systems of living: On the one hand you had the Muslim, Arabized plantation-owning Swahili, and on the other was the freedom-loving but property-less Waboni.

Which were the happier people? Was it the Muslim with his eternal woman palaver and religious rites or the carefree, far-ranging pagan Boni? It would be hard to say. Certainly the latter had his hard times. His hunting and snaring did not always prosper, and when that was the case, he had no store of food to fall back on, as did the Swahili plantation owner. On the other hand, bountiful nature provided the former with a store of things that cost nothing but knowledge on how to find and use them.

Then, too, the Waboni had not the money-lender—that bugbear of mankind—to contend with, for the very good reason that no one would advance him anything. And, of course, the tax-gatherer—perhaps the greatest of life's worries—could not soak him on anything, for there was nothing to tax. It seems to me, in fact, that the Waboni comes nearer to being a really free man than has anyone else.

Take for instance his hunting equipment. It costs but a few hours of patient but loving toil to fashion a bow. His ammunition—arrows—is far better fitted to do its job than anything he could acquire for money, and it is to be had for but little toil. The poison with which he furnishes his big-game arrows comes from the forest. As he wanders a free man through the limitless bush he, like the fisherman, has that priceless thing—hope. I consider his lot an enviable one, but only so long as he resists the insidious poison of possession of property.

There is one possession he cannot help having, female children. Should he father two or three girl children, inevitably they will come under the ever-roving eye of some plantation-cum-harem owner. There will be negotiations, bribes, flattery, and promises. A father may succumb to these. The price is high, for although they are pagan, they are quite a good-looking people and very virtuous. Extremely so, one might say. One might go further to say incredibly so, when one considers what goes on in their camps, which you cannot call villages.

I had been hunting far into the interior with a family group, and, as we shifted camp every two or three days, I had my camp-bed right in among the people. There were a number of girls of all ages. One in particular was a very prepossessing creature. To me, she looked rather mature to be unwed, so I questioned one of the men about her.

"Why was such a fine-looking girl not married?" I asked.

"She is," he replied, "but she is still a virgin."

I pricked up my ears at this and asked how that could be.

"The husband hasn't paid up in full," was the answer.

"Do they sleep together?" I asked.

"Of course they do," he laughed.

"And she is still a virgin?" I asked.

"Yes," he said, "if her husband took her before he had completed the purchase, he would not only lose the girl but all he had previously paid."

Some continence, I thought. As I still could hardly believe it, I determined to ask her father about it.

I found papa very proud of his daughter, inclined to boast about her.

"Do you really mean that they sleep together and she still remains a virgin?" I asked him.

For answer, he called his daughter. Obediently, she came while swinging an empty water gourd with that lovely poise given only by the balancing of loads on the head. She stopped in front of us while her father said something to her in their own language. She laid aside the gourd and was about to lie down when I realized with horror what it was all about.

"No! No!" I laughed. "I believe you. Splendid," I said, "she's a fine girl."

It must have been true! At any rate they were quite willing to put the matter to examination.

Abu Dali
Abu Harraz
Dar-Tagalla
Hedebab
ABYSSINIA
AFAR
DANAKIL
Debra Tabor
Amhara
Mota
Shoa
Ankober
Antoto
Kobbo
Helle kaka
Shonga
Tana
Bahr-el-Arab
Shilluk
Nuer
Sobat
Nasser
Goba
Baro
Dembo
Jur
Meshra-er-Rek
Bongo
Abu-Kuka
Khor Kohs
Kaffa
Bonga
Ushulle
Golda
Omo
Doko
Arusi
Lado
Bari
Rimo
Dufile
Tarrangolle
Karamojo
Stefanie L.
Samburu
Borani
Libana
Ndoruma
Kibali
Tangasi
Bomokandi
Wadelai
Sanga
Momfu
Nepoko
Aruwimi
Albert Nyanza
Unyoro
Coja L.
Elgon
Kahunga
Stanley Falls Stat.n
Ruwenzori
Uganda
Mengo
Nyiro Mt.
Lorian L.
Lykipia
Kaple
Bugoma
Albert Edward Nyanza
Kenia
Oda-Boru-Ruwa
Naiwasha L.
Kikuyu
Machako
Kism
Massa
Wanga
Witu
Lamu
Kipini
Malindi
3900
Victoria Nyanza
Bukoba
Kivu L.
Ruanda
Ukerewe L.
Natron L.
Utim
Kilima Njaro
19226
Teita
Mombasa
Ugombe
Masali
Unyamwezi
Ujiji
Kawele
Urambo
Tabora
Igonda
Ugalla
Uganda
Kakoma
Uyanzi
Kondoa
Usambara
Pemba I.
Pangani
Zanzibar
Saadani
Bagamoyo
Dar-es-Salaam
Mpwapwa
Ugogo
Usagara
Kawende
Ukonongo
Karema
Mpala
Makijombo
Mandala
Lukuga
Rungwa
L. Leopold
Urori
Uhehe
Mahenge
Ubena
Mafia I.
Kassali L.
Viano Mts.
Mweru
Kasongo
Kibanga
Riba-Riba
Urua

Slaving and Raiding in Karamojo

CHAPTER 30

The following are letters that Bell wrote or received about slaving operations, raiding, and the conditions he found in Karamoja, Uganda, during his five years there.

Extract from correspondence of the Chief Secretary, Uganda Protectorate, Entebbe (dated 5 March 1940) to Walter Bell:

". . . Your existence and activities in Uganda, particularly in Karamojo, are, of course, well known to all of us who have come after you and we are sending to you a copy of a letter which you wrote to Ormsby in 1906 from Omani-Mani, which describes in detail the difficulties which you were encountering at the time with Swahili raiding parties, and which provides a most interesting vignette of conditions in Karamojo during those far-off days. We have the original manuscript letter preserved here in our library together with a copy of your book, *The Wanderings of an Elephant Hunter,* which is still in wide demand and which still remains a text-book for those who aspire to follow in your footsteps.

". . . you have, of course, our permission to quote. . . ."

Here Bell inserts a short explanation:

The country of Karamojo is that part of the map lying to the north of Mount Elgon (fourteen thousand feet). At the time of which I write, it had no white administration at all. The tribes were entirely free to do as they liked. They paid tribute to no one. They fought their neighbours on all sides and they fought among themselves. Every village was heavily stockaded by man-proof fences, and all stock was brought within the stockades by nightfall. A further disadvantage was there were no powerful chiefs with any sort of authority; every village was on its own.

The people were rich in cattle, goats, sheep, and donkeys. Besides milk and blood, they cultivated and grew millet—red and white—sim-sim, and a little tobacco. To render the latter transportable, it was made into bricks by pressure and, they said, a light binding of cow dung.

The country was really a high ridge running parallel with the lower valley of the Nile on its western side and flanked on the east by the thorny wastes surrounding Lake Rudolph.

The low-lying and in some places swampy Nile country contained enormous herds of elephants. In the wet season many of the aged bulls wandered from these herds up to the high, drier country of Karamojo, there to enjoy fresh tree-browsing without the pestiferous hordes of cow elephants that made life so difficult nearer the Nile. For years there was a considerable pick-up of ivory from natural causes alone, and the ivory was of the finest quality, and the supply was augmented by the native custom of snaring elephants.

Now to snare a wild bull elephant is quite a contract, as one can imagine. As far as I know, these people are the only ones to have mastered the art. It must have taken possibly centuries of trial and error to arrive at a successful solution of the problem. I have described the whole affair in The Wanderings of an Elephant Hunter.

Added to the natural pick-up of ivory in the bush where tusks had lain for years and years as the natives could find no use for them, there were tusks from the snared elephants as well. The natives regarded the tusks to be of even less value than the bones of the skeleton from which at least a certain amount of fat could be obtained.

The time came when traders penetrated the area. At first they were received in the usual fashion, with spears. Then when it became known that elephant bones, as they regarded tusks, were wanted and would be paid for in iron wire, brass, copper wire, and in beads, everyone rushed off into the bush to find the long neglected but now valuable tusks.

After some years, the supply began to dwindle. Prices soared. Finally, the natives decided that trade goods were no longer acceptable. Henceforth, ivory would be forthcoming only for cows.

Where were the traders to turn for cows? No one sold cows voluntarily. The traders had guns hadn't they? Why not combine forces and raid cattle? As many as six hundred guns could be gathered together, and these combined with one thousand, five hundred or two thousand spearmen as auxiliaries made a practical certainty of success. Raid after raid was carried out, and the price of a tusk rose to ten or twelve cows.

******

Bell sent this next letter to Ormsby, the government representative at Mbali, the then farthest outpost. It lay on the southern slopes of Mount Elgon. In the letter, Bell tells Ormsby of the raids taking place in his area.

SLAVING AND RAIDING IN KARAMOJO

Mudingo (one day's march beyond Mani-Mani)
February 28th, 1906

Dear Ormsby,

Herewith some interesting news. When I arrived at Mani-Mani on the 15th of this month, I got information that the Swahilis had—during my absence—raided Dabossa and had lifted some one thousand, one hundred head of cattle. Not content with that, they had again gone to Dabossa but have not yet returned. Here at Mani-Mani I found nobody but Shunde and Abdulla Karone and a few lesser spirits. On the second day I called them to my tent and asked them what they thought I should do about this raid. They made no attempt at hiding the fact. They said the *shauri* (affair) was on me. I then told them if they would return all the cattle to the Dabossa, I would not say anything about this raid.

At first they seemed greatly relieved, and when I asked them how the cattle had been divided, they told me that Minya Kombo had passed through with one hundred head on his way to the Turkwel River. I hear he has since bought some ivory there, almost certainly with Dabossa cattle. Also that Bwana Madaba had taken one hundred and thirty, of which they showed me one hundred and three here at Mani-Mani that had been put to graze with the Karamojo. Also that one hundred and thirty head had come with three Karamojo boys of Bwana Simba and that these were at Maroto, which is one day from Mani-Mani.

As regarded the other *tajir*s (rich men) concerned in the raid, it was proposed to call them to Mani-Mani, there to have a big *shauri*. I then told Shunde to write a letter to them, telling them to come to Mani-Mani. I gave them ten days to give me an answer. On the 17th, Shunde sent the letters off. Yesterday, the 27th, Goshe turned up. To-day, there being no news of the others, I have decided to send you all the information I can, in the hope you will do all you can. The Dabossa have always been a decent lot, and it is pretty rough on them to lose their cattle—on which they almost entirely depend for food—to these swine.

As far as I can gather, the raid started thus: When I told Bwana Madaba that if anyone raided Dodosi, I would see that justice was done. Bwana Madaba, Simba, Ponda, Kombe, Faman, and Abude then wrote a letter or letters inviting Goshe to send his guns as they were going to raid Dabossa.

After all, I had said nothing about the Dabossa; I had only warned them about the Dodosi. The above-mentioned sent between them about one hundred and fifty-six guns. The accounts vary slightly.

With the guns were some Dabossa boys, two of whom cleared out when near Dabossa. They went like Hades into their own country and told the Dabossa that the Swahilis were coming to *piga* (raid) them.

At night the natives tried an attack on the Swahili camp but, unfortunately, only succeeded in spearing four men, one of whom died. Next day the Swahilis tried to make peace, probably with the idea of repeating their old trick of firing suddenly on a large crowd of natives in camp. However, the Dabossa were not having any of it. Then the Swahilis fired and the miserable natives, although numbering thousands, cleared out to a man, such is the terror inspired by a gun among these people.

Some one thousand, one hundred head of horned cattle were taken, four thousand sheep and goats, besides some donkeys. The cattle were brought down to headquarters at Morongole where they were divided. When Shunde, Abdulla Karone, and Minya Simba saw the cattle, they resolved to be also in it. A second raid was planned on a decidedly larger scale than the first. Their two big *dawa*s (medicine men or priests), Malimu Nasibu and Malimu Mkunda—the latter quite an old man—have gone on the still-absent raiding party. . . .

The list of names I have attached are the big people; they have innumerable lesser lights who take goods from them. I am now on my way to Dodosi and confidently leave this business in your hands.

This raiding is not a thing of to-day only, as you will see from the list I have provided of twelve such raids.

It is with great diffidence I mention anything with regard to any policy pursued by Grant (provincial Commissioner Jinja Province), but I think his fining the Swahilis a trifling sum for raiding the Turkana has done more harm than good as they now think it is only a matter of money.

I need hardly point out that almost every day cattle are being lost to the Dabossa as the Swahilis are buying up ivory at any price, ten head of cows for a tusk, besides what they eat. I have been told by one who was on the raid that a great many women and children were speared by the Karamojo who went with the raiders. If you come, you won't see a single head of cattle at Mani-Mani settlement itself. The numbers of cattle given above as taken by each *tajir* I don't for a moment believe. . . .

I am telling the Swahilis I am sending this letter, so if you happen to notice an unusual exodus, you will know the cause. Their only trails are the old one to Mumias and the new one to Mbale.

Please let me know what you are going to do.

Yours very sincerely,
W. D. M. Bell

******

After this rather long and rambling letter—about the only one I wrote in those days—I will relate what happened to the second raid that was still out while I was writing the note to Ormsby.

About three months before, I had gone down to Mbale with a lot of ivory. The traders had thought to themselves that no one with so much ivory will return. He will retire and go to his own country to settle down. Now we can get really busy and raid Dabossa properly.

Actually, I had no wish to leave the country at all, and after the boys had their fling and a month's beer drinking and had spent all their money, we had replenished our stores at Mbale, sold the ivory, and returned once more to the *barra* (wilderness) to continue the hunt. Of course, we soon heard from native sources that the raiders were once more on the war path. Hence the above letter to Ormsby.

In reply to my letter, O. told me the Government could not see its way to further commitments and that I should do what I could to stop the raiding. He also said that it should be clearly understood the authorities would not be responsible for what might happen. He sent me a letter, however written in Kiswahili, the proper grammatical sort, which I remember we had some difficulty in reading being more familiar with bush Swahili. In this letter he told the traders that they were to obey any orders I might give anent the subject of raiding.

There were hard, strong men about in those days, and memories of what had happened in the recent mutiny of native troops were still fresh in people's minds. So when I read out this letter to the traders, they were somewhat impressed, I think, although I had no force at my disposal with which to compel obedience. I always go on the assumption that the other fellow is rather more scared than you, yourself, are. I determined to catch the returning raiders red-handed and with their booty, all the while pretending to be on the trail of elephants just as usual.

At a certain place the Dabossa trail scaled an almost precipitous rift that ran for many miles across the country. There were several places where the walls of this rift could have been scaled by lightly loaded men and active native cattle. Judging that the raiders' intelligence would be at least as good as mine, and probably infinitely better, I felt certain they would have been informed by their countless spies of my movements and, maybe, of my intentions. Therefore, in the disposition of my interceptors, I posted four boys on the main trail, thinking the raiders would never be so foolish as to use it, while I occupied the other possible routes up the escarpment with sundry small parties of watchers.

The orders to all these boys were on no account to start firing on these raiders, for, as I have said, we had no force with which to command anything. My safari armament consisted of some twenty Snider .577 caliber, single-shot breech-loaders, a very ancient type of army rifle and the first breech-loader, in fact, to supersede the muzzle-loaders. Unfortunately, only Martini-Henry ammunition was available, and as this stuff was a .450-calibre-bullet-cum-.577-case and although it fired, Heaven alone knew where the bullet would go.

Behind this futile little force, however, were my own personal rifles, a .275 Mauser and a .303 British ten-shot rifle. Should it come to a show-down, I had little doubt of the result even against four or five hundred guns. For above all, I had the invisible but all-pervading influence of the sundry strong men, alluded to earlier in this narrative, behind me. I just felt the raiders would not resist by force. I went on with my hunting, my base camp in daily runner communication with my outposts.

Confident as I was, it was a bit of a shock and anticlimax to find a runner arrive in camp to say that the headman, whom I had left on the main trail with three boys, had corralled the whole raid—lock, stock, and barrel. Cattle, sheep, goats, and humans were all being held.

Damnation, I thought, *they'll never be able to hold them.*

With this thought in mind, we rushed along through the bush to the main trail. Luckily, I had the sense to leave two boys to watch the trail I had expected the raiders to take, where they duly intercepted some bright lads sneaking past with some modern rifles long since stolen in far-away Nairobi from some visiting sportsman. Though savage beyond measure in dealing out death and destruction to the fire-armless natives, they simply took it lying

SLAVING AND RAIDING IN KARAMOJO

The people were rich in cattle, goats, sheep, and donkeys.

down when confronted by even porters representing in any way, however remote, the Government.

What a scene unfolded itself when we arrived at the main trail camp! Here were my lads on a perch of rock overlooking the plains below them. All around the vast arena were camped the raiders; hundreds of fires were burning; and thousands of cattle browsed peacefully among the dust clouds made by the herds of goats and sheep. Luckily, there was a strong spring of water at this place.

I learnt that my headman was down among the raiders at their camp. We descended the escarpment where, indeed, the only water sufficient for such a mob lay, and we made camp right in among the throng. Here we found our headman standing over a pile of fire-arms of every description while shouting orders in true sergeant-major style.

Meanwhile a group of big-shots sat under a shady tree muffled to the eyes in their robes, seemingly accepting of the sudden reverse in their affairs with that fatalistic dignity all true followers of Allah appear to acquire. They could so easily have said "To Hell with you, Bwana Bell," and gone their way. We could not have stopped them. They must have known that, yet they attempted nothing. I read them the Riot Act, and they merely said, "Inshallah."

All right, it was now time to find out what was what. I asked, "How many women have you?

They produced a dozen or so. It was a safe bet they were concealing some, so I blustered a bit. Finally, we collected eighteen, but many were no doubt missed. The women were all clothed in something or other—muffled up their heads and bodies—so it was hard to tell if they were captives unless they themselves wished us to know it. White men are so sap-headed in these matters. So those who wished to remain with the raiders—and there were some already captivated by the wearing of clothes—remained with them.

It was extremely hard to get a really true account of what had happened on the actual raid. One could but collect as many accounts from as many different people as possible. Some talked freely enough while others were pretty tight-lipped. Most of the Karamojo auxiliaries had slipped away to their villages.

I asked Pyjalé to find out how many would be going through the tattooing for killing a male or a female. He told me at the next big dance there would be a chance to count the new blood-red ostrich feathers that are worn on these occasions and, of course, any new tattooing would be conspicuous as they take great pains to keep the cuts open with dirt so as to acquire a large cicatrice at each cut. The big shots would not talk at all.

Some of the accounts from my own men were terrific. They had friends and acquaintances among the humbler of the raiders, and these men said they had taken the Dabossa people quite by surprise as they had not been expecting another raid so soon on top of the other one. It was infuriating to think that if I had not left the country this raid might never have taken place.

According to most accounts, the raiders attacked at dawn. All over these parts the villages are heavily stockaded. Much labour is spent in digging in the hardwood tree trunks so close together that nothing can get through them and so high that climbing them is difficult. The wood on these stockades is extremely hard and will turn or stop any of the older type of lead bullet. The best chance, therefore, of securing the cattle is at dawn, for then they are ejected from their cramped quarters in the middle of the village and are milked outside.

And cramped it is. It can be imagined that by the time the necessary number of huts and pens is provided for humans, corn, goats, sheep, calves, and space for perhaps five or six hundred head of cattle, things are a pretty tight squeeze. Not an inch is wasted.

From all accounts two villages were surprised and overwhelmed simultaneously. The cattle were first driven off and then the inmates were dealt with, most of whom had hurriedly shut and barricaded themselves in their stockades. Since this was a strong raiding party, they evidently thought they could remain on the battle ground and defy any concentration of spearmen. It was easy to set fire to the huts by throwing in burning brands over the top of the stockade.

As the natives had no bows and arrows and could not throw their stabbing spears, the villages were soon ablaze. Their position close up against the stockade and their proximity to each other all helped the attackers. As soon as the village was well alight and the fire beyond any possible hope of being extinguished, out the miserable wretches had to come. They were immediately shot or speared by the waiting raiders.

The auxiliaries as always are the most blood-thirsty in these affairs. The more they kill, the fewer left to breed enemies seems to be their philosophy. To this urge is added that frightful incentive for privileges. It's necessary to murder to get the longed-for tattooings and to wear the much-coveted blood-red ostrich feathers at dances. Combine these with the privileges the wearers are accorded by the young unmarried girls—privileges that cannot be withheld or denied—all amounted to a very real and potent check on over-population.

Frequently one would see a dozen young bloods flogging a protesting girl with switches, lacing her squirming young naked body without mercy. One would be told, after breaking up the little party, that she had notions, being swelled-head for example, or perhaps she had shown too marked preference for some particular beau, and, in fact, had sought an exclusive arrangement.

The Dodosi refused to give up the cattle entrusted to them.

Had it been left to the ever women-hungry Swahilis, I don't think any young women would have been killed except those who were already pregnant. Once these native women came under the spell of clothes, and that of an easier way of life, they would never of their own free will return to the slavery of the toilsome life in their own villages, a life that made hags of them quite early in life. There were exceptions, of course.

These were rare but undoubtedly proved that a few of them, at any rate, were capable of that passion we call love between the sexes. Such a case was that of a certain girl who fled to our camp. Hard on her heels came a Swahili *tajir* (rich man). He said the girl—a native of Karamojo—was his wife. Asked how this "marriage" came about, it transpired he had "acquired" her. The girl said she had been taken on a certain raid but not by this particular *tajir*. He had merely bought her from her capturer; therefore, it was not a marriage at all.

I pointed out to the *tajir* that his case stank strongly of slave-dealing, and he knew what that meant. I told him he was lucky to get off with only the loss of the girl, and had him forthwith ejected from camp with warnings that any further attempt to regain his "wife" would have ominous consequences. Well, that girl returned to her native lover, and I only hope she never regretted it. I have my doubts. It would be a superhuman passion that could withstand the grinding toil and the yearly baby that is the native African married woman's lot.

By this time we had made a huge pile of all the firearms on a ground sheet, and I started to make a list of them. Some of the modern double-barrel rifles bearing the names of famous London makers could have told an interesting story had they been capable of speech, other than that of death-dealing. Some undoubtedly escaped us, sneaked off through the bush. The two boys I had left at the exit where I thought the raiders would use arrived with three such sneakers-past.[1]

What an assembly of stolen guns there were! Their origins ranged from Egypt and Ethiopia to the Belgian Congo and the Rhodesias. They were largely junk and badly neglected, of course.

After listing the arms and such ammunition as could be gathered in, I had, of course, to hand everything back to the Swahili. Much of the ammunition had been fired in the free-for-all affray, and some of the remainder no doubt buried hastily in the bush. Having no mandate to dispossess these people of arms that had been misguidedly allowed them by Government for the protection of their supposedly peaceful trading missions, I could do nothing else. So once more they went their way to plot and plan and lie and intrigue, to soak in sex in their comfortable permanent camps. All I could do was to keep the cattle, sheep, goats, donkeys, and such few humans who were willing to return to their homes.

Pyjalé had, meantime, been off calling up responsible men of the Dodosi tribe to take over the cattle for safe keeping until such time as we could establish relations with the owners of the stock. They came with great alacrity. Cattle are in these people's blood. I kept impressing upon them that they were only to hold them in safe custody for maybe a month.

In their desire for livestock, they frothed and quavered at the mouth at seeing so many enemy cattle. They simply could not restrain themselves. They

---

[1] A slightly different version of these last two pages can be found in chapter 2 of *Incidents from an Elephant Hunter's Diary.*

quarreled with each other for possession, and I had to have their spears removed and parked under guard or there would have been another free-for-all on the spot. I began to wonder how we should ever induce them to part with the cattle again when we required it of them.

The booking of all these cattle was a laborious affair. Hundreds of little sticks had to be cut. Each stick represented ten cows. A Dodosi notable would cut out a hundred head while I wrote in a book his name and against it so many cows and bullocks. Then he would be handed ten sticks tied in a bundle. This was to remind him of the number he would have to return when called upon to do so. It took days to get through the sheep and goats, and I was heartily sick of the whole business—especially as it interfered with my hunting activities.

My boys were emphatic that the Dodosi would never give up the cattle again, but Pyjalé was just as emphatic that they would. The writing in a book and then reading out the man's name and the number of cattle given in his charge was a mysterious affair to these savages, and it smacked strongly of "medicine" (magic).

******

Soon we were alone and peaceful and could once more resume our own ploy. We still had the women captives, which we reckoned to send home as soon as our hunting should take us within a distance from their country that would be reasonably safe for them to traverse. We were on good terms with the Dabossa as we had returned cattle to them on a former occasion.

As we weaseled our way through the bush wherever elephant trails led us, these captives soon grew fat and blooming. Having nothing much to do and plenty of elephant meat and fat, they soon began to show every sign of enjoying life once more. When delivered to their own people, it was certain they would be very much plumper than when they joined us. As to all the reasons for this plumpness, perhaps it would be better not to enquire too closely. I did what I could and put a guard on them at night, but bush life lends itself to philandry. Who knows, many a Dabossa may be going about to-day with a "foreign" look.

Before we sent off our captives to their homes, more than one of them expressed the wish to remain with us, pleading that their people had been killed in the raid. Knowing the lot of an orphan among these tribes made it a difficult matter to decide. It was determined to get rid of them before any further complications arose.

When, therefore, we found ourselves within a day's march of the nearest village, four of them were sent off with an escort. They were instructed to establish relations with the Dabossa notables and to tell them we were prepared to return their cattle as in the former raid.

Now Pyjalé and a few of our *askari*s (native soldier) had to go back and rout out all the cattle left with the Dodosi. While waiting for these to arrive, I thought it would be a good idea to use this abundant manpower to search for elephants, pointing out to them they had nothing to eat, anyhow, and that we could not possibly feed them except if we found some elephants. About a hundred men scattered through the limitless bush with the result that in three days I got thirty-six good bull elephants. Not only that but every tusk was brought in the day it was shot. These results illustrate how plentiful and obedient were the Dabossa, while awaiting their cattle, anyhow.

Then a runner arrived to say that, as usual, the Dodosi refused to give up the cattle entrusted to them. We sent another runner to say that we were following hard on his heels with all the Dabossa spearmen, and that they, the Dodosi, would not only lose their acquired cattle but their own as well and that every defaulting Dodosi would be shot. We knew from former experience that the defiance was beer-induced and would soon subside. And so it went. Bluff is a grand thing . . . when it comes off.

Soon we had all the cattle, so potent was Pyjalé and his interpretation of the meaning of that mysterious writing in the book. How much one owes in these affairs to one's native interpreters can hardly be computed. They think up exaggerations that one would hardly dream of, let alone use. The story for instance, that once a man's name is entered in a book no matter where he hides he can be found and dealt with. It is a pity that education destroys all these illusions.

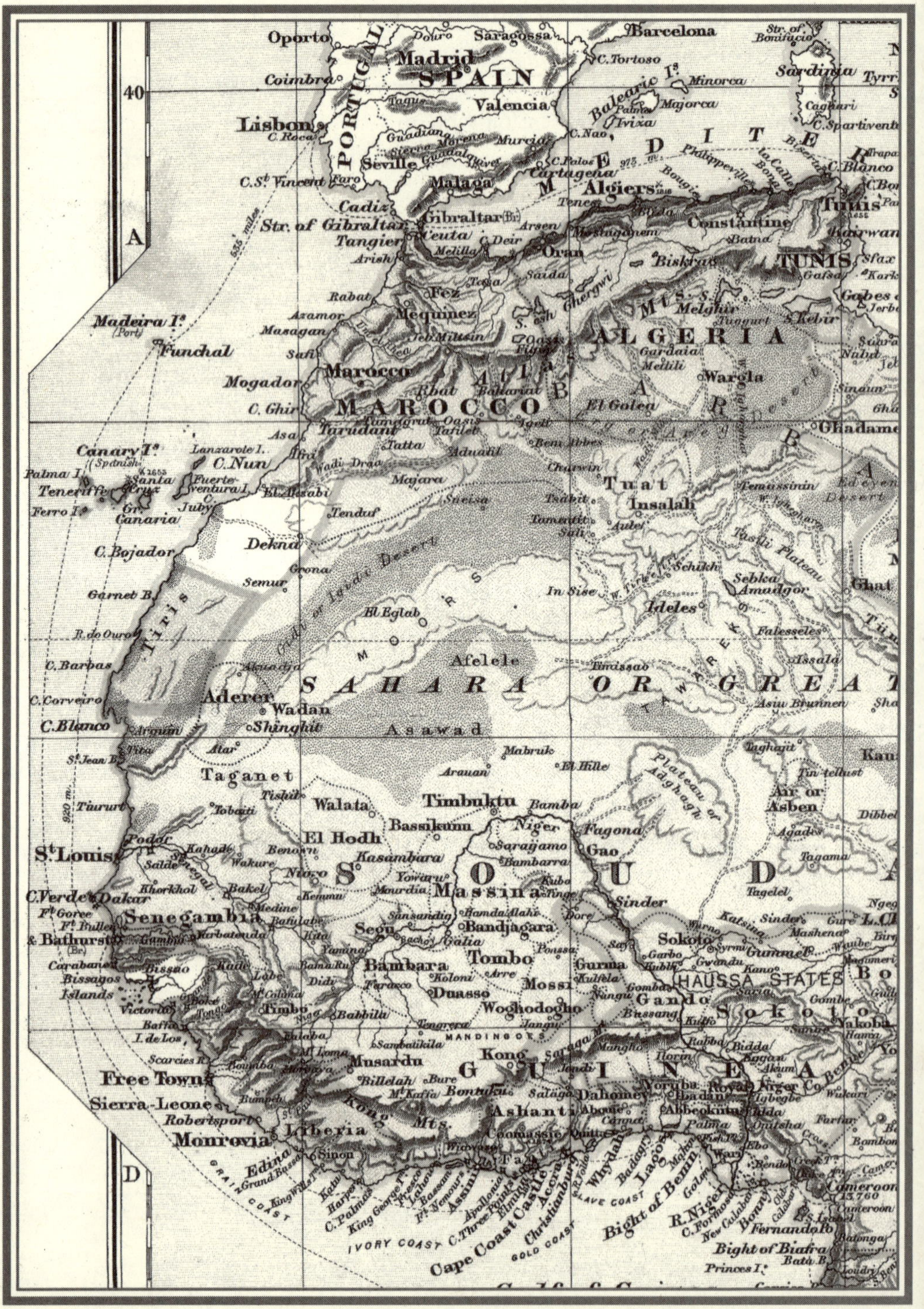

Oporto
Douro
Saragossa
Barcelona
Madrid
SPAIN
PORTUGAL
C. Tortoso
Coimbra
Balearic Is.
Minorca
Majorca
Iviza
Sardinia
Cagliari
C. Spartivento
40
Valencia
Lisbon
C. Roca
C. Nao
Seville
Murcia
C. Palos
Cartagena
C. St. Vincent
Faro
Malaga
Algiers
Philippeville
Bona
La Calle
Bizerta
C. Blanco
Tunis
Cadiz
Gibraltar (Br.)
Str. of Gibraltar
Ceuta
Tangier
Melilla
Arish
Oran
Mostaganem
Constantine
Batna
Biskra
TUNIS
Gafsa
Sfax
Gabes
A
Fez
Rabat
Azamor
Mequinez
Mazagan
Safi
Madeira Is.
(Port.)
Funchal
Marocco
Mogador
C. Ghir
MAROCCO
Tarudant
ALGERIA
Gardaia
Melili
Wargla
El Golea
Tafilet
Tatta
Asa
Igeli
Beni Abbes
Ghadames
Canary Is.
(Spanish)
Lanzarote I.
C. Nun
Palma I.
Teneriffe
Santa Cruz
Fuerteventura I.
Ferro I.
Gr. Canaria
C. Juby
El Aesabi
Wadi Draa
Majara
Tuat
Insalah
Temassinin
Tenduf
Aulef
Sali
C. Bojador
Dekna
Semur
Grona
Schikh
Sebka Amadgor
Ghat
Garnet B.
In Sise
Ideles
El Eglab
Tiris
R. do Ouro
MOORS
C. Barbas
Afelele
Timissao
SAHARA OR GREAT
C. Corveiro
Aderer
Wadan
C. Blanco
Arguin
Shinghit
Asawad
Atar
St. Jean B.
Mabruk
El Hille
Araouan
Taganet
Plateau of Adghagh
Air or Asben
Agades
Tichit
Walata
Timbuktu
Bamba
Tiurut
Tobaiti
Bassikunu
Niger
El Hodh
Fagona
Gao
St. Louis
Podor
Salde
Kasambara
Bambarra
Wakure
Benaun
Nioro
SOUDAN
Massina
C. Verde
Dakar
Khorkhol
Bakel
Medine
Tagelel
Sinder
Ft. Goree
Ft. Bullen
Senegambia
Bathurst
(Br.)
Bandjagara
Sokoto
Segu
Katsina
Mashena
Carabane
Bissagos Islands
Bissao
Bambara
Tombo
Gurma
Mossi
HAUSSA STATES
Kano
Gando
Sokoto
Yakoba
Timbo
Duasso
Woghodogho
Victoria
I. de Los
Bussang
MANDINGOES
Musardu
Kong
Bidda
Scarcies R.
Free Town
Sierra-Leone
Robertsport
Monrovia
Liberia
Kong Mts.
GUINEA
Bure
Bontuku
Salaga
Dahomey
Yoruba
Ibadan
Abbeokuta
Royal Niger Co.
Ashanti
Coomassie
Whydah
Badagry
Lagos
D
Edina
Grand Bassa
Sinou
GRAIN COAST
Harper
C. Palmas
King George Ft.
IVORY COAST
C. Three Points
Cape Coast Castle
Accra
Christiansburg
GOLD COAST
SLAVE COAST
Bight of Benin
R. Niger
C. Formoso
New Calabar
Bonny
Old Calabar
Cameroons
Fernando Po
Bight of Biafra
Princes I.
Bata B.

The Film Party

Chapter 31

My steamer very kindly made a brief call at Southampton to embark any passengers who might have booked for the West African ports on her scheduled run. It was just after the 1914 war and there were but few who would travel by a German line. Yet the ship itself was a marvel of labour-saving ingenuity. Split new, she was what is known as an intermediate cargo boat carrying a few passengers. Whereas such a boat would normally provide fair accommodation but poor fare, the Germans had struck a new idea—to provide first-class accommodation and first-class fare equal in every way to that on the most up-to-date liners with the added advantage that the crowds were avoided. There were some thirty passengers, all one class of course, of whom only five were British.

All these passengers were accommodated in single berth cabins. Every conceivable labour-saving device was employed, basins that emptied overboard, hot and cold water laid on, everything electric, fans, etc.

It was just as well for there were only five stewards. These men did the cabins, waited at table, served in the smoking room, and formed the band that played nightly until midnight and into the small hours whenever there was a party night.

These parties were great affairs: Liquor was good and cheap, and many of the passengers were women. Married or single, they seemed to be out to enjoy themselves to the utmost and they were all over the British contingent. Contrasting the gloomy air of the latter with the exuberant jollity of the German element, one would have thought that it was the Germans who had won the recent war.

Among the Germans there was a film-making party, presided over by a film magnate, who was going only as far as the Canary Islands thence returning home. The man in charge was a Major S. He it was who had former experience of Africa. They were all booked for Liberia, the Negro Republic, the only territory that would accept Germans so soon after the war.

This Major S. was an interesting man who spoke perfect English with an Oxford accent. He even looked like an Englishman, dressed like one, and would have passed anywhere for one. He told me he had spent the entire war in England as a spy. I could well believe it.

He divulged to me the story behind the film. It was curious mixture of romantic love and violence in African jungle, and an elephant had a great part in it—a white elephant at that.

Curious to know how he proposed to find a white elephant in Liberia, I asked him how he planned to do that. He said all that part of the story had already been shot in Tierpark Hagenbeck, a zoo at Hamburg, and with the aid of whitewash.

Another part of the story consisted of the raping of the heroine—that's her over there—he nodded toward a lovely German girl with a long, slim glass of beer in front of her across the smoking room—by native Africans.

"That's not going to be so easy," he opined. "I don't know how she'll take it, and the light is difficult anyway," he said.

"But surely," I ventured, "that part of it could have been done in Hamburg, too."

He looked hard at me.

"Have another?" I suggested.

"Look here," he said, "I've heard of you before. Aren't you an elephant hunter?"

I admitted the charge.

"Weren't you in Liberia before the war?"

"Yes," I told him.

"In Sinu Town?"

"Yes."

"Well! Of course! I heard about you."

Apparently relieved to find I was not a functionary of some sort or likely to be a rival, he went on to say that the main object of the expedition, as far as he was concerned, was the collecting of monkey glands. Professor Voronoff was at that time at the height of his rejuvenation experiments with the aid of sexual glands from animals and apparently there was big money in it.

As I understood the process, the glands had to be taken from the living animal, and I was therefore curious as to how S. proposed to capture them.

"Shoot them," he said. "We Germans have perfected a secret process of preservation. There's a fortune in it. But Herr XX (the film magnate) is nuts on this film. We are making it up as we go along."

As soon as we steamed into decent weather, we saw the film party at work. One of the scenes consisted of the finding a stowaway in the coal bunkers. It was most realistically done. The cameras were set up at one end of the deck, and a sailor

The Film Party

Among the Germans there was a film-making party, presided over by a film magnate, who was going only as far as the Canary Islands thence returning home.

came along hauling the stowaway by her golden tresses—for, of course, it was the heroine in boy's clothes—and she had seemingly overlooked hiding her long hair. In the process of being tugged along by the sailor, a very beautiful rounded breast was on display through her torn shirt. She was smothered in coal dust, too.

But something was wrong with this scene, and it had to be shot again. This time a gigantic and brutal-looking seaman took the place of the discoverer of the stow-away. Far better action was got with this man. He swung that miserable girl off her feet as he cursed and swore at her. So rough was he that

353

an excitable little cockney among the onlookers was with difficulty restrained from rushing at the huge sailor.

"I'll biff the great hulking brute," he said.

As he would have had to fly to have reached any vulnerable part of the sailor's anatomy, we had a good laugh.

I noticed that the cine camera operators looked through the centre of their machines as they turned the handles. I asked S. why they did this.

"They get the correct focus that way," he explained, "and do not have to move the camera back as the Americans do."

When I asked if I might see the apparatus more closely, he said that it was another German secret and they would not allow it.

When the ship arrived at the Canaries, everyone went ashore. The film party was to shoot some scenes, and some wanted to watch the film-making, which everyone thought great fun. Then there were others who wanted to do the town in the ordinary tourist fashion, i.e., calling at the pubs for a drink.

The natives thought the film party as good as a free show, and S. had no difficulty in getting plenty of local colour. What this particular part of the film was about was not very clear, but the sun shone and everyone laughed except the camera men who were always very serious, anyhow.

At the Canaries the film magnate was due to leave us. Before doing so, he gave a champagne party to all on board. A jollier party you never saw. Even the English unbent and became almost genial. Everyone got rather oiled, and the fun got pretty near to the bone. But those German women could certainly take it, however it might come. Heaven only knows where anyone slept that night.

The next morning the ship sailed after the film magnate had taken a most affectionate farewell of everyone. He had tears in his eyes as he embraced the star and starlets. He was a nice little man, that film magnate, and not at all what I had expected him to be.

All was grist to their mill apparently. For when we sighted a fleet of fishing boats off Cape Blanco, our skipper diverged from his course and slowed down to a stop near a boat flying the French flag. Apparently words were unnecessary. The Frenchmen filled a small boat with fish and came alongside without a word of greeting, hate in their faces. Also without a word, a sling was sent down by the German sailors. Up came some grand-looking fish and down went some sacks of potatoes. Still without a word, the exchange was effected, and we steamed away, the transaction having, of course, been recorded by the camera men.

One morning when we were expected to sight our destination, Liberia, I was up in the bows in pajamas. As dawn broke, it revealed a long, low line of mangroves, as dismal a sight as can be imagined. As I looked through the binoculars, a hot, sweet scent filled my nostrils. Glancing down, there stood the ravishing figure in silk pajamas of the star, all her lovely curves and breasts outlined by the breeze of the ship's way. It was the star all rosy with sleep.

"Well," I said, "how do you like the look of your new country"

"Is that Monrovia?" she said with horror.

"That's Monrovia all right," I said.

"Gott in Himmel!" she cried and burst into tears.

At the unloading of the film party's baggage onto a lighter [barge] alongside, I was an interested spectator. You never saw such an amount of ammunition, all done up in neat little tin-lined boxes. Stacks of it and stacks of firearms, too. *They must be planning something more than a war on monkeys,* I thought.

As I said good-bye to the skipper of that steamer, and while thanking him for the good time we had all enjoyed aboard his ship, I took one last good look at him. Yes, it was certainly the same man. There could be no reasonable doubt about it. No two men could so resemble one another. I was too shy to refresh his memory. This was the German skipper of a coastal schooner, and I had last seen him in bed with our mutual landlady in far off New Zealand some twenty-five years earlier.

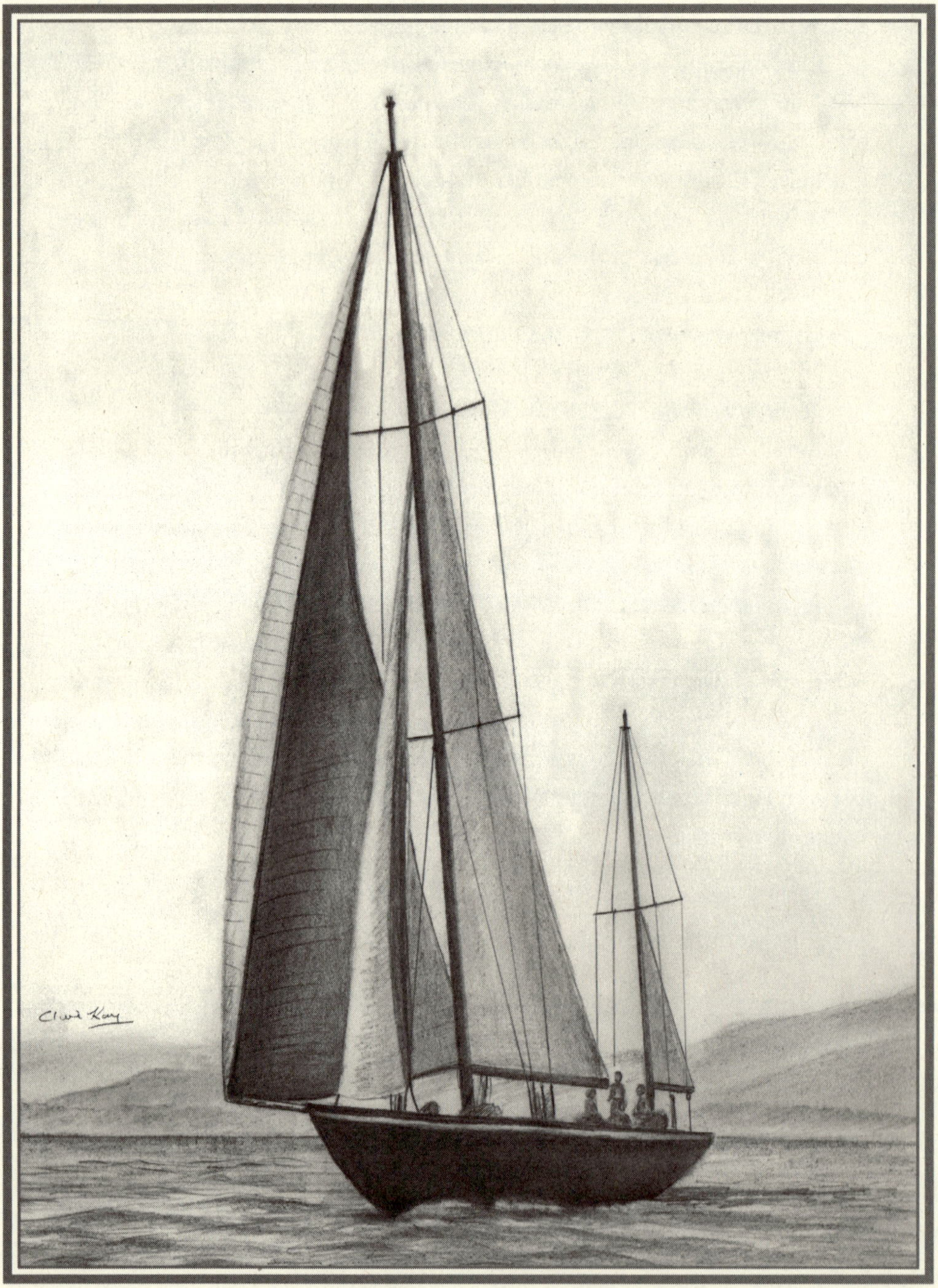

Miscellaneous Misadventures and Reminiscences

Chapter 32

Looking back on my hunting days, I find them to be singularly lacking in adventures. Certainly, at least once in the Yukon I was subsequently told that I had come very close to being shot. At the time it did not seem to me to be so, and I think my mates were wrong. It happed thus:

Two prospectors and I were traveling upstream in a Peterborough canoe when night closed upon us. We found that we were close to a shack of sorts, the kind chiefly used by dog teams in winter running the U.S. mail along the frozen Yukon to Cape Nome from Whitehorse. In summer it was occupied by a hunter who had a quite nice-looking and fairly young Indian squaw—Coppermine, I think it was. Well, we three dirty and tough-looking roughs were made welcome to the bunkhouse, and as we had meat we were quite happy. The squaw's man was absent on a hunt.

In due course we all turned in and were sound asleep when we were suddenly awakened by screams from the lady who was sleeping in the kitchen. With the thoughtlessness of extreme youth, I dived into the adjoining lean-to to find one of my traveling companions apparently trying to rape the lady. Although small, she was extremely tough and was putting up a stout show.

The "he" in question had had to lay aside his belt and six-shooter, probably because they held his pants and frustrated his design. At any rate on my entry he let go the girl although he was already in a strong strategic position, having got between her legs. On the instant she slipped away and into the bush. I sympathized with the chap, but all I could do was laugh as he drew his Colt. It is pretty hard to shoot down an unarmed lad, and so it proved to be. It was his companion who later told me that I had had a close call.

******

Over the course of my time in Africa, I killed one thousand—and a few over for full measure—crotchety, old bull elephants. I never counted the few cows that simply insisted on having it. I used to reckon that by and large each one of those thousand bulls cost me seventy miles of foot travel. My consumption of shoe leather was fantastic, averaging a pair every fortnight. A native African's horny soles lasted two months, thus proving more durable than the white man's shoe leather. Of course, his were growing all the time whereas my leather was dead.

Reminiscences of an Elephant Hunter

There was one rather disappointing aspect of this ancients-killing, and that was the phenomenal number of elephants I found with broken tusks. Some were broken short off by the lip, others halfway along, while many were worn right down.

The diameter of the world record tusks killed by Shundi's M'chagga slave with a muzzleloader on Kilimanjaro measured 23⅜ inches outside the lip. The tusks weighed 236 and 226 pounds when green. I had a dozen tusks that measured better than that, but all were broken or worn down. One pair of stumps measured 24⅛ inches. What they might have weighed had they been like the virgin in the fables, intact, no one can say. I think it is pretty certain they would have overtopped Shundi's weights.

******

I am repeatedly asked if I saw anything of the man-eating lions of Tsavo. When I first went through the Voi country, the natives of those parts made no complaints about lions. They used the lion—along with hyenas and vultures—much as we use morticians, that is, to remove the dead. At that time the natives were not on very neighbourly terms with white men. One or two robust characters had handled them roughly when they came demanding their customary *hongo* (passage toll). So, being white myself, I might not have heard of any unusual lion activity.

As the Kamba and Sanyr tribes were very efficient bow-and-arrow hunters, I think it improbable that they would have tolerated any nonsense from lions. Their hundred-pound bows used long, heavy arrows, and the three-inch barbed heads were covered with poison, so these people had the means to confront man-eating lions. I conclude, therefore, that the man-eating commenced with the arrival of the thousands of coolies from India, the construction gang for the projected Uganda railway.

******

When I was a lad of twelve, I went round the world. I would say my chief danger lay in avoiding being buggered, a danger be it said never contemplated by my worthy guardians when they so thankfully shipped me off. You will probably not want to refer to this, yet Lawrence of Arabia made a fortune out of his experience at the hands of the Turks.

Yet another pleasurable reminiscence is the ease with which one found oneself between almost any girl's thighs often to find a maidenhead in the most unexpected places. I suppose these girls thought—if they thought at all—that a boy of such immaturity was safe; there could be no harm in accepting the embraces of such a child. They often expressed surprise at such youthful ardour, and no doubt many of them learnt a useful lesson. So, you see there is nothing under heaven that has not its use in the design for living.

******

Dangers and adventures seem to see me coming and avoided me in the most annoying manner. I was having a beer and snack at a wayside pub in New Zealand once. Food consisting of beef, mutton, cheese, and bread was so abundant in that lucky country that it is served with every drink, or rather it stood in quantity on every bar. All you had to do was buy your drink, 6d, and fill up. Often hot dishes would appear—meat pies and whatnot. Your 6d drink entitled you to a free meal, a godsend to dead beats such as I.

One day I was enjoying my usual meal alongside a big, lusty bearded man when he began to converse. He was in his cups and began to argue about this and that and to blow off about his successes in fighting. Certainly, he looked husky enough. Presently he remarked on my colour—I was pretty well tanned by sun and wind—and finally announced firmly that he was of the definite opinion that I was a black boy.

My immediate reaction to this was quite spontaneous. I leant toward him with a hand on his enormous biceps and invited him in a whisper—so the barmaid should not hear—to come out and take his coat off. This seemed to pause the great blowhard.

Recovering, he said in a sort of wonder, "Don't you know who I am? I'm Basher of Basherville" or some such rot. Looking me up and down, he said, "I've killed men three times the size of you."

"All right," I said, glancing at the barmaid who was looking rather apprehensive—I flattered myself by thinking it was on my behalf. "Never mind all that. Come on out."

Well, he went off like a pricked balloon. He had about as much stomach for fighting as a castrated sheep.

I am terribly sorry, but I cannot help it: Those are the only sort of apologies for adventures that seemed to fall my way. That and stealing government property.

******

359

When I finally left Africa, Katie and I lived for a time in London. I took to living in the past as I found I could barely live in the present. I started to write, then to paint—you would never guess—elephants. I gave that canvas three of the loveliest bull elephants the most hectic dream had ever conjured out of Limbo. It passed, was hung in the Royal Art Exhibition of 1925, and sold, right off. I wish I had kept it.

Town life was getting me down, so we bought Corriemoillie, our little home in the Highlands. It was easier there to keep fit, and it was easier to cast back over the merry past. But just as in the Yukon, the midges [small flies] become a menace in July and August. Now that I was supposed to be civilized, I had no protective coating of grease-bound wood-smoke to protect me. So, naturally, Katie and I thought we would get a boat large enough to live on and spend the fly months at sea.

Out of a whole book of designs we fell in love with those from the board of one Olin Stephens. We used his design, after getting his permission of course, and had her built of steel in Aberdeen by a very competent yard, and I may say we have had immense fun out of it.

My wife found a lovely name for her, the *Trenchemer*, out of some historical work on Richard Coeur de Lion. King Dick had so named his galleon the *Trenchemer*, and as the original one was painted red, so we painted ours red, too. There is a very good but fiery Scotch whisky called "Red Hackle," and we found that it seemed to go well with the boat.

******

Of course, the answer to all this repining for the past lies, as ever, over the next horizon. I am not speaking of the blue horizons that used to lure me on and on, ever receding farther away. I speak of the horizons of science. There lie the unexplored lands for the youth of to-day. Better and better methods of preserving human life go hand-in-hand with bigger and better ways of destroying it. Then the final one, perhaps the most difficult one of all, will be how to set the blooming thing off.